Delivering Profitable Value

*A Revolutionary Framework
to Accelerate Growth, Generate Wealth,
and Rediscover the Heart of Business*

Michael J. Lanning

BASIC
BOOKS

A Member of the Perseus Books Group

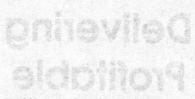

Library of Congress Cataloging-in-Publication Data

ISBN 0-7382-0162-6

Copyright © 1998 by Michael J. Lanning
Previously published by Perseus Publishing
Published by Basic Books, A Member of the Perseus Books Group

Published by arrangement with Capstone Publishing Ltd. Published simultaneously in Great Britain.

Set in 10-point Zapf Calligraphic

First paperback printing, March 2000

Find us on the World Wide Web at
http://www.basicbooks.com

Books published by Basic Books are available at special discounts for bulk purchases in the U.S. by corporations, institutions, and other organizations. For more information, please contact the Special Markets Department at the Perseus Books Group, 11 Cambridge Center, Cambridge, MA 02142, or call (800) 255-1514 or (617) 252-5298, or e-mail j.mccrary@perseusbooks.com.

Dedication

For Joan, Mike, Charley and Amanda

Contents and Plan of Book

The Introduction challenges the thinking manager to pause and ask, 'Does my organization often look for strategic opportunity in the *wrong* places? Does it seek to understand and improve customers' real experiences or does it gaze inward, as if into a managerial mirror?' For the manager who may answer even a qualified 'yes' to the latter part of that question, the challenge is getting the organization to stop contemplating itself and to start formulating strategy based on profitable delivery of superior value to customers. Unfortunately, conventional management theory (including the fields of strategy and marketing) does not solve but actually worsens this problem by encouraging managers to venture further *into* the managerial mirror. Managers are invited to consider a revolutionary but realistic alternative philosophy, framework and methodology for accelerating profitable growth: *Delivering Profitable Value (DPV)*. An example of a turnaround in a Hewlett-Packard business introduces some of the essential *DPV* concepts. The introduction also provides a sense of the resulting experiences organizations can expect from applying *DPV*. Finally, the introduction outlines the book's structure, the authority and experience on which it is based, and the kind of real world examples used to illustrate its argument.

Competent managers, who regularly compare their product and organization to competitors and earnestly solicit customers' opinions, can be deceived into assuming that they are adequately externally focused. This chapter urges managers to consider the possibility that their culture may nonetheless be overly fixated on the *product-supply* functions of developing, producing, and selling products and services rather than focused on understanding and profitably delivering customer experiences of superior value. This misdirected focus is an astoundingly common occurrence in organizations filled with intelligent, educated, and amply advised management. This chapter asks managers to consider this question: does this organization unconsciously ignore the true determinants of business success by conforming to the two dominant and fundamentally flawed models of management practice, the *internally-driven* and the *customer-compelled?* These are illustrated by the spectacular failure of Xerox in PCs, and the initial failed attempts to stop a business decline in one Weyerhaeuser business unit. In contrast, successful application of *Delivering Profitable Value* is illustrated by the latter's subsequent turnaround and, in greater detail, by an unusual model of success within the embattled Eastman Kodak.

Chapter Two – Customers' Resulting Experiences: Essence of a Real Value Proposition

This deceptively simple but incredibly powerful concept is explained, illustrated and defined in rigorous, actionable terms. This is the foundation upon which a wholly new perspective for thinking about business will be built. The rich and complex world of customers' resulting experiences, a world altogether different in kind and importance from the tired concepts of 'customer needs, requirements and expectations, and product benefits,' is revealed.

Chapter Three – The Good, the Bad and the Unintended: Every Business Delivers a Value Proposition

This chapter holds the complete definition of a *real* value proposition and discusses how fundamental it is to accelerating profitable growth. The VHS/Betamax example illustrates how *unconscious* of their value propositions managers can be. Accordingly, this chapter explains how to identify the propositions actually delivered. Some managers will assume value propositions concern only consumer businesses, but this chapter shows the equal relevance of the concept to industrial and commodity businesses.

Chapter Four – To Choose or Not to Choose a Complete Value Proposition, That Is Management's Question

This chapter discusses what must be done to *choose* a value proposition. Managers will easily recognize the difference between talking about customers and genuinely making a strategic commitment – the choice of a value proposition. Some propositions, including many winners, are *tradeoffs* – they include inferior experiences. Genuinely choosing a value proposition entails decisions that go beyond defining the customer and the resulting experiences they will derive. An industrial lubricants value proposition and numerous other industrial and consumer examples illustrate choosing a *complete* value proposition. The chapter provides practical tools for making this fundamental strategic decision.

Chapter Five – Some of What a Real Value Proposition Isn't 72

This chapter briefly dispenses with many of the concepts that can be confused with a value proposition. These include positioning, slogan, USP, mission statement, values statement, strategic intent, value discipline, and value added.

Chapter Six – Playing to Win: Choose Good Value Propositions 80

This chapter discusses choosing *winning* value propositions. Numerous examples show why organizations must deliver *superior experiences* to customers, rather than focus on having a superior *organization, product, or competencies*. Digital Audio Tape and several other ventures are shown to have failed, despite 'superior technology,' because they offered an inferior value proposition.

Chapter Seven – Provide and Communicate: Delivering Is More Than Lip Service 89

The purpose of choosing a (real) winning value proposition is to profitably *deliver* it. This perspective is quite different from the traditional view of a business as an entity that supplies a product. The chapter defines and illustrates (with Service Masters, Volvo, and others) the concepts of providing and communicating each resulting experience and argues that managers must think 'forwards,' beginning with customer experiences and ending with business design. This perspective is contrasted with employing the conventional *backwards* approach, which begins with internal resources or imagined advantages, advances to developing products, and ends with using marketing to convince customers to want those products. Advertising is discussed as an example of functions dominated by astoundingly internally-driven thinking and further misdirected by customer-compelled input. Much advertising is lauded as creative but demonstrably fails to work, since it does not help communicate a superior value proposition. The converse also holds. Illustrations are given from Nissan, Nike, P&G, NEC, British Airways, and others. A summary chart contrasts the value-delivery and product-supply focus.

Chapter Eight – Design a Business Forwards: the Value Delivery System 116

Chapter Eight introduces and illustrates in depth the central *DPV* framework. Southwest Airlines has been much discussed, but its real strategy and that strategy's derivation have not been coherently explained. They are here, through the framework of the *value delivery system* (VDS). Southwest, Sensomatics, Sony Walkman and other examples defy the conventional logic of management but beautifully and simply confirm that of *DPV*.

Chapter Nine – Staying Alive: Adjust and Recreate Your VDS 136

Here the reader learns to use the value delivery system (VDS) as a dynamic framework by which to flexibly reinvent one's business in response to a competitive and shifting environment. The Checklist for a Winning Business is presented. The means for courageously changing a business are demonstrated so that managers can avoid falling into the comforting but ultimately suicidal habit of 'leveraging' the organization's strengths until it is unable to compete. Small Glaxo's attempt to garner a small market share of antiulcerants, then dominated by SmithKline, is recognized for the tour de force that it is: a brilliant redesign of the VDS. Organizations must reinvent their businesses, but not in their own image. This chapter also distinguishes between the VDS framework and the Porter Value Chain, which is easily confused with but fundamentally different from the VDS framework.

Chapter Ten – and Now...Will the Real Customer Please Stand Up? The Value Delivery Chain 151

The complex, interconnected relationships among an organization, its customers, their customers, and others are made manageable by the *value delivery chain* framework. Unlike the conventionally accepted approaches of the 'supply chain' and 'value chain,' this *DPV* framework helps managers prioritize these entities by distinguishing the all-important *primary entities* from other *supporting* entities. The long chains of an LED maker, a Weyerhaeuser business, and a plastics manufacturer reveal that the primary entity can be further removed than it might at first seem. The case of Fidelity Investments further demonstrates the dramatic impact of understanding the identity of the *real* customer – the primary entity in the value delivery chain.

Chapter Eleven – Primary and Supporting VDSs: Control the Chain Reaction   159

This chapter discusses the crucial issue of enlisting the coordinated support of other players in order to deliver the winning value proposition to the primary entities in a chain. The concept of delivering both a primary value proposition to primary entities and supporting propositions aimed at securing the support of other entities in the chain is explained. An example from the world of chickens demonstrates the brilliant coordinated design of both the primary VDS and the supporting VDS to intermediaries, while the floor cleaning business provides an example of creatively changing the interrelationships in a value delivery chain.

Chapter Twelve – Don't Sell to Business-Customers: Improve Their VDSs Instead   176

This chapter discusses how to approach complex business-customers without making the common error reinforced by conventional marketing theory – overly focusing on the buying function rather than truly understanding the customer's business. Results can be dramatically more promising than those derived from a sole focus on the customer's buying function. Conner Peripherals and the early Compaq, Fidelity in pension fund management and others illustrate this potential.

Chapter Thirteen – Define the Firm's VDSs: Key Task of Corporate Strategy   180

The concept of understanding a business as a value delivery system in context of a value delivery chain is expanded to include corporate strategy. The reader learns how to understand corporate strategy in a wholly new light – as the definition of the firm's value delivery systems. General Motors's long history is used as a classic example of an organization with initially a clear-headed strategy that gradually lost sight of its businesses. *DPV* urges senior managers to define and redefine their enterprises' VDS's, despite the perspective of conventional strategy theory, which can lead them to believe this exercise too pedestrian.

Chapter Fourteen – Define VDSs Within the Context of their Market-Space

This chapter completes the picture of business strategy in the *DPV* perspective. A market-space is a group of related potential VDSs and their potential for wealth, while each related potential VDS is a *value delivery option* in that market-space. Corporate strategy must design, define, and choose the firm's businesses – VDSs – in each market-space where it chooses to compete. Those undertaking this task must remain cognizant of the interrelationship with other existing or potential VDSs in the same market-space. Managers who have understood Part One now understand what a fully developed strategy must be in order to profitably deliver superior value. Armed with this understanding, they are ready for the systematic methodology by which to formulate and implement such strategy.

Part Two – *How* to Deliver Profitable Value

Chapter Fifteen – Formulate Strategy by Identifying and Choosing Value Delivery Options

This chapter holds an in-depth, practical explanation of the methodology for strategy formulation that starts with identifying value delivery options in a market-space. *DPV* advocates replacing traditional market and industry 'segmentation' with this methodology. The chapter discusses how and why conventional segmentation is so different, so unnecessarily complex, and so much less strategically useful than this *DPV* methodology. In an HP example introduced previously, the organization uses the value delivery options approach to greatly simplify its understanding of the relevant market-space. Chevron, in a supposed commodity business – natural gas – identifies the value delivery options in its market-space, and dramatically improves profitability. Using the *DPV* methodology, managers evaluate the value delivery options identified, then choose the optimal combination of them for the market-space being explored. Determining the firm's strategy comprises choosing the market-spaces in which to compete and the primary VDSs to operate in each market-space, and identifying the capabilities that the firm must support across these businesses. The relentlessly practical character of the methodology is demonstrated by the HP Vectra computer. Discovery of the option that Vectra was unconsciously executing yields a realistic opportunity. A flowchart visually depicts the *DPV* methodology. A key element of this approach to strategy is the method of *becoming the customer*, which is discussed in detail in the next three chapters.

Chapter Sixteen – Stop Listening: Become Customers to Discover What They Really Want 216

The basic principles of the intuitive but systematic and fact-based method of *becoming* customers are summarized here. An illustration of discovering unexpected strategic opportunity in Kodak's data storage business is given. Despite the resources expended in the name of marketing research, satisfying customers, and competitive analysis, most such exercises do not actually lead organizations to an adequate understanding of customers' experiences for the formulation of business strategy. Other illustrations are drawn from HP, Polaroid, P&G, industrial lubricants, Honda and a Caribbean systems integrator.

Chapter Seventeen – Virtual Videos of the Customer's Life: Structured Method for Becoming the Customer 228

Examples of the 'virtual video' methodology for a UK petrol/gasoline distributor, for Australian camera specialty retailers and for HP order-fulfillment are offered. To become highly competent at developing innovative value delivery strategies, managers must learn to understand and analyze customers' real behavior and experience to the depth of these examples and beyond. This chapter offers pragmatic guidelines for conducting this unconventional but dramatically more productive form of market-space analysis, both for application to business customers and to consumers.

Chapter Eighteen – What's Competition Got to Do with It? Understanding Customers' Alternatives 254

Here, competition takes its place within value delivery strategy formulation. This chapter exhorts managers to stop asking the traditional competitive questions: 'What will competition do?' and 'What can we do better?' Instead, *DPV* urges managers armed with the knowledge of the potentially most valuable experiences to ask, 'How well could competitors and other alternatives deliver these?' FedEx's Zap Mail debacle is an illustration. The why and how of making virtual *competing videos* of the customer's life are discussed. Competitive analysis concludes *becoming the customer*.

Chapter Nineteen – Make Disciplined Choices: Implement VDS-Structured Business Plans 260

The final step in formulating strategy in *DPV* terms is to articulate the disciplined choices produced by the analysis discussed in the previous four chapters. Organizations now must write and commit to *real* business plans. These are structured explicitly by the value delivery framework and carry the power of senior management authority behind them. They are not peripheral exercises, but rather must determine the organization's structure, its success criteria, and all its resources, processes, and the development of capabilities. Managers are shown how to implement chosen VDSs and then to monitor, measure, and improve their design and implementation. The underappreciated power of realistically testing a VDS is illustrated with the New Coke blunder, seen in a more sober light than usual. Finally managers are urged to face again the fundamental questions of *Delivering Profitable Value*: to start the whole creative and analytic search for strategic insight all over again. For *DPV* is not a once-off process but a way of business life.

Chapter Twenty – What to Do Monday Morning?

A practical starting point, from which to start making an organization more capable of *Delivering Profitable Value*, is offered. Managers are urged to assess the extent to which their organizations understand and have answered the demanding questions of *DPV*, versus the extent to which they continue to rely on the product-supply-focused paradigm and its internally-driven and customer-compelled thinking. Then, they are urged to *act* – to muster the *will* to pursue breakthrough profitable growth by *Delivering Profitable Value*.

Conclusion – Lead Beyond a Few Improvements, Build a Great Company: Institutionalize DPV

In conclusion, managers are challenged to be ambitious, to insist on truly integrating the commonsensical principles of *DPV*. An example of one great company's success in truly institutionalizing many of these essential tenets of business philosophy over the long term is presented as evidence that this ambitious goal can be achieved. Managers are reminded that they must only stay focused on the few key questions that really matter in conceiving and leading businesses.

Acknowledgments

To begin, I would like to thank my family for their love, support and blind faith. In particular, more than everyone else in this long project: my wife Joan helped the most to keep me focused; my son Mike gave me the most useful comments; my daughter Amanda gave me the most hugs and kisses, each one needed. My son Charley encouraged me too, and made a special contribution. One summer evening two years ago, I was sitting with Joan on our deck writing and Charley, then nine, came up and asked me what this book was really about. I rambled on for a couple of minutes, trying rather inefficiently to explain it. Pensive, saying nothing, he went inside, then returned in ten minutes and said, 'Dad, I have an idea for what to call your book – "The Heart of Business!"' Joan and I exchanged that astounded look adults get when they realize that children often see the world more clearly than they can. The title includes Charley's idea, which helped me see what, indeed, this book is really all about.

Many other people helped in a myriad of ways for which I cannot here adequately express my thanks and sincere appreciation. Among these, however, I would first like to make special mention of the book's principal editor, Dory Bertsche, with whom it has been a great pleasure to work. Superb, she is easily the best editor I have encountered and a consummate professional. Dory worked very hard with me over the past 15 months and greatly improved the clarity and accessibility of the book. She also designed what I hope the reader will agree is a very useful index. While any mistakes or conceptual weaknesses are my fault, should the reader find this book clear, easy to read, and lacking unnecessary redundancy, much of the credit is Dory's.

My good friend and colleague, French consultant and author Camille Vert, also deserves some real credit for this book, for it is only because of his persistent encouragement that I finally got serious about writing it. More important, his original management concepts, and aspects of his consulting experience, have greatly influenced my thinking. Camille's insightful 'Industrial Chain Method' especially helped shape the value delivery chain framework and other elements of my work.

Thanks to Douglas Fox for first suggesting, 25 years ago at Procter & Gamble, the phrase and idea of 'becoming the customer.' In addition, numerous clients, members of my firm *The DPV Group*, and friends have very helpfully commented on drafts of the book. These include Glenne Harding, Miller Macmillan, Kip Knight, Mike Halpin, Eric Berggren, Will Fraser, Steve Puls, Steve Furbacher, Andrew Griffiths and joel Epstein. I'd also like especially to thank Steve Puls for providing invaluable support and encouragement throughout this project. And my colleague Dan Draper has graciously rovided helpful, intelligent commentary on every draft over the past two years. Many other clients and colleagues have also influenced my understanding and contributed to elements of the book.

I want to warmly thank Ed Michaels of Mckinsey & Company, who originally inspired me to develop new concepts and then strongly supported my creation in 1983 of the value delivery framework, the foundation of this book. My former partner of ten years Lynn Phillips also deserves credit for my later, much fuller development of the value delivery ideas. Starting in 1986 when he first saw them, Lynn recognized the potential of these ideas, then did a great deal in our executive education practice to popularize them (as our course *Building market-Focused Organizations*, or *BMFO*) and to support me in further developing them. It was Lynn's original idea to develop and focus on, in our practice, several of the case examples I have used in the book, and he helped me learn about and develop some of them. moreover, earlier in my writing of this book we had planned to work on it jointly, and Lynn did provide helpful comments on an early draft.

Many thanks to Richard Burton and Mark Allin, principals of Capstone, my publisher for outside North America, who gave early, sustained and patient support. Likewise to Nick Philipson, a great champion for the book and Executive Editor at my publisher for North America, Perseus Books. Thanks also to Tom Fryer of Sparks in Oxford who did a terrific creative, professional job in designing, typesetting and providing some final editing, all unde time pressure, and to Perseus's Julie Stillman for her helpful editorial input. I would also like especially to thank my Administrative Assistant Lauren Frye for years of loyal support and long, ofter strange hours of hard work on this project. And thanks to Roselyne de Chevron-Villette for much kind administrative help in Versailles.

Finally, I'd like to thank five more people: my Mom and Dad, who taught me compassion, and think critically and liberally; Mix, wherever you are, for getting me into this in the first place; Massimo Ruosi who taught me more than anyone else about creating and managing a business; and John W. (I know where you are) for being another Dad and for asking me many times, 'Mike, aren't you done with that book yet?'

A Brief Overview of *Delivering Profitable Value*

Most business enterprises entering the 21st century must search for breakthroughs in profitable growth. But they had better look in the right places. The richest, though not the most obvious, place to search is in the world of potential-customers' *resulting experiences*. In fact, a business is best conceived and managed as the intentional delivery of a chosen scenario of resulting experiences to some group of potential customers. If these customers find that scenario of experiences (including the price) to be superior to their alternatives (even if it includes *tradeoffs* versus those alternatives), they will give the enterprise their revenues. This scenario of resulting experiences is the real meaning of the often misunderstood concept, the 'value proposition.' If the enterprise can deliver a superior value proposition at a total cost that is below the revenue it gains, then the business succeeds. Thus, a winning business should be understood as the profitable delivery of a superior value proposition, a simple but profoundly different paradigm than that which sees a business as the supply of a product (or service).

The central framework of this book conceives of a business as an integrated system entirely oriented around the delivery of a chosen value proposition. That is, a business should be defined and managed as a *value delivery system* (VDS) rather than by the conventional model of a *product-supply system*. A *product-supply focus* should be replaced by the deceptively simple but fundamentally different *value delivery focus*.

In addition, it is crucial for many organizations in complex businesses to focus on the delivery of a superior value proposition to customer entities that may not buy anything directly from the organization. A consumer products company, for example, sells to consumers through intermediaries such as retailers. A building-supply maker may sell to building owners through intermediaries such as contractors. Such organizations need the coordinated cooperation of intermediaries in order to deliver the necessary value proposition to the *real* customer. Therefore, a firm's value delivery systems often include the actions and resources of other entities outside the firm. Here, the concepts of a *value delivery chain* and of *primary* and *supporting value delivery systems* are used to manage these complex relationships.

The book defines corporate strategy, which, properly understood, consists of discovering, designing, choosing, and using corporate resources to support, the firm's businesses – its primary value delivery systems. These must be understood and managed in context of their *market-spaces* – the other businesses with which the firm's primary value delivery systems may interact.

How does a firm creatively formulate winning value delivery strategies? First, to discover the most valuable customer experiences, managers should use the method of systematically *becoming the customer*. This means to explore, observe, analyze, and redesign creatively the actual experiences potential customers do and could have. This exploration is radically different from conventional market research. Using this basic method, managers forsake traditional market segmentation in favor of systematically *identifying value delivery options*. Then they make a *disciplined choice* of which value delivery systems the organization will implement. All functions, resources, and capabilities are then developed, managed, and measured according to these designed and chosen value delivery systems. This methodology for discovering and formulating innovative strategy is wholly different from focusing on the competitive superiority of an organization's products, resources, and skills or from *listening to customers* and doing as they request.

Understanding, developing, and managing businesses in this way is *Delivering Profitable Value (DPV)*. The book draws on numerous value delivery focused firms, other writers, my experiences, and those of my colleagues in *The DPV Group*. Fifteen years ago, I created the seminal value delivery concepts of the value proposition and value delivery system. I have since further developed this philosophy, framework, and methodology. It is my hope that the reader will recognize the power of this revolutionary and realistic approach to profitable growth and the rediscovery of the real heart of business.

Beyond the Looking Glass

The events most critical to a business happen outside the firm managing it. These are the events that the customer experiences as a result of using and interacting with the firm's products, services, and actions. Yet these *resulting experiences* and their implications often escape the real attention of managers in conceiving and executing business strategy.

While underappreciated, this concept of a resulting experience is simple to understand. Consider the experience some customers get as a result of using automatic teller machines (ATMs), versus that of using a human teller in their bank. They can rely on getting cash in less than two minutes, at any time, any day, at many locations. As a result, their lives are a little improved. Compared to the traditional human-teller alternative, customers spend less total time getting cash, rarely disrupt their schedule to rush to the bank before closing, and virtually never find themselves without cash when they need it.

In total these customers, by using ATMs instead of going into a bank, have perhaps six resulting experiences. They: (1) get cash as accurately as they would from the human teller; (2) save a significant amount of time; (3) reduce disruption in their lives; (4) decrease the number of incidents of being out of cash. However, they also: (5) incur a slightly higher chance of getting mugged and (6) often pay some ATM-related transaction charge. One of these resulting experiences is equal to the alternative of using a human teller; three are superior; two – including the price – are inferior. The superior experiences outweigh the negatives; using ATMs is in net a superior proposition to the customer.

A proposition has some customer-perceived value; thus it is a 'value proposition.' Customers select the superior one: the combination of resulting experiences, including price, that in net will have the greatest value for them compared to alternatives. By delivering a superior value proposition, a firm wins those customers' preference and so their revenues. Whenever a firm delivers a superior value proposition at a cost (including its cost of capital) below the price, that business generates wealth. It follows that a firm's actions and resources in any business should be determined by an explicit decision of what value proposition to deliver and how. This is managing business from the perspective of *Delivering Profitable Value*. Unfortunately, it is all too easy to manage businesses from a very different perspective.

As if gazing ever lovingly into a mirror, a great many firms focus almost entirely on their side of the firm-customer relationship. They continuously ponder themselves, thinking about their products and services, their production resources, and their processes. They may compare themselves to competition and earnestly solicit customers' opinions. However, they analyze and act without real regard for the crucial determinant of success. For the managerial mirror does not reflect real customer experiences. Therefore, the strategic questions of value delivery are neglected. What are the most important experiences potential customers have today, and how much could we possibly improve them? What profitable value proposition should we (our organization and other entities with whom we must cooperate) therefore deliver? And how should we provide and communicate these experiences, at a cost that allows us to generate wealth?

Instead, managers often ask, 'What products or services should we create, make and sell, and how?' These questions must eventually be answered, but they are the wrong starting place for business strategy. Because they are asked too soon, managers answer them using quite different criteria than a choice of profitable value proposition. Thus, they frequently use criteria such as 'What can our firm do at lower cost or that differentiates our product versus competitors?' Or 'What should we do that will most leverage our existing skills, technologies, and assets?' Or 'What must we do to match the benchmarks established by leading competitors?' Or 'What do customers say we should produce, and how do they say we should make and sell it?' Or 'What do customers say we should do to increase their satisfaction with us?'

Such criteria dominate most approaches to business strategy. They allow organizations to develop, produce, and market products or services without deciding or often even understanding the resulting experiences for customers. The firm still delivers a value proposition, but it is an unintended and often unconscious outcome rather than the deliberate driving force of the business. This backwards approach is often completed by an after-the-fact writing of some superficially constructed, product-positioning statement, perhaps even (unjustifiably) called 'our value proposition.' But fundamentally, managers are focused on supplying their product, not on delivering a real value proposition.

Operating a business without deeply understanding and actively managing both sides of the firm–customer relationship in an integrated fashion is somewhat akin to a physician treating a patient without understanding their condition. Asking the patient to self-diagnose and recommend a treatment does not correct that ignorance of their condition.

Similarly, inadequate understanding of customers' experiences does not imply a lack of *input* from them. Many firms request and listen to input from their customers. Rather than *listen to* customers so much, managers need to *become* customers. This means, not asking customers for direction, but systematically learning what it is like to live the customer's life; to be, think, and feel like the customer. Then and only then can managers infer what the most valuable resulting experiences *could* be for that customer.

The way firms often manage businesses might even be called egotistical.

Thoroughly self-absorbed, egotists can only understand relationships in terms of themselves. In any relationship, egotists' only concern is how they are perceived, how they are performing, what they are accomplishing. Egotistical firms may obsessively compare themselves with competitors, but the subject is the egotist, not the customer. Some egotists may also compulsively solicit the opinion of the customer, constantly asking how they rate and how to rate higher. However, the egotist is still not the least interested in customers or their real problems and aspirations. The competitors and the customer only serve as mirrors in which the egotist can further regard himself. The egotist fails in many relationships and can't understand why.

In Lewis Carroll's *Through the Looking Glass*, Alice is so fascinated by the images in the looking glass that she goes through it, into a world where backwards logic and nonsense rule. Many business organizations, because they do compare themselves to competitors and they do analyze customers, count themselves externally focused and do not recognize their behavior for what it really is: a perpetual stare into the managerial looking glass. In that looking glass, only the organization's products, resources, and processes can be clearly seen, not the real life of customers. Even if customers hold up the looking glass for the organization, by rating them and making many suggestions, the organization still focuses on itself. Unfortunately, much of orthodox management guides managers not away from this looking glass but rather deeper into it. The strategy and marketing fields and other management thought provide a stream of varied rationalizations for a continuing focus on the organization's products and how to supply them rather than on the resulting experiences the organization, in order profitably to grow, must deliver to customers.

However, just understanding the resulting experiences customers currently have is a deceptively simple challenge. To discover potential experiences that some customers *would* value, even if they are unaware today, is more difficult. So is making disciplined choices of which experiences to deliver (and which not) and exactly how. These are highly demanding creative and analytic capabilities that must be deliberately built and nurtured by a firm's leadership, but rarely are.

To understand customers' experiences truly and then formulate and execute business strategy entirely in those terms, managers must get beyond the managerial paradigm of the looking glass. To accelerate profitable growth, they must design each of their businesses around a disciplined choice of a winning value proposition. Most do not.

And managers should wonder, *why* not? Indeed, this book is intended to awaken a degree of *anger* at the extent to which strategies are formulated without more than the most superficial understanding of the questions posed by *Delivering Profitable Value*. These questions are, in some sense, intuitively obvious. But upon reading this book, experienced, open-minded managers, it is hoped, will acknowledge that these are decidedly *not* the questions by which business strategy is commonly formulated and executed. Most organizations (bolstered and distracted by the conventional wisdom of strategy and marketing theory) conceive and manage their businesses without regard for these questions. Many good managers are exasperated with the status quo, and more should be. They desperately want their organizations to become adept at systematically discovering and aggressively pursuing breakthrough growth opportunities. To such managers, this book proposes a comprehensive, practical, yet altogether revolutionary alternative for pursuing that ambitious objective: the philosophy, framework, and methodology of *DPV – Delivering Profitable Value*.

Turning protocol analyzers into network advisors

In 1990, Hewlett-Packard's Colorado Telecomm Division (CTD) was in trouble. CTD's 'Protocol Analyzers' (PAs) helped computer managers analyze network malfunctions. In the mid-1980s, CTD's new PAs produced much more network data than competitors, which allowed network managers to diagnose malfunctions more quickly. By 1990, however, CTD had gone six years without a new product. Competitors had attacked niches, steadily eroding CTD's leading market share. Since 1987, CTD had slipped from the highest profit and growth division in its HP group to the lowest profit, fastest shrinking.

CTD's new product efforts had been frustrating. Projects leveraged CTD's strength (as the company saw it): producing more network data for analysis than competitors could. However, as the diversity of networks increased, niche competitors designed PAs that produced large amounts of data and included features that customized data to the customer's specific network, applications, or maintenance organization. CTD would discover, months into a project, that they had missed an important feature. The project would backtrack and reach the market too late, or simply grind to a halt. Division leadership thought R&D objectives needed to reflect customer understanding better, so CTD tried elaborate planning exercises to identify customer-desired features.

They divided customers by their industry-type, kind of network, applications used, etc. and tried to identify what features these various customers wanted from their PA. Surely this would work – it would be customer-driven! Instead, it led to long statements committing all things to all people, which failed to clarify R&D objectives better. At the same time, CTD's later generation PAs increasingly had numerous features and functionalities that exceeded competitors' products but which most customers did not seem fully to appreciate.

In 1990, CTD tried a new approach to their strategic dilemma. They started with exploring a 'day-in-the-life' of a series of customers to see problems through their eyes. This focused not just on network managers, the traditional 'customer,' but on network-maintenance staff (the real users inside the customer-entity, from CTD's perspective) and even on the immediate customers of network management – the employees using the network. This time, CTD did not ask what PA features customers wanted but instead spent hours at customer sites 'becoming' users, managers and their customers. *Becoming the customer* is different from *listening* to customers. For CTD, it meant studying what customers tried to do and how, including the users' diagnosis and repair of network malfunctions and including their frustrations, compromises and inefficiencies. To accomplish this, CTD sent inter-functional teams to interview network managers, the users in maintenance and their customers, as they did their jobs in various installations. From these explorations, CTD discovered the scenarios that customers in different situations would most value.

In this way, CTD discovered that many in network maintenance were increasingly overwhelmed by the network complexity and by pressure from their customers, the network users, to maximize availability (uptime) of the network. CTD also discovered that the scenario of experiences these customer entities truly needed was *not* to be provided by PAs with ever more data to analyze. Rather, they needed maintenance staff to isolate a problem quickly and then implement a fast practical solution. This produced an insight upon which the entire CTD organization was then rigorously focused. Rather than 'making and selling Protocol Analyzers,' CTD redefined its business as 'delivering, to network-maintenance organizations running complex, critical network systems, the maximum possible network availability (uptime), via superior problem isolation, at a similar price versus competitors.'

This relatively simple conclusion became CTD's value proposition, driving actions in technology development, product design, procurement, manufacturing, packaging, distribution, selling, advertising, service and support, and pricing. Thus, CTD conceived of its business as a *value delivery system*, in which all of these functions were reoriented to focus on one objective: to deliver profitably – *provide* and *communicate* – the newly chosen value proposition. This insight dramatically changed CTD's strategy and culture. Many were profoundly uncomfortable with this at first, since this shift moved away from CTD's (and their personal) strength. Yet the Division found that it could develop the appropriate technology to deliver this value proposition much better than its competitors. CTD introduced the 'Network Advisor,' a product which de-emphasized data to be analyzed by users and instead isolated and identified network problems. It showed the user the problem, a good solution, and how to implement it quickly. This new product redefined the business, caught the competition off-guard, and produced a dramatic turnaround in CTD's business.

Prior to adopting a more *value-delivery* focused approach, CTD, like most businesses, had been *product-supply* focused. That is, they focused on developing, producing, and marketing a product (or service) rather than on *choosing, providing* and *communicating* a superior value proposition. Despite the common use of the word 'value' in management jargon, the value-delivery focused perspective as defined in this book is rarely practised. Rather, the product-supply orientation dominates management practice today and its underlying theories. Most often, organizations, as CTD did, manifest this perspective by being 'internally-driven,' eager for any rationale to cling to the apparent safety of their past strengths. Internally-driven managers seek competitive advantage in the way products or services are made and sold, in assets, technologies, costs, or functional skills that competition lacks. They do not seek it in the value proposition they will deliver.

In an attempt to transcend this internally-driven myopia, many, like CTD, pursue what they often see as the only alternative: commit to anything and

DPV: a proposed paradigm shift

Abandon the conventional view of a business as:

A product supply system

Develop the product	Produce the product	Market the product

- Internally-driven and customer-compelled criteria determine what product to supply and how:
  - be different from competitors
  - be lower cost
  - utilize the organization's competencies/assets/advantages
  - do what the customer (any and all) say to do
  - be excellent/world class.
- Supplying this product determines revenues and costs.

And adopt the more intuitively obvious but revolutionarily different DPV view of a business as:

A value delivery system

Choose a value proposition	Provide this value proposition	Communicate this value proposition

- General management explores value-delivery options, then makes a disciplined choice of a profitable, superior value proposition.
- All functions, products/services and relationships with other entities are single-mindedly designed, managed and measured so that chosen customers actually derive and perceive the superior proposition.
- The delivery of this value proposition determines all revenues and costs.

everything customers suggest, or the 'customer-compelled' path. Just 'be close' and 'listen to' the customer, promise 'total satisfaction' and 'do what they say,' beckons this siren song. But despite listening enthusiastically, the customer-compelled organization still fails to understand the resulting experiences customers would most value. It asks the same wrong questions that the internally-driven organization asks (how to produce and market what product), but now it wants *customers* to answer. Most organizations find the customer-compelled path impractical and are driven back toward the traditions of the internally-driven organization, disillusioned and discouraged.

Even as its market share eroded, CTD thought it was focused on both competitive differentiation and customer needs. While leveraging CTD competencies, it designed, often at the buyers' request, PAs with more and more features. Only when the division focused on freshly analyzing and improving the *experiences* of their actual users, the network maintenance staff, did the turnaround begin.

Many organizations find themselves engaged in a frustrating effort to blend these two flawed approaches – internally-driven and customer-compelled. These are just different sides of the same product-supply coin; both are flawed because they are not value-delivery focused. Managers either do whatever the customer says unless it violates an internally-driven mandate, or follow internally-driven agendas until a customer complains. This awkward dance seems to some like a striving for balance, but misses the fundamentally different alternative: the value-delivery focused approach of *Delivering Profitable Value (DPV)*.

Why *DPV?*

This book puts forth a comprehensive and distinct approach to the formulation and implementation of business strategy that is aimed at achieving breakthrough, long-term profitable growth. The central framework in that approach defines a business as the delivery of a value proposition, rather than the dominant definition of a business as the supply of a product.

The term 'value' has been widely used in the discussion of management concepts, but differently than its use here. The idea of creating value for shareholders, for example, is important but different, since value as used here refers to value for customers. That concept of creating value for shareholders is complementary to *DPV*, however, as will be discussed later. Value is also used frequently in strategic frameworks, notably in the ideas of value added and the value chain. These notions, regardless of semantics, are firmly rooted in the view of a business as a product-supply system, focusing on the value of a product and of the processes and resources that supply that product to customers. Value in *Delivering Profitable Value* concerns a very different notion, a difference of fundamental importance to business strategy. It refers to the value, as compared to alternatives, of the resulting experiences customers derive by doing business with the organization. This difference in perspective means that an organization bases its decisions about products and services and how they are developed, made, and distributed entirely on the profitable superiority of the resulting experiences for customers.

Equally great is the difference between the philosophy, framework, and methodology of *DPV* and the endless parade of simplistic nostrums that prescribe promising everything and anything to customers. For *DPV* advocates truly understanding customers' experiences by exploring and studying them in order to improve them profitably. And *DPV* is about disciplined choices. These choices are the strategic decisions to deliver some experiences and to not deliver others, to some customers and not others, in order to maximize the long-term profitable superiority of value delivered.

This *DPV* approach is developed from the perspective of how to create and define businesses successfully rather than that of how to improve the utilization of existing resources marginally. Thus, managers are asked to approach their businesses in the true spirit of entrepreneurialism. Much that is written on entrepreneurial behavior focuses on the importance of freedom from bureaucratic control. But the interpretation of *DPV* emphasizes the entrepreneur's lack of baggage of a subtler kind. The successful entrepreneur feels no duty to leverage some corporate resource or perceived competitive advantage, or to survey customers to find out their less than imaginative 'needs.' Rather, many entrepreneurs who succeed do so because they are free to invent a business designed entirely to improve their potential customers' situation profitably.

While relevant to starting a business from scratch, this perspective of creating a business is no less relevant to improving ongoing businesses where massive investments in assets and capabilities are already in place. Large complex business organizations that understand, apply and ultimately institutionalize the principles of *Delivering Profitable Value* will greatly increase their capability to generate the long-term growth and wealth creatively, in new and regenerated businesses, that characterize a great company.

Specifically, managers in an organization that genuinely adopts *DPV* will learn:

- when and why to say *no* to customers, *no* to internal agendas, and *no* to competitive aping dressed as 'strategy'
- to use a powerful methodology for systematically discovering non-obvious strategic insights hidden in the current experiences of potential customers
- to apply a framework for bringing inescapable clarity and a disciplined choice to what the organization is going to actually do – and not do – to deliver superior value profitably to customers

- how to formulate and execute strategy coherently in the context of the often long and complex chains of supplier–customer relationships, thus using value delivery to:
  - prioritize strategically where in this chain the organization should focus, and
  - win the cooperation and coordinated action of other players in the chain
- to stop using simplistic formulae to escape the complex analytic and creative challenge of formulating corporate and business-unit strategy; and to stop evading real decisions by imposing a chaotic overdose of every known managerial fad upon the organization.

On the other hand, understanding, internalizing, and acting on the principles of *Delivering Profitable Value* also represents a significant *tradeoff* for leaders and their organizations. *DPV* is not two- or even twenty-minute management and it does not contain the three or nine easy-tricks-to-corporate-success-this-quarter. Actually to use, let alone fully institutionalize, the principles presented in this book is without doubt hard work, which requires some measure of courage and faith to persevere in the face of inevitable frustrations and setbacks. Moreover, adopting these principles means letting go of many managerial assumptions about the dynamics of making a business successful. But the value to an organization of rediscovering the real heart of business far outweighs this price.

DPV is offered here as a genuine paradigm shift. Once understood and accepted, I believe this perspective of *DPV* has a revolutionary effect (for the better) on the whole world view of any open-minded manager interested in creating profitable growth. At the same time, many managers will find the ideas in *DPV* not to come from Mars but rather to be already intuitively familiar, as if coming from the reader's own experience. Though the phrase *paradigm shift* has certainly been overused, my colleague Miller Macmillan has pointed out how apt its real meaning is for both the degree and subtlety of change in fundamental perspective that *DPV* represents. As Thomas Kuhn wrote, discussing paradigm shifts in the context of scientific history:

> 'Practicing in different worlds, the two groups [of scientists] see different things when they look from the same point in the same direction ...
> That is why a law that cannot even be demonstrated to one group [of scientists] may occasionally seem intuitively obvious to another. Equally, it is why, before they can hope to communicate fully, one group or the other must experience the conversion that we have been calling a paradigm shift ... [And] it must occur all at once (though not necessarily in an instant), or not at all.'[1]

***

The book presents the *Delivering Profitable Value* philosophy and framework first, explaining, illustrating, and contrasting it with conventional practice. A business is defined in the first 14 chapters of Part One by progressively developing the conceptual building blocks of *DPV*. First, Chapter One further discusses the paradigms that dominate management behavior and assumptions today – the internally-driven and customer-compelled – and contrasts them to the paradigm of *Delivering Profitable Value*. The connection between *DPV* and generating wealth (or, as it is sometimes called, creating shareholder value) is clarified. The internally-driven and customer-compelled models are then contrasted with a detailed example of an organization applying *DPV*.

Then, in Chapters Two through Six, the concept of value proposition is thoroughly explained in rigorous and actionable terms. The discussion begins with the essence of a value proposition –customers' *resulting experiences*. This is followed by the notion that every business delivers some value proposition, but most organizations do not know what propositions they inadvertently deliver. An organization must take real strategic responsibility by specifically *choosing* the value proposition in each business. This is a disciplined choice that many organizations imagine they make; few actually do. Finally, the relevance of competition is explained by discussing the absolute requirement that a value proposition, to be successful, must be *superior* to the customer's alternatives.

Chapters Seven through Nine develop the larger and even more important framework for creating, defining, and managing a business: the *value delivery system*. A business must *deliver* each chosen customer experience. Delivering the value proposition can most intuitively and rigorously be understood as *providing* and *communicating* the value proposition. This leads to the definition of a business as a *value delivery system* (VDS), the central framework in *DPV*. The VDS must be designed and dynamically managed over time.

Chapters Ten through Twelve expand the value delivery framework to encompass the whole complex chain of entities in which most organizations must operate. This chain is explained in *DPV* terms as a *value delivery chain*. An organization must understand and deliver superior value to an array of related entities in the chain, including suppliers, immediate customers, their customers, and other indirectly influential entities. Identifying the most crucial of these entities and their interrelationships is necessary to successful strategy. Most organizations put far too much emphasis on the most immediate entities, those that directly buy the organization's products and services. Correspondingly, they tend to place too little emphasis on ensuring that more important entities further away in the chain derive the value proposition that is necessary for the organization's ultimate business success. In addition, organizations often fail to recognize the crucial importance of securing the cooperation and coordinated action of other players in the chain. Chapter Eleven offers a solution to these problems: the concepts of *primary* and *supporting* VDSs. The primary VDS is the framework for creating and managing a business in *DPV* terms, for it encompasses the delivery of a value proposition to the most important – the primary – entities in a value delivery chain. This delivery includes the actions of other entities in the chain, thus requiring the organization to design the supporting VDSs to secure cooperation of those supporting entities. Chapter Twelve emphasizes that delivering a winning value proposition to a business customer, anywhere in a chain, demands *improving* that customer's own VDS.

Finally, in Chapters Thirteen and Fourteen, business strategy in *DPV* terms culminates in corporate strategy. A firm's leadership should see its most important roles as defining and redefining the firm's primary VDSs, and as supporting the building of the capabilities needed to implement those VDSs. In addition, these VDSs must be understood and designed in the context of their *market-space*, the set of other related potential VDSs with which they may interact. A *market-space* is more than the conventional notions of a market: a group of customers or a group of customers and their demand for some product. It does include a set of customers, but as part of a set of potential, related businesses or value delivery systems. Numerous examples illustrate the principles that constitute this different view, this value-delivery focused philosophy of corporate strategy.

Part One thus proposes that a firm's strategy should consist of its choice and design of the primary value delivery systems it will implement within each market-space where it will compete. Part Two proposes a comprehensive methodology to formulate and execute such strategy without getting bogged down in the internally-driven and customer-compelled traps of the conventional approaches to formulating business strategy. The methodology of *Delivering Profitable Value* is based on two essential principles. First, strategic *value delivery options* must be identified by systematically *becoming* customers in relevant market-spaces. Then, a *disciplined choice* of the winning options, the firm's primary VDSs, must thoroughly determine all the organization's actions.

Applying *DPV*, an organization first identifies, in market-spaces worth exploring, the businesses it could pursue. Each market-space is thus analyzed to identify the organization's strategic options in it – the potential primary VDSs. This can be compared to but is very different from the common meaning of the terms 'segment' and 'segmentation.' This analysis entails systematically becoming potential customers, estimating what competing value propositions customers will have available, and then gauging the capability gaps the organization must close to execute the identified winning VDSs profitably. It includes quantifying the opportunity and challenge that the potential businesses represent and then choosing the optimal combination of them. The *DPV* methodology draws in some ways upon but differs dramatically from conventional methods of segmentation, market research, competitive analysis, and the prioritizing of capabilities or competencies. Chapters Fifteen through Eighteen discuss in detail this fundamentally different, value-delivery focused approach to formulating business strategy.

Chapter Nineteen explains how *real* business plans should commit the organization to executing, measuring, and adjusting its chosen design of businesses and associated capability building. Lastly, Chapter Twenty suggests some concrete first steps to begin the process of formulating and implementing strategy by the principles of *DPV*. Organizations that learn to deliver profitable value in this comprehensive, disciplined fashion and continuously improve this ability will leave the internally-driven and customer-compelled behaviors behind. Such organizations no longer develop or execute business strategy in a managerial looking glass. They steadily build the profound organizational capabilities to discover great value propositions and to deliver them in a brilliantly coordinated fashion. As a result, they enjoy a much higher probability of achieving dramatic long-term growth and sustained generation of wealth. And they have more fun.

The reader will already have noticed that *DPV* uses plenty of vocabulary and concepts common in management practice, yet with many significantly different twists. As Thomas Kuhn noted:

> 'Since new paradigms are born from old ones, they ordinarily incorporate much of the vocabulary and apparatus, both conceptual and manipulative, that the traditional paradigm had previously employed. But they seldom employ these borrowed elements in quite the traditional way. Within the new paradigm, old terms, concepts ... fall into new relationships one with the other.'[2]

Whence DPV?

The book is based on sufficient authority and expertise in this area. I first created the seminal concepts of value proposition and value delivery system in 1983–4, while with McKinsey & Company. I spent seven years there as a strategy consultant, after a like period in brand management with Procter & Gamble. That original work was an attempt to reconcile two perspectives. In the value delivery framework I took much that was essential in my brand management education, including the central importance of shaping a business around customers' real experiences, and combined it with McKinsey's systems thinking that saw a business as an integrated system of interrelated resources and functions. McKinsey's business-system framework (the basis, as acknowledged in Michael Porter's 1985 book *Competitive Advantage*, for the more widely popularized Porter value chain) was focused on *supplying a product*. The value delivery system focused instead on *delivering a value proposition*.

My work was sponsored by a senior Director of McKinsey, Edward G. Michaels, who challenged me to develop a new framework that would orient strategy more centrally around customer insight. Ed, one of the best consultants I've ever encountered, pushed the value delivery thinking, and the genesis of *DPV* thus owes much to him. Subsequently, McKinsey has developed and widely used the value delivery framework. Meanwhile, the phrase 'value proposition' has become commonplace in business, although rarely accompanied by its actual, non-trivial meaning.

In 1987, about to leave McKinsey, I met Lynn Phillips, a teacher on Stanford's business school faculty. Then-Mckinsey partner Elliot Ross had introduced him to the framework in the form of a presentation that Michaels and I had titled *Building Market-Focused Organizations*. Lynn encouraged me to develop and use further the calue deliver ideas as the basis of a course and executive education practice. He and I formed a partnership and taugh that course (called *Building Market-Focused Organizations*, known ove the years as *BMFO*). We and our colleagues in Lanning, Phillips & Associates (LPA) presented it to over 20,000 executives in over 60 client firms worldwide over the next decade. Thus, Lynn provided executive education and advice to numerous clients mentioned in this book. As Ed Michaels had earlier, lynn pushed my thinking in many aspects of the value delivery concepts for a decade. The full development of *DPV* thus also owes a debt of gratitude to Lynn, who independently continues to teach *BMFO*.

Over the past 25 years, good fortune has provided me with a broad and rich mix of raw material from which to draw in creating and thinking about this *DPV* philosophy, framework, and methodology. My line management, consulting, and teaching experience includes computer systems and related products and services, consumer packaged goods, textiles, apparel, telecommunications, beverages, banking and investment management, forest products, retailing, chemicals, pharmaceuticals, petroleum and gas, transportation, consumer and industrial imaging products and services, health care, professional services, and various other industries. *DPV* draws heavily on that experience and on the similarly diverse experience of my colleagues. In the past three years I revised the articulation of the entire value delivery framework and methodology, in the process of writing this book. That exercise also led to the formation of the strategy consulting firm, *The DPV Group*, which is entirely devoted to helping clients discover, understand, and apply the *DPV* approach.

The book makes extensive use of examples. Some of these concern well-known strategic innovations or failures, on which other observers may have commented before. However, the object here is to explain that they can best be understood through the lens of *Delivering Profitable Value*. Kuhn pointed out:

'All historically significant theories have agreed with the facts, but only more or less. There is no more precise answer to the question whether or how well an individual theory fits the facts. But questions much like that can be asked when theories are taken collectively or even in pairs. It makes a great deal of sense to ask which of two actual and competing theories fits the facts better.'

For example, many have noted the surprising triumphs of businesses such as Southwest Airlines (SWA) or Glaxo Wellcome's blockbuster Zantac. Some leading strategic thinkers have tried to reconcile the unconventional behavior of these firms with their undeniable success by saying that these firms differentiated their business models, that they were 'contrarians' who won because they did things differently. But this principle cannot help managers create innovative strategies! The important question is why did these differentiated business models, which contradicted converntional strategic doctrine, actually work? Likewise, some have tried to explain these successes as reflecting great service and unflinching adherence to each customer whim. But this theory fails to explain why these innovators made key decisions in contradiction to unambiguous customer expectations. Supported by learning from SWA's founder (Rollin King, who has lectured on SWA as part of BMFO classes) and by consulting work with Glaxo in the late 1980s, this book will explain why these firms really succeeded. They discovered innovative resulting experiences customers preferred, often despite what those customers said before experiencing them. Heedless of violating industry conventional wisdom and strategic orthodoxy, they designed and executed with discipline the brilliant delivery of these experiences. As Rollin King commented in endorsing LPA and BMFO,

'At Southwest Airlines, delivering superior value to our target customers is the cornerstone around which we have built our success. Every employee in the company is engaged in the effort, not just the marketing depatment, After being exposed to it [the value delivery framework], it all comes together and makes it much easier to pass on to new generations of management. The only problem with their material is that now our competitors may learn why we have been killing them in the markeplace all these years!'

Many other examples of successes and failures that enliven the argument in favor of *DPV* populate these pages as well, from a diverse range of firms including Federal Express, Fidelity, Sony, Perdue Chickens, British Airways, Kodak, Procter & Gamble, Microsoft, BHP, General Motors, Volvo, Hewlett-Packard, Apple, Coca-Cola, Sensomatics, Service Masters, and numerous others.

However, among the most important examples discussed are ones where the specific *DPV* framework and methodology have been deliberately and successfully applied, such as in the above example of CTD. The success stories discussed in some depth include: Chevron's US natural gas business (since merged with NGC Corp); Glaxo's Zantac; Weyerhaeuser; several HP businesses including reseller distribution and PCs; and several Kodak businesses.

The natural gas business, for example, appears to be as pure a commodity as one could find. What could there be to a winning value proposition except for price? Steve Furbacher, now President of energy firm Dynegy Midstream Services (subsidiary of Dynegy, Inc.), commented on Chevron's use of the *DPV* approach.

> 'As General Manager of Chevron's Natural Gas Business Unit (NGBU) in the early 1990s, we used the DPV concepts to help us rethink strategy and develop the market-focused capabilities needed to improve results in a commoditized business. Along with our Total Quality program, we used the DPV concepts to genuinely transform the NGBU culture. Our people learned to understand and reinvent our businesses from the perspective of what customers would really value – different both from trying to sell them what we want to make and from asking them to tell us what they think they want. In customer satisfaction we went from the bottom quartile in our industry to number two out of about 40 ranked companies. In bottom-line performance we increased margins some 40 percent, worth over $15MM annually.'

In the late 1980s, Hewlett-Packard was on the verge of giving up on Vectra, its attempt to enter the PC business. The management team first assumed that it desperately needed to analyze and segment the entire PC market, but a faster, more practical application of the *DPV* methodology was in order. Using a rifle rather than a shotgun, a targeted exploration of customers' experiences revealed a very interesting value proposition that Vectra, unbeknownst to HP, had inadvertently delivered to a small set of customers. Recognizing the much larger strategic option this discovery represented, the Vectra team was able to breathe life into the nearly dead business. This paid off in the long-term, as HP's PC business stayed alive and later became a success to rival its great printer business.

Also in the late 1980s, Glaxo Welcome's (then Glaxo's) antiulcerant Zantac had already far exceeded management's original expectations and seemed to have reached a plateau. Using the *DPV* framework in a seminar forum, country management teams worldwide found that the key elements in Zantac's winning value proposition had yet to be truly communicated to many physicians. Refocusing on this proposition helped accelerate Zantac's growth again. Then Director of Glaxo Holdings, Franz Humer noted:

> 'This workshop revitalized the marketing and sales strategies behind our leading product throughout our subsidiaries around the world. It

clearly focused people's minds on what is important to maintain unprecedented growth of the world's most successful pharmaceutical product ten years after it was first launched.'

***

Many people find that *DPV,* on close examination, seems self-evidently reasonable. They often feel that, while they have never put the concepts together in this manner or expressed many of them in this way, they have on some level known and believed many of the ideas that make up *DPV.* Yet it is equally clear that fully adopting *DPV* would mean changing a great deal in most organizations. Among the dramatic changes it may entail are the way in which businesses are defined, success-criteria adopted, the organization structured, market-spaces explored for their strategic options, customers studied, competition analyzed, and resources, processes and functions developed and managed. Making these changes disrupts business-as-usual quite a lot more than trading-in last year's buzzwords for the newest collection, only to perpetuate the same internally-driven and customer-compelled thinking.

But for those not too timid of heart or lazy of mind, here is a way to act upon the truth about business. All thinking managers, those with both eyes open, will know it intuitively. For business is about the creative relationship between an organization, other players it must influence, and the organization's real customer. To maximize the chances of sustained success, businesses must be conceived and managed accordingly.

Notes

1   Thomas S. Kuhn, *The Structure of Scientific Revolutions,* University of Chicago Press, 1970, p. 150.

2   *Ibid,* p. 149.

3   *Ibid,* p. 147.

Understand the Heart of Business: What *Delivering Profitable Value* Is

Part One explains and illustrates how business strategy can be understood in terms of the principles of *Delivering Profitable Value (DPV)*. It discusses strategy at the individual business unit and the corporate level, when it is based on understanding a business as a *value delivery system*. Such a strategy recognizes each business as the disciplined choice of a true winning value proposition and the deliberately designed integration of all resources and actions around the profitable delivery of that proposition. This central framework of the value delivery system is then extended to allow strategic prioritization within the complex chain of customer-supplier relationships within which many businesses must operate. Finally, it is shown to be the proper focus of corporate strategy, which in its essence is defining, by market-space, the businesses – value delivery systems – by which the firm will grow and generate wealth.

Chapter One

Internally-Driven and Customer-Compelled Management Aren't *Value-Delivery* Focused

DPV, although based in part on numerous existing ideas, in its totality is relatively new. Once understood, *DPV* can light a new path to long-term business success. Far less traveled than the internally-driven and customer-compelled paths, this path is for those committed to succeeding by profitably delivering superior value to customers.

Most firms' behavior towards customers is internally-driven

Organizations do not behave in an internally-driven manner out of stupidity or ignorance. It is rather natural, for anyone inside a business organization, to view the business from the inside out: let's make a product (a 'good' one, of course) and then sell it to some customers. Moreover, the internally-driven organization usually does not altogether ignore customers and may, in fact, pay much attention to competitors and various other external issues. Much of conventional management theory reinforces internally-driven thinking by encouraging managers to formulate strategy unhindered by any serious analysis of customers' real lives and businesses. But there are two more fundamental reasons behind internally-driven behavior.

1   As compared to understanding customer experiences beyond the most superficial level, it is much easier to identify, measure, compare, and manage the characteristics and attributes of the organization's products and product-supply resources and processes.
2   Organizations are *in no hurry* to look too deeply into customer experiences, lest they find little competitive difference they can do little about.

Nonetheless, leaders who want businesses that consistently and profitably deliver superior value must help their organization recognize internally-driven decision making for what it is and force it out of their culture.

Internally-driven behavior essentially consists of attempting, consciously or unconsciously, to impose the organization's view and its outputs on customers with inadequate regard for what is actually most valuable to them. The organization makes whatever it is comfortable making or whatever it believes itself relatively good at making, as compared to competitors. This can result in profitably delivering superior value to customers, if the organization is lucky. That is, if the internally-driven organization happens to be competent at making and selling something that happens to deliver experiences of superior value, the organization happens to make money. But if the organization delivers a less valuable experience than some alternative, its luck has run out.

One important version of this behavior includes very close attention to competition. Such organizations manage by *competitive* strategy, focusing intently on the organization's position in its industry relative to competing forces. The organization works hard to exert superior power over these competing forces, which include customers and suppliers. It searches for the leverage to defeat competitors and force its own will on customers, hoping to *extract* customers' revenues rather than *win* their lasting preference.

There is a paradox here. By focusing so hard on exerting power, instead of understanding and profitably delivering superior value, an organization often *loses* power. By focusing instead on becoming customers, discovering and profoundly understanding what would truly be most valuable to them, an organization *gains* tremendous power. Power over competitors, suppliers, and customers.

Some internally-driven cultures are less aggressive. These organizations are not so inclined to focus on controlling customers and getting power over competitors. Rather, they remain firmly within their comfort zone, encouraged by the success the status quo has brought them. Their fondest wish is to be allowed to keep doing what they understand and do well without interruption.

For example, Xerox first succeeded through a bold gamble on xerography. In the late 1950s, dimwitted market research projected little demand for xerographic machines. Although at that time unable to sell the technology, the company bet that customers' low interest in xerographic technology did not reflect its potential value to them. As a result of this gamble, Xerox deservedly became a huge success. Then, as documented by D.K. Smith and R.C. Alexander in *Fumbling the Future*, internally-driven thinking gradually took over, costing Xerox part of its copier business and causing it to fumble one of the biggest ever technological opportunities.

Xerox had a proven formula for success in its highly successful medium and higher-speed copiers (30–70 copies per minute). These used dry toner – the powdered ink that is momentarily melted and then cooled at high speed to fix it on the page – and specially designed, customized parts. They were sold by a sophisticated direct sales force and supported by a high quality, extremely responsive service contract. Xerox leased these copiers, in effect selling copies, not machines.

Xerox used this same proven formula in its low-end copiers (typically 8–20 copies per minute) business. The low-end represented a small portion of the total copies that produced revenues, so the company placed a low priority on it. Thus, Xerox ignored these copiers' imperfections: too big, prone to frequent breakdown and very expensive. It didn't seem to occur to Xerox management to redesign this business with a focus on profitably increasing reliability and reducing size and cost of the copiers. Instead, Xerox stuck with the proven formula, imposing the distinct skills and techniques that worked in one business onto another less important but quite different one. As my colleague and imaging-business veteran Dan Draper points out, it took another 20 years for Xerox finally to introduce a family of low volume machines truly designed from the ground up for these users. Moreover, they have combined this product line with a service organization that is now truly tuned in to customers' experiences. But in the mid-1970s, Xerox didn't get it.

At that time, Savin/Ricoh led a Japanese assault on this low-end business. Savin used liquid toner, which did not have the cost and reliability problems of dry toner. Further improving cost and reliability, they designed the machine for maximum use of off-the-shelf, standardized parts. Much less expensive service contracts were needed, since machine downtime was a mere third of that of the Xerox machine. Savin/Ricoh eschewed the unnecessary cost of a direct sales force, using instead office equipment dealers who sold rather than leased machines. Overall, the net price per copy was well under half that of Xerox.

Savin quite effectively communicated the vastly superior value they provided. One ad displayed a Xerox copier's 'call key operator' button – which, when lit, indicates a machine breakdown – labeling it Xerox's 'feature that works best.'[1] By 1976 Savin claimed to have displaced Xerox as number one. So much for the low-end. This loss exposed Xerox, letting competitors in the door of every customer.

Meanwhile, over the next decade, Xerox invented some of the most impressive and ultimately important computer technology but essentially squandered it all. The company began with an exciting R&D vision, that of developing a whole new way of using computer technology to enhance thinking and communication in offices. As a result, Xerox invented most of the technologies that today make small computers reasonably easy to use and effective in communications. The output of Xerox's PARC (Palo Alto Research Center) personal computing research was simply astounding.

Xerox PARC was years ahead of anything even comparable. Consider that in the early 1970s PARC, arguably, really invented the first personal computer, the concept of distributed computing, the first graphics-capable monitor, the mouse, the first computer icons, the concept of windows on a screen, the first user-friendly word-processing program, the first use of the WYSIWYG (what you see [on the screen] is what you get [when printed]) principle, the first multitasking capabilities, the first local area network (Ethernet), the first object-oriented programming language, and the first laser printer.

The one thing almost as amazing as this bundle of spectacular innovations was that Xerox managed to do virtually nothing with it. Apple, then Microsoft, and eventually the rest of the IT industry made billions of dollars from the Xerox creations, but not Xerox. In retrospect, this was truly a great triumph of an internally-driven culture. Wedded to the Xerox way of making and selling copiers, the organization could not realize that its solutions for the low-end copier market-space were entirely wrong, until too late. In this copier-centric culture, the PARC technology seemed from another planet, even though senior management had requested it. As a result, these concepts were smothered, ambushed and hog-tied.

Trying to explain this bizarre failure, one former Xerox official who had opposed PARC's project later argued that the Alto (Xerox's PC) would have been too expensive. 'For the price that had to be paid, the Alto would not live up to customer expectations ... It wouldn't have been a successful business venture.'[2] This comment was based on a 1973 cost estimate, which assumed an extremely expensive laser printer would accompany each machine. By 1976, costs had dropped dramatically and a far less expensive printer solution was attainable. This didn't deter Alto opponents, however; that was the year the company decided not to introduce Alto. The logic was a bit like rejecting the telephone, car or refrigerator on the grounds that an early prototype looked expensive.

The company's visionary statement of aspirations[3] wasn't much help during this time. In the 1960s, CEO Joe Wilson said, 'We aspire to be a leader throughout the world in graphic communication.' In 1970, CEO Peter McColough stated, 'Our fundamental thrust, our common denominator, has evolved toward establishing leadership in what we call the "architecture of information."'[4] Apparently, making such a statement doesn't guarantee it'll sink in.

The organization didn't introduce anything for nearly a decade after inventing the Alto. The copier-oriented culture took over the PARC project, spawning endless battles over control of the technology. In late 1977 Xerox showcased the PARC technology at 'Futures Day,' an event designed to convince Xerox managers of the technology's worth. Although the PARC scientists were initially excited at this opportunity, one later recalled their disappointment:

> 'The reactions we saw in the wives were what we had hoped to see in the men. What was remarkable was that almost to a couple, the man would stand back and be very skeptical and reserved, and the wives, many of whom had been secretaries, got enthralled by moving around the mouse, seeing the graphics on the screen, and using the color printer. The men had no background, really, to grasp the significance of it. I would look out and see bright enthusiasm in the eyes of the women, and the men just asking, in a standoffish way, "Oh, can it do that?"'[5]

Later, someone in upper management thought maybe they could unload this distracting PARC technology, so they offered Steve Jobs of Apple a *tour* of PARC. Seeing the cornucopia of brilliant concepts, Jobs apparently exclaimed, 'Why isn't Xerox marketing this? You could blow everybody away?'[6] Xerox didn't sell the technology, but Jobs had seen the concepts, many of which, with the help of numerous PARC employees who joined Apple, later became the Macintosh.

Although certifiably internally-driven in this case, Xerox is a creative and intelligent organization. Another, more primitive version of internally-driven behavior consists of being *Imitation-Inspired*. An imitation-inspired culture has no clue what to do, so it imitates the most successful competition in its industry. Few managers would defend such a model any longer, but it still exists.

Also prevalent among internally-driven organizations is cost-controlled behavior. In this case, organizations are so inwardly focused that the outside world, with the exception of shareholders, is almost completely shut out. Paradoxically, cost-controlled behavior so narrowly focuses on cost that it doesn't even reduce cost very well. Unintentionally, the organization ignores the experiences of greatest value to customers. This leads to numerous false economies that increase costs over the long-term. In contrast, when managers *do* understand these experiences and define what the organization must do to deliver them, an organization can discover hidden, often dramatic opportunities to save cost.

The cost-controlled culture cuts costs democratically; all costs are equals. It therefore is likely to cut some costs that are essential for delivering the most valuable resulting experiences to customers. The cost-controlled organization doesn't notice this mistake because it doesn't identify and understand those experiences in the first place. Conversely, it sustains costs that are actually quite unnecessary for delivering the most valuable experiences. The organization may justify these costs by thinking 'We always do it this way' or 'our leading competitor does it.' This approach leaves virtually no chance for the organization to deliver a winning value proposition while incurring only the truly requisite costs.

Organizations must define and deliberately build the most important capabilities they will need to deliver superior value profitably in the future. But many managers have latched onto the idea of core competencies as an excuse for rationalizing activities with little connection to value delivery, at least in the real world. Reinvesting in processes and technologies simply because the organization can be relatively good at them can easily produce internally-driven strategies that reflect little understanding of the experiences customers would potentially value.

While wandering around in Looking Glass house, Alice met many odd but entertaining characters, many of whom are Chess pieces in an arcane version of the game that is woven through her adventures. One endearing fellow she meets is the White Knight. His Core Competence was falling off his horse.

> 'Whenever the horse stopped (which it did very often), he fell off in front; and, whenever it went on again (which it generally did rather suddenly), he fell off behind. Otherwise he kept on pretty well, except that he had a habit of now and then falling off sideways ...
>
> '"I'm afraid you've not had much practice in riding," she ventured to say, as she was helping him up from his fifth tumble.
>
> 'The Knight looked very much surprised, and a little offended at the remark. "What makes you say that?" he asked, as he scrambled back into the saddle, keeping hold of Alice's hair with one hand, to save himself from falling over on the other side.
>
> '"Because people don't fall off quite so often, when they've had much practice."
>
> '"I've had plenty of practice," the Knight said very gravely: "plenty of practice!"
>
> 'Alice could think of nothing better to say than "Indeed?" but she said it as heartily as she could.[7]

Internally-driven management begins not by asking what experiences potential customers would most value; it starts instead with what it likes to do or thinks it can do better than competitors. The internally-driven company knows what it does. It knows its products, services, technologies and its technological and operational capabilities. It knows its sales and marketing techniques and positional strengths. And it usually knows what its current buyers request and expect. What it doesn't know is the winning value propositions for each market-space in which it could compete. It therefore can't reevaluate what it *should* do except by very indirect indicators.

Lacking the focus on delivering superior value, the internally-driven organization can only repeat whatever worked before. Correlating actions and resources with past victories, the organization vainly hopes to find the key factors for success. When the internally-driven organization gets into trouble, it may change products, services, or processes but, without a coherent vision, it gropes for what it might want to accomplish.

Customer-compelled illusions: that's still *you* in the mirror

The great majority of organizations tend toward the internally-driven modes of management. Management usually realizes at some point that the organization's internally-driven processes and decision-making frequently frustrate or even infuriate customers. Most want to avoid this malaise and so naturally gravitate toward the apparent cure: the organization should be *driven*, not by our technologies and ingrained processes but rather by none other than The King – the customer. Go ask the customer, listen to them, do as they say, and all shall be well.

Yet this behavior provides only an illusory escape from the egotistical mentality of the internally-driven culture. Organizations commonly implement solutions without having defined the problem. Such solutions-in-search-of-a-problem are most often internally-driven, and are designed to leverage the organization's technological-, production-, or marketing-know-how, to increase its competitive differentiation, or to achieve a lower cost than the competition. On the other hand, customers' demands or expectations are sometimes used to define these supposed solutions. These customer-compelled solutions are usually no more likely to solve the right problem, however, than internally-driven ones, since a customer problem is still not well understood.

Both the internally-driven and customer-compelled organizations frame the same wrong question ('What products or services should we develop, produce, and market/sell, and how?'). Rather than answer this wrong question based on what we want to do, the customer-compelled approach asks the customer to answer this wrong question for us! This false panacea is no improvement, despite the passionate fervor with which some experts and their followers extol it. Customer-compelled behavior still only amounts to focusing on the organization, to asking the customer to hold the mirror while the organization continues to gaze into it. As such, organizations using this model fail to penetrate any but the most superficial understanding of the customer and their real experience.

Most politicians provide a vivid example of the customer-compelled mentality. Most politicians don't think through, articulate and win support for a coherent vision of society. Instead, they typically lurch from one position to the next based on the latest focus group or poll. Somehow, these same politicians are perplexed when the public finds them unprincipled and cynical.

In contrast, those rare politicians who have had lasting impact on societies, such as Lincoln, Churchill, Roosevelt, De Gaulle, or more recently Thatcher, Reagan, and Mandela, pursued visions they thought best for society. They sold their strategies, usually encountering great resistance and lack of understanding, not by reacting to public opinion but by convincing their public to believe in their vision.

Customer-compelled behavior regularly causes organizations to miss or reject great opportunity. When consulted about the great product and technological advances of this century, potential customers established a fine track record for almost always being wrong. It is difficult to imagine the complex set of experiences resulting from using an unfamiliar product or service. Customers confidently rejected the idea of computers, photocopiers, microwave ovens, cellphones, personal computers, voice mail, and many other initially dumb-sounding ideas without which they now wouldn't want to live.

Scott Adams, creator of the comic strip about the business philosopher Dilbert, discusses the traditional use of market research in projecting demand for new technologies, giving the following example of great 'historical uses of market surveys':[8]

Airline Survey (1920)

If you had to travel a long distance, would you rather:

A. Drive a car

B. Take a train

C. Allow yourself to be strapped into a huge metal container that weighs more than your house and be propelled through space by exploding chemicals while knowing that any one of a thousand different human, mechanical, or weather problems would cause you to be incinerated in a spectacular ball of flame.

If you answered 'C' would you mind if we stomped on your luggage and sent it to another city?

Similarly, customer-compelled inquiries can persuade organizations to adopt weak ideas. Repeatedly, consumers have responded with enthusiasm, in market research, to descriptions of environmentally friendly 'green' products. But when customers are confronted, in reality, with a product that doesn't work as well, smells funny, is hard to use and costs more, the market projections somehow fail to materialize. Many consumers told Kodak they couldn't wait to watch still photos on their TVs, and yet Photo CD hasn't quite caught on. Consumers wanting to seem reasonably sophisticated and open to new technology may unintentionally mislead the researcher.

Some managers assume that industrial, business-to-business buyers differ from consumer buyers in that they *know* what they need. Not much evidence supports this bit of wisdom. In fact, in complex industrial marketspaces, the buyer often obscures the identity of the more important actual users in the customer organization. Japanese computer companies invested heavily, in the 1970s and early 1980s, in very large computers – mainframes and super-computers. Any diligent study of computer buyers in corporations and governments in the 1970s strongly reinforced this focus. In the process, most Japanese computer companies missed the sea change to smaller computers.

Dutifully listening to customers prevents the organization ever gaining any real insight into the most valuable opportunities for those customers. Consider Weyerhaeuser.

In 1990, forest products giant Weyerhaeuser's particleboard[9] business was struggling to survive. Particleboard was a commodity; Weyerhaeuser's was no different than that of competitor Georgia-Pacific (G-P). A large particle board customer group used it to make less expensive furniture. These customers made clear to Weyerhaeuser's sales force what they needed. They wanted particleboard meeting industry quality standards, the right quantity, the right dimensions, on-time delivery, and a low price. Both Weyerhaeuser and G-P could meet the specs, but G-P enjoyed slightly lower costs and so earned acceptable returns at a price not sustainable for Weyerhaeuser.

Weyerhaeuser's sales force constantly *listened* to customers. The message was clear: price is what counts. So they duly concentrated on cutting costs. But Weyerhaeuser *and* its customers were wrong. Much better opportunities for both lay in rethinking the furniture companies' use of particleboard.

A multifunctional Weyerhaeuser team learned that using larger dimension particleboard could save customers the significant cost of gluing smaller pieces together. Yet the customers never requested thicker board since it had not been made before. Plants were designed to make only the thinner board; if feasible, producing thicker board would certainly require a slower, higher cost process, thus increasing the price per board foot. But of course, if the cost of gluing exceeded the premium paid for thicker board, the furniture company would get superior value even at a higher price.

Later, Weyerhaeuser discovered a similar opportunity to increase revenue by enabling these customers to use new, more attractive laminates. These laminates were previously difficult to use because of the imperfect particle board surface to which they had to be laminated. The company learned to discover such opportunities continually. In fact, they redefined their 'Composite Products' businesses by studying and redesigning, often with customer input, both the customers' processes and Weyerhaeuser's products.

The customer-compelled organization resists such an approach to customers. Managers often think, 'We can't go in and tell them how to run their business! We don't know as much about the furniture business as they do. If there were better ways to run their business and they needed something different from us, they would have asked us a long time ago.' To the manager making the statement, this seems highly respectful of the honored customer. But this attitude actually causes managers to shrug off the responsibility for profitably pursuing the customer's best interests.

Customer-compelled behavior seems to indicate a higher concern for the customer, but by focusing exclusively on meeting the customer's needs and expectations, an organization often ends up satisfying them *less*. By listening a lot less, by saying no, and by trying to understand what *would* be most valuable for a customer, an organization can often satisfy customers much more.

Customer-compelled behavior is often manifested by attention to the wrong 'level' in the 'chain' of customers. That is, organizations are often fixated on the most immediate entity (firm or department or individual) that buys the organization's product. Often the immediate customer's *customer* should really be the central focus of the organization.

Yet, organizations are often so intent on 'meeting customer needs' and 'totally satisfying' them that they cannot stop listening to the demands of immediate customers long enough really to understand the customer entity of real primary importance, further down the chain. In similar fashion, organizations may devote too much attention to the demands and perspective of those in the buying role. In the process, the organization does not devote enough effort to understanding the customer's whole business. This deeper understanding should include the people and functions within the customer entity who are most impacted by the organization's products.

An organization must use some criteria to select which customer requests actually to honor. In the absence of a specific chosen value proposition, the organization ends up doing what it thinks it can do, what it is good at doing, what matches its 'strategy.' Thus, the customer-compelled organization, with great intensity of interest, asks customers what they want, and then does what it would have done without such input.

Customer-compelled behavior does not help managers make real business *decisions*, only customer-oriented-sounding commitments. A winning value proposition is often a *tradeoff*, with some resulting experiences superior and some inferior to the customer's alternatives. The customer-compelled organization is unaware of this reality and is searching instead for total solutions, such as 'total satisfaction, quality, or service.' Total is better than partial, undoubtedly. But businesses can not deliver everything to everyone, ever. Pretending they can leads only to a facade of satisfaction.

For example, most airlines assure passengers that *they* are the airline most committed to passengers' total satisfaction. Among other measures by which the airlines try to prove their superior devotion, most work very hard at punctuality – on time departures and arrivals. Talking with a baggage handler recently about why bags sometimes end up on the wrong flights revealed an interesting perspective. 'You've got to understand,' he explained, 'what they [management of the airline] look at is – did the flight leave on time? I hear about it if I put an "on-time" in jeopardy by trying to get a few bags loaded last minute. So I see another flight in two hours to the same city, I'll often play it safe, throw your bag on the belt for the later flight. We all do that; nobody says nothing.' Result: the airline protects its on-time performance; the passenger arrives on time, only to lose a couple of aggravated hours waiting for their bag. (Moral: tip the bag handler at curbside check-in.)

Thus, organizations donning the satisfaction facade understand that they must *commit* to satisfaction and demonstrate this commitment to customers. But this is quite different from understanding that they must actually deliver experiences of superior value. Leaders must work hard to keep their organizations from falling into this confusion. Delivering a winning value proposition often requires convincing customers to accept some hard tradeoffs, not just innocuous pabulum. The satisfaction facade may frequently reflect indecision and a lack of clear commitment. As George Bush once said, 'All I was doing was appealing for an endorsement, not suggesting you endorse it.'[10]

Few organizations are exclusively internally-driven; fewer still are purely customer-compelled. Most organizations try to counteract the toxic effects of internally-driven behavior with a regimen of customer-compelled behavior.

Often, organizations sense that both types of behavior are flawed and so shuttle back and forth between the two. Indecision and confusion, ill-defined businesses, misguided restructuring, functional disintegration, wasted resources, and ultimately a lower probability of success are among the frustrating results.

The wages of internally-driven and customer-compelled behavior

Well, so what? Does it matter if a firm is internally-driven and customer-compelled to boot? Only if that firm cares about achieving the greatest possible success. For these behaviors inhibit an organization from developing the capabilities needed to deliver superior value profitably. Internally-driven and customer-compelled organizations do not recognize the central strategic importance of choosing for each business the value proposition it will deliver. It follows that these organizations are not designed to deliver a particular value proposition. Instead, organizations are structured around products, assets, technologies, skills, convenient groupings of customers, or some mix of these across its diverse resources. In addition, the measurement, reward, and accounting systems are not aligned with delivering a winning value proposition.

These constraints manifest themselves in three respects.

First, innovations in product and service (hereafter just 'product' for shorthand) weakly and inefficiently enhance the delivery of superior value. Technology and product development are not informed by an in depth familiarity with the detailed experiences of customers, especially the potential users of the product. Instead, the marketing or sales function supposedly analyzes customers' needs and passes these requirements on to R&D so that they can meet them. Or perhaps R&D asks customers directly to detail their own requirements. Even worse, R&D may be charged with differentiating the organization's product versus its competitors. All too frequently, the organization explicitly encourages R&D to develop products that leverage the technological skills the organization deems most important.

Second, organizations dramatically under-utilize non-product/service resources by failing to use them to enhance or even transform customers' experiences. Like R&D, these functional entities in the organization are too isolated from the real experiences of customers. They may be bombarded with customer suggestions, satisfaction surveys, and the like. But manufacturing/operations, after-sales service, support, logistics, billing and so forth rarely gain anything more than a superficial glimpse of customers' real lives. Often these functional entities are told they need not understand customers deeply. Marketing determines customers' needs; R&D creates products that meet them. These other functions should simply minimize costs and customer complaints. (Then people are surprised to find these functions acting internally-driven.)

Finally, the customer-communications functions fail miserably in communicating superior value propositions. Advertising, sales and other communications-oriented functions are not expected to convince potential users of superior resulting experiences. These organizations discount such mundane objectives and as a result, judge advertising campaigns by their popularity or 'creativity' (as measured by marketing awards) rather than their ability to communicate the right value proposition and build a business. Similarly, the sales force, with an exaggerated appraisal of the importance of 'relationships,' is not guided or expected to communicate a specific, agreed value proposition. Furthermore, these organizations devote a disproportionate amount of analytic attention to the quantitative aspect of communications. Management and their consultants worry greatly over media or sales coverage plans; the focus is on which doors to knock and how often. Deciding what message to convey, a decision critical to ultimate success, is not accorded strategic significance.

Organizations may not fail as a result of these shortcomings. With luck, they may manage to deliver some winning value propositions profitably. Most organizations, however, hindered by such poor value delivery ability, will generate far less wealth than they could have otherwise. Of course, these firms may still survive. General Motors, IBM, Philips, Xerox, AT&T, Siemens, Texaco and countless others make huge mistakes, miss enormous opportunity, but have survived. Obviously, many other firms have eventually disappeared.

Delivering profitable value is about making money

> *'The engine which drives Enterprise is not Thrift, but Profit.'*
> John Maynard Keynes, 1930

> *'Ohhhh, I get it! It's a profit deal!!'*
> Steve Martin, in the movie *The Jerk*

The framework and methodology of *Delivering Profitable Value* rest on the starting assumption that a firm should manage its businesses to maximize the long-term wealth they generate for that firm. 'Maximizing' means, of course, doing so within the ethical and legal boundaries set by the stakeholders of that firm. To this end, each business in a firm should be given the clear primary objective of maximizing over the long-term the value they deliver to customers at a cost allowing profitable returns – that is, allowing generation of wealth.

Over time, a firm *must* generate wealth, meaning it must gain revenues that at least match its total costs, including the cost of capital invested. Otherwise, a firm withers and eventually disappears. In principle, by generating wealth, the firm will continue to attract capital and be able to compete, survive, and even grow. Thus, in *DPV*, 'making money' is meant in the sense of the 'economic' definition rather than that of the 'accounting model' of profit. The economic definition essentially says that a company's market value is determined by discounting its expected cash flows back to a present value, at a rate reflecting the company's cost of capital. This notion of measuring a firm's financial success in terms of the real wealth generated for the firm's owners was first articulated by economists in the 1960s. It was originally popularized by the consultancy Stern Stewart, under the term 'EVA' (Economic Value Added) and later further popularized by Marakon Associates as 'VBM' (Value Based Management). Many people also currently refer to 'creating shareholder value.'

The principles of *DPV* are wholly in accord with this rational measurement model (although not with some proponents' tendency to go overboard and assert that a corporation need *only measure* EVA or wealth generated in order to manage its businesses). To avoid confusion of terms, given the central use in *DPV* of the term 'value' in reference to what is delivered to customers, the phrase 'generate wealth' is used exclusively in this book when talking about making money.

This outcome, where a firm generates wealth, is usually in the interests of most of the firm's stakeholders, including its owners, its employees, its leadership, its suppliers, customers, and indirectly society at large. This outcome is often *not* in *everyone's* best interests, however. When a business succeeds, it frequently displaces some other firm, resulting in at least short-term losses (of money, jobs, power, etc.) for other people. On balance, however, society gets more value. Railroads, slide rule makers, and mainframe computer companies have all suffered due to other companies succeeding at their expense. But society is a better place with cars, planes, calculators and small, personally controlled computers. It is healthy for democratic society that the companies who create improvements are rewarded, not stymied. And it is likewise necessary that the mismanagement of large companies does not go unnoticed by the Invisible Hand.

It is incumbent upon the owners of a firm to define the ethical boundaries within which it is OK for the firm to generate wealth. Important as that debate is, this book will not argue what those boundaries should be. Rather, *Delivering Profitable Value* assumes that, within those boundaries, firms should single-mindedly pursue the generation of wealth. *DPV* then turns to the (not so) easy part: how do you do that?

The whole object in *DPV* is, ultimately, to generate wealth. The proposition here is *not* that a firm should profitably deliver value because that's nice for customers, but that it should do so in order to generate wealth. The most effective way to generate wealth, to make money in the long term, and thus to keep a firm strong and growing is by profitably delivering superior value. This is a bit more easily said than done.

Integrating *DPV* as an organization's way of business life is non-trivial. Like most significant change, it is neither quick, painless nor without risk. However, it requires neither a miracle nor the dawning of a new age to improve dramatically an organization and its ability to make money. On the other hand, a little magic can come in quite handy.

Down-under magic: example of using *DPV*

As Eastman Kodak faces some of its most intense competitive threats ever, it can learn much from the remarkable success of one of its small country organizations, Kodak Australasia, in rethinking and redesigning its delivery of value propositions in the consumer market.

For many consumers, the experiences of viewing their photos contain some measure of real magic. People are frequently known, during a fire or other disaster, to insist on saving their photo album ahead of far more expensive items. Research has shown that when photos are given as gifts, these can be incredibly valued, despite their low cost. Who knows exactly why, but one psychologist ventured that 'people need photography' because:

> 'We remember visual things imperfectly. They're ... subject to distortion and decay ... Sometimes the real event becomes less important than the record of it.'[11]

In her book *On Photography*, Susan Sontag commented on magic in photos:

> 'Our irrepressible feeling that the photographic process is magical has a genuine basis ... a photograph is not only like its subject, a homage ... It is part, an extension of that subject.'[12]

However, to get these rewarding experiences consumers must first go through a rather long 'journey.' They will need a camera and the right film for the occasion. They must understand how to use the camera to capture the right images, then take the film to a photofinisher to be processed, choose processing options, and finally retrieve an envelope of prints and negatives. Then the consumer may make copies or enlargements, crop a print, frame some, etc. At last, the pictures can be enjoyed.

Some consumers find the rather long and complex journey interesting and even enjoyable. For a much larger number, the journey is a hassle that inhibits them from enjoying and doing more with photos. The difficulty, complexity, time demands, and the uncertainty of results at the end of this journey leave many consumers discouraged, a bit intimidated, and often disappointed. Winning in such a business, it would seem, might focus on enhancing consumers' awareness of the magical experiences possible at the destination of this journey, while dramatically improving the journey so consumers can get there more easily, more often.

Kodak sells the products and services that are used in this journey, distributing them through retailers. But unlike most consumer markets, the retail environment plays a major role beyond product distribution. What happens in a store can make the journey much less difficult, the eventual result more often pleasing; or it can do the opposite. Kodak should therefore have great interest in consumers' retail experiences. The traditional view, in contrast, has held that Kodak was in the product-defined businesses of film, cameras, paper, photofinishing services, chemicals and equipment. 'We're not retailers,' Kodak executives like to tell people. However, Kodak's experience in Australia, and more recently elsewhere, demonstrates the power of defining businesses in terms of the integrated delivery of customers' most valuable resulting experiences rather than in terms of the design, sale and distribution of products.

Traditionally, through the 1980s, Australian consumers obtained most of their imaging products and services through two retail channels: camera stores and pharmacies. Two broadly defined groups of consumers existed, then as now. The more serious photographers, the hobbyists or 'enthusiasts,' enjoyed or at least studied the photographic process. They were more likely to be male and tended to favor the camera-store channel. Consumers in the much larger 'snapshooter' group consumed less product and service. They were less interested in the technology of photography, but did want pictures of their memories and events. Snapshooters were somewhat more likely to be female and tended to buy both film and photofinishing through their pharmacy.

Then in the early 1980s, the 'mini-lab' arrived, a photofinishing laboratory able to fit into a small retail space. Retailers could develop and process film on-site in only an hour. Slow to react at first, Kodak began seriously to lose market share to others who capitalized on the growing popularity of one-hour service. Then, led by Drs Will Fraser and Ziggy Switkowski, Kodak Australasia (KA) put together a well-conceived and executed response, named 'Kodak Express' (KEX). The KA organization bolstered this initiative until it delivered a brilliant value proposition to consumers. As part of that effort, Kodak also learned to deliver a superior value proposition to KEX retailers, motivating and helping them deliver the right value proposition to the consumer.

KEX was a runaway success. By the early 1990s Kodak had recovered its market share and profit and in 1991 KA was even the first winner of the Australian Quality Prize.[13] The organization's confidence had been restored.

From blowflies to Wizards

There remained work undone, however. In 1992, Kodak Australasia (KA) was first exposed to the framework and methodology of *Delivering Profitable Value*.[14] Now KA formed cross-functional business teams, each focused on a major retail channel, e.g. KEX, camera stores, pharmacy, food, duty free. Leadership understood that the products were the direct sources of revenue, but they gave these retail-defined teams – called value delivery system (VDS) teams – real power as businesses. Using that power, the VDS teams determined the resulting experiences KA wanted consumers to have, then designed delivery of the value proposition to the channel that would support those consumer experiences. Relentlessly studying retailing, the VDS teams spent a lot of time working closely with and learning the business of their retailers and studying the consumer's real experiences in that channel.

At this time, the future of one channel, the camera store, seemed bleak. Their traditional customer was the enthusiast, a breed no longer growing rapidly. Walking into a typical camera store of this period, a consumer might find a gentleman behind the counter, perhaps 45, wearing glasses and a comfortable cardigan sweater. Cameras and related equipment fill the store window; the bottom shelf is covered with a fine residue of dust and perhaps provides a few blow-flies (a large Australian species prevalent in summer) their final resting place. Little sunlight penetrates the clutter of equipment and signs in the window, resulting in a rather dim ambiance. A photo enthusiast might wander in and have an interesting chat about the 60 or so different lenses scattered about the shop.

Less often, a young mother of two might drop in. A snapshooter, she usually doesn't go into camera stores, instead using the pharmacy or the Kodak Express to buy film and processing. But she's thinking of buying a new camera for her husband. While she's there, she'd like to ask the expert's opinion on why some of the photos she recently took didn't turn out as well as she'd hoped. She could have asked the clerk in the KEX or the pharmacy, but surely they don't know as much as the camera-store man. He answers her questions, wearied by their evident naïveté. His answers are a little too technical for her quite to make sense of them. He does, however, suggest she try a different brand of film, rather than the Kodak film she had been using. He's an expert; so he must know what he's talking about. She leaves with two rolls of non-Kodak film, no camera, no real answers to her questions; but at least she's been made to feel a little stupid.

By the early 1990s, Kodak had not given the camera stores much reason to love it. Down the street from the typical camera store might be a KEX, taking business with its 1-hour service that he doesn't offer. Across the street is a pharmacy, which now offers the same 1 or 2 day service offered by the camera store at a very low price. Kodak even owns some stores of their own. Some partner. Meanwhile, though Kodak had implemented innovative programs for other channels, it had done very little to help give this channel a basis to compete. Not surprisingly, Kodak's market share in this channel was much weaker than in most others, and dropping.

The preceding 15 years had witnessed a trend of business moving away from the photo-specialty channel. Some argued, why invest in this channel? It will continue to have a hard time competing against the mass merchandising retailers. One could also make the argument that many of these stores were poorly managed small businesses without the resources to improve. Some stores actually blamed Kodak for their problems and expected Kodak to support them by helping them price-compete against the bigger retailers. But with the future seeming to point toward highly efficient new channels, shouldn't Kodak just read the writing on the wall and focus on the channels where the volume was headed?

The KA team didn't think so. First, while what seemed to be strategic thinking may have encouraged Kodak largely to ignore this channel, the team realized that camera stores have a disproportionate influence over consumers. If camera stores recommend a film to use, enthusiasts will be influenced directly and snapshooters will often be influenced by the enthusiasts. And if a camera store clerk tells a snapshooter what film to use, the snapshooter will usually listen. So the camera store VDS team realized it must get these stores to align closer with Kodak film.

But then the team asked a more important question. What role could the camera store play in improving the consumer's experience, besides simply supporting Kodak film? Since the snapshooter respects the expertise of the camera store, is there an opportunity to make this retail environment a *helpful* rather than intimidating and off-putting experience for this consumer? Snapshooters are too often disappointed with their photos, too often intimidated by the complexity and technology, and too often unaware of the magic – the fun and marvelous experiences – they could have with photos. Snapshooters would be happier with their photographic experiences and probably would seek more of them if they were more often successful, more confident, and more aware of these great experiences. If, moreover, they found Kodak instrumental in helping them through the journey to this magical destination, so much the better for Kodak's market share.

The team began to view the camera store as something far more than a troublesome, fading player in the industry. The camera store, with its credible expertise and ability to present the whole range of photographic possibilities, could have an extremely important impact on the snapshooter's experience. But the blowflies would have to go.

While the camera store channel had its problems, many of the owners were bright, ambitious entrepreneurs who desperately wanted to change things. The team decided to involve these retailers early in the development of value delivery plans and, to restore some fun, excitement, and maybe even magic to this important channel, the team named the program Wizard. In early 1993, the group held a conference in Sydney to talk about how Wizard stores might pursue the snapshooter in addition to their traditional enthusiast consumer. There, Wizard members learned the *DPV* framework and methodology.

They were encouraged to *become* the snapshooter and to help their staff do the same. These retailers began to ask themselves, what's it like for the snapshooter to walk into one of our stores? What would it have to be like in order to win that consumer, capture their imagination, and give them a great experience? If we could make that happen, could we still serve our traditional enthusiast? If so, could delivering a great value proposition to the snapshooter revitalize our businesses? If so, what would Kodak and we have to do?

The Wizard team – storeowners and Kodak managers – developed many insights that helped Wizard become another big success for KA. For example, observing and analyzing the snapshooter's experience when picking up a print order, the team discovered an opportunity. Typically, a camera store would usher the snapshooter out, once the transaction was complete. Yet snapshooters have a strong urge to *look* at their photos as soon as they get them. Rather than maximizing transaction efficiency, why not invite them to spend a few minutes examining their photos instead? This is a golden opportunity to congratulate the consumer on particularly good shots or to suggest additional uses. 'That would look *great* in a nice frame!' Of course, opening an envelope of disappointing photos is another opportunity. That consumer may be discouraged, blame their own incompetence, and put away the camera until at least next Christmas. Here's an opportunity to *save* a consumer – show them how to get better results or maybe offer re-processing.

Wizard was a great success. One of the more innovative and dynamic Wizard members, Larry McInerny, dramatically turned around his business during the three years following the Sydney conference. Though competing against 18 other photo outlets on the same street, most offering much lower prices, McInerny's Wizard camera store now commands over 50 percent of that local market. One of the many small things that contributed in a big way to his success was that McInerny put chairs and tables just outside the shop, so consumers could sit while examining their photos, perhaps over a cup of coffee. He says, 'Now they can sit down, have a look and hopefully they'll come straight back in,' where his staff can *talk* with them about their prints.

And from Digital Print Stations to Image Magic

At the same time that KA was developing the Wizard program, Kodak in Rochester had created an array of new digital-imaging technologies, though some had yet to find a good home in the marketplace. One promising product was the Digital Print Station (DPS). This high quality scanner could produce a high quality reprint on the spot and could fit in a small retail outlet. Where DPS was tried in various markets around the world and simply sold to retailers, it often sat without enough consumer interest to justify it. However, KA recognized another great opportunity and launched a test market to use Wizard as the context in which to make DPS a success.

The team began by reexamining the consumer's experiences and their relevance to DPS. The early thinking on DPS was that consumers would be delighted to use DPS themselves to make a reprint or enlargement. At last consumers could more conveniently make reprints. But as the team experimented further, they continued to contemplate the magic of photography that they wanted to help snapshooters enjoy. DPS would be convenient, yes, but what is the desirable consequence of making that reprint? Partly by experimenting in Wizard stores, the team gradually realized that the retailer needed to show the snapshooter what great looking results they could get with DPS. They also realized that the emphasis should not be how good DPS is but how great it would be to have a framed enlargement and how great it would look on, say, the dining room wall.

The DPS team also began noticing in early store tests that older consumers were bringing in a lot of old photos to make fresh copies. Research showed that many consumers had very old, very precious photos but had only one copy of these and no negative. With DPS they could safely get a great reprint, enlarge, and frame it.

The team launched the concept as Image Magic, heavily leveraging the Wizard program. There, Image Magic could be fully explained by store staff and materials which, with advertising, illustrated the system's capabilities: enlarged and cropped prints, removal of red-eye, and other enhancements, all of which would make the print great for a frame. In-store staff and materials and advertising also showed how those old, one-of-a-kind prints with no negative could be made into a great, framed enlargement, all without any risk to that precious print. It 'never leaves your sight,' the advertisement promised. As Larry McInerny said:

> 'The Image Magic has been just fantastic for us. The advertising is bringing people in here in droves; they're digging out old photos out of everywhere and even [many] new photos, with the zoom and crop and red-eye features. And because we have trained staff, we can talk to the consumer; when they pick up their photos, we can say 'ah, gee, that'd be

*fantastic, come and take a look at this and we put it on the Image Magic,
show them what it would look like and when you crop it down it looks
like a completely different photo; the people are just over the moon
when they see those results.'*[15]

Of the more than 500 prints made with Larry's Image Magic each month –
more than enough business to pay for the actual machine quickly – he estimates that about half leave with a frame and that two-thirds of *those* have a
matte. During the period of developing the Wizard, Image Magic and related programs, the entire photographic retail category in Australia/New
Zealand increased by about 4–5 percent and KA's profitability increased significantly.

By starting with and returning regularly to the right fundamental questions, getting to the right answers is a lot easier. Searching for a profound
understanding of how to make customers' real life experiences more valuable for them leads ultimately to a good place for any company – making
money. Now we'll turn to a more detailed exploration of what those questions really are and how to really answer them. Profitably.

Notes

1   Douglas K. Smith and Robert C. Alexander, *Fumbling the Future*, W.
    Morrow, New York, 1988, pp. 184–6.
2   *Ibid*, p. 177.
3   Or, 'strategic intent,' in today's parlance.
4   Smith and Alexander, *op. cit.*, p. 177.
5   *Ibid*, p. 208.
6   *Ibid*, p. 240.
7   Lewis Carroll, *Through the Looking Glass*, St. Martin's, New York, 1977,
    pp. 175–6.
8   S. Adams, *The Dilbert Principle*, HarperBusiness, 1996; pp. 141–2.
9   'Chip board' in the UK.
10 *Bushisms*, Workman Publishing, 1992, p. 40; February 3, 1992, to Colo-
    rado governor Romer, at a governor's conference, after Romer attacked
    a Bush proposal as not reflecting the position of many governors.
11 Susan Sontag, *On Phoography*, Anchor, New York, 1990, p. 85.
12 Susan Sontag, *op. cit.*, p. 156.
13 Equivalent to the US Baldridge Award, or Japanese Deming Prize.
14 Through the executive education course *Building Market-Focused Or-
    ganizations*, or BMFO.
15 Kodak Australia interview of L. McInerny, 1996.

Chapter Two

Customers' Resulting Experiences: Essence of a *Real* Value Proposition

Those who would make a business succeed face crucial decisions. Most important of these, yet most overlooked and poorly understood, is a disciplined choice of the *experiences* the business will cause some intended customers to have. These are the resulting experiences a business delivers, and they are the essence of a value proposition.

Properly understood, business is very much about the exploration and improvement of customers' real life experiences. The traditional concepts of 'needs, requirements and benefits' share important common ground with resulting experiences. However, the differences are considerable, as the conventional concepts focus too much on what the business does or on superficial, vague ideas of benefits or needs. Managers must put down the looking glass long enough to understand deeply and act decisively on the specific experiences customers would most value.

This chapter offers managers the criteria necessary to articulate resulting experiences in the depth they deserve, in contrast to the neglect they receive. Only with this foundation can organizations truly understand value propositions and why their delivery is at the heart of business.

Where the real action is: customers' experience

When someone uses a microwave oven to reheat food, the following series of events may happen. First, the food is cooked in a pot in a traditional oven. It is then put in a bowl and placed in the refrigerator. The customer later takes the food from the refrigerator, puts it directly on a plate, and reheats this food in the microwave. In about five minutes, they eat the food, which probably tastes pretty good. To clean up, they wash the original pot, the bowl, and the plate.

Without a microwave, this person would take the food from the fridge, put it in another cooking utensil, and heat it for about 25 minutes in a traditional oven. In this case the food might dry out and stick to the utensil. Then this person would put the food on a plate and eat it.

By using the microwave, the customer eats the food about 20 minutes earlier, does not have to wash the additional utensil (which may be difficult to wash), and enjoys better tasting food which has retained its moisture. These microwave experiences include events resulting in some consequences that are better than the traditional oven experience. These better experiences come, of course, with the drawbacks of shopping for, finding space in the kitchen for, perhaps learning how to use, and maintaining this extra oven, this microwave. And all of these resulting experiences come at the price of *buying* the microwave. Microwaves have succeeded because the value to customers of the resulting experiences, including the drawbacks and the price, was in net superior to the current experiences.

Potential customers of any product have various relevant experiences, including their current experiences and others that they may not have yet had. A superior value proposition offers a scenario of resulting experiences, which is, in net, an *improvement* over the other scenarios of experiences available. Neither internally-driven nor customer-compelled methods work well in discovering these scenarios. To do this, managers must *become* customers, rather than *listen* to them. Honda, for example knows this to be true.

A team of Honda employees is staked out in a parking lot of a grocery store. At a distance, they videotape scores of consumers performing the same task: loading groceries into the trunk (boot outside North America) of a car. Different cars, different consumers, different grocery bags. Back in Tokyo, Honda engineers and other managers, designing the next model, watch these videos. Some consumers are seen struggling to get the bags into the trunk. Some arrange their plastic bags to keep them from tipping over. At night, some peer into the trunk as they try to arrange bags in the back of the trunk. A few pause, rest a bag on the edge of the trunk wall, and then have to lift the lid again after it partly closes. For a few others, the cart slowly rolls a few feet away from the car as they load it. For some, the whole process goes along without a hitch.

These motorists are not *telling* Honda their trunk needs or their desired benefits in a trunk. They are simply living part of their car experience. Watching these videos, the Honda engineers and other managers vicariously live that experience as well by putting themselves in the consumers' shoes. They can see and feel what is imperfect in the consumers' experiences. Then they can envision how a far superior trunk-loading experience would look for these motorists.

A team of engineers from a maker of computer workstations performs a similar exercise. They observe, document and analyze aircraft engineers designing an aircraft by building models and simulating parts of the design on computer. In recent years, the aircraft engineers' computer-simulation ability has speeded and improved their design process, yet they are still unable to simulate some of the largest, most complex design elements. They eventually build physical prototypes that let them view and analyze whole systems within the design, such as the electrical system. But they cannot 'walk through' the plane, viewing the whole system at once.

In addition, some steps of the design process occur sequentially, making it difficult for the engineers to collaborate as fully as they would like. If several engineers could view the simulation data simultaneously, they could discuss and work on it together instead of reacting iteratively to each other.

The workstation team interviews the aerospace engineers at length. They map their processes and capture their frustrations and compromises. In this, the workstation team tries to understand the imperfections of the actual experiences of this potential workstation-customer. The team is not studying buying habits; rather it is studying the aircraft maker's business and how the use of computers fits into that business. Similarly, the team is not surveying the aircraft maker to find out its key buying factors, needs, or desired benefits for workstations or computers. Rather, the team is trying to understand what a better computing experience, one that would make the aircraft design team and their company more successful, would look like.

Criteria for a resulting experience

A resulting experience clearly is:

1. An *event* (or sequence of events), physical and/or mental, which happens in the customer's life as a result of doing what some business proposes
2. The end-result *consequence* of this event for the customer
3. In *comparison* to a customer's *alternative* experience, either superior, equal, or inferior
4. The *value* for the customer of this relative consequence
5. *Specific and measurable:* one can objectively determine if the customer experienced the events, consequence, and value compared to alternatives.

A resulting experience is *not*:

6. About 'us,', i.e. NOT products/services or their attributes, features, advantages, differentiators; not our plans, resources, assets, capabilities, processes, functions, reputation or descriptions of excellence
7. A *vague, ambiguous topic or platitude,* e.g. NOT superior, total, outstanding, or unsurpassed quality, service, satisfaction, performance, convenience, partnership, reliability, timeliness, productivity, or responsiveness.

Delving deeply into customers' current and other available experiences is the only way an organization can discover which experiences will be superior for the customer. But searching for a superior combination of resulting experiences to deliver requires that those individuals performing the search first understand precisely what a resulting experience *is*.

What a resulting experience *is*

A resulting experience includes one or a series of related physical or mental *events* that happen in the life of the customer, whether a business or consumer customer. These events happen at least in part due to the actions of a business organization. They ultimately have an end-result *consequence* for the customer, in *comparison* to some alternate experience the customer perceives. An experience is thus *superior, equal* or *inferior* to that alternate experience. This difference versus the alternative has some *value* to the customer. Finally, to be useful for a business, an experience is *measurably specific*.

A resulting experience includes events, leading to a consequence

The event that is part of a resulting experience may be a specific act, like listening to music on a CD, or a process, like assembling a colored TV-console. It may be a physical or a mental event. A customer watching a movie engages in physical behavior – sitting in a theater with eyes fixed on the screen – but some of the most important events happen inside their head (except when the film is an action film, during which very little happens inside the head). The movie-goers watch and listen, become mentally and emotionally involved, identify with characters, and imagine themselves 'there.' They are amused, shocked, awed, terrified, and inspired to buy the 23-piece promotional toy collection … or whatever.

An event can be simple, like enjoying a consistently tender chicken dinner provided by a particular brand. However, the events in an experience may be complex, with one event leading to another. Managers must learn to peel the layers of the onion until they adequately understand the true end-result consequence in that experience.

To business users in the mid-1980s, for example, Hewlett-Packard's laser jet printers delivered an experience consisting of a more complex series of events. Compared to dot-matrix printers, users could produce documents with darker, more contrasting blacks, and more sharply focused characters. This made users' documents easier to read and, as a result, they communicated more effectively. If we peel the onion even further, it is reasonable to say that many users could use these more effective communications to persuade others more easily and thus could be more successful. In such a case, one must identify and describe the *whole* experience, including the entire series of related events as well as the end-result consequence. No one event (such as 'makes blacker blacks' or 'makes users more successful') constitutes the whole experience.

Managers learning both to discover and to deliver resulting experiences to customers will find it helpful to ask the question, 'so what?' If one can still ask this question about a resulting experience, the onion has probably not yet been peeled enough. There is likely a further consequence in this experience, not yet defined, which must be understood.

'So what?' would have been an instructive question for those admiring IBM's classic marketing strategy for its PCs in the late 1980s. Wanting to reassert power in this market, IBM announced with much fanfare a strategy of differentiating its PCs through a product feature – the Micro Channel – which only IBM's PCs would be privileged to contain. The problem with the Micro Channel was that it did little, if anything, at the time for the experiences any PC user might value, and so it made a similarly insignificant contribution to IBM's fortunes. In contrast, this question led Kodak Australasia to discover a key to Image Magic's success (see Chapter One, pp. 37–8). Consumers would be able to make an enlargement themselves easily with Image Magic, but still, so what? Even more important was the end-result consequence of enjoying a great-looking framed enlargement on their wall at home.

In some cases, however, there is a diminishing return in further defining consequences. The 'so what?' question can also surface that point of diminishing returns, the point at which the important end-result consequence has been adequately defined. A computer might allow faster calculation, saving users some amount of time. One *could* go on to study what they actually do with this saved time. Do they write more reports or make more phone calls? Whatever the answer, so what? If the answer would help unearth the whole experience and its value, then it's worth asking the question; if not, you can stop peeling the onion.

It's important to ensure that events actually lead to the apparent consequence. A potentially valuable experience for South American newspapers, for example, would be to shorten their complex image-production process. Such an improvement would allow images, such as a color photo of last night's winning soccer goal, to be added right up until the paper's deadline. In consequence, circulation and profits might grow.

An integrated digital imaging system, which affects image production time, might be just the solution for these newspapers. However, a supplier of these systems would need to determine the exact links between each of these events in order deeply to understand this potential experience. How *much* production time could be reduced and how much is needed actually to allow more timely images? Roughly how much might this increase circulation? A substantial reduction in image-production time might not allow many later insertions. If so, no great consequence would result. Conversely, enough time saved could allow a paper with no color images from last night's game to produce editions with all the latest coverage in color. Perhaps this result would substantially bolster circulation.

In some cases, several quite different events, which constitute separate experiences, have the same ultimate consequence. For example, a component-supplier may sell to a customer who is a final-product manufacturer. The component's design might allow its use by the customer in three different final-products, leading to lower inventory requirements and thus lower costs. At the same time, the components may be received within three hours of planned assembly, which also reduces inventory levels. Both are experiences, with the same kind of consequence (reductions in the customer's inventory levels), that are best understood as two separate, though obviously related, experiences.

On the other hand, using that single component in three different products may also lead to another event and a different ultimate consequence. Using just the one component may simplify quality testing on the customer's final product, resulting in the consequence of a higher quality product. Although here the initial event (using just one component in three products) is the same as above, it led to a different next event and a different ultimate consequence (higher quality rather than reduced inventory). This experience is again best understood as separate from those above.

A consequence is relative to alternatives, making the experience either superior, equal or inferior

Customers often can obtain comparable experiences from similar suppliers or from those producing completely different products. They sometimes can create the experience themselves. Or they can live without it. The end-result consequence of the events in an experience must be understood relative to all of these alternatives that are available.

A customer's resulting experience is superior if the consequence is preferable for that customer. Hartmann Luggage delivers some superior experiences to the frequent traveler. Many customers find this rugged luggage lasts for a relatively long time without significant damage, even with the abuse the best airlines give it. When a piece of luggage *is* damaged, authorized repair shops fix it, usually under the warranty and quickly, and return the luggage about as good as new. The consequence is that the luggage lasts longer and users have to replace it less frequently, a welcome improvement in anyone's life.

A resulting experience can be superior to a customer's alternatives in two respects: it is the same kind of experience delivered to a greater degree, or it is unique. Many motorists perceive that a Volvo delivers superior safety. Driving a Volvo is not absolutely safe but perhaps more so than most alternatives, so this experience is superior. American Express imposes virtually no limit on charges and provides nearly instant replacement for a lost or stolen card anywhere in the world. Competing cards all carry a limit, and your vacation will be long gone before they replace a stolen card. So AMEX delivers two unique experiences, both improvements over the alternatives, and thus both superior.

In some cases, a resulting experience is superior by being *less* of something. The graphical user interface (GUI), invented by Xerox, popularized by Apple and sold by Microsoft, is said to make learning and using PCs easy. Nothing actually comes close to achieving true ease of use when it comes to computers, but compared to the old DOS interface, a GUI like Macintosh OS or Windows is far less tortuous.

Obviously, resulting experiences are often not superior. Profitably delivering superior value requires understanding and often deciding to deliver resulting experiences that are only equal or even inferior. In many markets, several competitors deliver very important resulting experiences that are essentially equivalent. Firms managed as commodities often implicitly reflect the inaccurate assumption that no experience, except for price, *can* be made superior. Often such experiences are worthy of great attention, however. Even a small change may make an experience superior or inferior, and thus can have a potentially significant impact on a business.

Many successful businesses deliver a mixture of superior, equal, and inferior experiences. In the late 1980s and early 1990s, Microsoft's DOS operating system (OS), including 'Windows,' defeated Apple's Macintosh OS. DOS delivered some superior and some equal experiences to office-dwelling users. By using DOS, customers could use any IBM-compatible computer, common in most offices. If they used the Mac OS, they had to buy and use a Macintosh computer. Its incompatibility meant documents and files could not be very easily shared between it and the other IBM/PC-type computers in the user's office. To avoid this consequence, the customer would have to ensure that *all* of their computers were Macintosh. And Macs cost more. DOS users could also access the larger number of software applications written for DOS/Windows.

Once a user has learned an application available on both DOS and Mac OS, like Microsoft's own Word and Excel, using the two operating systems was similar. In this, the two provided an equal experience. However, DOS users had to accept one inferior experience: it was more difficult to learn and to use, which made users somewhat less productive and more ill tempered than if they had used Mac. The superior experiences and price advantages of DOS, however, overwhelmed this inferior one and thus Apple.

As you might expect, a superior consequence has some positive value relative to the alternative; an equal experience has a neutral relative value; and an inferior experience has some negative relative value. For example, a paper-company might switch to using a boiler that produces steam that transfers heat to paper more uniformly. As a consequence of this greater uniformity of heat transfer, less paper may be damaged. This leads in turn to less paper lost in production and less bad-quality paper getting through to the paper company's customers. The cost saved in lost paper and the revenue gained by better average uniformity in paper shipped, constitute the value of this resulting experience.

Often, however, understanding with any accuracy the real value of an experience for a customer is not easy. The question to answer is this: what *would* the customer perceive as the value of the end-result consequence of this event, compared to alternatives, if they could experience it? This is quite different from asking how much the customer is currently ready to pay. *DPV* is partly about analyzing what the value of certain potential resulting experiences would be and how they can best be delivered.

A resulting experience is measurably specific

To be useful for an organization, a resulting experience must be described in actionable terms. It must be possible for the organization to determine whether or not the experience has been delivered to the customer. If a motor oil business concludes that motorists can 'protect their engines better, leading to longer engine life than with any other motor oil,' the business has articulated an experience specific enough to be measured. That is, one could determine that it was or was not delivered. However, it is often more useful to quantify an experience.

The more precisely an experience can be defined, the less room for confusion inside an organization when trying to deliver it. It is therefore desirable, though not absolutely necessary, to be as *quantitative* as possible when describing a resulting experience. A thorough quantitative description includes the actual event or events the customer will experience, the consequence these will produce and the value this will have, all in comparison to the customer's alternatives. A motor oil may protect engines more than other oils 'leading to on average a 10 percent longer engine life.' If this is enough impact to win customers' preference, the organization can focus single-mindedly on this objective.

Consider the tenderness of a chicken, a resulting experience not easily quantifiable or even measurable. A more consistently tender chicken dinner is, however, a superior experience. And, customers can *tell* us if they find a chicken dinner more or less tender. Likewise, customers can try to tell us how much they think they value this experience. And one can infer over time from their real behavior how much they will *pay* for this superior experience, which provides a more direct measure of its value.

Resulting experiences are often hard work to discover but are usually easy enough to understand once discovered and articulated clearly. Yet, conventional management practice most often does not focus on this deceptively simple idea of customers' experiences.

What a resulting experience *isn't*

Instead, organizations usually identify what customers supposedly want or demand, thus missing the mark in one of two ways. Using internally-driven or customer-compelled methods, they often identify characteristics of the organization and its products, rather than customers' experiences. Or, they may identify broad, generic topics of customer needs or benefits. While these generalities usually offend no one and may even feel good to those claiming them, they are so unspecific and ambiguous that they provide no actionable direction for a business.

Experiences are not about 'us' – not attributes of the product/service or the organization's resources, functions, processes, reputation, etc.

Several years ago, in a *DPV* seminar,[1] managers of a medical diagnostic instruments business debated whether they had clearly articulated the experiences delivered to their users, doctors in hospitals. Some participants insisted that the group certainly had. These individuals produced as evidence a description, issued by marketing to field sales, of 'the benefits to your customers' of the company's new cardiac monitoring system, which read as follows: 'higher capacity Winchester disk (now 84MB); ... can store more patient records; ... faster throughput of patient data; ... faster printing; ... printing via PCL5 ... for full disclosure printing; ... 8MB RAM on-board in the [name of the product] ...'

This statement implies some resulting experiences: storing more records, with faster throughput and faster printing may lead to good things. But what might they be? For example, perhaps diagnosis will be more accurate, in that perhaps physicians will make fewer false positive diagnoses, resulting in less time and money wasted on additional unnecessary testing or even inappropriate medication. Or perhaps diagnostic accuracy won't be affected, but the speed with which a diagnosis occurs, and thus the patient's comfort, will be much improved. Who knows? Probably not the field sales reps and possibly not even the people who wrote it. Although the latter are quite knowledgeable, the organization had not decided what explicit resulting experiences to deliver.

The distinction between a resulting experience and some attribute of an organization is not difficult to understand. Yet many organizations regularly name such attributes as reasons why customers should buy their product or service. This tendency does not evince an inability to comprehend the distinction. Rather, management theory fails to make the distinction and thus it is not taken seriously in practice.

The terms 'benefit,' 'need' and 'requirement' are frequently used by managers in a context somewhat related to resulting experiences. The term 'benefit,' especially, is used by some in a way consistent with resulting experience. In fact, the genesis of the seminal *DPV* concepts was influenced importantly by the management principles of Procter & Gamble in which 'benefit' was a dominant strategic concept. However, 'benefit' is generally used too loosely in management theory and practice, without rigorous definition, and with no relation to the concept of a resulting experience.

Besides offering a description of product or service attributes, the term benefit is also used to mean what a business will do. For example, several years ago an internal team in a large global chemical company conducted a review of the strategies of various businesses within the firm. Learning little about what the business units offered customers beyond products and prices, the team asked the units to state more clearly what benefits they gave their customers. One unit's report characterized the typical response. It asserted that they offer to large pharmaceuticals 'the following benefits today:

- We sell them [a certain chemical] they cannot make
- We dispose of all their waste material
- We have responsive, flexible, global logistics.'

The question unanswered in this response is 'what are the resulting experiences to which these benefit statements may be relevant?' The chemical allows the customer to make their own chemical reactions at a lower cost than if they did not have it, but other chemical firms offer it as well, so the consequence is actually equal to the alternatives. By disposing of the customer's waste material, the chemical firm may eliminate the customer's direct disposal costs and perhaps some environmental liabilities. The team speculated that perhaps the business could dispose of this material more completely than was possible with a competitor, thus reducing the customer's cost and risk by a greater amount. But the benefit statement certainly fails to indicate whether this is the case.

The third statement is perhaps the most obtuse. Competitors supply customers locally, delivering on short notice, so that customers can make last-minute production changes without incurring high inventory costs. The firm in question, however, supplies these customers from a distant region, and so cannot match this experience. 'Responsive, flexible, global logistics' sounds good but is a euphemism for a somewhat inferior experience. Articulating this fact would be far more helpful to managers than obscuring it as a benefit.

Many descriptors commonly presented as customer needs or benefits are really only a description of the organization's product or of what the organization does. First mention must be given to 'Quality' and 'Customer Service.' These terms are often considered crystal clear when in fact they are amorphous and vague. Even worse, they connote vague characteristics of the product and the organization more often than those of experiences. Quality often describes how well-made a product or service is, while customer service most often refers to a process the business performs. Some customer experience may result, but it is not described by these words. Examples of these descriptors include:

- speed
- power
- leading-edge technology
- compact
- light weight
- durable
- reliable
- responsive
- technical support (i.e. it is available/given)
- on-time delivery
- fast service
- on-time performance

Another set of concepts frequently presented as a benefit or need is even further removed from the customer's experiences. These are qualities of the organization, often created by researching customers with questions such as 'what do you look for in a supplier (or brand)?' They are usually good characteristics, that is characteristics customers vote for, and they may actually help deliver some experiences. But they are *not* experiences customers will have. Some typical examples follow:

- trustworthy
- a stable company
- in this industry for the long-term

- good reputation
- a Brand(s) (i.e. our product is, or, we have)
- technical expertise
- a knowledgeable Sales Force
- product innovation
- a technology leader
- committed to partnerships with our customers.

All these characteristics describe the product, the organization, or how they will perform, not what experience the customer will have. They may lead to a resulting experience, may show up on market research as what customers want (or expect, require or need); but resulting experiences they are not.

Similarly, resulting experiences are not equivalent to advantages or differentiators. These terms usually describe good characteristics the product or organization has that the competition lacks and not some experience a customer will have.

Not *just topics or superficial, vague generalities and platitudes*

While organizations often describe themselves instead of resulting experiences, they also often substitute ambiguous and thoroughly unactionable concepts. A resulting experience must be more specific than a mere topic. A chicken consumer might value tenderness in a chicken dinner; a petroleum company might value lowering maintenance costs. These topics are closer to resulting experiences than are product features or a knowledgeable sales force. But they are not expressed in specific terms, which compare them to some alternative and thus provide some notion of their value.

The strong tendency is toward the superficial and imprecise; after all no one can disagree with a platitude. However, to construct a useful value proposition, managers must articulate resulting experiences that can be understood relative to the customer's real alternatives, and then deliberately delivered and measured. A great deal of what passes as benefits or needs, however, is nebulous, offends no one, is never wrong *per se*, and not surprisingly adds virtually nothing of true meaning. Three of the most classic phrases to which organizations are urged by popular management theory to swear allegiance, as if a strategy panacea, fit into this category: quality, service, and customer satisfaction. In this same category are many others nearly as-popular, such as: performance (or price/performance), reliability, convenience, relationships, trust, one-stop shopping, ease of use, easy to do business with, comfort, and appearance.

'Performance' is a broad topic that relates to some possible resulting experience. Perhaps, in a computer, it may refer to speed of operations, perhaps leading in turn to the ability of the user to perform operations they otherwise could not have. Or perhaps it leads to the user saving significant amounts of time in performing operations. Or perhaps it means less irritation and distraction from having to wait several seconds between specific operations.

'Reliability' could mean a product will always perform the same way, perhaps reducing uncertainty and thus allowing a user to understand better how to use it effectively. Or it could mean it never breaks down, thus saving the user repair costs. Or perhaps it never (or rarely) malfunctions, thus damaging a project. Or something else having to do with 'reliability.'

What is the consequence of 'one-stop-shopping?' Is it that a customer will save time in the actual shopping experience by being able to get everything in one shopping 'stop?' Or does it really mean that by purchasing several related products or services from one supplier, the customer can count on that supplier standing behind the products, taking responsibility for all of them working? Therefore, does it mean that when things go wrong it will be easier quicker to get them fixed? A distributor could sell a customer all the component products in some system but different makers may manufacture those products. In this case, it may well be that the distributor *cannot* do a good job of repairing the system. Yet the customer can still buy all the products from one distributor. Does that make this 'one-stop shopping' also? Without precisely defining the experience, including the consequence, all of these terms are ambiguous and thus useless.

What a resulting experience can include

To appreciate better this fundamental building block of *DPV*, it is useful to consider some of the possible variations in resulting experiences. These are discussed below.

Experiences can be directly observable or invisible

Some experiences are a direct result of features and are relatively straightforward to observe. A Swiss Army Knife gives access to many tools helpful in everyday or emergency tasks, like repairing equipment, camping, administering first aid, practising self-defense and, most important, opening a bottle of wine. Moreover, these tools are carried in a remarkably compact package and endure despite years of heavy usage.

Natural Gas Clearinghouse delivers a less observable, and yet real experience. They ensure that an industrial user's supply continues unabated even during shortages. The experience they provide is the virtual elimination of the chance of a plant shutdown. It's a hard one to touch, but it's worth a lot to the customer. An experience occurring within a customer's mind is even harder to describe and measure. For example, a customer staring motionless at a TV may experience entertainment; or, may be becoming brain dead. It's hard to say.

Experiences can be pragmatic and rational or ... not

The value of some experiences may be emotional rather than practical. Those consumers who place a higher value on a photo album than on more expensive items are not irrational; they just place a high value on an emotional experience.

A lot of nonsense clouds managers' minds over the distinction between product features and image. Some tobacco companies believe that many smokers wear their cigarettes, in a manner akin to their clothes. The image associated with a particular brand says a little something about the personality of that consumer. Some smokers would rather a cigarette associated with a tough, masculine, independent cowboy who lives with his horse, riding through the rain in the desert. Other smokers prefer a cigarette that says they, like other women, have 'come a long way baby' (that is, all the way to cigarettes; wow, what next?).

For smokers, these experiences are real, regardless of how unconnected they are to product features. They are real even though they don't make you masculine or liberated. The experience of associating oneself with a certain type of person, taste, or lifestyle is real and in some cases has value for customers. Beyond this intuitively obvious fact, mystifying the supposed magical power of selling a product by image is silly. It leads organizations to forsake the search for legitimate resulting experiences and instead to associate their products with some vapid, meaningless image.

Experiences can be part of the 'journey' to the 'destination'

Customers often must go through a journey of experiences to reach the destination, the experience for which they are buying the product or service. Although easy to overlook, important experiences happen during the journey. Some journey experiences occur at the same time as the destination experience, but are clearly subordinate to it. These include difficulty, convenience, reliability, and risk. The destination experience one may want from a cell phone is to make calls from locations not possible on the conventional network. Experiences subordinate to this could include how well one can hear, how long the battery lasts, or how difficult the phone is to carry, given its size and weight.

Changes in business customers' costs or their ability to generate revenue can comprise resulting experiences

The price a customer pays is a resulting experience. So are all the other non-price, cost-related experiences that result from doing business with an organization. A customer's ordering/buying, learning, installing, holding in inventory, maintaining, disposing, or handling/using costs can all be influenced.

Cost-related resulting experiences can be quite subtle. A particular steel maker might develop a superior understanding, in some aspects, of how an auto-body manufacturer must work with steel to form a car body. The steel maker may then cut and deliver its steel, and give technical support to the car-body maker, in a way tailored to reduce some steps in the customer's manufacturing process. Compared to using a competing supplier, the manufacturing time, and thus the cost to produce the car body, may be reduced. Such an experience, moreover, might be more valuable than other experiences that accompany it, such as higher costs for handling the product or higher price.

Some costs may not entail saving money *per se* but affect the *risk* of losing money. Of course, financial services companies regularly deliver such experiences. A savings account pays a low return but entails little risk; a junk bond or investment in certain derivatives offers the reverse tradeoff. Customers frequently bought IBM products despite a price premium to enjoy a lower probability of a much more expensive event – a disastrous system crash.

A customer may also value the experience of reducing the uncertainty of a cost. Enabling a customer to count on a fixed price for an extended period of time in a market where prices tend to fluctuate unpredictably can provide a cost-saving experience. By knowing with certainty the price they will pay, a customer may save inventory and production costs otherwise required to protect against price fluctuations.

Similarly, helping a business customer increase their *revenues* can constitute important resulting experiences. For example, a business could help customers make products that provide a better experience to *their* customers. Or one could help business customers improve the communication of

---

What a resulting experience can be

1 Directly observable or invisible; but it must be real.
2 Pragmatic and rational; or, not.
3 Part of the 'journey' to the 'destination'.
4 Changes in business-customers' costs or in their ability to generate revenue.

their value propositions. A business might also help business customers to understand their markets better and to refine their value propositions.

Is resulting experience just new jargon for old marketing terms like benefit or need? Not quite

Benefit, need, value, and some other related terms are certainly common in marketing and strategy literature. However, their definitions and use only reinforce the conventional ignorance and neglect of the resulting experience concept. Conventional theory simply does not put the concept of the customer's experience anywhere near the center of attention. As discussed and used in the conventional approaches, the concepts of benefit and need do not explicitly *exclude* the customer's experience. But they are casually used at least as often to refer to 'us' (the ever beloved subject), the attributes of the organization's products and its resources. When these concepts *are* used in reference to some customer experience, it is often in much too vague terms. Generally speaking, this conventional theory makes little or no mention of the notions of defining an explicit event and its consequence in comparison to specific alternative experiences with some relative value in measurably specific terms.

Conventional management theory clearly accords importance to the concepts variously called benefit, need, value, differentiation, and others. All have some vague relationship to the concept of the customer's experience. *DPV*, however, places supreme importance on this concept. Accordingly, *DPV* contends that a consistent, rigorous understanding of this central notion is crucial to managing a business. However, resulting experiences are not actionable in isolation. They belong in a larger business context, for they are part of the proposed exchange between a business organization and customers. Next we turn to that larger context, the value proposition.

Notes

1   Then titled *Building Market-Focused Organizations* (BMFO).

Chapter Three

The Good, the Bad and the Unintended: Every Business Delivers a Value Proposition

The hidden fulcrum of business strategy is the value proposition. Yet most organizations have not yet discovered it or begun to understand and use its full strength. This chapter will begin to develop this central concept in some depth, aiming to show how a value proposition is the essence of any business, whether or not the organization is aware of it.

What it is

Essentially, a value proposition is the *entire set of resulting experiences* (discussed in Chapter Two), including some price, that an organization causes some customers to have. Customers may perceive this combination of experiences to be in net superior, equal, or inferior to alternatives. A value proposition, even if superior, can be a 'Tradeoff,', i.e. one or more experiences in it are inferior while others are superior. Two aspects of value proposition bear clarification here: the 'customer' and 'price.'

Who the customer is

A value proposition can focus on a single customer or a very large number of customers. Whichever, customers all have one thing in common: the combination of experiences and price in a business's value proposition is the most appropriate one for this business to offer them.

The term 'the customer' is used generically here. In some markets one can unambiguously identify customers as the people immediately interacting with the organization. For a retailer, the shopper is clearly the customer; for a law firm, its clients. In some businesses, however, the immediate customer is a business with customers who may have customers, etc., thus forming a chain of customers. Sometimes a customer several levels removed from the organization should be considered as the primary customer, while others who more immediately interact with the organization are best understood as intermediaries. These issues are developed in depth later.

Here it is important simply to realize that a value proposition can be focused on either primary customers or a set of intermediary customers. The principles of a value proposition discussed in this chapter hold regardless of where the proposition's customers reside along the chain.

Price: special case of a resulting experience

Price refers simply to the money the customer pays in order to obtain all the other resulting experiences in a value proposition. Price, like other resulting experiences, can be preferable or not. A higher price is usually an inferior experience, for example. As defined here, price does not include any other cost incurred by the customer. In articulating a value proposition, separating price from any other kind of cost reduces the opportunity for ambiguity and confusion. These other costs, such as operational costs or cost of ownership (e.g. maintenance, inventory, training) are instead expressed in other resulting experiences. If a customer's costs are made lower by doing business with some organization, this is a superior experience.

A value proposition usually includes a single overall price. However, in some complex propositions, the customer may pay several separate prices for different products or services that are all part of delivering that proposition. In this case, it often makes sense to cite each of these separately as part of the overall value proposition articulation.

In some value propositions there is no price, that is, the customer makes no monetary payment. In some complex chains, e.g. healthcare, one customer may pay a price and get some resulting experiences while another gets various other resulting experiences without directly paying a price.

A business is the delivery of a value proposition

In most general terms, a business is some activity whose purpose is to make money, or generate wealth for the firm, through some exchange with one or more customers. The fundamental contention of *Delivering Profitable Value* is that a business can only achieve this purpose by delivering some profitable value proposition. An organization may operate one or more businesses. In the *DPV* perspective, each business consists of the delivery of a single value proposition. An organization (firm, division, business unit, etc.) may operate only one business, in which case it delivers a single value proposition. If it implements a number of businesses, then by definition it delivers the same number of value propositions. There is a one-to-one correspondence between businesses and value propositions delivered. The concept of having one value proposition for a multi-business organization is thus meaningless.

This *DPV* perspective does not define a business as its products, services, or processes. Rather it recognizes these things as parts of a business. Nor is a business equated here with an organization, i.e. a firm or business unit. An organization, including its people and all other resources, is an entity. An organization may create and operate businesses. And a business is the combination of resources used and actions taken by the organization, including all costs incurred, plus the resulting experiences a set of customers gets, plus the revenues the organization thereby gains. All this is the delivery of a value proposition.

To 'deliver' a value proposition means causing, intentionally or not, a customer actually to have and be aware of the experiences in that proposition. This delivery consists of two basic functions: 'providing' and 'communicating' the value proposition. *Providing* it means that if and when the customer actually accepts the proposition, thus buying and/or using some product or service, the customer will actually have the experiences, including the price, in that value proposition. *Communicating* that value proposition means that before, during, and after accepting it, customers understand, appreciate, and believe that they will have those experiences.

The value proposition that a business delivers determines its commercial success. The value proposition is not a side-show or one of several key factors important for a business – its delivery is the *whole* show.

An often-told tale is Sony's defeat by Victor in the video cassette recorder (VCR) market. Sony introduced Betamax at nearly the same time that Victor introduced VHS. Most analysts say that Beta's playback picture quality was noticeably superior to that of VHS, whereas the recording picture quality of both was about equal. However, most VCR usage involved playing rented movies; recording was then only a small piece of a VCR's overall use. Yet despite Beta's sharper, clearer playback picture, VHS won handily.

Using either VCR required videotapes recorded on the respective standard, either Beta or VHS. So when early VCR owners went to their movie rental store, they needed to rent a movie on the standard appropriate to their VCR. Rental stores, of course, had no enthusiasm for carrying two versions of every movie. Because VHS got into the market slightly ahead of Beta, video stores began carrying primarily VHS movies early on. Sony may have been somewhat overconfident given their so-called superior product and so may have reacted too slowly to the VHS lead. In any case, consumers realized that, even if Beta were somewhat superior in picture quality, they wouldn't be able to rent as large a selection of movies with a Beta. Consumers continued to buy VHS even after Sony introduced and began communicating Beta's superiority. This reinforced video stores' behavior and the cycle ran on until Beta's situation was hopeless.

Much has been written about this case: how could the inferior product win? Why didn't superior quality win the day? Does this evidence the mysterious powers of marketing over product superiority and quality? Does this demonstrate that first movers always win? Does it mean that distribution channel strategy is more important than product strategy? Does it show, yet again, that consumers are not too rational, easily fooled by all that marketing into picking the inferior product? A simpler and more useful way of understanding this case is to realize that the consumer was confronted with two alternative value propositions, one clearly superior. Beta's value proposition was, in effect:

- The consumer should buy a Beta VCR, rather than a VHS.
- They can record material with about the same picture quality as VHS.
- They can rent or buy and watch movies. Picture quality will be even a little better than VHS, with consequence of moderately greater viewing pleasure for those movies. The value of this superior experience would justify a moderate (15–25 percent?) premium in the VCR price.
- However, they will find far fewer movies to rent or buy, with the consequence of much less often being able to watch the movie they want to see and often not being able to watch anything they want to see.
- The price of the rental/purchase is about equal versus VHS.

There is no mystery in VHS's victory. *The superior value proposition that is actually delivered always wins the customer's preference.* And if the cost to deliver that superior value proposition is sufficiently less than the revenue it produces, it generates wealth. This is not to say that the winner always has the most honorable and deserving management or the superior product or the smartest marketing department or any other factor other than the only one that ultimately counts: the superior value proposition. The consumer, much editorial to the contrary notwithstanding, simply acted rationally. They used more common sense than some of the convoluted analysis offered to explain this case. And perhaps more than Sony used.

It only confuses this case, as it does many, to interpret it as product superiority versus distribution or marketing issues. In *most* cases, a small head start in distribution is no killer advantage. Superior products win day in and day out despite coming into the market later than their inferior competition. In most cases, and many in Sony's own history, a late introduction of a superior product has little impact on its ability to deliver a superior proposition. In this case, however, VHS's head start initiated the video stores' and ultimately the consumers' reaction, which proved fatal for Beta.

Some analysts also wonder if Sony failed in its consumer marketing, as well. A reasonable speculation, instead, is that many consumers who bought a VHS had already heard and were inclined to *believe* that Beta machines produced a somewhat better picture. Sony probably succeeded in communicating this superior experience. However, this superior experience paled in comparison to the problem of movie-availability.

Similarly, it wastes time to wonder if the VHS victory proves that being a first-mover is the magical formula for businesses to follow. Despite a plethora of examples that demonstrate the ability to win as both a first mover and a follower, much marketing and strategy literature poses such momentous questions as if some generalized algorithm for success can be deduced. Being first in the market is good if it helps profitably deliver a superior value proposition; if it doesn't, it isn't. In this case, being first *was* very helpful for VHS *because* it set in motion a set of reactions that delivered a decisively superior experience: movie-availability. It was not helpful because first movers have more fun.

The question to ask is this: did Sony/Beta deliver a superior value proposition? And the answer is no, it did not. So it lost. Of course, VHS did not have a flawless value proposition. The VHS value proposition, like many winners, was a tradeoff – partly superior, partly inferior, and partly equal. But in net, it was superior.

The conventional, product-centric perspective sees the product, instead of the value proposition delivered, as the business. It evaluates whether the product is superior and then considers how well the product is sold, distributed, and marketed. *DPV* simply treats product, distribution, advertising, and all other variables as important because and only because they may affect the value proposition delivered.

Most organizations are not familiar with the concept of value proposition as defined here and do not know or deliberately decide what value proposition they deliver. But this lack of awareness does not change the fact that every business delivers some value proposition; nor the fact that every business succeeds or fails as a function of the cost of that value proposition and how it compares in customers' minds to the alternatives.

Value happens: the *de facto* value proposition

Any organization that attempts to sell something delivers a value proposition, *de facto*. That value proposition may be a winner or a loser, but the organization delivers *some* value proposition by virtue of being in business. Organizations need not worry, '*Should* we deliver a value proposition?' More useful is to ask, 'What proposition *do* we deliver?' This may lead to the even more interesting, 'What proposition *should* we deliver?'

In the early stages of a business, an organization may only plan or develop products without yet actually selling anything. There is no *de facto* value proposition at this point. As soon as something is offered for sale, however, a *de facto* value proposition starts being delivered. Some or even all customers may have a perception of the value proposition they *would* get from a business before they have even bought its product or service. People who have never owned a Mercedes may perceive some fairly clear set of experiences they think it delivers. The *de facto* value proposition delivered to them then is solely a function of what has been communicated. Once customers *have* bought and used the relevant products and services, however, they are influenced by what has been communicated *and* provided.

It is useful, for any business, to know what *de facto* value proposition is delivered. Why is the business doing well/struggling? The answer always lies in what value proposition the business has been delivering, compared to competing alternatives, and in considering the costs of delivering it.

Sometimes significant improvements of a *de facto* value proposition result from simply understanding it. By precisely articulating the *de facto* value proposition delivered, one may identify and cut costs that were assumed necessary for its delivery but in fact are not. The organization often can then redirect those resources to delivering better experiences.

For example, one soft-goods retailer reengineered its shirts in the early 1990s to perform better in an international apparel trade group's quality testing. The quality standards, not surprisingly, were almost entirely about durability – how threads, seams, buttons, and fabric held up under simulated wear-and-tear. Each component was subjected to rigorous pounding, yanking, twisting, and hammering. The effort was a success; the testing proved the retailer's improved shirts able to last *years* longer than its rival's.

But what experiences were delivered to consumers as a result of the improved quality? Well, research indicated that this retailer's shirt, like that of its rival, was already lasting longer than most consumers currently *kept* it. The retailer, with its newly indestructible shirts, did not deliver *any* different experience to the customer, except perhaps to professional wrestlers wearing them in the ring. On the other hand, the improved quality did increase costs. The same research discovered that many consumers actually preferred the retailer's garments (before shirts were made guerrilla-warfare-ready) because they were more *comfortable*. They had a softer, smoother feel to the skin and fit a little better. Yet toughening shirts did nothing to enhance this experience. Performing this research and articulating the *de facto* value proposition helped the retailer draw a very useful conclusion: perhaps some of the cost of immortalizing shirts would be better invested in comfort.

Answering the following questions reveals the one or more *de facto* value propositions currently delivered by an organization. It is often important to understand the *de facto* propositions delivered to both primary entities and intermediaries. So one might answer these questions for consumers and then again for retailers, for example. Moreover, if answers to the second, third and fourth questions vary significantly among customers, the organization is actually delivering several value propositions, each of which should be identified and separately articulated.

The *de facto* value proposition

1   What customers do business with us (directly or indirectly)?
2   What do they buy or use and what actions must they take to do so?
3   What are the best alternatives they perceive? If they did not do business with this organization, what would they likely do instead?
4   What resulting experiences, including price, do they get by doing business with us rather than selecting their best alternatives?

***

Many managers first exposed to the value delivery framework assume their organization knows its value proposition well. Understood properly, that is rarely the case. The concept is so deceptively simple on the surface that managers just can't believe they don't have it written down, somewhere. This is compounded by the tendency to trivialize the concept. Since 1984, when I first created the concept, the phrase has been popularized and used unaccompanied by an understanding or explanation of its full meaning. Often, the term 'value proposition' has been misinterpreted as the simplistic marketing notion of positioning, the meager content of which is largely antithetical to the term's true meaning.

As a result, some in an organization may put forth a statement they are happy to *call* their current value proposition, but it rarely answers the above questions of the *de facto* value proposition. Many such candidate 'value propositions' do not explicitly answer *any* of those questions. Most at least fall short of answering the fourth (what resulting experiences do the customers get?), not meeting the *Criteria for a Resulting Experience* (p. 41).

Moreover, even when some in an organization may have an answer to these questions, even more rarely do several managers in the organization, especially in various functions, understand and agree on those *same* answers.

But after discovering that the organization does not have a clearly defined, consensus view of its *de facto* current value proposition, most managers also begin to realize they have also not answered the even more pressing question: what value proposition(s) *should* this organization deliver?

If an organization is to take responsibility for its own fate, it must learn what a *complete* value proposition means, then face the responsibility of making the disciplined *choice* of what complete value propositions to deliver.

To Choose or Not to Choose a Complete Value Proposition, *That* Is Management's Question

To choose genuinely a value proposition is to make the central decision of business strategy, for a value proposition defines the precise objective of a business. To make this choice, an organization must formally decide to actually deliver a particular value proposition at some specified point in time. The organization may fail to deliver the value proposition chosen or may change its strategy and adopt a different one. Still, a chosen value proposition does not state a fuzzy aspiration; it completely and absolutely commits the organization to its real delivery.

The complete value proposition

answers the following questions:

1 What is the specific *timeframe* for delivering this proposition?
2 Who is the *intended customer* who will derive the resulting experiences chosen in this proposition?
3 What do we *want* them to *do* in return for the experiences they will obtain? (What purchase and/or usage of products/services and any other major behaviors we want them to exhibit?)
4 What is the best competing *alternative*(s) they will have available?
5 What resulting experiences, including price, *will* they experience, including equal or inferior ones, ensuring each is:
   - an event or events in the customers' lives, resulting from doing what we want them to do, with some end-result consequence for them in comparison to their alternatives, this relative consequence having some value, all expressed in measurably specific terms
   - *not* a description of us, characteristics of our products, services, processes, resources, functions or general excellence; *nor* a vague ambiguous topic or platitude.

This commitment must be as unambiguous and specific as possible. It is therefore necessary to *complete* the choice of a value proposition by specifying the context in which the organization will deliver some set of resulting experiences. Thus, choosing a complete value proposition requires an organization to make five interrelated decisions.

Internally-driven and customer-compelled organizations make many decisions, the body of which they call a strategy. But the choice of a complete value proposition is usually not among these decisions. It is the will and courage to face the defining choice of a value proposition that distinguishes an organization managing out of the looking glass from these others.

Yet a chosen, complete value proposition does not a business make. It helps to choose a *winning* proposition, of course. But actually to *use* a value proposition, to act on this choice, an organization must design and then implement the rest of a business – the actions and resources with which to *deliver* that proposition.

The ultimate choice of complete value proposition and the design of its delivery are iteratively interactive with each other. That is, designing the delivery of a proposition often brings about refinements in the proposition itself. One usually cannot choose a winning proposition without considering the design of how it will be delivered. But before finally implementing that design, managers must take on the responsibility of truly choosing a complete value proposition.

Five questions of a complete value proposition

A complete value proposition is *about* customers but *for* the organization. It is not addressed to customers, nor a way to communicate to them. It is not even primarily about what the organization will communicate to customers, although it must drive these communications. Rather it articulates the essence of a business, defining exactly and completely what the organization fully intends to make happen in the customer's life.

Once and future strategy: what timeframe for this proposition?

An organization must commit to a specific, measurable result, not just identify some vague issues or goals. As part of ensuring that specificity, it must decide *when* a value proposition will be delivered. This helps commit the organization to actually delivering it, instead of merely working on it.

Obviously, the winning value proposition for a business may need to change over time. Trying to write one value proposition to cover both the short and long-term only encourages vague, unactionable mush, such as,

'We will reduce our customers' repair costs.' Very good. But how much and versus what alternative? 'Some this year, more next year, striving ever toward our goal – zero repair costs and the best in our industry!' Exciting; and perfectly vague.

The organization might want, for example, to strive to deliver one specific level of repair cost next year and a different one in three years. The organization should then articulate two propositions, one for each timeframe, in each case specifying the repair costs the organization actually intends the customer to experience, as compared to their best alternative. Then managers can determine whether they have truly made and should make the real commitment of choosing this proposition. 'Are we or aren't we actually going to deliver this specific proposition? If so, we must do it at this specified time. Will we?'

Specifying a timeframe distinguishes a business' long-term strategy from its short-term strategy. In doing so, this helps reveal the frequent reality that there *is* no long-term strategy. Expressing general aspirations to improve continuously in the future makes it easy for managers to delude themselves into thinking they have a long-term strategy. Articulating the short-term value proposition, and then determining how it should be changed or replaced in the long-term, helps solve this problem. That is, assuming long-term changes involve something more specific than to 'get even better!'

Consider a manufacturer of plastics used to make auto bumpers and body panels. The manufacturer might conclude that the auto makers would greatly value lowering the average vehicle weight, thus better meeting government mandated fuel efficiency goals. If the plastics company believes it can deliver a 1 percent weight reduction next year and a 3 percent reduction in three years, two propositions, one for each period, are far more useful than a single proposition committing to delivering 'ever better vehicle weight reduction.' To succeed, the plastics company may *need* to deliver that 3 percent reduction in three years, in which case its engineers need far clearer direction than 'ever better.'

The discipline of specifying a timeframe counteracts the managerial tendency to think, or at least speak and write, in idealized superlatives. As the world adopts new transmission technologies for cellular phones, providers will eventually offer service with virtually no interruptions. For the next few years, however, users will still be plagued by frequent disconnections, voice 'drop-out,' inadequate decibel volume, cross-talk from other conversations, and stupid popping noises. Therefore the near term value proposition a cellular provider should *choose* includes these far-from-perfect experiences. The same provider may well choose a longer-term proposition that includes nearly perfect conversations, but such an experience has no place in the short-term proposition.

To whom? *The intended customer*

To what entities or individuals does the organization intend the business to deliver resulting experiences within the specified timeframe? An organization may choose one value proposition focused on its primary customer and another related one focused on intermediaries. For example, Sony needed to think through the proposition to potential VCR consumers, its primary customers, a related one to movie rental shops and another one to consumer-electronics retailers selling VCRs. For each of these groups, the question to ask is this: 'Which of these customers are the intended customers, the subject of this value proposition?' For Sony's consumer proposition, for example, they needed to decide *which* consumers to target. Likewise, for the proposition to rental shops, *which* shops should be the intended customers in that proposition.

This question is *not* 'Who uses the product or service now and who wants it?' Intended customers could have no idea that the organization or its products even exist. They are simply the customers with whom the organization *intends* to do business, within the specified timeframe. These are the potential customers for whom this value proposition is most appropriate.

An appropriate intended customer for the microcomputer (the PC), in the 1970s, should have been: the hundreds of millions of knowledge workers worldwide who would be more productive by writing, analyzing, storing, and communicating information via a computer. Instead, many in Apple and elsewhere in the computer industry assumed the intended customer would be the 60,000 or so hobbyist engineers then interested in kits to build their own computers. These were the people asking for and interested in a personal computer. But they weren't even relevant to the right potential customer – almost everyone else. Of course, when asked, everyone else would laugh at the idea of owning a computer and explain patiently that they had no need for one. Yet personal computing could potentially deliver superior experiences of great value versus the alternatives.

Chapters Ten–Twelve discuss the interrelationships between delivering value propositions to primary, intermediary and other customers. In addition, Part Two of this book discusses in detail *how* an organization can choose its intended customers. At this point, simply realize the importance of deciding and articulating who those customers are as part of the complete value proposition.

What does the business want the intended customer to do?

A complete value proposition describes the exact behavior the organization wants and needs the intended customer to exhibit within the selected timeframe in return for the resulting experiences delivered to them. This behavior includes the products/services the customer must buy and/or use. But that's not all. An organization may want a customer to change significantly their behavior, such as a business customer's operations. For example, Weyerhaeuser did not simply need furniture companies to buy its particle board product (see Chapter One, pp. 26–7). The company wanted furniture makers to implement the following two changes:

- Furniture companies would stop buying thin dimension boards and gluing them together to make thicker dimension legs. Instead, they would close those gluing lines, reallocate those resources, and buy thick dimension board from Weyerhaeuser to make the legs.
- In addition, they would buy Weyerhaeuser's smoother board and apply the specialized ultra thin laminates to it.

Going beyond customer-compelled thinking sometimes means asking customers to do something difficult and uncomfortable. Consider banks whose complex computing environments limit access to customer information, in that the form and timeframe in which information is available leaves something to be desired. In these organizations, long established, mainframe-based computer systems house a myriad of databases for customer accounts, transactions, and profitability. These systems are often closed, i.e. it is hard to add other makers' products that could improve data access.

IBM might ask such a bank to stay tied-in to IBM's mainframe and systems guidance, slowly gaining better access to applications and databases. Workstation makers like Sun, HP or DEC might ask the bank to move quickly toward a more open environment, like the ones they offer. The integrated data access offered by these organizations would provide better identification and service of the most promising customers. However, most banks view this fast and radical change with trepidation. Giving a workstation maker a central role in 'enterprise computing' seems risky compared to using IBM with its decades of experience in this role.

The path of less resistance for the workstation challengers to follow is the easier proposition for the customer to accept: move slowly, giving only a little business to Sun or HP as a cautious experiment in a better computing environment. But, of course, this also gives IBM more time to improve their own open system offerings. Will the workstation makers' window of opportunity close while they wait for an increase in the bank's comfort level? Should they then propose more dramatic, riskier moves for the bank? The answers to these questions are critical to success of the challengers. Thus, deciding exactly what an organization wants the customer to do can be as important as understanding the customer's resulting experiences.

Often without making a *disciplined choice*, many businesses automatically try only to win the customer's preference rather than work to increase total market consumption. Of course, this is the only option in many cases. However, some markets, though considered mature, have great potential for growth given the right value proposition.

The US coffee market showed no growth a few years ago. But lurking within this apparently classically mature market was the latent desire to drink great coffee in a pleasant but simple atmosphere. Then, Starbucks of Seattle introduced a retail chain that superbly romanticized coffee drinking. The chain presented the best varieties of exotic fresh beans, freshly ground expertly on the spot. Customers were encouraged to sit, drink one of the endless varieties of latte, cappuccino, or espresso, and enjoy the aromas and quiet jazz in an urbane but simple, relaxed atmosphere. This experience fueled tremendous sales of fresh beans that the consumer took home. Starbucks added drive-through facilities at some outlets. Tiny versions were appended to complementary retail environments like book stores. Other retailers followed suit. Consumption soared in this not-so mature market.

The consumer still-photography market may present such an unrealized opportunity. Developed economies' photo consumption seems mature. Yet some consumers use 10 or 12 film rolls per year while others with similar demographics and lifestyles use 2 or 3. No inherent limit constrains these consumers, but many are not fully aware of the pleasure they can get from imaging. Many have had disappointing experiences with photos or are intimidated by photography's complexity. If someone were to help them succeed more often and get more enjoyment and fewer hassles from imaging, significant total market growth may be possible. But it is only attainable by choosing to make this happen as an element of a value proposition. Kodak, in their innovations in the retail environment and the recent introduction of the Advanced Photo System, is currently working to capture this opportunity.

What are the best alternatives these customers will have?

If they do not do business with us, what will they most likely do instead? What will they perceive as the best alternative for them? Whatever the answer, a value proposition must give them the reason to do what the organization offering it wants instead.

Here is where *competition* fits into choosing a value proposition. An organization must understand the value proposition customers can have if they don't accept the value proposition of that organization. This alternative experience presents the competitive threat. As defined here, a competitive threat is not some combination of the competitor's products, resources, and capabilities. To deal effectively with a competitive threat, an organization must benchmark and beat the competitor's value proposition, regardless of how they otherwise compare.

Often, the best alternative lies not with another firm making a similar product but with another technology or with just doing nothing. The PC customer's best alternative in the 1970s was to use no computer. The best alternative to a growth-oriented value proposition from Kodak, for the consumer using 2–3 rolls of film per year, is to remain the same. The winning value proposition must beat these competing alternatives as well.

What then will be the customer's resulting experiences?

The preceding questions provide the context for the value proposition. Within that context, this essential question regarding resulting experiences can be answered in actionable, unambiguous terms. That is, for the specified timeframe, if the intended customer does what the organization wants and does not choose an alternative, then what resulting experience will be delivered to this customer?

As is the case with the other questions of the complete value proposition, answering this one requires making a disciplined choice. This question is not, of course, an invitation to make customer-compelled promises of everything customers might want a business to deliver. Management must determine what combination of resulting experiences, including price, to deliver and this includes what *not* to deliver as well.

Many winning propositions are *tradeoffs*

Some experiences may be equal or even inferior to the customer's alternatives, and thus provide a tradeoff for the customer. But to deliver a profitable value proposition, this combination of experiences must, for the intended customers within the specified timeframe, be in net superior to the alternatives and be profitably deliverable.

Choosing a tradeoff value proposition is not evidence of failure. Delivering an inferior one generally is. So is delivering a superior one at higher total cost than the revenues it produces. Rather than agonize over not achieving total customer satisfaction, organizations should heartily embrace the opportunity to deliver a tradeoff value proposition, if it's a winner.

Many tradeoff propositions simply reflect the fact that the organization *cannot* deliver some experience as well as the customer's best alternative. More than a few managers, all victims of customer-compelled philosophies, cannot bring themselves to admit, let alone write down, an inferior experience their business delivers. A few others are so internally-driven that they hope marketing will either fool the customer into thinking the inferior experience superior or into looking the other way until it's too late. So these managers find it dangerous to say or write down anything but hyperbolic self-acclamation for their business.

It is more realistic and useful, if one's goal is to make money, to acknowledge the inescapable inferior experience by writing it into the complete value proposition. After all, it's merely a simple truth on the paper, not some incantation that will make the business wither and die. It actually helps a manager confront the inferior experience(s) and say, 'OK, so despite this, how can we profitably deliver a superior value proposition? Let's see, where's the *superior* part?' In fact, managers should search aggressively for creative tradeoff opportunities. Sometimes great success comes of deliberately denying customers a resulting experience or delivering an experience less well or thoroughly than is possible.

Better us than you – a brief illustration

Recently, an organization competing in the industrial lubricants market developed a complete value proposition. The market in which the organization competes is very price competitive and characterized by low margins. The intended customers in this case perform machine lubrication and related maintenance with their own maintenance staff. These customers tend to be primarily focused on other production issues, despite the need for a disciplined and focused capability in maintenance-lubrication on complex, heavily used machinery. Less than optimal maintenance-lubrication can result in a range of potentially avoidable production costs, such as higher levels of unscheduled and scheduled machine downtime. Furthermore, the cost of handling and disposing lubricant oil, on the rise due to environmental protection issues, presents another potential cost-savings opportunity.

The organization believed itself capable of profitably helping its customers achieve a large part of these potential cost savings. And it developed a value proposition which reflected that belief. The level of specificity in their value proposition below is a good illustration of a complete value proposition (data is disguised, shown illustratively here).

Choosing is an internal commitment to deliver the *best possible* proposition – but no more

In choosing a complete value proposition, an organization formally decides to deliver it exactly as stated. It is no longer an option, something under consideration, or a set of experiences the organization will work toward delivering. Therefore, 'what we want the customer to do' and the 'experi-

An illustrative industrial-lubricants value proposition

Timeframe. We will deliver this proposition for at least 2 years starting in 1997

Intended customers. Manufacturers with plants using machinery vital to operation, requiring lubrication as part of maintenance. In these plants the cost impact of maintenance-lubrication is substantial but they are not close to optimizing lubrication tasks.

What we want them to do. Replace current lubrication processes with our total lubrication-management service; contract to us all lubricant procurement, inventory-management, maintenance and disposal and actual lubrication procedures; buy all lubricant from us, increasing our share +20–30% in this portion of the market.

Best competing alternative. Continue buying lubricant oil from us or competitors, pursuing lowest bidder, while performing all maintenance in-house.

Resulting experiences. Their total production costs will decrease dramatically, roughly 1.5–2.5%, worth far more than the price. Specifically, customers will experience:

1 3–5% less *unscheduled* downtime due to machine component wear and machine failures currently caused by inappropriate maintenance-lubrication procedures. About 10–20% of this avoided downtime results in avoiding temporary line shutdowns, thus actual lost production; the rest reduces inventory and redundant-machine costs incurred now to keep this downtime from line shutdowns. This experience results in total production cost savings of 0.8 to 1.2%.

2 10–20% less *scheduled* machine downtime caused by use of inferior lubricants with shorter drain intervals, thus avoiding direct maintenance and part replacement (e.g. ball-bearing) costs, worth another 0.3–0.6% total production cost savings.

3 Over 25% lower direct cost of lubricant waste disposal, since disposal will be handled by us rather than a contractor plus less tangible long-term regulatory and liability costs, caused by less than optimal safe disposal, worth another 0.2–0.3%.

4 Lower overall procurement costs worth about 0.1–0.2% associated with:
    • inaccurate, untimely payment of lubrication invoices
    • storage and retrieval of lubrication invoice information
    • overtime caused by non-electronic handling of these tasks.

5 Lower inventory and environmental compliance costs, worth an estimated 0.1–0.2%, caused currently by drum delivery of lubricants, to be replaced with bulk delivery.

6 An inferior experience is the partial loss of direct control by plant management over lubrication process and some resulting anxiety, but little actual economic impact.

Price. Annual fee, proportional to lubricant volume, about 40% below total cost savings customer realizes from above and includes +5% premium versus current lubricant price.

ences they will derive' must be doable. It is counterproductive to commit to delivering more than is presently possible.

Committing only to that which can be delivered frustrates some managers. 'Shouldn't we always strive for more?' Of course. So strive to deliver the most superior, profitable value proposition *possible*.

Conversely, a value proposition should *not* be reduced to what can be *guaranteed* to a customer. An organization's realistic proposition may go beyond what the organization would explicitly guarantee. Managers should also remember that choosing a complete value proposition only entails an *internal* articulation – not a communiqué to customers. It is a statement by which to design and guide an entire business. It thus may be long and not necessarily the height of entertainment.

Most organizations do *not* in fact choose a complete value proposition. They rarely articulate answers to the all of the complete questions. When managers do come close to a full articulation, rarely does the whole organization agree and commit to those same answers.

Three tests of choosing: has our organization really chosen a value proposition?

1 Has our organization articulated the answers to the questions of the *complete value proposition*, including experiences that meet the *criteria for a resulting experience*?

2 If so, has this complete value proposition been formally adopted as the driving element in our strategy for this business, agreed by all functions and departments to be the basis for actions, priorities, and resource allocation?

3 If so, is this value proposition clearly known and understood by virtually everyone involved in every function in our organization?

Thoroughly answering the second and third questions involve the larger frameworks of the value delivery system and value delivery chain. The reason behind choosing a value proposition is that it allows an organization deliberately to design all the actions and resources so as to deliver that value proposition, i.e. to design the whole value delivery system. Moreover, while everyone involved in this business within the organization must understand and buy into the value proposition, frequently entities outside the organization must also. Often, suppliers and intermediaries between the organization and the intended primary customer must help deliver the proposition. Nonetheless, these three tests help determine whether an organization has made the disciplined choice of what value proposition to deliver, a choice fundamental to business strategy.

Chapter Five

Some of What a Real Value Proposition *Isn't*

Without a full understanding of the concept, a value proposition can be equated with some other widely used but quite different business concepts. Moreover, since its creation in 1983, the phrase has worked its way into fairly common usage, but has been generally unaccompanied by its intended meaning. Therefore, to clarify further this central construct of *DPV,* the value proposition is contrasted in this chapter against some important concepts with which it should not be confused.

A value proposition is not a positioning, a slogan, or a USP

A value proposition is not another name for the message an organization should communicate to customers. Choosing a value proposition should indeed determine that message, and that message should help convince the customer of the resulting experiences they will have and why these are superior. However, that chosen value proposition should also determine everything else about the business that is important.

A marketing concept popularized by advertising execs Al Ries and Jack Trout, 'positioning' is how an organization explains a product to customers. It has at best an indirect connection to a value proposition. As Ries and Trout defined it:

> 'Positioning starts with a product ... But positioning is not what you do to a product. Positioning is what you do to the mind of the prospect. That is, you position the product in the mind of the prospect.'[1]

A product can be positioned or repositioned using a variety of characteristics, most of which are something other than the resulting experiences a customer will have. It could be positioned in terms of its relative market share (Hertz is #1, British Airways – the World's Favorite Airline). Or who uses it (here's a movie star who uses this credit card!). Or attributes it has that competition doesn't (largest! oldest! best at positioning!).

Broadly speaking, positioning is the way an organization wants to make customers perceive the product. But a chosen value proposition is the decision as to what experiences the customer will have, not how customers should be made to think about the product. Moreover, the communication of a value proposition concerns those experiences and why they are desirable, not simply anything that affects the product's position in the customer's mind.

The poor beleaguered marketer often views positioning as a powerful tool. Change the position of our identical product in the consumer's mind relative to those other identical products, and – voila! – we create distinctiveness. With any luck, we fool the customer into buying *our* identical product. Thus success is based on a marketing-manufactured distinctiveness, not on any experience of superior value. As a way of 'separating the customer from their loose change,' to quote Ted Levitt, this certainly beats the trouble of superior value delivery.

Marketing professionals sometimes lament the negative stereotypes of their profession. Yet it is no wonder why people often think that marketing honors deception as a clever business practice when you consider the subtle deception of positioning. A value proposition concerns itself not with the product but with the customer's behavior and experiences. The object of a value proposition is not to make the customer see something that isn't there. The object is to conceive a real scenario of experiences that is superior.

In a narrower sense, positioning comes down to writing a slogan. Slogans are not necessarily bad. If General Electric brings good things to life, it's probably harmless to say so incessantly. Likewise with Apple's 'the power to be your best' or 'Merrill Lynch is bullish on America' or 'IBM means service.' But confusing a slogan with a value proposition is *not* harmless. Admittedly, the concept of a slogan is easier to understand than that of a value proposition. This may explain why interpretation of the term is sometimes reduced to the absurd level of a slogan. However, as the reader will have discerned, a value proposition is not a slogan.

The Unique Selling Proposition (USP), on the other hand, is an intelligent approach to the role of a few well-chosen words in business. The concept was invented in the mid-50s by the Ted Bates advertising agency and popularized by its leader Rosser Reeves in the classic *Reality in Advertising*. It argues that advertising must articulate and convey a unique reason for the consumer to buy what is being advertised. A USP is such an articulation. USP is a very reasonable concept, one which all advertising professionals claim to have known since the age of three. Based on the almost complete lack of USPs in today's advertising, most of them seem to have forgotten it at age four. Advertising effectiveness would be greatly improved if professionals would actually use it instead of merely paying it homage.

However, the USP is written for the customer and does not provide strategic guidance to the organization. Like the product's design and features, like the organization's manufacturing assets and all other resources, the USP comes after and is driven by the value proposition. A well-chosen proposition should determine a well-written USP. Thus a USP is not a value proposition, but it can be considered the manifestation of one in advertising.

Not a mission statement, statement of values or strategic intent

Mission statements can be helpful, despite the tendency to write air-headed fluff and call it our mission. A mission statement might define very broadly the market or kind of markets in which the organization intends to compete. Markets should be defined by the customers and type of experiences relevant to them. Procter & Gamble is primarily focused on markets of consumers and the experiences associated with keeping their personal environment clean. Merck focuses on patient consumers and health professionals, and the health-restoring and health-sustaining experiences of value to them. A mission statement may usefully prescribe limits within these markets. Merck might constrain its means of value delivery to what pharmacological substances can do. Or it could decide that it's acceptable to include other forms of health-care value delivery, such as operating HMOs. A mission statement can also indicate the broadly defined goals of the organization, such as the size and rate of growth it wants to achieve, its required return on investment, and other, non-financial goals such as safety for employees.

None of this, however, constitutes a value proposition. A proposition can help *achieve* a mission by delivering some particular experiences to particular customers in return for their money. A value proposition, together with how it will be delivered, constitutes one business. That business is part of a strategy through which attainment of a mission is pursued. When an organization operates more than one business, the difference between a mission and a value proposition becomes even clearer. A mission statement can usefully guide a collection of businesses in the same organization. Not so for a value proposition, which drives a single business.

In recent years, a variant of mission statements has emerged: the values statement or statement of corporate values. This is sometimes just another name for a mission statement, but it often addresses broader issues the firm wishes to articulate. It more likely touches on questions of ethics or community involvement, for example. Some managers might mistakenly associate these statements with a value proposition, given use of the word value.

Obviously, however, the word value takes on a different meaning in the two phrases.

According to a *Fortune* 1993 article on the subject of value statements, one incentive for their recent proliferation in the US is the 1991 federal sentencing guidelines for crimes such as bribery. 'Companies can reduce culpability by showing they have a compliance program, including a values statement.'[2] In the case of mail order clothing firm Hanna Anderson, one of their stated corporate values was 'Social Action: We will research specific opportunities for Hanna to contribute to the community.' This led to an innovative program of buying back clothes from consumers whose infants had outgrown them. The clothes were then laundered and donated to needy families. This program did contribute to the community. Moreover, the point was not lost on consumers.

Mostly, however, a value statement produces a harmless, vague exhortation to employees. After several iterations, one firm came up with 'inspire active participation in the growth of everyone to benefit our business.' At GM's Saturn division, employees participated in articulating a 'commitment to customer enthusiasm' (upgraded from the first draft, which was only '... customer satisfaction').[3] Harm only ensues when people conclude that this statement means they do not need a real business strategy, based on a real value proposition.

The most common characteristic of all such broad statements is their vacuity and downright silliness. Too often, such statements end up sounding too much like the Mission Statement Dilbert's boss wrote for his group:

> *'We enhance stockholder value through strategic business initiatives by empowered employees working in new team paradigms.'*[4]

Adams helpfully defines them as 'a long awkward sentence that demonstrates management's inability to think clearly.'[5] *Fortune*'s Farnham cites some gems, all from real corporate values, mission, vision, and similar kinds of statements:

> *'We will strive to achieve average long-term top-quartile performance within our chosen sectors.*
> *'We will promote personal growth through cleanliness.*
> *'We will achieve results in a planful way.*
> *'We will seek and develop long-term relationships with key customers who offer potential for multiple major projects during the Strategic Time Frame.*
> *'We impose on ourselves an obligation to reach beyond the minimal.*
> *'Buy-in from colleagues and supervisors will be sought.*

'Our intent is to be the world leader in moving people and material vertically and horizontally, over relatively short distances.'

In the category of very broad slogans intended to inspire greatness resides the more intelligent concept of 'strategic intent' created by Hamel and Prahalad. In essence this concept means, 'an obsession with winning at all levels of the organization, ... [something that] envisions a desired leadership position and establishes the criterion ... to chart ... progress.'[6] It is also 'an animating dream ... [the] dream that energizes a company.'[7] Some examples are: 'Komatsu set out to "Encircle Caterpillar." Canon sought to "Beat Xerox." Honda strove to become a second Ford ...'[8] And 'The dream of British Airways ... was to become "The World's Favourite Airline."'[9] These are all very well, but they are rather broad goals.

The strategy field and its practice in management consulting has a habit of analyzing businesses at great length only to announce a rather broad and uncontroversial objective, like 'we should really increase market share – a lot!' The hobgoblin plaguing smaller minds, figuring out *how* even to begin achieving the objective, is postponed until the mundane stage of *execution*. In reality, the difficult and more critical part of strategy is deciding how profitably to cause customers to change their behavior. This decision, choosing the value proposition and designing its delivery, is not petty execution; it is the essence of realistic strategy.

Unfortunately, when mission/value statements and the like become more specific, they often harbor internally-driven thinking cloaked as strategic thinking. Missions can be used to specify products, technologies, competencies, distribution channels and manufacturing assets to be deployed. However, they usually lack any notion of the appropriate value propositions to deliver. Yet not only strategy but also marketing seems to endorse this internally-driven approach. Kotler's marketing textbook asserts that a company's mission

> *'... is shaped by five elements. The first is its* history ... *[from which it] must not depart too radically ... second is the* current preferences of the owners and management ... *Third,* the market environment ... *Fourth, the organization's* resources *determine which missions are possible ... Finally, the organization should base its mission on its* distinctive competences ... *[i.e.] its core competence.'*[10] *[Italics in original.]*

At least the 'market environment' merits a mention among these criteria. After issuing such a mission statement, the marketing department might then be tasked with writing supposed value propositions, positioning statements, or *something* that rationalizes these largely internally-driven decisions.

Undeniably, much internally-driven and customer-compelled thought occupies many of these statements. A real, chosen, complete value proposition plays a different role and is focused on quite different topics. However, one genus of these statements that can usefully be associated with value proposition is the 'vision' for a single business. While many visions share some of the more unfortunate characteristics of the statements discussed above, the idea is often used to mean that a business should have a vision of its future. What does the organization want this business to accomplish? On what should it single-mindedly focus?

These are not bad questions to pose and *DPV* would argue that the answer for any single business should be: the choice of value proposition. To be clear, a typical vision statement is not a value proposition, as defined here. However, the instinct to want a clear vision of a business is a good one. That vision should consist of deciding, for a specified timeframe, who the intended customers are, what we want them to do in comparison to what competing alternative, and what resulting experiences they will thereby derive. And of course, all should be such that the business generates wealth.

Not a value discipline

Michael Treacy and Fred Wiersema's article on Value Disciplines and their 1995 book, *The Discipline of Market Leaders*, suggest that there are three strategies for companies to select. Each is what they call a value discipline: operational excellence, product leadership, or customer intimacy. While these three descriptions seem closely to echo Michael Porter's earlier classification of three generic strategies – low cost, differentiation, and more customized niche – they are not at all similar to value propositions. Nor do they articulate types of value propositions.

However, after reading their book, one might draw the conclusion that value disciplines are indeed meant to be types of value proposition. Their introduction states their 'task: to introduce, define, and develop three concepts ... The first is the value proposition ... The second, the value-driven operating model, is that combination of ... processes, ... systems, ... structure ... that gives a company the capacity to deliver on its value proposition.'[11] The three 'disciplines' are the third concept and seem to be presented as three kinds of value proposition and as three kinds of 'value driven operating model.'

Specifically, they say, the value proposition of the company following the 'operational excellence' value discipline is 'low price and hassle free service.' The proposition to customers from 'product leadership' firms: 'the best product, period.' And the proposition of 'customer intimacy' adherents is, 'We have the best solution for you – and we provide all the support you need to achieve optimum result and/or value from whatever products you buy.'

Whether or not these formulae constitute bold new strategic directions, the reader will easily recognize that they are not value propositions. There is no hint of a choice of timeframe, exactly which customers the business will pursue, what the business wants them to do, or what their alternatives are. The value disciplines do not infer resulting experiences, except for indicating a lower price with operational excellence than with the other two. Beyond price, they are a mixture of vague platitude and general descriptor of what the organization will do.

Readers should also understand that DPV is *not* a redefinition of concepts belonging in any part to Treacy or Wiersema. On the contrary. Not only do the two claim to 'introduce, define and develop' the value proposition, but also their definition of 'value driven operating model' seems to parallel the 'value delivery system.' That announcement should not be misconstrued to mean that Treacy and Wiersema first created and/or developed the concepts of value proposition or value delivery system.

Not the value added

The term value has a long history in economic discussion. It is so burdened with baggage that its meaning is not highly precise, but the essential meaning is nonetheless relevant to the concepts of *Delivering Profitable Value*. One of the more unfortunate pieces of baggage is the term *value added*. Value added refers to the materials, features, services or other resources added to a product at any given stage of production and distribution. Raw material enters the manufacturing system, and at each stage of production something new is added, thus adding value until finally a finished product results. Those who buy it may add further to it before reselling it, perhaps as part of a more complex product or service. Value added strategies purportedly differentiate a commodity; one adds value to the commodity, perhaps through features and services customers want, thus differentiating the product. In fact, the concept antecedes the generic strategy of differentiation in the industrial organization school of strategy. A value added strategy is supposed usually to lead to a higher cost and a higher price.

Some people may instinctively assume that the value proposition is equivalent to this value one adds to a commodity product. Of course, this is not the case. A value proposition, properly understood, is the essence of any strategy, whether the product involved is considered, by whatever measures, identical, inferior, or superior to other products. The value proposition is neither the product nor the costly differentiators one adds in the hope of making it more appealing.

Delivering a value proposition does not necessarily require adding anything to anything. In fact, one might deliver a winning value proposition by *taking away* materials or features or services from some base product. Moreover, the value in a value proposition is the value in the customer's experience, not the value in the product. It is the experience of the customer that must be differentiated.

***

The heart of business is *Delivering Profitable Value*. To develop effective business strategy therefore organizations should understand and concentrate enormous energy on the choice of a complete value proposition for each business. To be understood well, this idea of a value proposition must be distinguished from various other concepts with which it can be too easily confused. Once managers understand what one is, and what one isn't, however, it is time to be sure that the one they choose is a *good* one. For, the application of *DPV* means playing to win.

Notes

1   Ries and Trout, *Positioning: The Battle for Your Mind*, New York, Warner Books, 1982.
2   Alan Farnham, "State your values, hold the hot air," *Fortune*, April 19, 1993, p. 53.
3   *Ibid*, p. 54.
4   Adams, *The Dilbert Principle*, op. cit., p. 37.
5   *Ibid*, p. 36.
6   Gary Hamel and C.K. Prahalad, 'Strategic Intent,' *Harvard Business Review*, May–June 1989, p. 64.
7   Hamel and Prahalad, *Competing for the Future*, HBS Press, Cambridge, MA, 1994, p. 129.
8   *Strategic Intent*, op. cit., p. 64.
9   *Competing for the Future*, op. cit.
10 Philip Kotler, *Marketing Management*, Prentice Hall, Englewood Cliffs, NJ, p. 66.
11 Michael Treacy and Fred Wiersema, *The Discipline of Market Leaders*, Addison Wesley, Reading, MA, 1995, p. xiv.

Chapter Six

Playing to Win: Choose Good Value Propositions

The purpose of choosing a complete value proposition is to deliver it and thereby succeed as a business. Therefore, an organization needs to choose *good* value propositions – winners. A winning, complete value proposition meets two interconnected criteria: customers must find it *superior* to competing alternatives and the organization is able to deliver it at a low enough cost to generate wealth for the firm.

Know one when you see one

A good value proposition:

1 Is *complete* – answers the *Complete Value Proposition* questions (p. 62), meeting the *Criteria For A Resulting Experience* (p. 41).
2 Would clearly be *superior* in net to intended customers' alternatives, *if* we actually delivered it. The 'superior' criterion is applied to
   - not every experience, but the whole proposition in net
   - not necessarily our products, resources or competencies, versus competitors, but rather the value proposition.
3 Could produce *more revenues than cost*, if we delivered it.
4 Is *possible* for us to deliver in the relevant timeframe.
5 Is in net *smart* for our enterprise to deliver, after considering the *indirect impact* it may have over time and on our other businesses.

Would this value proposition be *superior*, assuming it was delivered?

A complete value proposition is superior if the intended customer finds the combination of resulting experiences delivered within the specified timeframe superior. To determine whether this would be the case, each purportedly superior experience must be evaluated individually as must the combination of all experiences. Though it may seem a straightforward, almost trivial exercise, the distinction between a superior value proposition and one destined to fail can be quite subtle.

Equal is not good enough

To be profitable, a value proposition almost always must be superior. This superiority is also absolutely necessary for sustaining profitable growth. Some people may assume an equal value proposition sufficient for success. Parts of management theory, especially the industrial-organization microeconomics school in the strategy field, reinforce this view. Firms characterized as 'equal to competitors' are said to succeed if the 'industry structure' is favorable. Closer examination shows that 'equal to competitors' usually does not mean the firm delivers an equal value proposition. These 'equal' firms only succeed because their businesses deliver superior propositions.

Sometimes a business may offer an equal value proposition to new customers, but actually offer a superior one to existing customers. These businesses originally won customers by delivering superior value and keep them now because of some inferior experience the customer would undergo if they were to switch to a competitor. This cost of switching may be emotional rather than pragmatic. For example, several General Motors car lines long ago stopped attracting new customers, but retain third or fourth generation customers who may enjoy the family tradition of owning this car line more than they would owning a superior car.

And of course, a business with lower costs may be able profitably to charge a lower price for a product that delivers equal or inferior experiences, but thereby deliver a value proposition that is superior overall.

Businesses deliver truly identical value propositions much less frequently than would be commonly assumed. If several businesses actually do offer identical value propositions, however, customers will have zero preference among them. In that case, microeconomic theory says, rightly, that the market will then drive down prices. A business can still make money, in theory, if it can sustain a significantly lower cost position and if competitors cannot find any way to deliver a superior experience. These conditions exist far more often, and last far longer, in economists' theoretical models than in the real world. However, even this theoretical situation precludes sustained growth, which is only possible by giving some customers a reason to change their preference, i.e. by delivering superior value.

Superiority of experiences, not of organizations

Given the importance of superiority, managers must be able to judge whether a proposition is, in fact, superior. A judgment more difficult than it may appear, it is often made wrongly because the conventional mindset leads to misunderstandings. Superiority of *what*, versus *what*? The real question here is whether the actual customer experiences will be superior to competing alternative experiences. The quite different question posed instinctively by the conventional approach is whether the organization is superior to the competition's organization.

One version of this classic misunderstanding is to assume, in effect, that if a business delivers *more* resulting experiences than competitors, this business must be superior. In the 1980s, the retailer Sears added the Dean Witter stock brokerage to its offering. Many Sears customers use brokerage services, so the Dean Witter offering was viewed as satisfying a need. No other retailer made this offer. Ergo, superiority. However, to deliver a superior proposition, one of two things had to happen. Either the investment experience alone had to be somehow better in a Sears store, or the combination of experiences had to create some synergistic experience with a valuable consequence, such as saving time. It is hard to imagine how investment advice would be *better* delivered in Sears. And few customers found synergy in shopping for a lawn mower and trash can, changing stock portfolio, and topping off the morning with a new toilet seat cover.

Comparing product performance attributes, as often happens in technology-intensive businesses, is equally misleading. In fact, as described by *The Economist*, observers of new technology have noticed what they think is an important phenomenon. Products that supposedly fill a market need, deliver what they promise, and whose manufacturing costs are reasonable, sometimes fail anyway. How could this be, they ask? Consider Philips' and Sony's introduction of Digital Audio Tape (DAT) in 1987, which followed their success with compact discs. Ten years later, DAT's failure seems a mystery, since the technology is purportedly superior. *The Economist* explains this phenomenon as follows:

'...*they were not sufficiently better than the established alternatives.*

'*Since the success of CDs, venture capitalists have introduced a rule of thumb, known as the 10× rule, to help them decide which ventures to back. They ask...'Is this thing ten times better than what it is replacing?'*

DAT can, it seems, be explained on this basis.

'*DAT has advantages over both CDs and tape cassettes (which survived the CD...in part because [the Sony] Walkman allowed them to do things that CDs could not). Digital tape beats CDs because it can record music instead of just playing it. And it beats cassettes because its sound quality is better. Unlike CDs, though, DAT bombed.*

'*The received wisdom is that it was killed by record companies ... afraid it would be used to make pirate copies ... But other technologies (including CDs) have been resisted by record companies and succeeded. The real reason therefore seems to be that it simply did not pass the 10× rule.'*[1]

However, DAT did not fail because the value proposition was not 10× better. The value proposition was not *any* better. Consider the supposed advantage over CDs: the consumer could record on DAT. So what? The consumer could not replace CDs with DAT on this basis; they still needed a CD to record it onto the DAT. Concerning the customer's actual resulting experience, a question: *what* advantage?

Cassettes succeeded because consumers could record music from phonographs onto a cassette, then listen to the cassette in conditions where a record could not be played, such as while jogging with a Walkman or riding in a car. The CD narrowed this difference, since one could listen to CDs on a portable 'Discman' or, as was increasingly common by the late 1980s, in a car CD player. The only situation where a CD would not work well was in situations with a lot of movement, such as running or other sports and exercise. Cassettes survived partly because of this application. But why didn't DAT replace cassettes in these situations?

By 1989, the consumer could easily buy pre-recorded cassettes. Many had already recorded some of their music from phonographs or CDs onto cassettes. For consumers to use DAT instead of cassettes in sports situations, they would have to jettison their cassettes and cassette players, in effect starting completely over, in order to get better sound. But while running or riding an exercise bike, how likely is the difference in sound quality to be appreciated? How about a 0.1× rule?

Abilities are *not* more important than results

Thus, organizations often search for superiority in the wrong places. Contrasting an organization's visage in the looking glass with that of its competitors will produce some misleading, if sometimes comforting, observations. Another manifestation of this way of thinking is to assume that using a core competence means a business is superior. According to the widely accepted doctrine, a core competence is one that competitors cannot match, i.e. we're better at it. Managers often confuse superior ability with real competitive superiority. For only if an ability helps an organization to deliver a superior experience is the ability usefully superior.

Obviously, there is a positive connection between how capable an organization is at delivering an experience and how that experience will compare to alternatives. However, an organization must place the highest priority on the customer's actual resulting experience and not on the capability or even core competence with which it is delivered. It is like the joke told among some physicians, where the surgeon notes, admiring his competence, 'The operation was a complete success! Although the patient died, we kept him in perfect electrolyte balance throughout!'

Kodak's Photo-CD technology is an impressive creation for which the company has found innovative applications in non-consumer markets. Initially intended to have a major impact on the consumer imaging business, it allowed consumers, with purchase of a special video-CD player, to view still photos on a TV and to store photos electronically. But the anticipated consumer impact did not happen. However, Hamel and Prahalad cite this case as an illustration of the power of leveraging competencies that other firms lack.

> '... top managers ... must ask, 'Given our particular portfolio of competencies, what opportunities are we uniquely positioned to exploit?' The answer points to opportunity arenas that other firms, with different competence endowments, may find difficult to access. For example, it would be hard to imagine any other firm than Eastman Kodak creating a product like Photo-CD, which required an in-depth understanding of both chemical film and electronic imaging competencies. Canon may understand electronic imaging and Fuji may understand film, but only Kodak had a deep understanding of both.'[2]

Managers should be wary of applying superior competence without some notion of how it will help the organization deliver a *superior* value proposition. Few consumers recognized the superiority of buying an expensive CD player, waiting an extra week before getting the prints back, and paying much more for photo-processing in order to view stills on TV. As a result, Photo-CD lost Eastman Kodak several hundred million dollars. While not *overly* important, these little details of the *long-term business results* from competency-driven strategy may deserve attention. Hamel and Prahalad recommend taking away a different lesson:

> 'The ultimate success of this product is less important than the lesson its managers learned about how a synthesis of skills residing in seemingly disparate businesses could be combined to create new competitive space.'[3]

A capability to do something others cannot do is sometimes fun but is not a good substitute for superior business strategy.

Could we profitably deliver this proposition?

Achieving sustained profitable growth requires delivering truly superior value propositions, as has been discussed. However, a winning value proposition must indeed be possible to deliver at a cost below the revenues it will produce. Of course, often one can only determine this possibility after designing the whole business. That is, an organization usually must have some idea of how it would deliver a proposition before estimating its cost and making that determination. Later chapters address the issues of delivering a value proposition and determining how to deliver it. Here, it is important simply to emphasize that no value proposition is a winner unless it can be delivered with revenues exceeding costs by enough of a margin to generate wealth. The potential revenue from delivering a proposition, the means necessary to deliver it, and its possible costs must all be taken into account.

Could *this proposition produce revenues above total cost?*

Deciding that a proposition would be superior is one thing; sometimes it is quite another to determine if it will produce enough revenues to cover its cost. This can especially be the case with a new, unproven proposition and even more so if delivering it will require a daunting investment. Frequently, making such a judgment entails assessing whether some new experiences will be sufficiently superior to alter significantly the behavior and attitudes of intended customers.

At the time Federal Express introduced its initial value proposition, most of its potential customers had not used overnight service, for two good reasons. These office workers were unaware of such services, which were then bought only by the shipping department or mail room in a company. And the services that existed couldn't consistently deliver packages overnight. Then-industry leaders Emery and Airborne were called air-freight forwarders. They picked up packages from the shipping department, drove them to the local airport, booked space on commercial airliners, and then delivered the packages in the destination city. Less than 50 percent of packages reached their destination by the next morning.

But FedEx designed a new approach based on a network using only its own planes and employees. This approach enabled FedEx to deliver over 90 percent of packages by next morning. The network cost several hundred million dollars. But FedEx was right that this would deliver an experience of real value to millions. FedEx told their story, the overnight courier market exploded, and FedEx won the major share of it. The network's cost was far exceeded by revenue.

Could *we deliver it, given conditions at time of delivery?*

If an organization articulates a value proposition that is to be delivered in the future, that organization need not ask 'Can we deliver this today?' or 'Does this use our current advantages or capabilities?' The relevant question is 'Can the organization build the capabilities needed to deliver it profitably by the relevant timeframe?' While Detroit was still laughing at Toyota in the 1960s for shipping their silly little cars to the USA, Toyota was just beginning to think about what it would take to win in the luxury end of the market. Toyota certainly did not have the capabilities in place then, but steadily built them until their introduction of the Lexus twenty years later.

In some cases, the most viable value propositions for an organization may require building fundamentally new capabilities, rather than building on existing strengths as Toyota was able to do. British Airways, when facing privatization in 1980, had few capabilities on which to fall back, beyond their expertise in alienating passengers and losing money. BA, to the British flying public, stood for Bloody Awful at the time, but since Her Majesty's government had always been willing to subsidize the national flagship airline, the losses and mediocrity had never troubled BA. The Iron Lady ended this party; BA then had to *compete*.

BA did a truly great job of thinking through the value propositions it would need to deliver and the capabilities required to deliver them. They conceived of the Club World business-class experience, for example, but realized they would need to transform the entire culture and build wholly new systems and infrastructure to deliver it. The visionary leadership of the airline realized, however, that with enough focus and commitment over several years, all the changes could be accomplished and the new capabilities built. Anything less, they realized, would not allow the firm to deliver the two or three critical propositions it needed to compete. By the late 1980s, BA had succeeded, becoming the world's most profitable airline.

However, if an organization concludes it could not deliver a given value proposition then of course it must return to the drawing board. And if it determines it could deliver a superior proposition but only at a total cost that exceeds the total revenues it would generate, then this *may* not be a good value proposition. It certainly will not generate wealth for the firm, looked at in isolation and only for its specified timeframe. Before positively or negatively assessing a value proposition, however, it may be important to consider its indirect profit impact.

Will the proposition indirectly impact profit?

A value proposition that is profitable in its own right, however, may not *always* be a winner for the organization as a whole. For delivering it may affect other businesses. Or it may affect the organization's ability to deliver winning propositions for the same business in the future.

For example, consider a chemical company selling a plastic that requires an unusual chemical component, produced by that same company in limited supply. That chemical is therefore critical to the delivery of this value proposition. If the organization were to entertain the notion of another business delivering a value proposition that also requires some of that precious chemical, it would have to consider this second value proposition's effect on the first. Delivering this second proposition might negatively impact the plastic business's ability to produce the plastic and thus reduce its profit. So, to understand fully the impact of delivering the second value proposition, one must consider the affect on the first business's profit.

Delivering one value proposition may also compete with other propositions the same organization is already delivering in the same market. In the 1940s, Procter & Gamble first created a synthetic clothes-washing soap – detergent – that washed clothes significantly better than soap. The company considered launching a new brand using the breakthrough technology. However, P&G held more than half of the clothes washing market at that time, and some argued strenuously for holding back the technology. Competitors would rush to match the new technology, of course, with unpredictable results. In the ensuing instability, P&G would be hard pressed to come out with a better share of the market than it then had. Why not let sleeping dogs lie? This reasoning lulls many companies into leaving themselves vulnerable to destruction.

Howard Morgens, largely the creator of the brand management system and then CEO of P&G, rejected this play-it-safe strategy. Even with P&G's strong position, he recognized the risk of competitors' delivering the improvement first and so risked the company to reach the consumer first. The company launched the detergent brand, called Tide. Competition did follow, and soaps were virtually wiped out inside two years. But after the dust (OK, soap powder) had settled, P&G had actually reestablished an even stronger market share by leading with the new technology. Morgens thus established one of the basic strategic principles that guide P&G. The company would bet long term on delivering the most value possible, as soon as possible, into any market, rather than hanging back. Even though some strong existing businesses may be hurt in the short term, the company believes its total array of businesses in a market will be stronger in the long term. From a long-term view, delivering the new value proposition outweighed the potential damage to the existing businesses.

A profitable proposition can also affect the reputation of other businesses. Hewlett-Packard, with its reputation for reliable equipment, might lose more than it would gain by selling a cheap, unreliable device, even if that cheap-device proposition could generate a lot of revenue.

Conversely, one proposition may increase the credibility of another business' proposition. HP's laser jet business has been hugely successful in its own right, but it has also helped pave the way for Vectra, HP's PC. Once people grew accustomed to HP as the standard for printers, it seemed more natural that HP might make a good PC as well.

Or a proposition may strengthen relations with distributors or other entities in other businesses. Kodak's proposition to hospital radiology departments thus modestly helps its record-keeping business with the same hospitals. Or, a proposition may use underutilized assets built for another business, thus improving that business' costs.

Just as delivering a value proposition may affect other businesses, it may also affect the same business in a timeframe beyond that of the proposition. Many Western firms ignored this simple concept in the face of Japanese competition. Over and over, Japanese firms have entered markets at the less profitable end.

For example, in the late 1960s, the Japanese entered the North American market with economy-sized cars. Detroit auto makers were so enamored of large cars' higher margins that they reacted far too slowly and casually. Detroit seemed to understand the small car as a form of bait and switch – if you bought one, it would be so shoddy that you'd be desperate for a good (i.e. big) one. To compete strongly against the Japanese then would have meant improving small cars, reducing sales of their far more profitable whales-on-wheels. However, Detroit's penalty was that a whole generation of consumers became fans of Japanese car companies because of superior experiences, like doors that usually closed. Many came to assume that *any* Japanese car, including luxury models, must be better made as well.

***

This book urges managers to devote enough energy to make the disciplined choice of a real value proposition. However, value propositions do not mean much in isolation. It is their *delivery*, their providing and communicating, that makes businesses. We therefore turn next to what businesses must really do – provide and communicate value propositions.

Notes

1   'Being digital is not enough,' *The Economist*, September 28, 1996, p. 100.
2   Hamel and Prahalad, *Competing for the Future, op. cit.*, p. 32.
3   *Ibid*, p. 85.

Chapter Seven

Provide and Communicate: Delivering Is More Than Lip Service

Conventional business theory advocates a focus on supplying a product. It does not support the view of a business defined and managed by a chosen value proposition. So how are managers to reconcile the traditional develop-produce-sell business system framework with the value proposition? Some will be tempted simply to tack on the idea of a value proposition to the conventional product-supply framework, a rationalization as an afterthought, without actually changing much of anything. They may even go so far as to issue a slogan or two, which is duly inspired by this supposed value proposition. But in reality, adding a slogan or even a well-written value proposition after the fact of the business' design misses the point of *Delivering Profitable Value* entirely.

It is not much better, however, to 'choose' a value proposition, then develop, produce and sell a product more or less 'consistent' with it. One can hoist a value proposition like a flag and insist that everyone salute it, but this will not much change an organization's behavior or chances of success. Rather, to go much beyond lip service and genuinely deliver a chosen value proposition, all aspects and elements of the business must be specifically designed to *provide* and *communicate* each resulting experience. Along with choosing a value proposition, these are the truly essential functions of a business.

Conventional understanding of a business: a system of functions that supply a product

Operating any business requires various resources. These may be physical objects – a product, plant, truck, store, brochure, a TV commercial – or a process – order fulfillment, distribution, product service-and-support. Departments within an organization, typically called functions, produce and manage these resources. R&D, Manufacturing or Operations, Distribution, Finance, Marketing, and Sales and Service are among the more common functions. Others, often supporting the main functions, include Human Resources, Information Technology, Legal, Quality Assurance, and Public Affairs.

Typically a business is understood as a system of such functions supplying a product. All the functions are focused on developing, making, or marketing/selling it. The *subject* of the business is not a value proposition and how to deliver it, but rather the product and how to supply it.

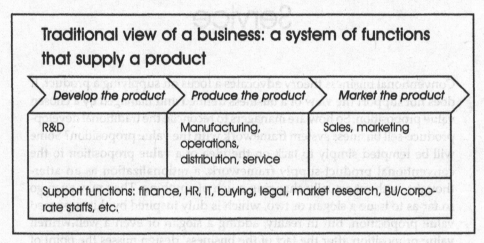

Traditional view of a business: a system of functions that supply a product

Develop the product	Produce the product	Market the product
R&D	Manufacturing, operations, distribution, service	Sales, marketing
Support functions: finance, HR, IT, buying, legal, market research, BU/corporate staffs, etc.		

This framework poses questions that can be answered without a choice of value proposition. Consider developing the product. What should it be? How should it perform? What features should it have? How big should it be? Has fast should it go? How should it look? These questions can all be answered *without* explicitly deciding what resulting experiences the product should help deliver. Instead, principles like the following are relied upon in answering such questions:

- leverage our new technology
- achieve the low cost position
- differentiate the product
- use our core competencies
- listen to the voice of the customer, give them what they want and need.

In producing the product, should the organization contract the manufacturing out to another company? Should it produce components and let customers assemble the final product? Should it carry inventory of the over 2000 variations of the product in the catalogue or only carry the 320 which constitute 80 percent of orders? Should it make and ship the other 20 percent 90 days later, or discontinue them? Which products should be manufactured in multiple sites versus manufactured in only one and then distributed globally? Criteria for answering these questions might include:

- achieve low cost position in our industry
- maintain highest quality
- do it the way the customer wants it done (read my lips: satisfy the customer)
- produce it the way that leverages recent investments in technology
- keep the plant at full capacity, or otherwise maximize utilization of assets
- produce it to stay on budget, regardless of consequences.

And in marketing and selling the product, what sort of sales force, of what size? How should they be trained? What should their presentations contain? On what should the advertising campaign focus? Rely on such time honored tenets as these, and you can't go wrong:

- sales reps know each customer and meet their needs; every customer is different
- relationships are everything; let sales handle each one
- customers only buy on price
- we're customer intimate – we give them whatever they need
- we're using branding
- we need creative advertising that's different and popular with customers
- our channel partner does the selling.

Any of these sound familiar? Under the conventional perspective, products will be developed, manufacturing and operational decisions will be made, and selling activities will be performed. These decisions will ultimately deliver some *de facto* value proposition, a proposition which is the result of chance, not deliberate intent.

The traditional product-supply framework is so deeply ingrained in most of business culture that many managers may simply decide to add a value proposition to it. In other words, management would answer the questions posed above, and then decide what value proposition the resulting product-supply system implies. Obviously, this is not the same as choosing a value proposition. Others may try to use a value proposition to guide the application of this traditional framework. Thus: choose a value proposition, then develop, produce and sell a product consistent with it. In effect, management says, 'Here's our value proposition; as we determine what product to develop and how to produce and sell it, let's keep this value proposition in mind.' This might be more useful than the first approach. But the traditional mindset, with its seductive, internally-driven and customer-compelled logic, usually prevails even if a value proposition is both guiding principle and touchstone. Managers will still primarily try to develop, produce, and sell a product rather than deliver a value proposition.

Organizations need a different framework that redefines the basic business functions in value delivery terms. A business should be understood as a system of functions that deliver a value proposition: *choosing*, *providing* and *communicating* the value proposition. Products are still developed, made and sold, but not based merely on vaguely complementing or being reminiscent of the value proposition. Rather, these products, resources and activities are designed and deployed based on the specific requirements to provide and communicate each resulting experience in the proposition profitably. They are not deployed based on creating the best product or on how best to develop, produce, and sell.

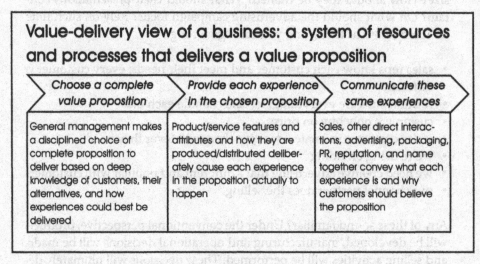

Value-delivery view of a business: a system of resources and processes that delivers a value proposition

Choose a complete value proposition	Provide each experience in the chosen proposition	Communicate these same experiences
General management makes a disciplined choice of complete proposition to deliver based on deep knowledge of customers, their alternatives, and how experiences could best be delivered	Product/service features and attributes and how they are produced/distributed deliberately cause each experience in the proposition actually to happen	Sales, other direct interactions, advertising, packaging, PR, reputation, and name together convey what each experience is and why customers should believe the proposition

To deliver a value proposition, provide and communicate each resulting experience

The functions of providing and communicating the chosen value proposition shape, guide, and control all of the business' resources and actions. These functions transform the value proposition's somewhat abstract description of customer experiences into concrete products, assets and processes the organization must deploy.

Providing a resulting experience requires causing the event or events in that experience actually to happen in the life of the intended customer. Those events then lead to some consequence relative to competing alternatives, with some value to the customer. The focus of providing is to make those events occur. In order to do so, an organization needs one or more vehicles with which to cause the events. In most businesses, a product is just such a 'providing-vehicle.' But it is the *result* of the product, and not the product itself, that matters to the success of the business. The features and attributes of a product interface with a customer to bring about the specific events in a resulting experience. Any other asset or process which influences or helps the event in an experience to occur is also a providing-vehicle. A package, a service that maintains a product, a customer-training program, an instruction manual, an order fulfillment process, or a distribution network can all be providing-vehicles for some resulting experience.

Communicating a resulting experience means ensuring the intended customer understands two things: (1) what resulting experience the organization believes will happen if the customer does as the business wants; and (2) the reason they should believe the experience will in fact happen. 'Communicating-vehicles' are needed to enable this function. A sales presentation, an advertising campaign, a product's appearance, packaging, a trade show, word-of-mouth, or public relations can all be vehicles carrying some message to the intended customers. The content of the message – facts, logic, evidence – communicate the experience, i.e. bring about the customer's understanding of it, its value and the reasons to believe it will be provided.

From the *DPV* perspective, building capabilities in an organization consists of obtaining or creating the required providing and communicating vehicles for each business.

Consider a relatively sophisticated market, buffeted by the discontinuities of technologically intensive evolution in the global marketplace: homemade lemonade. A potential customer, Stevie, is riding his bike when he sees a sign on the side of the road. On this sign, placed there by local seven-year-old entrepreneur Amanda, is written, 'Queen of England Lemonade – cool down with a sweet lemony, thirst-quenching taste, only 25 cents – good enough for the Queen of England!' Hot and thirsty, Stevie stops his bike, buys some lemonade for 25 cents, and drinks it. It tastes good and quenches Stevie's thirst. These two simple resulting experiences, plus the one of paying 25 cents, have been both communicated and then provided to Stevie. Thus the value proposition was delivered.

To provide an experience is to cause the customer actually to go through it. The most important vehicle for providing an experience is usually a product or service, though often it is not the only vehicle used. Amanda's lemonade was the main vehicle by which Stevie was caused to go through the sweet lemony taste experience. But she also needed to set up a table near the road; she needed a pitcher, ice, and cups; and she had to stand behind the table and pour. The product was necessary, but only because it was a vehicle to provide resulting experiences; moreover, it was not the only vehicle. Experiences are not useful because they help sell a product; products are useful because they help provide experiences. A product carries its specific features, such as lemon and sugar, to the customer, helping cause them to have some chosen experiences. Thus a product is a *providing vehicle*.

To get and use these providing vehicles, however, Amanda needed other resources that could produce them: the grocery store, the kitchen, and, most strategic – Mom. These resources produced the lemonade, ice, pitcher, and cups. In addition, Amanda hired her ten-year-old brother Charley to ferry more lemonade from the kitchen to the roadside stand. Charley, an unwilling partner until offered payment in form of the newest Nintendo 64 game, supplied the logistics process, another providing vehicle.

To communicate the value proposition also required some vehicles, again produced using resources. The sign, including its copy, was produced and erected at the table by Charley. It communicated not only the experiences of good taste and a quenched thirst, but also the price. Passing customers would also see Charley drinking a cup, licking his lips in an effort to convince them of its superior taste. Because of these vehicles, customers were convinced that drinking Amanda's lemonade would give them a good taste and quench their thirst. Amanda, having both provided and communicated a sustainably profitable value proposition, took the company public and recently sold a major stake to Bill Gates, roiling lemonade stock-market values from Tokyo to London.

Think forwards: experience to delivery-vehicles to resources

Both *DPV* and the conventional perspective acknowledge that a business includes products, resources, and processes. The conventional perspective, however, assumes these are the natural starting point for determining what proposition is delivered. The *DPV* perspective begins at the end-results desired for the customer, at the value proposition. It then designs what must happen to provide and communicate that proposition, defining the products, services, and other necessary assets and processes. Finally, it *then* creates, obtains, and aligns the appropriate resources to produce these vehicles.

Because the *DPV* approach works from the end to the means, it is truly forward, not backward thinking. However, the traditional approach of beginning with the organization and moving outward toward the customer, while it seems rational, is profoundly backwards. It starts with the means and tries to find the end that fits. A chosen value proposition determines requirements for providing and communicating it, which in turn determines the required vehicles. The vehicles must not be allowed to determine what value proposition to deliver.

By thinking forwards, an organization can properly design how to provide a value proposition. Service Masters, for example, understands the difficulty experienced by large institutions in managing their janitorial function. Janitoring tends to be less than inspirational. Turnover and absenteeism are high, substance abuse and other health problems frequent, general morale low. Respect for janitors and self-respect among them tends to be low. A large institution, such as a hospital, has a lot of headaches in trying to manage this function. So Service Masters devised a value proposition that would give these large institutions the resulting experience of a well-performing janitorial staff without the headaches. The company asks to assume responsibility for its potential customers' janitorial tasks. The customer, say a hospital, also pays an annual fee. The first year's fee is slightly below the customer's previous year's costs; subsequent fees are guaranteed to decline steadily. A comprehensive set of cleanliness and hygiene measures is immediately put in place and continues during the contract.

To provide these experiences, Service Masters hires most of the janitorial staff at the hospital. Those who do well have an opportunity to earn more and to move up to a supervisory position. They have the opportunity to supervise an entire hospital staff and ultimately a region. They are trained and taken seriously as potential supervisory talent. Motivation, a basis for respect and self-respect has a transformational impact on attitude and job performance. Turnover and absenteeism are so improved that productivity skyrockets, bathrooms and hallways are cleaner, the total staff is smaller and better paid, and non-salary costs are lower.

The providing vehicles in this case are not simply janitorial service and the human and other resources that make up that service. Rather, the vehicles include a detailed understanding of what events have to be different for the customer in that service. Service Masters' deep insights into why those events are so difficult to make happen are perhaps the most valuable vehicles in this case. Providing Service Masters' value proposition may seem mundane in contrast to a semi-conductor manufacturer or an international law firm. However, Service Masters has made consistently outstanding returns precisely because designing and building these providing vehicles is powerful yet far from trivial.

Often customers use a product within the context of a larger product or system. In this case, complementary providing-vehicles must exist. For chip maker Rockwell to provide one of its winning value propositions requires not only its chip. The modem in which the chip operates and the fax machine in which that modem works are also providing-vehicles that complement Rockwell's own product.

In like fashion, a product and other providing-vehicles may not provide a chosen experience if the customer does not have the appropriate capabilities. Read a typical software user's guide to see how little regard can be given to helping customers use a product. On the other hand, Kodak Australia's Wizard camera stores focused on involving, educating, training, and helping the consumer to be more successful with photography. This input to the customer is less tangible than a product or service but can nonetheless be another powerful providing-vehicle.

Providing a resulting experience

When an organization provides a resulting experience, the specific *event or events* in that experience actually happen in the intended customer's life

One or more providing-vehicles, via features, attributes, or other elements that interact with the customer, cause the events to happen

Providing-vehicles may include:

- Products/services and other resources and processes
- Information, education or other influences on the customer.

This or other organizations may produce the vehicles, using various resources.

Effectively *communicating* a value proposition is also part of thinking forward. Volvo's successful value proposition of the 1970s and 1980s centered on a safer experience. If involved in an accident, driver and passengers were somewhat less likely to be injured in a Volvo than in competing cars. The main providing-vehicle was of course the car, with its attributes relevant to safety. Volvo's roll bar in the roof made occupants safer if the car were to roll. Extra high gauge metal absorbed more impact energy, leaving less for occupants to absorb. In a collision, the engine collapsed accordion-style, absorbing energy while doing so, and then dropped down to slide under the front seat, a somewhat improved experience for front seat occupants. Volvo was also first to include rear seat belts as standard equipment.

To communicate this superior-safety experience, Volvo *told* intended customers about it. But merely *telling* the customer about an experience doesn't constitute communicating it. Getting customers to believe the experience will really be provided is the important part of communicating. Accident and injury statistics helped Volvo convince people somewhat, but that wasn't enough to convince them. So Volvo explained, over and over, in its advertising, brochures and sales presentations, how the car is designed and manufactured to make driving a safer experience. In this case, a large part of communicating the experience was explaining how the experience is provided. Furthermore, while the boxy, heavy appearance of the Volvo created an inferior experience, it was necessary to provide the safety experience. It also served as another communicating-vehicle. The body style, straight out of tank-design school, connoted superior safety.

However, Volvo seems to have taken its collective eye off the road. Instead of continuously improving how it provides and communicates a superior safety experience, it has drifted into trouble recently. Other makers now also focus on safety and recent safety innovations that should have been led by Volvo, such as air bags and anti-lock brakes, were not. In addition, a few years ago the company injured its credibility in communicating safety. It ran an ad showing a Volvo under several heavy vehicles, not being crushed. Small detail problem: it had been reinforced (to 'save production costs'). Its communications lately have shifted to telling motorists that actually Volvo is a sporty, stylish looking car after all. Somewhere along the way, a winning value proposition slipped away.

Organizations sometimes fail to convince their customers of the experiences they provide and then draw the wrong conclusion from their failure: that the experience is not important enough to the customer. Often, this is not the case. While the customer has been told about an experience, they either don't understand or don't have adequate reason to believe it or both. The communication is defective, not the experience itself.

Businesses based on new technologies frequently fall into the trap of blaming the customer for not understanding their value proposition. Most often, it is the high-tech organization that hasn't chosen, let alone understood, a winning value proposition. They love their new technology, produce it, and launch some perfunctory 'Marcomm.'[1] Then when one in a million potential customers buys their new doodad, they explain this result with adoption curve theory. Adoption curve theory is based on the observation that only a few people try a technology at first; they are followed by a few more until, if it succeeds, eventually everyone does. Adoption curve theorists see this as a natural order. Early adopters are the innovators while the vast majorities who adopt later are the laggards.[2]

Another interpretation is this: to most potential customers, many new technologies start out *providing* a miserable value proposition and *communicating* none at all. New technologies are often high priced, full of bugs,[3] very difficult to learn how to use and likely to break down often. On the other hand, the customer assumes all the risk. If you buy it, it's guaranteed to be yours no matter how worthless it turns out to be. To add insult to injury, the Marcomm conveys several pretentiously convoluted techno-features that only engineers or serious hobbyists can decipher.

For the large number of new technologies which fail, who were the dummies in this tale? Perhaps not the 'laggards' who wait until the thing actually works and comes at a price below military contractor standards, and until they have some vague notion of why they would want one. Marcomm doesn't usually communicate the value proposition to the laggards. Rather, as the bugs disappear and the price declines, the laggards discover the ex-

periences it provides through encounters with a few brave souls who have
used the technology.

Communicating a resulting experience

When an organization communicates a resulting experience, the intended
customer understands two things:

1 What experience the organization believes will happen in the customer's life:
   • What event or series of events will happen
   • Their end-result consequence, relative to competing alternatives
   • The value to the customer of this relative consequence.
2 What the reasons, if any, are for believing that this experience will indeed
   happen if the customer does what the business wants.

One or more communicating-vehicles convey a message that causes the
customer to understand these two things.
   These communication vehicles could include sales presentations, relationships, advertising, product appearance, packaging, word-of-mouth, publicity, trade shows, product documentation, etc.
   The organization or others may produce these vehicles, using various resources.

Advertising frequently is or should be the chief communicating vehicle
of a winning proposition and so can be decisive in a business's success. A
huge portion of advertising, which is developed irrationally and cynically
and makes little or no contribution to the business using it, obscures this
fact. It is further obscured by the trivial attention that much of management theory and management accord the topic.

Almost all functions, including advertising, cling to a persistent rationalization for keeping the function unfettered by any real chosen value proposition. Advertising would by no means be the only function transformed by
using the value delivery system framework. R&D, manufacturing, marketing, sales, information-technology, human resources – all the functions tend
to pursue agendas unguided by a real value proposition. But advertising
provides a good case for all functions being managed to provide and communicate a value proposition rather than reflect the managerial looking glass.

Case in point: insist on advertising that helps communicate the chosen value proposition

Because organizations often do not choose real value propositions for their
businesses, one might expect a large portion of advertising either to com-

municate a weak proposition or to communicate a strong one poorly. However, the business world would be lucky if this described the state of affairs, for a large portion of advertising does not communicate any part of any kind of value proposition whatsoever. Despite the myth that most advertising focuses on communicating product benefits, the truth is closer to the opposite. The beliefs and assumptions underlying much of the commonly accepted practices in managing advertising are among the more striking examples of self-indulgent gazing into the looking glass.

These beliefs include irrational, unfounded theories of persuasion. They include an amazing collection of myths and pure folderol about what works in advertising, about its role and powers, and about the ability to measure its effectiveness. Underneath this widely accepted, fatuous canon of unsubstantiated gibberish, moreover, lies a highly cynical attitude of indifference. Advertising can and sometimes does play an extremely important, fascinating, and legitimate role in helping deliver profitable value. But far too much of advertising is managed with no belief in such a role. Instead it is managed with one or more of these aims: to be popular and socially approved, to win awards, to feel creative, and to shirk any accountability for the success of the business, no matter how wasteful and counterproductive the advertising.

However, this negative state is not primarily the fault of advertising professionals and the agency industry. The irresponsibility is in the management of the organizations who pay agencies to produce and deploy ineffective advertising. On the one hand, the whole function is underestimated in its strategic significance. Most strategists sniff their noses at so lowly a field and many managers follow suit. On the other hand, a great many marketing and general managers who buy advertising services positively embrace the fundamentally cynical attitudes and the irrational nonsense and sophistry that pass as conventional wisdom about advertising.

As with product innovation, recognizing and using the principles of *Delivering Profitable Value* can make advertising dramatically more effective. Advertising must be understood and managed as an important part of a value delivery system, not as some autonomous art form or as a game played for the amusement of managers. It must be managed creatively, with discipline and with demanding standards, so that it helps to communicate, and sometimes provide, a chosen value proposition.

Stuff and nonsense[4]

A number of related, wrongheaded beliefs pervade the mismanagement of advertising. Many advertising professionals know better, but a great many do not. Worse, the preponderance of marketing professionals, who are the agencies' clients, do not reject most of these unfounded assumptions. One of these beliefs is that a rational, factual or logical approach to the content of advertising is counterproductive. Only something ethereal and elusive called brand image really works. This belief, which has always been held dear by many in the advertising field, seems to be growing in acceptance. One commentator summarized the trend:

> 'The old ads got your attention with an appealing image. [Then] they would celebrate the product's virtues...[but now] there is an almost total obsession with images and feelings and an almost total lack of any concrete claims about the product and why anyone should buy it.'[5]

This belief is an extension and triumph of sorts, of a long-standing philosophy held by many who work with advertising: the product, the benefits it might offer, the actual experiences customers might derive by using it, are of no real interest to customers. Who cares about some stupid product, be it a car or shoes or insurance or soap? We in the know, we realize these products are all the same anyway, and their dumb features and what-not are *bor-ing.* These are the 'product skeptics'[6] that not only prevent effective advertising but also generally make the delivery of profitable value more difficult. They do not believe that there is an interesting story in the relationship between the organization's product and the customer's real life. Therefore, much advertising has relied on 'borrowed interest,'[7] the use of marching bands, babies, dogs, alluring women, cars on top of mountain peaks, *anything* that might lend the product in question some interest on the part of the customer. Anything except the story that communicates to the customer the resulting experiences they will get from the product or service advertised.

A complementary belief is that advertising has awesome manipulative powers, that it is capable of subconsciously controlling customers. Vance Packard's 1957 bestseller, *The Hidden Persuaders,* claimed that advertising was secretly brainwashing people. Hidden in the magazine ad's image of ice cubes, in a glass next to a brand of whiskey, was a subconscious message about sex (i.e. drink this, get sex). His unsubstantiated imaginings struck a popular chord and have been absorbed by several generations of management and by the general public as self-evidently true. This exaggerated and mystified perception of advertising's power, combined with the product skeptic's belief in the necessity of borrowed interest, resulted in the mythology believed by most advertisers today. A successful ad must follow a particular formula. The most important piece of this formula is a topic wholly unrelated to the product or to anything resembling a value proposition. This gets the customer's attention. Then, the ad calls on the massive power of advertising to command the customer to 'buy' the product. This lesser piece is usually accomplished by mentioning the product in the last few seconds of a commercial or perhaps by sticking the product name in an obscure corner of a print ad. The thinking underlying this formula argues that the last bit about buying the product only gets in the way of the interesting bit.

Reinforcing this tendency is the rationalization that times have changed, a classic explanation in the industry for why advertising should be freed of the need actually to sell anything. A 'creative revolution' was announced in the 1960s, again in the early 1980s and again in the early 1990s, each time finally liberating advertising copy from the old-style, product-oriented boring stuff. The more recent of these revolutions was purportedly driven by two forces: consumers have more media from which to choose and a remote control with which to tune out advertising; and, products are all becoming the same.

According to *Forbes*, the Unique Selling Proposition (USP), 'the sensible notion that advertising should highlight that aspect of a product that distinguished it from its rivals – and trumpet the value of that attribute *ad nauseam* ...'[8] used to be accepted doctrine on Madison Avenue. Evidence of such acceptance is dwindling, however. The director of brand planning at a large agency explains the increasing disappearance of the product or what it might do for the customer:

> 'We are just trying to convey a sensory impression of the brand and we're out of there...USP is a great theory, but what do you do when most products come to market without a visible point of difference? We're communicating a different type of information today – a feeling of what the world is like, and if you identify with that feeling, maybe you identify with the advertised brand.'[9]

Do you share our feeling of what the world is like? If so, you should buy our product, which is identical to all others, of course. The reason for this approach is attributed to the limitation placed on advertising by the sameness of products. General management and marketing professionals do not necessarily reject such tortured logic. But the problem may reside within the managerial imagination, not within the products. Consider current Nissan advertising. The most famous spot in the campaign, as described by *Forbes*, 'shows a hip boy doll stealing the cute girl from a nerdy boy doll with the help of a cool toy car.'[10] As reported in the *Wall Street Journal*:

> 'It was, by many measures, the most successful TV commercial of 1996. Time magazine and Rolling Stone crowned it the best ad of the year. Oprah Winfrey devoted a segment to the young West Coast admen who created it. Sony is planning to turn the ad into a pilot for a television

series. The commercial was TBWA Chiat/Day's 'Toys' ad for Nissan, in which a toy soldier falls from the jaws of a dinosaur into the seat of a tiny sports car. For all the good press, though, there was a problem: While the ad was playing, sales were falling.

'In September 1996, when the ad made its debut, U.S. sales at Nissan fell 2.7% compared with the same month in 1995. Sales then fell 10.2% in October, 4.2% in November and 1.6% in December. Business improved in January after Nissan started pushing big incentives to counter archrivals Toyota and Honda, which had introduced new models. To Nissan dealers across the country, the message was clear: many people loved this commercial and others like it, but the ad campaign seemed to have a life of its own, detached from the business of selling cars. "It isn't anything that makes anyone go out and say, 'Hey, I need to go buy a Nissan,'" says [another dealer] in Irving, Texas. The Nissan campaign tells a great deal about the state of the advertising industry today. More than ever before, agencies are scrambling to make ads that create a buzz but have little to do with the products their clients sell.'[11]

In an interview with *Forbes*, Nissan's USA President Bob Thomas explains the company's exciting advertising strategy:

'Our proposition is that we're going to show you who we are, and the more you know about us, the more you'll want to have a relationship with us ... They're not interested in hearing from us that we make better cars – they wouldn't believe us anyway.'[12]

The *Journal* described Mr Thomas as concerned that, 'Our imagery ... wasn't at the same level as our sales.'[13] He apparently wanted to change Nissan's image from that of 'the company that always discounts its price.' So Nissan turned to agency TBWA Chiat/Day, a leader of the latest surge toward unrelated-images-as-advertising.

'Nissan's marketing team wanted to use an actor to portray Yutaka Katayama, the original, quirky head of Nissan's U.S. operations. [Retired, he is] still revered inside Nissan for bringing the U.S. the first affordable Japanese sports car, the Datsun 240z. "He would be the brand connector," [a Chiat/Day exec] says. "It's much easier to be stewards of Mr K's heritage than it is to be the manager of a financial statement."'[14]

Inspiring. But will the advertising even reveal that this character is the great Mr K or who he is? Oh, please! Don't bother us with such details; we are cre-a-ting.

> '[One ad] features a mysterious journey down an asphalt road cutting
> through a weird landscape. An actor repeatedly pops up with a sign
> reading '"mile." Another ... follows a young boy chasing a stray base-
> ball into an old barn. He falls through a trap door into a garage stuffed
> with Datsuns and Nissans. There, he runs into Mr K, who moves from
> one car to another at a superhuman speed. "Life's a journey. Enjoy the
> ride," he tells the boy.'[15]

Many people are fans of these creations. On the other hand, some find them
weird and lacking purpose. Pulitzer Prize winning humorist for the Miami
Herald, Dave Barry lacks the requisite sophistication to appreciate such creativity; or else his readers do. Claiming to have surveyed them for the commercials they hate most, one among many included Nissan:

> '... here's a bulletin for the Nissan people: Nobody likes the creepy old
> man, OK? Everybody is afraid when the little boy winds up alone in the
> barn with him. This ad campaign does not make us want to purchase a
> Nissan. It makes us want to notify the police. Thank you.'[16]

For the toy car in the masterpiece spot in the campaign, the agency

> '... picked a version of Nissan's famous long-nosed Z car. Unfortunately,
> Nissan was getting ready to discontinue that model, but the auto maker
> wasn't worried ... The ad made its debut Sept. 9, and set off a storm of
> ovations. "Lee Clow [legendary head creative at Chiat/Day] has nothing
> left to prove," declared a headline in USA Today. Entertainment Weekly
> hailed "the year's most turbo-charged spot." Oprah Winfrey gushed about
> how "critics are calling Nissan's car commercial one of the most enter-
> taining things on TV – and it doesn't even use real actors!" She then
> revealed that one of the dolls wore a custom-made Wonderbra.
>   'Meanwhile, viewers began calling Nissan with requests for prod-
> ucts connected to the ad. By mid-March, the company had sold more
> than 25,000 T-shirts featuring the dolls and the little car ... All that
> excitement, though, was lost on many Nissan dealers. Toyota ... was in
> ... a roaring fall, thanks to a new Camry backed by lower prices. Honda
> ... was aggressively pushing a new Civic. Meanwhile, Nissan had no
> new models to promote, making this "an ideal time to launch the brand
> campaign," says ... a vice president for the auto maker.
>   'Many Nissan dealers, though, were mystified by the campaign, par-
> ticularly the Toys ad. "I thought it was a great commercial, but they
> were trying to advertise a car they don't make anymore," says [one deal-
> ership general manager] "It didn't sell cars."'[17]

Meanwhile, those hobgoblins of the little and uncreative business mind – sales and market share – continued to decline.

> 'Finally, under pressure to hit sales targets for the fiscal year ended in March, Nissan resorted to offering heavy discounts – exactly the image Mr Thomas wanted to avoid … Some dealers are relieved. "Now I can start selling cars instead of dogs or pigeons," says [an owner-dealer] referring to the animal stars of two recent ads for Nissan. Retorts … Mr Clow: "That's car dealers. They're forever bitching about something … There are always people that like to damn things that are new."
>
> '[Referring to the advertising campaign's failure to generate sales and the decision to revert to price discounting after all,] "It wasn't a mistake, it was, 'We're going to go back and do this differently,'" Nissan's Mr Thomas says. What's more, Mr Thomas says the company was never counting on the Mr K ads to sell cars in the short term. Instead, he says, the commercials should boost the value of the Nissan brand. The ad agency says its research shows that Nissan 's "advertising awareness" and "brand likeability" rose as the ads aired last fall.'[18]

Advertising that associates a brand with a certain feeling or impression that is totally unconnected to any experience the customer might have as a result of using the product may be effective in some cases. The psychology of motivating people is certainly not understood well enough to rule out the possibility that such advertising somehow works on occasion. But anyone who claims that this is a surefire approach to advertising efficacy is dreaming, and if they claim to know how to do it, they're having a major hallucination. Claiming to be building 'brand-image,' advertising such as Nissan's actually communicates no value proposition. In reality, *successful* advertising that is cited as pure brand-image building usually communicates resulting experiences to the customer. It may do so without talking about product features, but that doesn't mean it isn't communicating a real value proposition. Consider Nike.

Nike's rise was propelled partly by innovative products that helped provide a value proposition focused on helping athletes perform to their maximum. It was also propelled by advertising which helped communicate this proposition. Nike's tag line, 'just do it,' did not extol shoe features, but it aptly captured what amateur athletes always tell themselves in order to get through a tough workout or the exhausting end of a competition. Nike was telling consumers that its shoes were the best with which to 'do it.' To make that message more credible, Nike told consumers that the world's absolutely *best* athletes consistently prefer those shoes.

Air Jordans, Nike shoes named for Michael Jordan, were endorsed by the most spectacular basketball player ever seen, a man who could take off in his Nikes and seemingly fly, twisting and floating freely above the basket. Nike picked out Jordan early, before he became the full-fledged superstar he is now. Of course, having an athlete endorse a product is an old concept, but Nike took the concept further and did it better. Some of the early ads featuring Jordan also featured film director Spike Lee playing the role of 'Mars Blackmon.' Mars was a would-be basketball star, hopelessly short, nerdy, bespectacled, and unable to fly. Mars and Jordan would play one-on-one with predictable results; Jordan would soar to unbelievable heights in his Air Jordans. Mars would then declare, 'It's gotta be the *shoes!*' Consumers knew it wasn't *really* the shoes, but those Air Jordans seemed to *help* Michael a bit, and they looked *bad* (i.e. good). After a great play on playground basketball courts, people were heard joking, 'It's gotta be the shoes.'

Bo Jackson, a phenomenal two-sport athlete, endorsed the idea that Nikes were *the* shoes for cross-training and for playing any sport imaginable. This notion appeals to young athletes who usually play several sports. Nike used humor in these commercials as well. 'Bo Knows' was the catch phrase. Bo Knows Baseball (wearing Nike's). Bo Knows Football (Nike's). Bo Knows Weight Lifting. Bo Knows a list of increasingly obscure sports. But consumers got the point.

In scores of more specialized sports, for which millions of amateur athletes wear shoes, Nike consistently presented the indisputably top performers endorsing Nike. The company solidified its mystique as a winner and proved itself able to pick winners when Nike correctly predicted (and bet $35 million) that Tiger Woods would become an unprecedented ultra hot superstar, and not just a phenomenal golfer. As with many fashion items, Nike's success bred success; it became cool and fashionable around the world just to wear Nikes. Just as some people wear Calvin Klein jeans because they like the association with high fashion or some people smoke Marlboro because they like the association with rugged cowboys, such advertising helped *provide* a valuable experience to many customers, an experience by association. Nike's problem is that much of its market share rests on the crest of this fashion wave it created; and waves, especially those made of fashion trends, have a way of crashing. The recent US advertising campaign by the national dairy association asks consumers, 'Got Milk?' A variety of engaging, adult, interesting, and amusing people are presented as loving milk and sometimes craving it when they can't get it. They have to have it because it's a natural, healthy, and great-tasting drink. That taste is, moreover, unique. This advertising does not create some irrelevant image from which milk can borrow interest – it treats the idea of milk and of drinking it as the thing that's interesting. Similarly, a few years ago, an ad with raisins dancing and singing to the tune 'Heard it on the grape vine' convinced many kids that eating raisins was fun and cool. Both of these successful campaigns focus on the customer's experience.

None of this successful advertising justifies a disconnect between the organization's product offering and the actual experience of the customer. The value proposition communicated by advertising may not be primarily a function of product features, but it does *not* follow that advertising can be effective without communicating *any* value proposition. Moreover, the doctrine that some vague notion of brand-image is the modern formula for effective advertising rests partly on a false dichotomy. Supposedly, the only alternative to presenting vacuous, irrelevant images to the customer is to torture them with product features. This false choice ignores the possibility that advertising should, instead, communicate a value proposition. And if the objective is to create advertising that utterly fails to communicate any value proposition, product features can be just as effective as image. For example, a recent British magazine ad depicts a car on what seems to be a drawbridge, with important features printed above it (and a patent application number unpretentiously listed by each):

> '*Traction control system with engine power/ABS intervention under inferior grip conditions … Refined structural rigidity for reduced torsion while cornering … Enhanced brake feedback and elastokinematic front suspension for continuous control on split friction surfaces.*'

Watch out for those split friction surfaces, and for phoney ads. In addition, watch out for advertising developed with the belief that no value proposition need be chosen to develop effective advertising.

Reinforcing this enormous confusion is the convenient belief that good advertising means creative advertising. Only a fool would vote against creativity, surely. But what exactly is creativity in business? From the *DPV* perspective, creativity in this context includes any new, innovative, non-obvious way better to understand or deliver a winning value proposition. Creative advertising finds a fresh, clever, memorable, persuasive way to communicate the chosen crucial resulting experiences that will win the customer's preference over time.

In Japan in the 1980s, NEC ran a television commercial for its industrial robots showing several competitors' robotic arms trying to pick up an egg. The hand of one robot closes around the egg, but not tightly enough, and leaves it untouched on the table. The second lifts the egg a few inches but loses it, and it breaks on the table. The third robot grabs an egg and crushes it immediately. Then, under the gently swinging voice of Frank Sinatra, the NEC robot approaches an egg, picks it up, swivels it around for 360 degree viewing, pivots over to a frying pan, taps the egg on the edge of the pan, deftly opens the egg at the crack over the pan, dropping the contents into the pan to form a perfect frying egg, and tosses the broken shell into a trash bin. This display was continuous action; there were no cuts in the scene. For the last ten seconds or so of the ad, the announcer gives more information about NEC's robots, which is reinforced by text appearing across the screen. In the background, the robotic arm confidently puts the last three eggs on top of a 12-level pyramid of unbroken eggs.

After viewing this ad, could a potential customer, a manufacturing engineer for example, begin to draw some tentative conclusions about the resulting experiences s/he might get from using an NEC robot rather than others? Yes, of course. This is true creativity in advertising because it brilliantly, freshly, and delightfully brings to life the value proposition.

In the fatuous doctrine prevailing in the industry and among many client managers, creative means something quite different. It means whatever is satisfying for the creators of the advertising. This attitude personifies the egotistical, self-indulgent gaze into the looking glass. And this from a function and industry supposedly in love with the customer! Advertising that makes the advertiser and the agency look creative, hip, and cool and so makes *them* feel good about *themselves* is an outrageous affront to the principles of business. Advertising should be giving the customer a basis for preferring the organization's offering, not building egos in the organization. Some, who fancy themselves defenders of creativity, will howl that this attitude stifles cool advertising. When advertising wins awards and plaudits for creativity, but fails the business, thus wasting the efforts of thousands of employees, suppliers, and others and throwing away the shareholders' investments, is that creative? When the company falters, laying off thousands and harming countless careers, is that cool? Yet winning approval, creative recognition, and popularity play an absurdly dominant role in advertising, a role that is rationalized as a belief in creativity. As Jim Jordan of agency Jordan McGrath, Case & Taylor lamented several years ago:

> '... pre-empting a powerful position to sell a lot of goods or services is simply not very high on the agendas of a lot of advertising agencies. The truth is that more copywriters and art directors in agencies create advertising for their reels[19] than they do for their clients. The work they do is often designed more to sell the creative person to his next agency than it is to sell the product to the next customer. Many creative people recommend the stuff they think will look best on their reel without regard to its potential effect on their client's sales. Now you may say ... "Oh sure ... some flaky creative would try that but his management isn't going to let him get away with it." Don't kid yourself. Agency managements are often no better...Agency principals perceive that their agen-

*cies will get more business if their work is perceived as chic, on the cut-
ting edge, funny or entertaining than it will if the ads merely sell a lot
of stuff.'[20]*

Another widely held and complementary belief in the prevailing philosophy is that effective advertising means popular advertising. Advertising can
be very popular, highly rated by customers as 'good advertising' or 'advertising I like,' and also be effective. However, the correlation between the
two is not very strong. There are many examples of popular campaigns
failing and unpopular ones working. The 'Joe Isuzu' campaign for Isuzu
cars was wildly popular for over a year, during and after which Isuzu sales
and market share continued a steady decline. One of P&G's most unpopular campaigns was 'Mr Whipple,' who kept telling shoppers 'Pleeeeease ...
don't squeeze the *Charmin.*' Because so many people hated Mr Whipple,
managers within P&G and its agency were desperate to find a campaign
that could beat it. But it took years and scores of test campaigns before the
brand could come up with anything that didn't *lose* to Mr Whipple (that is,
lose market share) in a test market. All things being equal, a business is
better off with advertising that people like. But it is irrational to favor popular advertising over that which builds the business.

Many believe that advertising need not, or even should not, communicate a value proposition, even when the business can provide a superior
one. This belief sometimes deludes managers into believing that a business
does not *need* to provide or communicate a superior value proposition, so
long as advertising builds some vague image. Consider British Airways in
the early 1980s when the company was first learning to compete profitably.
BA's agency at the time, British Saatchi & Saatchi, was then the hottest advertising shop and probably the leader of the then-latest incarnation of the
creative revolution for brand-image. Saatchi spent a small fortune and made
a bigger one producing lavish ad spectaculars with exciting special effects,
all designed to give BA a new image. BA seemed ready to invest in the new
images. Never mind the detail that no superior value proposition had yet
been chosen; perhaps exciting advertising would work instead. One famous
such effort, 90 seconds long, showed the entire island of Manhattan, sky
scrapers and all, majestically descending over London from about 5,000 feet.
Londoners were shown looking up in amazement at the startling and awesome sight; flight controllers guided Manhattan in for a landing at Heathrow.
The voice-over explained, 'Every year, British Airways fly more people to
more countries than any other airline. [Dramatic pause, more in-coming
instructions] In fact, every year we bring more people across the Atlantic
than the *entire* population of Manhattan. [Pause] British Airways – the
world's *favourite* airline.'

Actually, as the national carrier of Britain based in London, it would have been hard to do less than ferry the most customers internationally. But that didn't mean customers had good reason to *want* to fly BA. 'World's Favourite Airline,' of course, meant nothing more than that BA was, well, big. Gary Hamel and C.K. Prahalad celebrate BA's decision to become the Worlds' Favourite Airline as a shining example of a strategic intent, BA's 'animating dream.' However, BA was already big at the time Margaret Thatcher forced the firm radically to redefine itself. The problem was that BA was awful, in a *big* way. BA had not yet developed a winning value proposition, a problem not solved by supposedly spectacular advertising.

Another popular rationalization, for purportedly image-building advertising that is actually vacuous, is the widely held belief that advertising cannot be asked to do too much anyway. According to this view, it supposedly can only build what is called *awareness*, which usually means little more than the percentage of customers who have heard the brand name. Managers should unhesitatingly reject this pathetic rationalization for mediocre or ineffective advertising. Consider the advertising British Airways began using after it had developed and could provide a great value proposition.

In 1981, BA had not yet fully defined the experiences it would eventually have to deliver in its Club World business class offering to long-haul passengers, but the company knew it needed to reinvent itself in order to provide a superior value proposition. By 1986, BA had developed, in Club World, what was arguably the world's best business class experience. This proposition focused on making a business traveler's trip so relaxed, restful, comfortable, and conducive to working that the traveler would arrive more ready to conduct business successfully than on any other airline. The introductory advertising campaign brilliantly told BA's new Club World story. In the commercial aired in the UK, four executives sit in an executive meeting room somewhere in London. One of them, apparently the more senior, looks most embittered:

> 'So. Two years in New York and he thinks he can tell us how to run things. Well; we won't have it,' says the exec. Second exec responds: 'It's alright; I've fixed things. He's traveling overnight – on the redeye'. Cut to another executive, apparently the intended-victim, in a limo on a Manhattan bridge the evening before, heading for the airport in New York. Cut back to London, where a third exec worriedly asks: 'Not first class?' Second exec says, 'Of course not; company policy.' A knowing smirk spreads across the face of one of the other execs. Then cut to the New York airport BA desk, where the intended victim is checking in with no one in line ahead of him. He is showing his Club World ticket. Second exec in London comments, with some relish, 'By the time he gets

in [intended victim is shown his seat on the plane by the stewardess, who takes his coat], he'll be exhausted.' *Intended victim sits down in the large plush Club World chair, clearly surprised and delighted with how comfortable it is. First exec in London says: 'And he won't have had time to incorporate those figures I sent him in his report.' Intended victim works easily, with calculator and paper, on the large seat tray. First exec says, 'He'll be hungry [a rather good looking leg of lamb is on intended victim's plate, and the stewardess pours a glass of red wine] and* tired.' *Intended victim reclines way back, clearly about to catch some restful sleep. Second exec says: 'I've arranged for the chauffeur to bring him straight here,* not to the hotel.' *Third exec, darkly yet gleefully, says: 'Like a lamb to the slaughter, gentlemen!' In walks the intended victim, giving a distinctly up beat:* 'Good morning!' *He opens his briefcase and begins organizing his materials while standing. He doesn't look terribly exhausted. As his briefcase opens, his leather luggage tag with 'Club World' on it becomes visible. Voice-over announcer says: 'Club World delivers the businessman ready to do business. First exec, with his best predatory smile, asks hopefully: "Pleasant* trip?" *Intended victim pauses as if he hadn't thought about that, then says:* 'Yes, thank you!' *The malevolent grin slowly drops off the first exec's face, as the reality of Club World sinks in, unhappily for him.*

Though many details of Club World's early service are of course common today, BA was well ahead of the pack when the fully developed Club World was introduced. It played a major role in BA's remarkable success. This advertising needed no borrowed interest. It helped build an image, but the image entailed a set of strikingly superior resulting experiences for the long-haul business traveler who wants to arrive ready to do business. It built awareness, but not just of a brand name or of an airline's dream to be big or of flying metropolises. This advertising built awareness of the details of a superb value proposition. Advertising should be held to this standard of communication, not allowed off the hook on the grounds that it can't be expected to do too much.

Another classic misconception bolsters this rationalization for mediocre or useless advertising: effectiveness of advertising simply cannot be measured. In the 1940s, the Chairman of UK chemicals giant ICI declared that he knew that half of his advertising dollars were wasted; he just didn't know which half. *The Economist*, in a recent, brief survey of the state of knowledge about advertising, continued its traditional agreement with this supposedly undeniable truth by titling the piece 'Advertising – Which half?' It started by poking fun at Claude Hopkins who, 70 years ago, articulated very commonsensical principles for effective advertising, which have been widely ignored ever since.

'"The time has come when advertising has, in some hands, reached the status of a science ... no other enterprise with comparable possibilities need involve so little risk" [wrote Hopkins who] would have been disappointed to find ... that advertising remains woefully hit-or-miss. Even well regarded ads can misfire ... Measuring the effectiveness of advertising is ... much harder than it might seem ... you need first to be clear about what it is meant to do...[one view is] advertising is about creating and then nurturing brands.'[21]

The essay goes on to explain how difficult advertising effectiveness is to measure. But in reality, it is not particularly difficult, and there is no reason why it should be. Creating effective advertising is not easy, but measuring its effect on sales, market share, and long-term customer attitudes is a very straightforward exercise. It is simply one that the vast majority of organizations and the academic world, secure in the more comfortable belief that advertising is so mysterious a field as to be impossible to gauge, have not bothered to do. This is silly.

An advertising campaign communicates something to those who see it. This can be readily measured by various reliable research methods. If an organization has chosen a value proposition (and that's a big if), it is quite easy to measure the extent to which advertising communicates some part of that proposition. In addition, if the value proposition is a winning one, then communicating it will increase sales and market share. This is again straightforward to measure. Yet there is no shortage of excuses in organizations for not using these measures to assess the effectiveness of advertising or any other variable in a value delivery system. The common perception, one formed more by illusion than by reality, is that other variables make it impossible to read the impact of any one variable. P&G, for example, constantly measures every variable in the marketplace and conducts hundreds of carefully controlled test markets every year. Despite the same difficulties facing other firms, P&G's experience has proven that such measures can very consistently predict results. That firm is demonstratively far more successful, as a result of this intensive testing, than it otherwise would be.

With care and hard work, advertising's effect on the long-term strength of a business can be measured. Some organizations unwilling to make the effort may find it more convenient to declare a mediocre and useless ad campaign above the vulgar reach of any measurement.

Organizations get the advertising they deserve

And who is to blame for the sad state of advertising? The fault lies less with the advertising industry and more with the client organizations and conventional management theory. Managers often ignore advertising or treat it as a toy. Rather than demand that it work hard to communicate a chosen value proposition, much of management seems inclined to accept the mythology that puts it beyond the reach of rational principles.

A manifestation of this attitude, whereby managers do not take advertising seriously, is the confusion between strategy and execution in developing advertising. Many managers make decisions between campaigns without distinguishing what they are judging. The first question should be, 'What value proposition is the advertising meant to communicate?' Second, managers should ask, 'How well was that proposition communicated?' Instead managers freely mix the two issues. This extends not only to judging and developing campaigns but also to hiring and firing agencies. In the typical three-ring advertising circus, several agencies present potential ad campaigns to the client. One agency implicitly assumes one strategy, and another assumes a different one. Usually neither *strategy* is well articulated, even if the execution is somehow impressive. Too often, the client executives decide which executions they liked the most (or perhaps the one that gave them the best feeling about what the world is like). As Jordan commented:

> '... But in fact some advertisers themselves encourage this ... thinking ... Our agency finished second in a new business review and one of my own people ... sort of blamed me because I had insisted on doing work that would sell more of the product and build the brand equity and ... even insisted on ... testing it to prove [it] ... And my associate said "That's not what they want. They want to walk out of that presentation room feeling entertained and amused" ... my colleague may have been right ... The prospect said that our work had been right on the money. But the winning agency's work was "hilarious."* [22]

When a product fails to work in the marketplace, it is rare that all the R&D engineers, manufacturing managers, and sales and marketing executives who worked on the product are summarily fired. It is even more rare, though somewhat more frequent of late, that senior executives get their comeuppance for years of strategic blunders. But when business is weak and advertising is being used, it is perfectly accepted practice casually to fire the agency. Notice where this squarely puts the blame. This is all consistent with the nonsensical suggestion that advertising is a mysterious black art. In this view, one tries an agency for a while; if they perform, magic. If not, put the account up for a review (invite the circus). There is nothing commonsensical in this approach; it simply allows the organization to shirk responsibility. The firms that get the best advertising results establish long-term relationships and make clear the strategy that the agency will help execute. The agency may well help shape strategy. But it does not do so with a total lack of direction and then take the blame for poor business results.

Management theory offers little help for this sorry situation. Of about 1500 pages of Michael Porter and Hamel/Prahalad's three tomes on strategy, advertising is mentioned in passing on perhaps a handful of those pages. To say that the strategy field treats the topic as unimportant overstates the emphasis given it by that field of study. Marketing, of course, is assumed to own this topic. Yet, the marketing discipline seems to have no quibble with the disregard in which strategy holds advertising. At the same time, the marketing discipline seems unperturbed by the rampant disregard in advertising for giving customers any reason to prefer the advertised product. Always ready to accommodate the fashion of the time, marketing does little or nothing to counteract the irrational and cynical attitudes that pervade the approach to this important function.

The internally-driven and customer-compelled philosophies create and perpetuate a great divide between customers' real life experiences and the workings of this classically important function. But that divide can be closed. Not just advertising, but product innovation and all other functions must be managed explicitly and rigorously by a completely designed value delivery system. 'What value proposition do we want to deliver, and how, to the intended customer?' The answer to this question must guide every function.

***

DPV posits that a business should be understood as a system of functions that deliver a value proposition rather than a system of functions that supply a product. This means that choosing a proposition must not simply be added to the product-supply framework. Rather, the functions of providing and communicating the chosen proposition must supersede the traditional functions of developing, making and selling the product. They must be used to integrate a business around a single clear vision, the chosen value proposition.

The three functions – choosing, providing, and communicating a value proposition – should determine the design and control of all products, resources and processes in a business. Together, they constitute the central framework of DPV by which any business should be understood, designed and managed: the *value delivery system*.

The product-supply versus value-delivery focus

Issue	Fundamental focus:	
	Product-supply	Value-delivery
Central topic of business strategy	What product to supply and how to supply it profitably	What value proposition to deliver and how to deliver it profitably
Main tasks of a business	Develop, produce and market (sell) the product	Choose, provide and communicate the chosen value proposition
Purpose of customers	Give revenue in return for a product	Give revenue in return for the other experiences in a value proposition
Purpose of a product	The source of profit, by its supply to customers	An often-helpful or even crucial resource to help deliver the chosen value proposition
Purpose of a value proposition	An often-helpful or even crucial way to help sell the product	The source of profit, by its delivery to customers
Organizing principle by which to structure and manage resource requirements in a business	Resources. The requirements are determined by product and function, producing an unintended and unquestioned value proposition	The delivery of the value proposition. The requirements are determined by each resulting experience
Meaning of competitive advantage	Ability to develop, produce or market some product differently than competition, regardless of value proposition delivered	Ability to deliver a superior value proposition profitably, regardless of whether products and functions are different from competition
Focus of capability/competence building	Enhance the organization's advantages over competition in developing, producing or marketing a product	Build the ability to choose, provide and communicate the resulting experiences central to some superior value proposition

Notes

1   High tech for 'Marketing Communications;' i.e. 'advertising and stuff.'
2   The terms by which one proponent, Geoffrey Moore, describes the curve, in his book *Crossing the Chasm*.
3   High tech firms explain that this term means 'feature;' if a user pays for the upgrade eliminating the bug, its meaning becomes 'benefit.'
4   Alice's term for much she finds in Looking Glass House.
5   'Brands with feeling,' *Forbes*, December 16, 1996 p. 292.
6   This term and several others discussed in this section were created and developed by a staff group in Procter & Gamble called Copy Services. This group analyzed copy effectiveness over the past 35 years. P&G has studied what works in advertising and what does not far more than any other manufacturer, the ad industry, or the academic community. This says less about P&G than it does about how little has been done elsewhere to understand seriously this important element of business.
7   Also identified by Copy Services at P&G.
8   *Forbes*, op cit, p. 292.
9   *Ibid*, p. 293.
10 *Ibid*.
11 S.G. Beatty, 'Mixed Message: Nissan's Ad Campaign Was a Hit Everywhere But in the Showrooms,' *The Wall Street Journal*, April 8, 1997, p. A1.
12 *Forbes, op. cit.*, p. 293.
13 *Wall Street Journal, op. cit.*
14 *Ibid*.
15 *Ibid*.
16 D. Barry, *Commercials You Hate Most, International Herald Tribune*, June 2 1995, p. 20.
17 *Wall Street Journal, op. cit.*
18 *Ibid*.
19 The personal portfolio of a creative person, which shows their work.
20 J. Jordan, from a speech delivered October 28, 1991 to ANA Annual Meeting, Phoenix, Arizona.
21 'Advertising - Which half?,' *The Economist*, June 8, 1996, pp. 72–3.
22 Jordan, *op. cit.*

Chapter Eight

Design a Business Forwards: the Value Delivery System

DPV suggests designing a business from the choice of value proposition forwards, to the resources and actions needed to provide and communicate it profitably. Managers must reject the backwards thinking that starts with an organization's assets and strengths, then moves out in search of a customer. In this comprehensive, integrating framework, a business consists of a chosen value proposition, all processes and resources used to provide and communicate it, and all the revenues, costs, and profits generated by delivering it.

A value delivery system: a business		
The *value proposition*	How each resulting experience including price is *provided*	How each resulting experience including price is *communicated*
• Timeframe • Intended customer • What organization wants customer to do • Customer's alternative(s) • Resulting experiences, including price	For each resulting experience, what processes occur, involving what resources, such that it is actually experienced by intended customer? *Includes:* how is price provided (so customer pays that price)?	For each resulting experience, what processes occur, involving what resources, such that customer understands it and believes they will experience it? *Includes:* how is price communicated?
Revenue generated by delivering the value proposition	Costs incurred by providing the value proposition	Costs incurred by communicating the value proposition
Profit (loss) generated by this business		

Designing a business by chosen resulting experiences – Southwest Airlines

In the airline business, sustained profits are hard to come by. While it is doing well lately, from 1992 to 1994 the industry lost about $5 billion in the US and $15 billion worldwide. Since deregulation in the late 1970s, there have been over 100 bankruptcies in the US. Yet chronic overcapacity still plagues the market. But all the airlines *understand* the established strategic formulae for making money. Except one, that is.

Since Rollin King conceived of and, with Herb Kelleher's help, formed Southwest Airlines (SWA) in the late 1960s, they have gotten plenty of free advice. Through the 1980s, the advice was: hey, it's about time for Southwest to grow up and start acting like a real airline. This meant SWA was supposed to abandon its focus on short-haul flights (less than two hours) to become a full-service, long-haul airline like the majors. It was time to build a 'hub-and-spoke' system, whereby passengers are flown to a 'hub' city, maximizing sales on the profitable long-haul flights.

At the same time, even a cursory audit of customers' needs and satisfaction pointed to opportunities for immediate improvements in Southwest's service, improvements that would bring it in line with industry standards. Southwest received over 8000 complaints per year about its numerous inconveniences versus other airlines. Of course, one might expect this grousing with a low-cost strategy. But, if SWA was going to continue as a no-frills airline, it was still spending money that no cost-obsessed, no-frills operator would.

Southwest's management just didn't seem to get it and still don't. They've done things wrong strategically for over 20 years now and have had to pay some heavy penalties. First, they have fun. Indeed, Fortune Magazine's poll of January, 1998 found SWA ranked as the best US company for which to work. In a related anomaly, they make money. Since 1973, two years after starting operations, SWA has made a profit every year, a unique achievement in the industry. Scores of airlines following a low-cost strategy folded, while SWA thrived. When SWA entered a market, total air traffic often increased dramatically and SWA captured a major share of the larger market. Despite very frequent flights, seat utilization was consistently high.

In the early 1990s, when the industry was demonstrating one of its collective core competencies (losing money and blaming uncontrollable forces), SWA's consistently profitable performance finally turned heads. Its larger, purportedly more sophisticated competitors and analysts stopped laughing. By 1993, according to *Fortune*, the US Department of Transportation 'concluded that SWA had become the dominant carrier in the nation's busiest air travel markets and was the "principal driving force for changes occurring in the airline industry."[1]

King and the organization discovered an insight, a value proposition that, if it could be delivered profitably, would be a winner. Then they invented a business – or, designed a value delivery system – to deliver that proposition profitably. What was SWA's value delivery system, how was it different from the rest of the industry, and why has it worked? First let's examine what SWA didn't do, which was to conform to conventional wisdom.

The big airlines love their very efficient hub-and-spokes and enjoy reminding passengers of how many cities they reach.[2] Did this match customers' requirements? The industry's market research showed that frequent business travelers rated very highly the ability to connect to many cities, an ability well provided by the hub-and-spoke model. In addition, passengers wanted trips as convenient and comfortable as possible. They expected to check bags once, claiming them at the destination even if they were to connect on another airline's flight. They also expected modern, sophisticated airport facilities; the convenience of ticketing through a travel agent; reserved seating; optional first class; decent meals on board; optional airport lounges; the ability to change a flight, but still use the original ticket, even if it was issued by a different airline. And they expected cheery, smiling service. SWA met this latter expectation, but none of the rest.

Yet, SWA also failed to meet the requirements of the other conventional strategic formula – the low-cost airline. Michael Porter explained the two alternative strategies, as they are applied to airlines, in his 1985 book, *Competitive Advantage*. The cost-leadership 'no-frills carriers,' unlike full-service airlines, would among other features have: no ticket counter, used aircraft, high-density seating, nonunion pilots and flight attendants, and a charge for checked baggage. [3]

Frequent travelers will recognize that 'no frills' is really the service-industry's euphemism for miserable service justified by cost leadership. For airlines this means: consistently late arrivals; inconvenient, infrequent schedules at inconvenient airports and terminals; lots of lost baggage; no meals (or, worse, cost-reduced meals); dirty, old, poorly maintained planes that make passengers nervous; and the friendly enthusiasm one expects from underpaid, overstressed employees who resent, fear, and distrust their management.

But none of the above captures the essence of SWA's strategy, or even comes close. Consider the following aspects of SWA's operation:

- short haul flights only
- no hub and spoke system, all point to point service
- only one aircraft type, only one supplier (Boeing 737)

- use of secondary, older, less sophisticated airports: a long ride from airports with best connecting flights to distant locations; few flights to these hubs
- no reserved seats, no meals, no first class, no airline lounges, limited travel agent listings, no tickets (recently)
- no baggage transfer between SWA and other airlines
- no interchangeable use of tickets between SWA and other airlines.

Yet, in this same operation:

- very frequent flights (e.g. every 30 minutes to same city)
- baggage service (free of charge)
- full-service ticket counters and ticket purchase at counter or gate
- all full-size jets, among youngest and best maintained fleets and least mechanical or other delays, in US
- employees who constantly joke and perform antics – silly holiday-costumes, bad singing, hiding in luggage bins; CEO throwing peanuts on board
- industry-average salary levels (about equal to leader, American)
- 80 percent of employees are union
- cost per passenger mile flown about 20 percent below the best competitors
- prices comparable to the cost of driving and well below other airlines.

SWA contradicts both of the standard strategic models. How, then, can its success be explained? One glib school of thought attributes SWA's success to *great customer service* –the employees are really funny, and everyone tries really hard, and so customers get total satisfaction. Well, in a customer satisfaction study, would a few customers mention the aspects of SWA that do not totally satisfy them? One might even ask if they would *prefer* meals, reserved seats, interline bag transfers, or service to the hub airports. Perhaps 95 percent would vote 'yes.' (The other 5 percent must not have understood the question.) Is SWA management too dumb to correct this dissatisfaction, or could it be intentional?

The other popular explanation for SWA comes from the strategy field, which argues that SWA is really a master differentiator. A Harvard case study explained that SWA succeeded in 'differentiating itself through its focus on service, operations, cost control, marketing, its people, and its corporate culture.'[4] Let all businesses do likewise. But how should one know whether to differentiate all these functions and resources or only some and, more importantly, differentiate them in what ways? In this same vein, strategy theorist Michael Porter cited SWA as an example of his conclusion that 'The essence of strategy is choosing to perform activities differently than rivals do.'[5] Perhaps, but which activities, differentiated on what principle? Strategist Adrian Slywotzky's 1996 book, *Value Migration*, similarly attributes SWA's success to a 'different business design' – a point-to-point, low-cost design versus a hub-and-spoke, high-cost one. The industry's hub-and-spoke system, he declared, is now obsolete and SWA recognized this and went there ahead of the others.

And strategists Gary Hamel and C.K. Prahalad explain that SWA was simply much bolder, more willing to dare to be *different*, an example of the 'challengers' and 'innovators,' as distinguished from the 'laggards.'

> *'Only after [SWA] became the most profitable [US] airline ... did United and American challenge their long-held assumptions about how to compete. At worst, laggards follow the path of greatest familiarity. Challengers ... follow the path of greatest opportunity, wherever it leads.'*[6]

But how to find and recognize this path of greatest opportunity? Be a 'contrarian':

> *'In the airline industry, conventional thinking held that a hub-and-spokes route structure was far superior to a point-to-point network ... Once one discovers the conventions, then one can ask if there is any value in ignoring them ... [SWA] became the most profitable in the [US] by ignoring the hub-and-spoke convention. Contrarians find these conventions and use them as weapons against orthodox-ridden incumbents. To discover the future it is not necessary to be a seer, but it is absolutely vital to be unorthodox.'*[7]

Yes, it's hard to disagree that breakthrough ideas are more likely if managers look for creative opportunities to reject orthodox conventions. But how would one recognize the hub-and-spoke convention as something to reject? The hub-and-spoke *was* superior to a point-to-point network and still is for much of the market. It is unlikely to become obsolete any time soon, since it provides far better access to a myriad of distant locations far more efficiently than point-to-point could. The hub-and-spoke was the *innovation* in the early 1970s, Southwest, the laggard. Luckily, King didn't mistake *wings* for a convention of the orthodox-ridden incumbents to reject.

The solution to the Southwest enigma is clear and simple, when understood through the lens of the value proposition SWA delivers and how it is delivered. SWA is focused on an intended passenger, who makes a particular kind of trip, which the industry abandoned. It is not that the intended customer would value *flying short-haul*, but rather *making a short trip*. Prior to SWA's arrival in a market, typically more than half of such trips were made by car or by bus. Very often, however, customers flying short-haul are not making a short trip; they are flying short-haul to make a connection as part of a relatively *long* trip. SWA's value delivery system is entirely shaped to deliver superior value profitably to this short-trip customer.

Let's begin by examining the intended customer's experience prior to SWA, as discovered by the founder who *was* originally one of those very customers.[8] In the sixties, King, a pilot in Texas, started a charter airline, went bust, got an MBA, and joined a venture capital firm. He traveled constantly within Texas, observing lots of other frequent intrastate travelers. He recognized a common problem. The business traveler had two options. S/he could drive 175–250 miles between cities, which took four to six hours door to door. Or s/he could fly on Braniff or Texas International airlines. Driving often won. Both options took too long and flying cost more.

Jets could get a passenger from one airport to another in 45–60 minutes. But that didn't necessarily move a person from door to door much faster than driving would have. Off-peak flights were seldom, so a midday wait for the next flight could be two hours long. In some cases, the passenger had to fly to a hub (Dallas or Houston), change planes, and *then* fly to the destination. Moreover, flight delays were common. Braniff, the largest carrier in Texas at the time, ran a complex system. A connecting flight from Miami could easily be late, delaying the short-haul flight in Texas. Braniff of course made its money on the long-haul, so why bother with niceties, like punctuality, on the less profitable short-haul? Braniff was then affectionately known by many Texans as 'the world's largest unscheduled airline.'

But industry always makes progress. In Houston and Dallas, huge new international airports had recently been built. Unlike the old, small airports they replaced, these were great for complex hubs, allowing connections to hundreds of distant cities. Of course, for a customer wanting to go from Dallas to Houston, this provides slim benefit. But, a customer does get to spend 45–60 minutes driving to DFW, more time parking, and more time walking a mile or so to the gate. In Houston, Intercontinental provides another long walk, a long wait for baggage, and then a long cab ride to the office being visited. In net, a short trip could take, door-to-door, almost as long as driving.

It also struck King that while airline personnel smiled a lot and kept saying things like 'Have a nice day,' the effort was transparently artificial. Neither employees nor passengers seemed to have much fun. And, of course, one paid quite a lot more for these experiences than for driving.

Rollin couldn't help imagining how much better a short trip would be for lots of Texans if an airline would just focus single-mindedly on that one situation. To go, door-to-door, between Dallas, Houston, and San Antonio in only a couple of hours, without paying much more than one would for driving, would be a dramatic improvement. Why wasn't that possible? What if it was actually kind of fun to interact with the front-line people at the gate and on the plane, even to the point of laughing a little? What if they seemed to *want* you to have some fun on the flight? What if all this could happen on a flight as safe as those of the safest airlines? SWA created just such an airline: an unconventional venture that *would* provide exactly these experiences at a low enough cost and to enough passengers to be profitable.

A reconstruction of SWA's value proposition is shown on the next page. While SWA did not write this statement, it is meant to depict the *de facto* value proposition delivered by Southwest.

Let's begin with providing the first resulting experience. To keep the wait for the next flight short implies a high-frequency schedule. Flights leave Dallas for Houston every 30 minutes all day, for example. For every flight to be direct means no hub-and-spoke system and all point-to-point travel. All the flight delays caused by 'full-service' elements such as seat reservations, food, transferring bags, and interline ticketing, won't happen for one reason: SWA doesn't offer these elements.

Minimizing mechanical flight delays of course requires planes to work. Reliable, easy-to-maintain planes are a help. But an exceptionally skilled maintenance crew and constant availability of the right spare parts and equipment would help even more. The most direct way to ensure both is – to use only one type of aircraft. SWA only uses Boeing 737s, a reliable, efficient, short-haul craft. Keeping a relatively young fleet of top rate jets, maintaining them better than other airlines, paying flight and maintenance crews well, and running the planes all day on high-frequency schedules are not low-cost, no frills moves; they are designed to deliver the key resulting experience.

Delays also happen due to connections – waiting for connecting flights, holding flights for connecting passengers. So, no connections, no waiting. The larger the airport, the more air traffic delays; so, use smaller airports. How to guarantee 30 minutes to and from airports? Locate in secondary airports that are closer to urban centers. How to keep customers in the airport for only 15 minutes? Again, small airports. Much simpler check-in helps too: no connections, interline ticketing, baggage transfers, seat reservations, or tickets. Bag transfers, connections, and complex airports cause lost/delayed bags, so SWA has none of it.

To communicate this resulting experience, SWA tells customers that they are saving time versus driving or flying on other airlines. In advertising and through front-line employees, they explain that passengers save so much time *because* of how SWA operates: more frequent schedules, fewer delays

Southwest Airlines' value proposition

I Timeframe for SWA delivering this Proposition: Immediate, ongoing

II Intended customer: People, mostly business, who: potentially value making frequent trips between cities 150–300 miles apart and staying in the destination city (not connecting to another city); would greatly value minimizing total travel time and cost on such trips; mostly have a sense of humor; are in Texas, to be expanded to West/Central markets where value proposition can be delivered

III What SWA [SWA] wants them to do: Use SWA for these trips

IV Customer's perceived 2 best alternatives: Drive; or fly another airline

V Resulting experiences for *these trips* (of 150–300 miles) customer will have:
Superior experiences:

  1 Consistently save significant travel time, door-to-door, specifically will:

  • Wait under 30 minutes for next flight; always fly direct; experience delays on less than 10 percent of trips; spend under 30 minutes in surface travel to/from airports; spend under 15 minutes within airports

  • In consequence, save a total of 1–3 hours door-to-door on such trips; typically spend 90 minutes to 2 hours on SWA, versus 4–5 driving or 3–4 on other airlines; can allow additional trip in same day and/or more business/personal time

  2 Be much more amused during flights; specifically will:

  • Frequently: laugh at/with amusing diversions, jokes, and quips of frontline staff; have amusing conversation that makes them feel sincerely liked by staff; in consequence, be more amused, despite discomforts, be aggravated/bored less, than with driving or flying other airlines

Equal experience:

  3 Be as safe as on safest airline; specifically will:

  • Be less exposed to danger than in driving and no more so than on the safest US airlines

Inferior experiences;

  4 Be *less* comfortable (though for short period); specifically will:

  • Often sit in undesirable seat, depending on when check-in; only sit in coach; not eat; miss out on airlines' offerings of these; miss out on more comfortable car seat

  5 Some minor time *lost*; specifically:

  • May lose 20–30 minutes on a meal during trip; may lose some non-travel time getting a refund if switch to/from SWA after buying ticket

Price:

Close to cost of driving; at least 30 percent below other airlines

(partly thanks to no bag transfers, seat reservations, or meals), closer and faster airports, shorter check-in, and fewer bags lost. And winning the 'Triple Crown' helps this communication, too. On a monthly and annual basis, it

Resulting experience #1: save travel time (door-to-door)

Resulting experience	How resulting experience is provided	How resulting experience is communicated
Consistently save significant travel time (door-to-door):		Via advertising and staff, communicate the following:
• Wait less than 30 minutes for next flight	• High-frequency schedules, e.g. 30–45 minutes in between flights	• Schedules
• Always fly direct	• No hub; all point-to-point	• Always direct
• Delayed arrival on less than 10 percent of trips	• No delays from reserved seats, food service, interline bags/tickets • Fewer mechanical flight delays because only one reliable craft (737), higher skill, simpler maintenance, and better spare parts • No connections delays • Secondary airports, less traffic	• On-time (Triple Crown) and reasons: simplicity and inferior experiences
• Spend under 30 minutes surface travel to/from airports	• Secondary airports closer to work/home	• Time saved by closer airports
• Spend under 15 minutes within airports	• Small airports: shorter walk, shorter bag wait • No seat-reservations, connections, interline services, or tickets mean shorter check-in • No bag transfer, no connections, simple airports means fewer bags lost/delayed	• Quicker airport procedures, fewer bags lost (Triple Crown)

has repeatedly won this award, which it invented based on government statistics. A Triple Crown winner is best in on-time performance, bags lost, and customer service complaints. No other airline has ever won it even once.

Delivering this resulting experience, however, causes other, not necessarily desirable results for Southwest. It loses the hub-and-spoke, long-haul efficiencies. Connections are very inconvenient, although the *intended customer* makes none. The customer is less comfortable than on other airlines and may lose some time in obtaining a meal or a ticket refund. The value delivery system must explicitly reflect these undesirable results.

The second resulting experience, amusing the customer, requires getting serious. From the beginning, the firm realized that only a certain kind of person could naturally engage with passengers in an appropriately up-beat and slightly bizarre fashion. Therefore, SWA not only trains employees to make the passenger's flight an amusing experience; it very carefully screens employees to find the right personalities. Candidates are observed for sev-

Resulting experience #2: be amused

Resulting experience	How resulting experience is provided	How resulting experience is communicated
Be much more amused		
Laugh at/with amusing diversions, jokes, quips of front-line staff	• Hire staff who can humorously entertain passengers with jokes, costumes, songs, antics • Choose staff partly due to humor, comedic ability even when under pressure • Provide formal training and rewards for amusing behavior • Support experience from the top (e.g. CEO throws peanuts on board)	• Word-of-mouth; humor in advertising
In amusing conversation, feel sincerely liked by staff	• Staff converse frequently, treat customers with sincere warmth; hire/ reward/train sincerely warm conversation ability	• As above; originally in Texas: 'Love' theme ('SWA: The somebody else up there who loves you'), Love Stamps, Love Field

eral days in simulated, stressful situations. SWA employees play the parts of customers. Observers include SWA human resources and frequent SWA flyers. If candidates seem able to respond sensibly to difficult passengers, making them smile or laugh, they are hired.

SWA understood that keeping passengers laughing was a good idea, especially given other elements in the proposition. Passengers tend to be irritable anyway, but take away their meals, reserved seats, and first class option, and a sense of humor becomes priceless.

However, a less amusing tradeoff customers expect from low-price airlines is a lower level of safety. SWA always understood that this was the wrong tradeoff to make. No parsley on the rubberized microwave eggs this morning? OK. But creative cost containment through avoiding unnecessary safety procedures? Not at Southwest. Opposing conventional low-cost logic, SWA excels in safety.

Resulting experience #3:
be as safe as on safest airlines

Resulting experience	How resulting experience is provided	How resulting experience is communicated
Be as safe as on safest airlines	• Youngest fleet in US • Safer procedures: 　• No compromises in maintenance 　• High morale; well-paid, staff treated with respect by management 　• Simple operations (only 1 type aircraft, no hub, no connections)	• Long-term, low-key communication through lack of incidents. Some publicity re: youngest fleet • Occasional FAA safety reports, contrasting bad publicity for other airlines, especially 'low-cost' competitors

Inferior experiences are deliberately included in a chosen value proposition and so they are intentionally delivered as part of a designed value delivery system. They are not unfortunate accidents to be swept under the organization's rug. A business may decide not to emphasize an inferior experience in its communication to the intended customer. However, the value delivery system should actually clarify how an inferior experience is delivered, even if the organization wishes its value proposition delivered a better experience. In fact, articulating inferior experiences and how they are actually delivered gives the organization an opportunity to understand and even minimize the negative consequence in that experience. Moreover, hiding the inferior experience from the customer is not as obviously wise as some would assume. Trying to obscure the perception of an inferior experience often creates ill will in customers; honestly presenting them is usually smarter.

Inferior resulting experiences: comfort, time loss

Resulting experiences	How provided	How communicated
Be less comfortable flying	• No seat reservations, 1st Class, meals, or airport lounges	• Staff and PR explain this allows experience #1 and lower cost
Lose some minor time getting meal or ticket refund	• No meals or interline ticketing	• As above

SWA's inferior resulting experiences include significantly less comfort during the flight, some minor time lost due to meals and, occasionally, to ticket refunds. But what may seem to be the most inferior experience is missing from the above list. That is, customers wanting to make a connection to or from SWA must lose time in changing airports and/or checking in a second time. For these customers, those who take a short-haul flight as part of a long trip, SWA actually increases their total travel time. Why isn't this listed as an inferior experience in SWA's value proposition? Because agreeing to SWA's value proposition does not cause this experience. On a day when a person is an intended customer of SWA, s/he would only value taking a short trip, not a short-haul flight as part of a longer trip. So they don't lose time making connections – they don't make connections. SWA deliberately decided against delivering a winning proposition to long-trip customers.[9] Of course, if the same long-trip customer wants on a different day to take a short trip, s/he becomes the intended customer.

Another experience delivered by SWA's competition is the ability to get tickets through a travel agency. SWA saves millions each year in travel agent commissions by not consistently delivering this experience to passengers. Yet the lack of this experience is also missing from the list because it too is largely irrelevant. Many travel agents issue tickets on Southwest despite the lack of commission; for these passengers, of course, there is no difference. For the rest, the inferior consequence of this event is trivial at worst.

It is useful for a passenger traveling on a conventional airline to have a ticket prior to the trip. Otherwise they must buy a ticket at the airport counter, easily wasting 15 minutes, often much more. At SWA, buying a ticket is greatly simplified and rarely costs the passenger more than a minute or two. Most recently, the company has disposed with tickets altogether. The passenger simply pays the fare and boards.

The inferior experiences in SWA's value proposition are minor in comparison to the superior experience of substantial time saved. When the other resulting experiences, including paying a price close to that of driving, are added into the package, it becomes clear why intended customers are loyal to and satisfied with SWA.

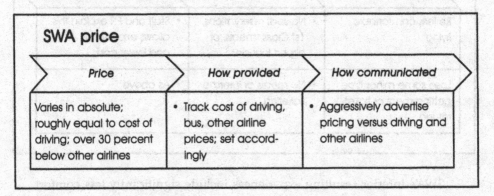

A great value delivery system is balanced and symmetrical, with virtually all elements complementary of one another. In the case of SWA, actions and resources that help provide the most important resulting experience (time saved) in the proposition do not compromise the other two superior or equal ones (amusing flights and unsurpassed safety). Yet, these same actions also create opportunities for a dramatically lower cost structure than full-service airlines and even lower than the no-frills, low-cost airlines whose strategies are so commonly confused with SWA's. A key component of SWA's low cost structure is its high utilization of aircraft. SWA turns around planes in only 10–15 minutes between flights, versus the industry average of about 38 minutes. The impact on a high-frequency schedule is dramatic; SWA uses at least a third fewer aircraft than it would if its turnaround time matched the industry.

How do they get this turnaround time? First, by not doing many of the things that slow turnaround. No time is lost on food service, reserved seating, or baggage transfers. Turnaround is much faster in smaller, simpler, lower-air-traffic airports without hub logistics. Second, unencumbered by meals, bag transfers, and the like, SWA has had over twenty years to hone the skill of performing a fast turnaround. Conventional turnaround performance is harder to measure and improve because other variables cloud the picture. Crews may be slowed waiting for transferred bags or late food service. Not at Southwest. So crews have the opportunity to become very skilled. One journalist described a typical turnaround in Phoenix:

> 'Wally Mills is watching the clock. At 3:15 [SWA] flight 944 from San Diego lands, on time … By 3:30, Mr Mills … and six other Southwest ramp agents must have this plane turned around and on its way … 'I think of this as a game,' [he] says 'I like to play against the [gate agents] up there working with the people to see if we can beat them.' With Indy pit-stop precision, workers attach the push-back gear to the Boeing 737, unload the Phoenix bags, load the ones for El Paso, restock the galleys and pump aboard 4600 pounds of fuel. A last minute bag costs the ramp crew the race with the gate agents, who have boarded 49 passengers. Then Mr Mills puts on a headset and prepares to direct the jet away from the gate. It is 3:29.'[10]

The experiences SWA *doesn't* deliver have further impact on its cost structure. Both using secondary airports and not operating a hub-and-spoke system save a tremendous amount. The same goes for the lack of food service, a seat reservation system, interline bag transfers, interline ticketing, and

Relative cost of Southwest's value delivery system

Overall relative cost	Differences in providing value proposition	Differences in communicating value proposition
Per passenger-flown mile costs are 20–30 percent below other airlines and close to driving	• 1/3 fewer aircraft needed (for same schedule) due to turnaround time (10–15 minutes versus 30–50) • No hub, no connections • No food, seat reservation, interline bags, or ticketing • Only one aircraft type • No mail or large freight • Skill of fast turnaround • No costs for: hub, food, seat reservations, interline tickets/bag transfers, 1st class, travel agency fees • Lower check-in, ticketing costs • Lower maintenance costs • One aircraft type • Fewer maintenance facilities • Simplified maintenance training	• Some efficiencies from strong word of mouth, free publicity over time • Price is enough to attract trial, superior experiences easily understood when customer tries; allows rest of value proposition to be communicated without heavy reliance on advertising • Front line staff's communication to passengers is also inherently efficient

travel agency commissions. And what about only relying on one supplier of aircraft? Conventional strategy wisdom would deride this as foolish, giving Boeing great 'supplier power,' with which they can supposedly capture the profits earned by SWA. However, it is Boeing who would be foolish to try to exploit SWA, probably one of Boeing's most profitable customers (the cost of sales to SWA could hardly be high, could it?) Boeing does not use its supplier power to hurt SWA's costs because Boeing understands a more realistic principle: the more that SWA succeeds, the more money Boeing makes.

This VDS even has efficiencies inherent in communicating the proposition. The dramatically low prices easily communicate a key part of the proposition. Customer trial, the staff, and word of mouth all communicate the rest of it very effectively and inexpensively.

***

SWA did not ask: 'What sort of airline should we build, with what schedules, planes, airports, on-board service, advertising and prices?' These are vehicles by which some value proposition might be delivered. Starting with experiences potential customers would value is a different route. Of course, King's original team didn't figure out the whole puzzle right at the beginning. It is an iterative process, with both mistakes and luck playing their roles. King and his team drew essential insights by intuitively doing what in *DPV* is called 'becoming the customer.' They closely studied and identified with the real life experiences of the potential customer. Then, thinking forwards, they created the value delivery system based upon those insights. Thus SWA works not because of some facile strategic formula or because of luck but rather because the whole system is designed from the perspective of the chosen value proposition. The value delivery mentality is about replicating this perspective in large complex organizations; it is not only for an entrepreneur starting a new business.

Design each value delivery system

While all organizations do provide and communicate some value proposition, most do not consciously choose one. Nor do they decide how to provide and communicate it. The VDS is a framework that describes the most critical functions of deliberately managing a business. These are the functions of trying, on purpose, to deliver a specific value proposition.

The VDS considers separately each resulting experience. For each resulting experience in the value proposition, the VDS describes the requirements for providing and communicating it. Product, service, sales, manufactur-

Designing a business as a value delivery system

Choose the Value proposition	Decide how the value proposition will be:	
	Provided	Communicated
• Timeframe • Intended customer • What we want them to do • Their best alternatives • Resulting experiences including price		
For each superior or equal resulting experience:	For each resulting experience:	
What events and relative consequence, of what value, must customer conclude they will experience?	What specific product attributes, features and characteristics are required to cause the events actually to happen in customer's life? By what product and service providing-vehicles should these attributes, etc. be made available? What changes must customer make in processes, resources, awareness and capabilities? By what educating or skill building providing-vehicles will we cause these changes? How should all these providing-vehicles be produced, by whom, with what implications by resource?	What information, logic, evidence must be conveyed so customer understands: 1 What the experience will be: • event or series of events • consequence, versus alternatives • value to customer of relative consequence 2 The reasons, if any, why they should believe the resulting experience will be provided? By what communicating-vehicles (product design, packaging, sales presentations/relationships, advertising, trade shows, etc.)? How and by whom should vehicles be produced? Implications?
For any inferior experiences: What events and relative consequence, of what value, must customer conclude they will experience?	If inferior experience is delivered, inferior to competing alternative, must decide: how provide it (same questions as above)? If it is an experience we deny, but is delivered by some alternative(s), we do not provide it	How ensure customer understands: • value lost is no more than it is? • good reasons (if any) for it, e.g. provides superior experiences? • they were not misled? • that in net the whole value proposition is superior?
For the price: What price?	What must happen such that customer actually pays this price?	How ensure customer understands price is no more than it is
Expected revenue from delivering this value proposition	Expected total cost of providing this value proposition	Expected total cost of communicating this proposition
Expected profit from this business in the timeframe		

ing, distribution and other functional requirements for providing and communicating that single experience are thus identified. Then, the next resulting experience in the proposition is described and its requirements identified. Two experiences may describe *different*, redundant, or conflicting requirements. When all the experiences and their requirements have been described, it is then possible to identify the overall implications for each product, resource, and function.

Some people ascribe certain winning VDSs to accident and luck. True enough for some successful businesses. So what should one do? Trust to luck? Hope for the best? Or try to manage the process rationally? Make disciplined choices, knowing that some will be poor choices. Choose a value proposition for a business, and decide how to align all resources and processes to provide and communicate it profitably.

VDS design and development is iterative

Strategy, reacting to changing circumstances, must evolve. Delivering a profitable value proposition does not require a perfect design from the beginning. It doesn't matter, in the long run, how wrong the original VDS was, as long as the business survives long enough to become a winning VDS.

Sometimes iteration in the design of a VDS comes with some pain. Consider Sensomatics, maker of the theft-prevention disk that is removed from merchandise upon purchase. If a shopper leaves a store with the disk still attached, a sensor sounds an alarm. Sensomatics has succeeded over time, but success came slowly.

In the 1960s, the founder[11] was inspired, as a grocery store manager, by a shoplifting attempt he tried in vain to halt. Shrink, loss from theft, is a major retail cost. Expecting a warm welcome for their first prototype, he was surprised to find not a single retailer willing to try the device – free. Resistance was related to department store security at the time. 'Floor walkers,' non-uniformed employees, walked the floor watching for shoplifters. At the time, Macy's had a security force larger than the police departments of all but the largest US cities. Sensomatics did not look quite innovative enough to compete with these vested interests. The firm finally had to *pay* a store $300 a month to try it. But, the test worked, shrink decreased, and Sensomatics got a break. A PX (the Army's stores for base personnel) agreed to a trial.

Sensomatics had designed the product with this equation in mind: for the product 'to work' meant 'to catch shoplifters.' The more caught, the more money saved. So the disk was designed to be well hidden within the garment. Unfortunately for everyone, one day the General's wife set off the alarm leaving the PX. She was not happy. In the great uproar that followed, the army tossed Sensomatics out.

However, Sensomatics learned from this incident and transformed their VDS accordingly. The superior experience was basically on target: make it harder for merchandise to leave unpurchased, with the consequence of less shrink than with floor walkers or other methods. Catching shoplifters had seemed the right focus, but Sensomatics realized that hiding the device was only *one* way to provide the experience. And they realized that this way also created an additional, inferior experience. Unlike the more discrete floor walkers, Sensomatics produced a loud, unattractive scene, thus severely alienating the trapped customer and putting off the onlookers. Even thieves are more profitably *deterred* than nabbed in plain view.

Sensomatics redesigned the disks and exit door sensors to be unmistakably visible. Sensomatics also provided this revised proposition by helping and encouraging retailers to *explain* overtly the security system to shoppers. The company carefully communicated the revised proposition as well, explaining and making believable the consequence of deterring without catching. Now only the dumbest shoplifters get caught.

Designing the VDS in uncertain or distant futures

A value proposition can be defined and assessed for some distant future timeframe, even with only a sketchy idea of how it may be delivered. One can also define how a proposition could be provided in the future, without determining exactly how to communicate it. But it is important to sketch a future value delivery system as fully as possible, despite uncertainty about that future. The internally-driven mentality wants to develop technologies, products, and infrastructures without bothering to figure out what VDS these might support. The convenient excuse that it's too far in the future to know about the VDS should be greeted with skepticism.

The Sony Walkman is a tale often told as an example of technology-driven triumph. No customer ever asked for a Walkman, but Sony made it anyway because of its technical abilities. Then the company, using marketing wizardry to make customers believe they needed the product, pressed it upon them. Rest is history. But the lack of a customer's request for a Walkman does not mean Sony wasn't focused on profitably delivering superior value, only that they weren't customer-compelled.

When Sony was spending hundreds of millions developing the Walkman, it was likely that they had conceived of few details of its eventual advertising campaign. They had probably not determined what in-store promotional materials would say. Maybe they had not even picked the name yet. These matters should not be confused, however, with the broad outlines of a value delivery system.

Sony invested development dollars in the Walkman because they *did* have in mind the rough idea of its value delivery system. The proposition was this: to be able to listen to very high fidelity music, including loud but very accurate 'true' sound reproduction in a mode that (a) doesn't disturb other people nearby; and (b) is highly and easily portable, with little hassle from size or weight. All of this could be had for under $200. They decided early on that cassette tapes were the appropriate recording medium, given their size, weight, and potential playback quality. If a cassette tape player could be made small enough, with small light earphones that put out high-fidelity sound, at a cost well under $125, this proposition could be profitably provided. If that proposition could be provided, Sony figured, it would communicate easily enough through word of mouth. That Sony thought of this proposition without the prompting of customers made Walkman a value delivery insight, not a technology-driven example of customer-free thinking.

CEO Akio Morita and other Sony executives had apparently noticed how irritating their own teenagers' loud (Sony) stereos were at home. And, as was typical of successful Japanese firms' executives, they had spent a lot of time in New York and other important cities where cumbersome, obnoxious portable tape players ('boom boxes') were common. Sony executives imagined a solution to these problems and established an ambitious product development effort to implement it. Sony's knowledge and skills in high-fidelity music reproduction and miniaturization made the project a natural one.

Initially, the company didn't know all the details of providing this proposition. Some important details of the Walkman VDS were developed after conceiving of the project. For example, Sony assumed the Walkman, like all tape players, had to include recording ability. However, they eventually found that the size, weight, and cost implications of the value proposition implied eliminating the record function. Then it dawned on them that this delivered only a trivially inferior experience. In other words, so what if the consumer could not record on a Walkman? It didn't matter that all competing players also record; it only mattered that the Walkman furnished a dramatically improved *listening* experience. This decision was an important refinement of the VDS.

And Sony no doubt thought little about advertising early on. But this should not be confused with the notion that Sony invented the Walkman with no concept of the value proposition it would deliver and roughly how they would provide it. Sony did conceive of a value proposition first and refined the details of providing and communicating it as they went along. This iterative process should not be interpreted as evidence of Sony's developing a technology without first conceiving of the VDS it supports.

It is convenient, and currently fashionable, to dismiss the question of designing the VDS until 'later.' Of course, product and technology research must continue without precise knowledge of a value proposition and its delivery. Broad, strategic decisions, such as acquisitions, sometimes don't allow the time needed for deep analysis. But the sooner an organization can sketch the general shape of the VDSs it may try to implement later, the better its chance of recognizing the difference between a major opportunity and a dead end.

***

A value delivery system is a business and so cannot be a static model. As the world changes, the value delivery system must also change. Using the VDS to manage a business dynamically for the long-term is the subject of the next chapter.

Notes

1   K. Labich, 'Is Herb Kelleher America's Best CEO?' *Fortune*, May 2 1994, p. 25.
2   Delta even made its slogan, 'Delta *gets* you there.' To some, this only raised an issue previously taken for granted. Then, in the late 1980s, Delta twice landed mistakenly at the wrong airport, so they dropped that slogan. Now it's 'Delta: we love to fly' which makes one think 'Great! And what's in that for me?' Recently, a vast cost reduction strained operations and some passengers now say Delta means 'Doesn't Ever Leave The Airport.' Perhaps they should go back to just getting there.
3   Michael E. Porter, *Competitive Advantage*, Free Press, New York, 1985, p. 78.
4   Quoted by Labich, *op. cit.*
5   Michael Porter, 'What is Strategy?' *Harvard Business Review*, November–December 1996, p. 64.
6   Hamel and Prahalad, *Competing for the Future, op. cit.*, p. 17.
7   *Ibid*, p. 99.
8   As related in numerous extensive interviews by King who has periodically guest-lectured in the *BMFO* course since 1989.
9   *De facto*, SWA delivers a secondary value proposition to some customers interested in saving money on a long trip even if they *lose* time, by hopping on SWA from city to city.
10 Bridget O'Brian, *Southwest Airlines is a rare air carrier: it still makes money*, *The Wall Street Journal*, October 26, 1992, p. 1.
11 As told in National Public Radio interview, July 1996.

Chapter Nine

Staying Alive: Adjust and Recreate Your VDS

To stay successful over time a business usually has to change. Its value proposition or the way it's provided or communicated may have to be changed to meet the threat of competitive value delivery systems. Organizations must design a *complete* value delivery system and evaluate whether it constitutes a winning business. But they must also be willing to reinvent their business, to redesign the value delivery system in the light of market changes, not in the light of their own comfort zone. They must rigorously and continuously challenge their business design to ensure it thoroughly reflects the disciplined choice of a potentially winning value delivery system for the relevant timeframe. This chapter will review this dynamic and constantly creative use of the value delivery framework. It will close with a clarification to ensure the reader does not confuse this framework with others, especially the business system and value chain concepts.

Choose completely designed, winning VDSs

For each business an organization implements or contemplates, it must make a disciplined choice of the value delivery system. Choosing a value proposition is ultimately inadequate unless done in this context. A complete VDS of course incorporates a complete value proposition. It also specifies how this proposition will be delivered, as such determining every important action and resource for that business.

The completely designed value delivery system

answers the following questions for one business:

1 What is the complete value proposition this VDS will deliver?
2 How will each resulting experience, including price be delivered:
  • Provided: What resources and actions will cause the customer actually to have each resulting experience?
  • Communicated: what will cause the customer to understand each resulting experience and the reasons for believing it will be provided?
3 What capability gaps must be closed and how will they be?

The checklist below suggests the questions by which to determine whether a VDS will generate wealth for the firm and thus whether it should be implemented.

Checklist for a winning business

1 Would it deliver a *superior* value proposition? If delivered as designed, do we believe intended customers would conclude that the value proposition is superior to their competing alternatives?

2 How much revenue would we expect?

3 Are we confident the organization can build the needed capabilities to implement it? This includes improving existing, as well as creating new, capabilities.

4 How much total cost would we incur? This includes the on-going cost of delivering the proposition plus the cost of building capabilities and including the cost of capital.

5 How much profit would this business generate, ignoring other businesses or later timeframes?

6 What impact, if any, would this VDS have on our *other* businesses? To what extent would conflicts or synergies from this VDS reduce/increase profitability of our other businesses?

7 What impact would this VDS have on *later* ones? Does it facilitate a longer-term, more profitable VDS, or compromise later ones?

8 What discontinuities may impact its success and sustainability? What changes in the market's environment could change the outcome of this VDS?

9 In *net*: is this a good VDS? Do we believe it will, long term, generate more wealth for the firm than not implementing it?

However, organizations cannot sustain a business by designing and assessing its attractiveness only once. To remain a winner, a business must be deliberately redesigned.

Avoiding ulcers: redesign the VDS to stay ahead of the competition

In 1976, the American pharmaceutical firm Smith-Kline-French launched Tagamet. Previously, over 10 percent of the world suffered ulcer disease with no effective treatment. Without curing the ulcer, Tagamet's H2 Blocker technology temporarily suppressed acid secretion so most ulcers could heal, although they were likely to recur later. A painful and frequently dangerous disease was fairly well controlled for the first time. Sir James Black, the

Scottish scientist who led the breakthrough work, later won the Nobel Prize. By 1981, Tagamet was producing over $500 million in revenue.

In 1981, mediocre performer British Glaxo was about the 25th largest pharmaceutical company. By the mid-1990s, its success in the ulcer market had made it one of the top three. The company, then Glaxo Wellcome, was the UK's most profitable firm. Smith-Kline (SKF), on the other hand, was shrinking fast in the early nineties and had to accept an inglorious merger with Beecham as a result. The design of the competitors' value delivery systems over time explains most of this reversal. Glaxo focused on improving delivery of the most important resulting experiences. SKF reacted with marketing tactics, did not redesign a superior VDS, and paid the price.[1]

Let's examine the initial *de facto* VDS for Tagamet. General Practitioners (GPs) in the developed world were the intended customers. The exciting value proposition to them centered on the first effective ulcer therapy in a safe and convenient form at a price that was high but generally affordable.

Tagamet was the commercial name for the compound Cimetidine. Clinical trials had shown that using one gram/day of Cimetidine healed 75 percent of patients' ulcers within 4 weeks and surfaced only minor side-effect safety issues. The dosing regimen was tied to meals because patients were accustomed to using antacids after meals. One 200 mg tablet after each meal and two more at bedtime totaled 1 gram per day. This regimen, prescribed for 4–6 weeks, was reasonably easy and thus convenient for the patient. This ease of use also helped with patient compliance. Of course, compliance (whether the patient strictly follows the necessary regimen) affects, in turn, the overall efficacy of the therapy.

SKF's own sales force did the detailing.[2] The company had a strong philosophy of growing steadily through its own marketing resources, rather than leveraging its technologies through licensing or other such agreements. As Tagamet succeeded, the company steadily built up its marketing resources. SKF also used advertising and, given the great breakthrough Tagamet represented, easily generated major publicity worldwide that helped educate GPs and patients to the newly available therapy.

Tagamet, the first billion dollar drug, was a spectacular success that catapulted SKF to the top ranks of pharmaceutical companies. Within a few years, one small cloud appeared over Tagamet's success, but it didn't seem too threatening at the time. The side-effect issues were found to be somewhat more significant than originally thought. It was known that Cimetidine interfered with enzymes in the liver. It turned out that this could cause an undesirable, and in some cases serious, interaction with several other drugs, e.g. anti-coagulants. It also had an anti-androgenic effect on a small portion of male patients, causing problems like breast enlargement and inhibition of sexual function. It also crossed the blood brain barrier, creating mental

1976 initial Tagamet value delivery system

Value proposition	How resulting experiences were provided	How resulting experiences were communicated
Intended customer: GPs for ulcer patients; want them to prescribe Tagamet versus other treatment		
Resulting experiences: First effective therapy, less than 75 percent healing in 4 weeks	Cimetidine H2 Blocker suppresses acid secretion, letting ulcer heal Easy to use (see regimen below), so good compliance	Detailing, journal ads, publicity: approved claims, healing evidence from clinicals
Generally quite safe	Only minor side effects for a few	Presented clinical trial results
Reasonably convenient to use	1 gram = 3 × 200 mg daily, 2 × 200 night, tied to meals (acid secretion)	Explained logical tie to meals, mimicking antacids
Price high but affordable		

disorientation for a few. Physicians tolerated such side-effects, however. Most drugs have some, and Tagamet's only affected 1–2 percent of patients. Drug interactions were avoidable and the other side-effects were not considered too serious.

By this stage, however, SKF should have fundamentally challenged its own antiulcerant business. Looking at Tagamet's value proposition, was there room for improvement? If a competing alternative were to deliver such an improved value proposition, how much profit might be at risk? Would such a threat be possible? To deliver such an improved proposition, what would be most important to change in the VDS?

If such questions had been asked, SKF could hardly have missed the fact that 75 percent healing in 4 weeks is hardly perfect. Would *more* of the active agent in the compound bring about higher efficacy? The side-effects may well be acceptable to physicians, but wouldn't a similar drug without such side effects deliver an obviously better resulting experience? If a higher dosage version were tried, would that make the side-effects worse? What about the ease and convenience with which Tagamet was used and the associated compliance? Is a regimen of eight capsules taken at four different times during the day the optimal combination of efficacy and ease of use? What was the medical basis for this four-time dosage and for the connection to meals? If the regimen were designed primarily to mimic patients' antacid habits, was this familiarity worth the inconvenience of four times a day?

SKF was not fortunate enough to ask and pursue such questions. Having succeeded in the ulcer market, the company looked elsewhere for new breakthroughs. It pursued new drugs in the related therapeutic area of Gastroenterology (GE) and also in cardiology and arthritis. Flush with cash, it launched an ambitious program of unrelated diversification, which was then fashionable. SKF bought into contact lenses, generic drugs, and a non-pharmaceutical instruments company. It increased investments in its low margin, management-intensive vaccine division, animal health, private laboratories, and over the counter drugs. But not ulcers.

When asked recently why SKF did not pursue a new antiulcerant, Sir James Black explained that they had already made a dramatic technical breakthrough and felt it very unlikely to make another one in the same therapeutic market. Only marginal improvements seemed possible. Unfortunately, marginal improvements were SKF's undoing.

Meanwhile, a Glaxo team had been searching for another H2 blocker. The team believed that if a similar molecule could be found that worked about as well as Tagamet and was patentably different, then a small share of this huge market could be captured. Opposition was strong inside the firm. As a generalization, physicians have traditionally shown considerable loyalty toward the pharmaceutical company that invents a new drug, especially if that drug is a breakthrough. Imitation drugs don't easily impress physicians, and they usually have had to compete on price. On the other hand, Glaxo did not have other, more exciting prospects. The H2 blocker team kept the project alive and developed the imitation compound, Ranitidine. Early indications from analysis of its pharmacology, animal studies, and early trials were that efficacy would be similar to Cimetidine but would have five times the potency per milligram. Most interestingly, it didn't seem to interfere with liver enzymes, produce the anti-androgenic effect, or cross the blood brain barrier.

Going into human clinical testing, Glaxo needed to select a dosing regimen. Here the team had to make a crucial decision about the value proposition Ranitidine would deliver. Administering more H2 blocker should, in principle, increase healing efficacy. The usual tradeoff involved in a higher dose, however, is that side-effects will also increase. The team decided on 300 mg per day, equivalent to 50 percent more than Tagamet's one gram regimen hoping to produce better efficacy results and still cause no side effects. Four-week results showed no side effects and 80 percent healing.

But the 5 percent directionally better efficacy was not strong enough to warrant a superiority claim.

The doubters in Glaxo believed that Ranitidine's small safety advantages would fail to excite most physicians, who would continue crediting SKF as the innovators in antiulcerants. Glaxo had only a small sales force in the key US market and had a weak presence elsewhere outside the UK. Ranitidine would obviously imitate Tagamet's regimen, tell its undramatic safety story, and compete on price, maybe winning two or three share points. However, Glaxo decided to launch Ranitidine, using the name Zantac, with an ambitious, unconventional approach.

First, the team made two changes in the value proposition versus what then seemed obvious: the dosing regimen and the price. Glaxo knew that mimicking the patient's after-meal antacid regimen didn't actually help heal the ulcer. In fact, Glaxo believed that in theory the H2 Blocker action may work better if in the system hours *before* eating. SKF seemed to think that, since taking the tablets after meals fit into existing behavior, GPs would find it an easy way to go. However, eight pills taken at four different times in the day was hardly easy for the patient. Zantac's regimen was just two tablets a day (called 'BD'), 150 mg each. In addition, Zantac's clinicals pre-scribed just 4 weeks of treatment rather than Tagamet's 4–6.

The Zantac team also went against the grain on price, arguing that a lower price would connote second-best, as well as strain the profitability of the project. Glaxo surprisingly priced roughly 30 percent above Tagamet, using pricing to help communicate superiority.

One of the most decisive choices Glaxo made was overtly and rather aggressively to communicate the most important superior resulting experi-ence in the Zantac value proposition. This decision, to emphasize strongly the lack of side effects caused by using Zantac in contrast to those caused by Tagamet, was less obvious than it may now seem. Physicians were tell-ing Glaxo that they would stay loyal to Tagamet, that its side effects were not very serious and did not affect a large portion of patients. In the abso-lute, this was probably a reasonable view, though one wonders what it must have been like for those few patients who had both the anti-androgenic and mental disorientation effects in the same evening.

The pharmaceutical industry's and the medical profession's aversion to mudslinging further complicated this decision. Competition among drug firms, then even more than today, was a polite affair. The European culture further inhibited comparative claims. Perhaps especially in a proper British firm, gentlemen simply did not go about *pointing out* deficiencies in another firm's product.

However, the Zantac team decided to go against the grain. They believed that, if forced to confront the side-effect comparison, many physicians would change their attitude. They would perhaps gradually realize that many of their patients, especially those of the male variety, would not have a difficult time choosing Zantac, given its at least equal healing efficacy. Likely Smith-Kline would cry foul over the violation of etiquette, but keeping the side-effect story out of the news would afford Zantac a similar lack of notoriety. In the sales force's detailing materials, in journal advertising, and elsewhere, Glaxo bluntly told this pivotal part of the value proposition story.

Finally, Glaxo further gambled by establishing licensing and partnership agreements in the US and Europe that overnight expanded the effective

1981 initial Zantac value delivery system

Value proposition	How resulting experiences were provided	How resulting experiences were communicated
Intended customer: GPs for ulcer patients; want them to prescribe Zantac versus Tagamet		
Resulting experiences: At least equal, perhaps slightly better healing than Tagamet, 80 percent versus 75, in 4 weeks	Ranitidine H2 Blocker; 50 percent more effective total potency (300mg/day, 5 × potency/mg); regimen better aligned with H2 Blocker action; regimen more likely followed	Detailing, journal advertising present approved claims, evidence for slightly higher healing, plus potency and compliance arguments
Safer – freer of side effects • No drug interaction concerns • No breast enlargement, sexual dysfunction • No mental disorientation	• Much less interference with liver enzymes • No anti-androgenic effect • Doesn't cross brain blood barrier	Aggressively reminded GPs of evidence for Tagamet side-effects; showed clinical data of none for Zantac; insisted it matters ('potency counts')
More convenient to use: • less frequent, fewer pills • less total time (4 weeks versus 4–6)	Shorter (4 weeks), simplified (150 mg BD) regimen aligns with Blocker action; uses greater potency	Explained better regimen logic and better effectiveness
		For above, aggressively expanded effective Sales Force size to compare favorably to SKF
Price over 30 percent higher	Announced price, by country	

size of the sales force to rough equivalency with SKF. In this way, Zantac immediately built the key communicating-vehicle for its aggressive superiority story.

SKF did not ignore this challenge, but seems not to have understood it. Seeing Zantac's simpler regimen from the regulatory filings, SKF moved to preempt this advantage by quickly changing Tagamet's regimen to just two capsules a day. However, the US Food and Drug Administration (FDA), the key worldwide pharmaceutical regulator, is conservative about an increase in total dosage of any drug, as an increased dose can mean increased side-effects. However, if a company requests simplifying its regimen while *lowering* total dosage, arguing that efficacy would not be significantly compromised, approval may come much faster. SKF went this route and changed Tagamet's regimen to 400 mg BD (totaling 800 mg, down from one gram) and reduced the regimen period to simply 4 weeks.

SKF was so successful in this preemptive move that soon after Zantac was introduced, Tagamet was just as easy to use as Zantac. In some countries, including the UK, the change was already in place before Zantac's launch. Some people viewed this as fairly embarrassing for Glaxo. But faces should have been red in SKF, not Glaxo. A business is an interactive set of actions and resources. A change in one element may affect others and the net output of the system. For this reason, when dynamically managing a business, it is critically important to stay focused on the whole value proposition and the priorities it dictates for the whole value delivery system.

Changing Tagamet's regimen to make it as convenient as Zantac's was important. But, as should have been obvious, staying at least as effective as Zantac in healing ulcers was far more important. Glaxo was already emphasizing the 80 percent healing rate and 50 percent higher total potency in Zantac's dosage. Physicians could deduce, without help, that despite the inconclusive clinicals, higher potency might be associated with a little more efficacy. Then SKF's sudden change made Zantac's potency 88 percent higher. Moreover, SKF was going to have to live with this move. Having argued that Tagamet was still effective at a lower dosage, SKF would have been hard pressed later to convince a skeptical FDA of an increase in dosage.

In addition, there was another context within which efficacy could be judged: maintenance therapy. Maintenance therapy should have been further cause for SKF to reconsider reducing dosage. It is painful and sometimes dangerous each time an ulcer recurs. Waiting for symptoms to administer therapy is, arguably, not optimal. Moreover, some patients are more likely than others to have recurrence, due to exacerbating factors such as intake of aspirin or certain diet and lifestyle factors. Therefore, it is reasonable to prescribe the drug indefinitely to some higher-risk patients as maintenance therapy. This effectively prevents most recurrence. Regulatory approval for maintenance therapy would be a separate process, including clinical trials that had not yet begun.

It seemed probable to the Zantac team that real differences in efficacy, due to greater acid suppression, might be easier to measure in the context of maintenance than it would in the acute (the initial 4-week) therapy. What if clinicals proved Zantac to be significantly more effective in preventing recurrence? A physician might well then reason that, despite inconclusive acute results, Zantac's higher efficacy in maintenance suggests a higher efficacy in acute treatment as well.

This scenario should have occurred to SKF. A way to preempt *this*, however, might have been to move toward a *higher* dose. Certainly, this would have taken longer to get FDA approval. Therefore, SKF would have lost the opportunity to preempt Glaxo on dosing regimen, but so what? Tagamet was not an unknown; it held 90 percent of the market and wasn't going to disappear overnight because of a dosing convenience disadvantage. Once SKF got approval for higher dosage, Tagamet never would have been seen as less efficacious than Zantac. At minimum, SKF should have kept dosage the same. It was a major blunder in the management of the VDS to damage efficacy just to beat Zantac to the punch on an experience of obviously lower priority.

Meanwhile, SKF actually made their safety problem worse. There was not much the company could have done about the fact that Tagamet had some side-effects and Zantac did not, but they only exacerbated the problem by making a lot of noise about it. They insisted to physicians that actually Tagamet was safe, as was evidenced by the large body of experience with it. Scintillating arguments such as 'Confident prescribing demands a solid basis' bombarded physicians. Endless journal ads touted the number of patients who had used Tagamet. All this drew more attention to an issue which could do SKF no good. Insisting on its safety could only raise physicians' awareness of Zantac's superiority and raise questions about SKF's willingness to admit a problem.

On top of these mistakes, SKF began reminding physicians that they could save the health-care system money by prescribing the lower-priced Tagamet. Given the lack of any other resulting experience that was superior for the physician, this price emphasis may have been seen as tacit admission that Tagamet was an inferior drug. In addition, with Glaxo rapidly creating a large sales force through licensing and partnering, SKF might have considered expanding its own through similar means, but remained confident in its SKF-only philosophy.

Against SKF's defense, Zantac's VDS quickly gained over 20 percent of the market.

Then Glaxo was faced with a decision between a conservative, evolutionary strategy and one with a much higher payoff and significantly higher risk, Glaxo could have chosen to enjoy safely its steady growth based on physicians' growing awareness of the safety issue. Or it could try to prove superior efficacy as well. The company could continue to invest in diverse markets, or it could bet heavily on the ulcer market, which was still dominated by a much larger player. It could remain comfortably UK-oriented and centralized, or it could rapidly globalize to address fully the worldwide ulcer market. Glaxo opted to go for broke, adjusting their strategy again to try to win outright.

Tagamet changes in value delivery system 1981–83 in response to Zantac

Value proposition versus Zantac	How resulting experiences were provided	How resulting experiences were communicated
Slightly less efficacy	Reduced dose 20 percent to 800 mg	Announced change; with price emphasis, may have implied lower efficacy
Moderately less safe	Side effects	Implied Tagamet really safer because of more experience – 'confident prescribing demands a solid basis.' Inadvertently exacerbated safety issue; price emphasis may have reinforced safety and lower efficacy
About equally convenient	Changed regimen: 400 BD, 4 weeks	Announced change
		For above, kept SKF-only sales
Lower price	Kept old pricing, now below Zantac	Began emphasizing low price

What Zantac first needed to deliver an unstoppably superior value proposition was better evidence that it provided at least equal, and probably slightly better, healing efficacy. Most physicians were holding onto Tagamet out of habit and loyalty, accepting SKF's best argument, which was, 'Why switch from a tried and true effective therapy?' Glaxo needed the opportunity to convince physicians that *nothing*, beyond price, justified continued preference for Tagamet over Zantac. Maintenance therapy was that opportunity, and Glaxo took it. The company sponsored two highly visible, large scale, multi-site, maintenance therapy clinical trials in the UK and US, which were overseen by Drs Gough and Silva, two of the world's leading gastro-enterologists. With such visibility, inferior results would be disastrous; even equality would be a major setback since it would lead physicians to conclude that Tagamet was just as effective after all.

Betting they would win, Glaxo took steps to invest more heavily in the ulcer market. The firm rapidly globalized, instituting an international board and decentralizing its organization. Country-defined business units were empowered to pursue growth aggressively. The firm refocused on GE and a few core areas, selling off distractions such as animal health, generics, and its distributor network.

Meanwhile, Glaxo pushed regimen convenience a further step, introducing a single nighttime 300 mg capsule. Confirming Glaxo's judgment, the Gough/Silva trials came in as decisive wins for Zantac. Gough and Silva both wrote papers declaring Zantac unequivocally superior in maintenance therapy efficacy. Finally, even with its higher price, Zantac could deliver a clearly superior value proposition. It grew to over a 40 percent share by the late 1980s. Now all that Glaxo had to do was push ahead full steam.

1983–86 Zantac improved value delivery system

Value Proposition	How resulting experiences were provided	How resulting experiences were communicated
As previous, except for resulting experiences versus Tagamet		
Superior healing: • Moderately better acute • Clearly better prevent recurrence	Ranitidine H2 Blocker; 88 percent more effective potency	Detailing, advertising, publicity for Gough/Silvis maintenance; clinicals plus potency argument, original clinicals; reduced emphasis on maintenance by late 1980s
Safer – as previous VDS	As previous VDS	Reminded GPs of side-effects
At least as convenient to use	Single night dose 300 mg capsule	Announced single-dose
Price: as previous	As previous	

However, in the late 1980s, a consensus began to form among Glaxo country marketing-departments: it was no longer necessary or productive to emphasize the efficacy and safety stories. Many believed then that communications should shift to convincing GPs that they could be confident in Glaxo and Zantac. The safety and maintenance efficacy stories had been told so often, this reasoning went, that physicians were bored and didn't want to keep being told the same thing over and over. Research purportedly showed that many physicians had rather cold inner feelings when they contemplated Glaxo, in contrast to warm ones when thinking of SKF. Rather than boring them further with the worn-out healing and safety stories, Zantac needed to convey its warm and nice feelings toward doctors. Journal advertising was developed to visualize soothing, emotionally warm environments (a Scottish lake, lined with pines, in one example), with exhortations to trust Glaxo and Zantac, now that it, like Tagamet, had been used by millions of patients.

It turned out, however, that the people *really* bored with the important resulting experiences were the people doing the communicating. Marketers, the sales force, and ad agencies found the same old story worn out, but how many physicians even knew this story yet? In pursuit of this answer, the company conducted research, which showed that typically more than half of GPs, even in 1988, did not know about Glaxo's claim of a superior safety experience compared to Tagamet, what that experience was, or the evidence for it. An even larger portion was not familiar with the maintenance efficacy findings. Moreover, countries typically were not pushing maintenance therapy very hard, apparently assuming neither market share nor market growth could increase much further.

Most Glaxo country organizations redoubled their efforts to communicate the efficacy and safety advantages and the rationale for maintenance. SKF meanwhile responded to Zantac's single dose capsule by introducing an 800 mg tablet. This was introduced as an amazing technical feat; ads dubbed it 'Gastrotechnology.' The journal ads continued touting the safety implied by Tagamet's '35 million patients.' And physicians were regularly reminded that Tagamet cost less. Ads compared Tagamet to Zantac as 'peas in a pod' (so buy the cheaper one); but increasingly, physicians stopped listening. Growing beyond the 40 percent share achieved in the late 1980s, Zantac achieved over 65 percent of the market, over $3 Billion, by the mid-1990s.

SKF was not cheated, tricked, or beaten by marketing gimmicks. The H2 blocker discovery merited the Nobel Prize and wealth, but it gave SKF no guarantee of sustained success. SKF should have been the one to search for a replacement to Tagamet. Cimetidine was wonderful, but 75% healing with some very irritating side effects for several hundred thousand patients in a cumbersome regimen should hardly have been cause for such complacency. Once faced with a severe threat like Zantac, SKF needed to look at its value delivery system as a whole, searching for improvements that would let it deliver the strongest possible proposition. If SKF had understood both its own VDS and Zantac's, it might have at least avoided creating a fatal vulnerability.

Glaxo was lucky. The company nearly let total victory slip away. Although Glaxo has not consistently applied the lessons of its own success, Zantac is a marvelous example of dynamically managing a value delivery system to maximize the opportunity for superiority.

Reinvent your business, but *not* in your image

A popular management belief that reinforces internally-driven behavior is that a business has a natural life-cycle and so will grow rapidly at first, then stagnate, decline, and finally die. Organizations are urged to manage these stages in the lifecycle. In a ridiculous case of self-fulfilling prophecy, these organizations often induce their own decline instead of rejuvenate a business. Like many strategy concepts born of analyzing historical microeconomic data, this theory confuses an observation of common behavior with an immutable law of the universe. It is rare, but not by any means impossible, to adapt a value delivery system to changing conditions and thereby sustain it over the long run. However, this outcome is unlikely for businesses managed with a constant expectation of imminent decline and death.

A corollary to the belief that businesses must naturally die is that differentiated ones must become commodities. Patents run out, the theory goes, and it becomes increasingly easy to get around them. Technology changes so fast that today's unique product is obsolete tomorrow. Furthermore, some products are inherently incapable of being differentiated. All this misleads managers to expect and inadvertently bring about the often-avoidable commoditization of their businesses.

Organizations often equate their businesses with products, which may well die or be matched by competitors. Imitating their own historical behavior, organizations become more competent at executing an increasingly irrelevant strategy. The belief in the life-cycle theory or the inevitability of commoditization reinforces these behaviors. Organizations would sustain profitable growth longer by realizing that a business is a VDS, not a technology or product or set of customers. They should look for opportunities to reinvent that VDS, based on freshly reexamining the customer's real experiences and alternatives.

The value delivery system: another name for the value chain? Hardly

A consensus in management theory has been that to maximize long-term success, a firm should manage its businesses as *integrated systems*. Any business is a *system* because its functions, resources, and processes interact with each other and thus affect the ultimate outcome. Obviously, these individual elements should not pursue disparate, inconsistent agendas. Unfortunately, they frequently do, which in turn sub-optimizes the performance of the system. But *how* should this system be integrated? The major schools of management thought propose various answers. All are variants on the product-supply system, discussed at the beginning of Chapter Seven, which sees a business as developing, producing and marketing a product.

McKinsey & Company, led by Fred Gluck among others, first pioneered the formalization of this framework in the late 1970s, calling it the 'Business System.' In 1985 Michael Porter published his framework, the 'Value Chain,' in his book *Competitive Advantage*. This recasting of McKinsey's business system further popularized the basic product-supply framework and its underlying logic. Porter introduced it as a way to describe a firm's business unit.

> *'Every firm is a collection of activities that are performed to design, produce, market, deliver, and support its product. All these activities can be represented using a value chain.'*[3]

Porter wanted to orient the business system framework more specifically around his generic strategies (cost and differentiation) and insisted on a much more detailed specification of the business functions. However, the value chain still treats a business as a system of functions/activities that develop, produce, and market a product.

While it is called a 'value' chain, reflecting Porter's notion that each activity must create value for customers through low cost or differentiation, it in no way specifies a value proposition that intended customers will obtain. Nor are the traditional functions oriented to provide explicitly or communicate such customer experiences. It still focuses on developing, making, and selling products, and not on delivering a value proposition.

In addition, the value chain or business system are commonly used to describe a business unit or even a whole company, regardless of how many distinct value propositions that organization may, in effect, deliver. Different value propositions, however, require different VDSs. To think that one VDS could deliver multiple propositions is a misunderstanding of the VDS framework. Such interpretation only reinforces the tendency to focus much more attention on supplying product and the resources by which to do so, rather than on real strategy – delivering a profitable value proposition.

The value delivery system, of course, was originally proposed by myself as a radical *replacement* for the business system. Rather than a product-centric framework, a develop/produce/market system, it proposes a value-proposition-centric 'value delivery system.' The value chain maintains a view of a business in terms of its functions for developing, producing, and marketing the product.

Therefore, to use the value delivery framework is not to give some new name to the same old product-supply functions and actions, nor to the superficially similar value chain framework that focuses on those old functions. To use the VDS is to rethink and redefine what a business does in terms of profitable value delivery. All the business functions must be understood and managed differently within the framework of the value delivery system. Those functions must serve that VDS, as providing- and/or communicating-vehicles. Instead, the key functions of most businesses are unconsciously operated in a non-integrated fashion, each function taking on a life of its own.

DPV thus does not reject but rather embraces this great central project of most mainstream management theory – to integrate strategically the functions of a business. The value delivery framework, however, shifts the focus of integration away from the product and from comparisons to competitors' product-supply systems, beyond the managerial looking glass and into the reality of potential customers' experiences. The value delivery system is a framework based on this intuitively obvious but commonly overlooked and disregarded perspective.

However, to apply the value delivery system framework in the real world, it is necessary to confront another question: 'Which intended customer?' In many markets, customers have customers, and sometimes they in turn have customers. Organizations have suppliers; other entities, such as regulators or suppliers of complementary products and services, also play a role. How can an organization formulate the value delivery system for a business with customers at all these different levels? It is time to understand who the *real* customer is and the accompanying implications for designing a winning value delivery system.

Notes

1   This section draws on experiences working with and interviewing Glaxo executives in the late 1980s.
2   The tightly regulated process of pharmaceutical sales calls.
3   Porter, *Competitive Advantage, op. cit.*, p. 36.

And Now ... Will the *Real* Customer Please Stand Up? The Value Delivery Chain

The value delivery system is a framework by which to define and manage the business relationship between an organization and customers. For simplicity, however, the framework has been treated thus far as if the only two players in that relationship were the organization and the customer. Of course, numerous entities are often involved, such as other business organizations, non-commercial organizations, individuals, and consumers. An organization may buy products from suppliers, then sell its own product to an immediate customer, who may sell it as is or incorporated into a larger product, to another customer. Each entity in this chain delivers one or more value propositions to customers further down the chain, until we reach consumers. A business may deliver value to customers at more than one level in the chain. To succeed, a business must decide where in the chain to deliver what value propositions and how to do so given the interacting and sometimes conflicting motivations of the various entities in that chain. This interconnected relationship among entities delivering value is best understood as a *value delivery chain*. In developing this concept, I have been greatly helped and influenced by the work of French consultant and author Mr Camille Vert, creator of the 'Industrial Chain Method.'

An organization should ask, 'Where in the value delivery chain are the greatest potential opportunities to deliver value profitably? Are there customers further out on the chain who could derive greater value from a different value proposition? What would the winning value delivery system therefore be? What actions and resources of the various entities, *including* our own organization, would have to be used to deliver it?

Organizations often assume too great an importance for the most immediate customers, thus failing to ensure that customers farther removed, who may be more crucial to the organization's long-term profitable growth, get the right value proposition. They sometimes focus too exclusively on the more distant customer, without properly understanding the intermediary customers. Rather than make a prioritized, disciplined choice within the chain, the customer-compelled instinct assumes that customers at all these levels should be totally satisfied.

Moreover, when organizations deliver value to customers at more than one level in the chain, they also fail to integrate and misunderstand how to prioritize these interrelated value propositions. Furthermore, when a customer entity is a business, organizations focus too much on influencing the purchasing function within it. Their efforts thus misdirected, they fail to understand and focus on delivering a winning value proposition to the customer's whole enterprise. In addition, the popular methods of 'value chain' and 'supply chain' analysis tend to look too narrowly at the chain. Value chain analysis seeks to find a level in the chain where the most profit is generated today, so the organization can participate there, instead of looking for the level where the biggest opportunity exists to increase value delivered profitably. Supply chain analysis focuses so hard on supply costs that it gives inadequate attention to the more strategically important issues of delivering more valuable resulting experiences.

To avoid these confusing errors, an organization designing a business must start by recognizing the value delivery chain and determining the most important level of customer entity in it, which is the level where the greatest value delivery potential exists. Customers at several levels may be crucial to the business's design and success, but the most important value proposition must be delivered to the most important level of customers. Recognizing this level in the chain is not always an obvious task, however. Doing so requires a thorough understanding of the value delivery chain structure.

Structure of a value delivery chain

Every business operates in a value delivery chain, but a chain may be simple or complex. To design a business, an organization must have a clear view of the structure of that chain. The relevant entities and how they must each obtain and deliver value must be identified. And the organization must determine the most important level of customers.

Different levels of customers; each delivers value to the next

In any value delivery chain, to the left of an organization may be suppliers, to the right an immediate customer, then their immediate customer, and so on. At the end of the chain resides some last relevant customer; this is the last level in the chain that is important for an organization to understand. In reality, levels may extend indefinitely but are only relevant if they could influence an organization's VDS. For example, British Airways' immediate customer is often an individual who belongs to some business, but that business and *its* customer are not very relevant to BA. However, industrial gases supplier Air Products must understand not only an immediate customer, such as medical equipment-maker Siemens, whose equipment uses these gases, but also Siemens' customer, a hospital, using Siemens equipment. This hospital is probably at the last relevant level in that chain. Entities at each level deliver value to customers at the next level. Each entity in a chain, except consumers, is thus a value delivery system.

At each level there may be many other comparable entities, which are often in competition.

In addition to these levels, there are often entities of importance to an organization that do not buy or sell that organization's product. They are not in line with the main levels in the chain, but they may be crucially important. Such *off-line entities* include regulators, legislators, governmental services, various politicians, the local community near a plant, standard-setting bodies, various kinds of thought-leaders, suppliers of non-competing products to entities in the chain, consultants, or third-party payers such as insurance companies. Usually these off-line entities are also VDSs in their own right and may be very important to understand.

Glaxo needed gastroenterologists to endorse the efficacy of Zantac and thus influence the GP physicians who actually prescribe the vast majority of antiulcerant. Similarly, Glaxo needed approval of the US FDA and other regulators in order to sell and make claims for Zantac.

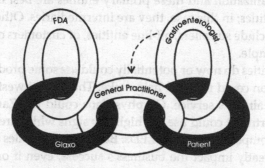

The relevant chain can be much longer and more complex than is often assumed. For example, one organization produces electronic components such as LEDs (light emitting diodes) that, as part of an electronic sign, can be remotely controlled to give motorists highway traffic flow information. A specialized firm designs, makes, and sells these signs to, for example, a state highway department. The state highway department is part of a state government whose concern, in principle, is the wellbeing of taxpayers and voters. The LED maker's immediate customer is clearly the sign maker. The sign maker's customer is the highway department, which delivers a value proposition to the state's taxpayers, especially highway-using motorists. The LED maker will certainly not sell LEDs to motorists, the state government, or the highway department. However, arguably all the levels in this chain are relevant for the LED maker to understand.

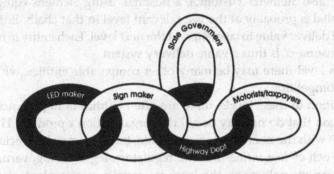

Recognizing primary and supporting entities

For each business, the customer entities at some level in the chain will be the most essential for the organization to understand. The proposition delivered to these customers will determine the business's success, even if the organization is only indirectly involved in its delivery and even if other customers in the same chain are more immediate customers. These most essential customers are *primary entities*. The more immediate customers between the organization and these primary entities are best understood as supporting entities; in this case, they are intermediaries. Other supporting entities may include suppliers, off-line entities, or customers of the primary entity, for example.

Primary entities do now or potentially could *use* some product or service the organization could make or help make. Thus, Southwest's passengers could use the airline's service. GP physicians could use Zantac. And the highway department could use the highway signs which are made in part by using the component maker's LEDs. But primary entities also make decisions that greatly impact the business's success, even if only indirectly. Their decisions may impact intermediary entities between them and the organization and thereby determine the organization's revenues. If the organization also can significantly affect the value proposition that these primary entities ultimately obtain, then it is crucial to the organization's success to *choose* and deliberately deliver that proposition.

Entities (organizations or individuals) which are at the most distant level in the chain where these criteria are still met should be considered the primary entity. For, it is the choice of value proposition to these customers that must shape the design of the business.

Clearly, the most immediate customer can also be a primary entity, but this is often not the case. Travel agents and corporate travel departments affect SWA's business, but the VDS must be focused on the traveler.

On the other hand, the primary entity is not necessarily the customer at the last level of the chain. Nor is it necessarily what is usually meant by 'end-user.' The patient was certainly important to the Zantac business and was the end-user, but was probably not the primary entity. Similarly, the motorist is the end-user of the highway signs that use LEDs, but the highway department is probably the last level where decisions will affect the LED maker's success. So the highway department is the primary entity.

Primary entities are furthest from the organization where potentially:

1 they use product the organization makes or contributes to making
2 the organization's profit is significantly impacted by decisions they make
3 the organization could affect the value proposition delivered to them, even if only indirectly through others in the chain.

Whenever the primary entity is separated from an organization by one or more levels in the chain, the levels in between can be understood as intermediaries. A channel of distribution is usually an intermediary between a manufacturer and its primary entity. However, intermediary entities are not *unimportant*. The maker of high-end hi-fi sound equipment typically needs a retailer to play a very involved role in educating the primary entity, helping custom design a system for that user, and perhaps installing and servicing that system.

Resisting distraction, focusing on primary entities

Whether internally-driven or customer-compelled, most organizations like to stay close to home and focus on the issue of supplying their product. Gazing into the looking glass, they often have trouble recognizing, in effect, how far away their primary entity actually is.

What's the consumer got to do with it?

Management theory has traditionally built walls between the principles that supposedly govern consumer versus industrial businesses. Not only do the principles of *DPV* apply fully to both, but often an apparently industrial business is in fact at the same time a consumer business. Often, consumers are the real but unrecognized primary entities at the end of a chain populated with industrial intermediaries.

When a chain is long and complex, with entities between an organization and the consumer playing important roles, the inability to see the key significance of the consumer is not surprising. Sometimes this inability reflects not the chain's subtlety but simply an organization's greater comfort with immediate customers. It's certainly easier to deal only with immediate customers, which are frequently more like the organization, itself. That is, these customers understand the organization's products, technologies, and processes. They, unlike the consumer, talk the organization's lingo. Consumers, by contrast, can even seem a bit exotic from the insulated perspective of an industrial-business organization.

The construction-materials industry is a good example of such a situation. The construction-materials industry supplies product to wholesalers who supply contractors who build houses they sell to homeowners. The industry usually focuses on the demands of builders, often as conveyed by the wholesaler, rather than on understanding homeowners. Because the homeowner doesn't directly buy any materials and doesn't know anything about them, the attitude goes, why waste time on them? Weyerhaeuser has good reason to.

Weyerhaeuser makes stress-tested beams for trusses in homes. These stress-tested beams cost more, but the manufacturer has developed a technology to test the strength of the beams so that this product is certifiably less likely to fail in critical applications. Such reliability is especially important in roofing. Builders can appreciate this reliability, whereas few home buyers would understand the first thing about stress testing or trusses. So, the industry treats the builder as the customer. However, the homeowner is clearly the primary entity. Many builders resist paying more for this product, since their customer, the home buyer, does not demand it. For Weyerhaeuser to justify its premium price, homeowners must be made aware of the resulting experience to them in the long-term cost of maintaining the home.

Even without the difficulties that industrial, operationally, or technology focused organizations have in thinking about consumers, there are plenty of opportunities to stay focused on the nearest possible customer rather than the real primary entity. Consider a plastics maker who supplies a molder who makes a console for a television manufacturer. The plastics maker may feel compelled to focus on the immediate customer, the molder. The molder has very good relationships with several key TV makers and can pick and choose among plastics suppliers. As long as the plastic maker keeps the molder happy, it can sell plenty of plastic. The TV maker knows, without any doubt, that their consumer prefers the appearance of the TV when it has been painted. The TV maker therefore paints the console after receiving it from the molder in an off-white, paintable condition. Several plastic makers compete for the ability to supply the molder. The molder is happy with this situation.

However, the TV maker incurs cost and manufacturing time to paint the consoles. The company manages worker safety, fire hazard, and other complicating issues as part of this process. The plastic maker could invent and produce a pigmented plastic that, if the molder changed its process, could give the molder the opportunity to present the TV maker with a pre-colored console that needs no painting. The plastic and the molding process would be more expensive for the molder; the console would cost the TV maker more. The molder may not have great incentive to change and may even face some risk in doing so. But the TV maker might get a substantially improved resulting experience from pre-colored consoles that is worth more than the price premium. Here the plastic maker's primary entity arguably is not the consumer but quite likely is not the molder, either. Again, of course, the plastic maker must also deliver an appropriate value proposition to the molder. But the primary entity is the TV maker.

Delivering a winning value proposition to the primary entity may not please the whole chain

A complicating factor in understanding the value delivery chain is the implicit assumption that an organization's task is to please the entities at *all* levels in the chain. Sometimes it is unavoidable, when delivering the most important value proposition in a chain, to deliver an *inferior* value proposition to entities at one or more other levels in that same chain. In fact, deliberately choosing to do so can be nothing short of strategically brilliant.

Fidelity Investments, which revolutionized individual investing in the 1980s, provides another example of rethinking the value delivery chain. Fidelity had sold mutual funds since its inception in 1946. Like other investment banks, Fidelity sold these funds directly to stock brokers who in turn sold them, along with other investments, to the broker's clients. The broker was the primary entity for an investment bank selling its mutual fund. If brokers liked the product, they used their retail relationship with investors to sell it to them. Then, in the 1970s, a different kind of young affluent investor began to emerge, and Fidelity recognized a new opportunity.

This young investor's parents had always used a stockbroker to make investments. However, many of these young urban professionals, just then earning the name Yuppies, had a different outlook. They were making a good living and were interested in making some investments. They wanted to retire early with a fat nest egg and fancied the idea of mentioning their smart investments to their friends. However, they worked long hours, did not want to spend too much time on investing, and only had the time free in evenings or on weekends. This customer would value efficient, accurate answers to their investment questions but would not value long conversations in the middle of working hours.

Yet, stockbrokers traditionally worked by chatting at length with the client about various individual stocks, and thus building the relationship. Brokers had not traditionally been available to clients outside of the nine-to-five, Monday through Friday timeframe. And brokers charged a hefty commission, or load, typically as much as eight percent.

Fidelity realized that this customer, not the broker, should be understood as the primary entity. Fidelity began offering mutual funds directly to the investor, bypassing the broker, at very low or no load pricing. They hired college educated people to man a toll-free service line, through which investors could get intelligent answers to questions during the hours they wanted; by 1986, this was a 24-hour service. Fidelity advertised directly to the investor, emphasizing the stellar performance of its top fund manager, the now legendary Peter Lynch, its wide portfolio of over 100 funds, and its efficient and convenient customer service. None of this met the expectations of the former 'customer,' the stockbrokers, and it failed utterly to delight them. However, Fidelity had placed themselves to ride the opportunity created by the bull market of the 1980s. The company grew from $5 billion in assets under management in 1977 to over $100 billion by 1989.

***

Once an organization realizes who the real primary entity should be, it must ensure that those primary entities are delivered the right value proposition. This is the primary value proposition, which is delivered by the primary value delivery system. This VDS includes actions by the organization but may also include those of intermediaries and others in the chain. To motivate these other entities to participate in this larger VDS, an organization must also deliver supporting value propositions to these other entities. Thus, to make money in a value delivery chain means designing both primary and supporting VDSs.

Chapter Eleven

Primary and Supporting VDSs: Control the Chain Reaction

Any organization wanting to implement a business successfully needs to understand *all* the entities in the relevant value delivery chain for that business. Designating one level in the chain as primary does not mean dismissing the other levels. Those entities that most crucially must experience the right value proposition in order for the organization to succeed reside at the primary level. To deliver this *primary* value proposition to these entities, an organization frequently needs other entities to cooperate. Intermediaries, suppliers or off-line entities often must take actions that, in conjunction with the organization's actions, result in the delivery of the right value proposition. Right from the organization's perspective, that is.

For the plastics maker supplying the molder (discussed in Chapter Ten), the winning value proposition must be delivered to the TV makers. Some molder must use the organization's plastic, and then a TV maker must use that mold. The organization thus must design a comprehensive strategy to win the cooperation and coordinated action of other entities in the chain. The plastics company must in effect implement a value delivery system that includes actions by molders and by the TV makers. This VDS delivers the winning value proposition to the TV maker, the primary entity in this chain. This VDS is thus a *primary* value delivery system. However, that primary VDS is larger than any VDS that the plastics-maker's organization literally owns or even totally controls because of the actions required on the part of other entities in the chain.

Making a primary VDS successful means motivating those other entities to play the role required by the primary VDS. Therefore, the plastics company must deliver separate, superior, *supporting* value propositions to molders. *Supporting* value delivery systems are needed. These *supporting* value propositions are meant to motivate these entities to play the roles required to help deliver the plastics company's primary value proposition to the TV maker.

In this regard, not only intermediaries but also off-line entities and suppliers deserve attention. Off-line entities do not buy or sell products that directly involve the organization, but may have a major impact on an organization's success. Frequently, off-line entities must be understood as part of the primary VDS and thus may require a supporting VDS focused on them. Similarly, an organization often should conceptually include the role of suppliers in designing and managing its primary VDS.

This chapter will develop these complementary concepts of primary and supporting VDSs, which together constitute a more complete framework for defining and managing a business. The possible composition of a primary VDS will be elaborated upon, including how the supporting VDSs must be understood as integral *parts* of the primary VDS.

Design the *primary* value delivery system

The primary value delivery system consists of the primary value proposition and all actions by the organization *and others* in the chain required to deliver it to the primary entity. When other entities in a chain must take actions and use resources in order that an organization's value proposition be delivered, the organization must design the primary VDS to *include* these actions and resources. Thinking this way requires remembering that an organization's business should not be equated with the organization itself or its products, but rather with the VDS that organization needs to implement. A business is not the things an organization owns; it is the delivery of a value proposition.

Chickens rethink their value delivery chain: a primary VDS

Let's consider a relatively simple example of transforming a business by rethinking the primary entity and implementing a new primary value delivery system. In the 1970s, Frank Perdue Chicken Farms transformed the chicken business in the Northeastern US. The story has been told before, with different interpretations, but is a clear example of reinventing a business by understanding the value delivery chain.

Perdue Farms, like other chicken farms and many agricultural businesses, had long been operated as a commodity. Frank Perdue was descended from chicken farmers and knew the industry well. But in the late 1960s, he determined to rethink his business. Perdue Farms had about $65 million revenues and thin, unreliable margins. Up to that point, a chicken farm made money as a function of its costs, the market commodity price for chickens, and to some extent the farm's relationships with distributors and retailers.

For a chicken farm, *the* customer was clearly the distributor or large retailer, who generally paid a market price to any farm, as long as the farm's chickens had passed the US Department of Agriculture's (USDA) quality inspection. With low enough costs, a farm could come under the market price and make a modest margin; with excess capacity in the region, a farm would just scrape by, often taking a loss.

Perdue's intuition suggested that it might be possible to have a bit more fun than this. He knew that consumers, not retailers and wholesalers, were the ones who finally bought, cooked, and ate chickens. He wondered why it wouldn't be possible to run a chicken farm as something more like a consumer goods business. What if he could determine what chicken consumers would most value about a chicken dinner? Would this likely include more than the USDA quality stamp? If so, could Perdue Farms imagine a chicken that would support such a dinner? What would the Farms have to do and what else would have to happen, beyond the Farms' direct control, to bring such a chicken into existence? What else, beyond the attributes of this imagined chicken, would have to happen to bring about that dinner? Who would have to make these things happen? What would it take to let the consumer know about this possible dinner? Could Perdue's modest commodity agricultural company make all this happen?

Perdue learned that some chicken farms in New England had recently achieved a somewhat higher price for chickens with a more consistently yellow skin color from some specialized outlets, such as butcher shops. Simple interviewing of chicken consumers in the Northeast revealed that a significant portion of them go out of their way to find butcher shops and other specialty outlets that have chickens with a rich, golden yellow skin tone. Asking these consumers to recount stories of a good chicken dinner, Perdue found that these consumers treasured a tender taste, preferred a golden color, and associated that golden color with tender taste.

Moreover, many of these consumers indicated that they could *not* count on getting the chicken dinner for which they yearned from the grocery store. Even when they did find a yellow chicken in the grocery store, these chickens would not always retain their rich golden color after the cooking process. Sometimes they became more of an off-white than a golden yellow. Correspondingly, the taste was not consistently tender but rather tough. These consumers certainly wanted to see the USDA stamp of quality assurance; no stamp, no sale. But they wanted more.

Perdue concluded that these consumers would go out of their way to get the experiences of cooking and eating a consistently tender tasting, golden yellow chicken dinner. He also concluded that a large number of consumers, a far larger number than the number of those already pursuing such chicken dinners, would respond to the same opportunity if they wouldn't *have* to go out of their way. Consumers talked as if they would pay a significant premium, as much as 25-30 percent, to achieve these other resulting experiences. Talk is cheap, but Perdue Farms decided to bet on the existence of a large group of consumers who would significantly value this improved chicken dinner experience.

Perdue Farms proceeded to reinvent every aspect of the chicken business, thinking forwards from the starting point of a tender tasting, golden colored chicken dinner with USDA-approved quality, offered at a price premium. The firm reexamined every element in the process of getting a chicken dinner onto a consumer's table from the perspective of achieving a tender taste and the appearance to match. As a result, scores of procedural steps in the operation of the farm were changed.

Perdue also determined that not freezing the chicken was crucial. This went against the grain of the industry, which had long before significantly cut distribution cost without hurting quality (as defined by the USDA inspection process) by distributing chickens frozen. Freezing allowed much more efficient transport to the wholesaler and/or retailer. Rail and truck were used to ship large quantities to the retailer, who could then efficiently distribute the frozen chicken to stores. Distributing *fresh* chickens would surely be a backward step in achieving cost leadership and a backward step in technology. Why, chicken farmers hadn't delivered fresh chickens in thirty years, when freezing technology hadn't yet been developed! But Perdue thought differently. The company put in place vans that would deliver directly to stores overnight, thus increasing cost and placing Perdue somewhere in the 1940s, technologically speaking. This generated considerable chuckling throughout the industry.

But what about those customers? The commodity mentality would quickly lead others in the industry to conclude that consumers have no intelligent opinion on a technical issue like distribution and that instead the demands of the wholesalers and retailers are the important consideration. Not Perdue. Instead, Perdue understood that its primary value delivery system had to focus on the consumer and that the actions of retailers must be put into that context. However, Perdue understood clearly that the retail entities were beyond Perdue's direct control.

So Perdue began by approaching upscale butcher shops that were already more interested than the chains in selling a truly higher class of chicken. This approach allowed Perdue to start building a reputation for superiority in chickens, a reputation which was enhanced by the limited availability, i.e. only at the finest butchers. Later, armed with this reputation, he would approach the supermarkets from a position of established demand.

Finally, he also realized he had to speak directly to consumers, the primary entities in this strategy. He therefore took the then bizarre step of hiring an ad agency to develop advertising for Perdue Chickens. The rest of the industry saw television advertising for chickens as perhaps the most

Initial Perdue Chickens primary VDS to consumers

Value proposition	How resulting experiences were provided	How resulting experiences were communicated
• Intended primary entity: chicken loving consumers in NE US • What Perdue wants them to do: buy/prefer Perdue to others		
Resulting experiences: A more consistently tender tasting chicken dinner	• Hybrid chicken developed for genetically more tender taste • Special procedures developed to enhance tender taste: hatching, classical music in living quarters; temperature/humidity controls, etc. • Diet designed and tested to enhance tenderness • Special processing procedures, including no freezing • Distribution by van overnight to allow fresh, not frozen, chickens • Retailed only by up-scale butcher shops prepared to handle fresh, not frozen	• Label on chickens saying 'Frank Perdue' and 'Fresh, not frozen' • Golden color connoting tenderness • Butchers tell consumer Perdue chickens are the most tender; up-scale outlets imply same • Diet story: fresh corn, marigold petals, Norwegian herring, cookie meal, fresh well water, etc. etc. ('a chicken is what it eats') • Advertising, various media, tells how Perdue chickens are raised, fed, distributed to be more tender tasting • Perdue, spokesman, tells many (strange) things Perdue Farms do (others don't) to make their chickens more tender • Selling line: 'It takes a tough man to make a tender chicken'
A more consistently pleasing appearance: golden colored skin	• Diet designed with extra xanthophyl content	• Same diet story as above, emphasizing result is yellow skin
Safe, equal to competing chickens	Followed USDA regulations	• USDA stamp of approved quality
Price: about 20–30 percent higher		

amusing of Perdue's eccentric ideas. Even the ad agency found the assignment a bit exotic. Perdue, without the help of sophisticated marketing professionals, pushed the agency to develop advertising that told consumers about the unusual things Perdue Farms was doing to raise chickens. Perdue believed this would give consumers a credible basis from which to understand why Perdue chickens were more tender than others.

The agency took to their assignment with increasing interest. The head creative partner in the agency spent considerable time following Perdue and other managers about the Farms and was rather awed by their tough insistence on getting every detail just right. But the agency was befuddled. How could they bring this story to life on TV? Then one day, he listened to Perdue go on about how tough he and his management were in their approach to chickens. As Perdue spoke, it dawned on him that Perdue was not just an unusual chicken farmer; he actually looked ever so slightly *like* a chicken, as well.

Thus was born the first CEO-spokesman ad campaign, featuring Perdue explaining how Perdue Farms feed their chickens 'fresh corn, Norwegian herring, cookie meal for dessert, nothing but fresh well water ... unlike the diet of most chickens.' Perdue explained how his chickens were only distributed fresh, not frozen, to keep them tender. Ads showed Perdue rejecting a chicken for not being yellow enough. Rounding out the campaign was the pithy line 'It takes a tough man to make a tender chicken.' Consumers were amused and convinced, at least enough to give Perdue chickens a try. A fast growing number found that, sure enough, these chickens were more consistently tender tasting and golden colored.

After establishing a good reputation and proving that his value proposition could work, Perdue approached the supermarkets. They did not want to handle fresh chickens, especially those labeled with Perdue's name and distributed directly to their stores. However, Perdue Farms argued that a supermarket would clearly make more money carrying Perdue birds than not because they had a proven demand and commanded a premium price. There was enough margin for the supermarket to cover their higher handling costs and still make a good return on an item that would help draw consumers to the store. Furthermore, the supermarket risked losing customers and chicken revenues by not carrying Perdue, as they did with any strong brand. Perdue therefore rolled out a second phase with supermarkets as the chief retail channel.

Second phase Perdue Chickens primary VDS to consumers

Value proposition	How resulting experiences were provided	How resulting experiences were communicated
Same as earlier		
Resulting experiences: Same as initial	Same, but now in supermarkets: • Accepted by supermarkets, van direct to store, versus through warehouse • Special handling by retailers as fresh, not frozen	Same, but now: • advertising emphasizes availability in supermarkets • supermarkets agree to present the product under Perdue's label
Same as initial	Same as initial	Same as initial
Price: about 10–15 percent higher		

A *supporting* VDS reflects the primary VDS

Winning the cooperation of supermarkets was crucial to Perdue's success. To get them to play the required role, Perdue designed and implemented a supporting VDS. This included a value proposition that asked the supermarkets to go along with these actions and offered two superior experiences in return. Supermarkets would attract more consumers to the store and generate higher average chicken revenue. The store would attract more consumers because Perdue's chickens were becoming well known and preferred by consumers who would therefore prefer a grocery store that carried them. Chicken revenues would be higher because stores could charge a premium for these chickens. On the other hand, some retailer costs would be higher, such as handling fresh rather than frozen chickens. Also, Perdue's chickens would not strengthen the store's own brand name, and the price the store would pay to Perdue was above that demanded by competing chicken farms. But in the end, the value of the superior experiences outweighed these inferior ones.

To *provide* the two superior experiences to the supermarket, Perdue had to supply the stores with the right chickens and ensure consumers would look for them. Perdue chickens would be the right chickens — more consistently tender tasting and golden yellow — via all the providing-vehicles defined in the primary VDS. Of these vehicles, retailers had to participate and cooperate in the crucial area of presenting the chickens fresh to the consumer. This meant they had to accept store-direct, fresh distribution and then present the chickens as fresh in the store. To ensure consumers would look for these chickens, Perdue used its advertising campaign, the Perdue reputation built-up earlier in butcher shops, and the Perdue label. Again, the supermarkets had to cooperate in this last action, by acquiescing to use Perdue's label rather than their own. Note that, in context of this supporting VDS, these latter actions and resources *communicated* the consumer experiences, but were also vehicles by which to *provide* the retailer's superior experiences.

Perdue Chickens: supporting VDS to supermarkets

Value proposition	How resulting experiences were provided to supermarkets	How resulting experiences were communicated to supermarkets
Supporting customer: supermarkets • What Perdue wants them to do: buy Perdue chickens, fresh, store-direct, Perdue label, 10% premium		
Resulting experiences: Superior: Attract more consumers and increase chicken revenues with higher consumer price, because consumers will prefer and look for Perdue chickens	• Perdue/store provide more tender taste, golden color [see primary VDS] so consumer prefers Perdue • Perdue/store communicate VP [see advertising, label, upscale stores in primary VDS] so consumer looks for Perdue	Sales force demonstrates that: • consumer wants primary VP • Perdue and store can deliver it • consumer preference will provide the promised resulting experiences to the store
Inferior: handling cost, no store brand identification	• Fresh distribution • Perdue labeled	Sales force shows that superior experiences outweigh these
Price: about 10–15 percent higher		

To *communicate* these same superior experiences to the supermarkets, Perdue had to convince them of several things. First, he had to convince them that consumers would really value the experiences in Perdue's primary value proposition. Next, Perdue had to convince them that Perdue's chickens, sold with the supermarket's help in the manner Perdue proposed, would in fact provide these experiences to the consumer. And they had to be convinced that Perdue's value proposition to the consumer, again communicated with the retailer's help, would be communicated well enough so that consumers would indeed be hunting for these particular chickens. Perdue also had to convince the supermarket that the value of the superior traffic and revenue experiences outweighed the inferior experiences. Perdue's initial success in upscale butcher outlets and the demonstrated willingness to invest in this radically new chicken strategy helped convince supermarkets to buy into Perdue's value proposition throughout the Northeast.

By the mid-1970s, Perdue Farms had grown to a dominant position in the northeastern consumer chicken market with over $600 Million revenues and with much higher margins than those experienced in the sixties. Today Perdue has over a $2 Billion business and continues to be very profitable. It is sometimes argued that Perdue transformed the chicken industry simply by making chickens of higher quality. Another popular interpretation is that he 'changed the strategy gameboard' by introducing branding and the discontinuity of TV advertising, thus differentiating his farm from others. Both perspectives misunderstand that Perdue, in effect, redefined the primary entity, understood them and the intermediaries well, and accordingly implemented a superior primary and supporting VDS.

Perdue Farms succeeded because of a winning value delivery system. The company identified the right primary entity, the consumer, chose a winning value proposition to that primary entity, and decided how to provide and communicate each resulting experience in that proposition. Perdue also realized it needed the supermarket chains to play a major role in this primary VDS, a role that those supermarkets would never have requested or even accepted, initially. So to win the cooperation of this vitally important intermediary in the value delivery chain, Perdue designed a superior value delivery system for the supermarkets.

A hierarchical relationship: supporting and primary VDSs

A primary VDS determines its supporting VDSs

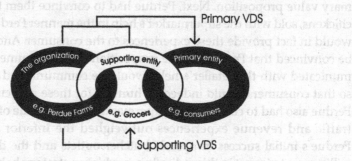

A supporting VDS is designed to cause the supporting entity to act as indicated by the primary VDS.

A supporting VDS is not independent. Its priorities are determined by the primary VDS, while reflecting what is possible to cause in the supporting entity.

Primary VDS (using Perdue example)

Value proposition	How resulting experiences will be provided by Perdue and by grocer	How resulting experiences will be communicated by Perdue and by grocer
Resulting experience: e.g. more tender taste	What Perdue must do to help cause this experience (products, services, assets, processes to be deployed); _ e.g. hybrids; not frozen What one other entity in chain, grocers, must do to help provide resulting experience: A: Accept store-direct B: Sell fresh, not frozen	What Perdue must do to help communicate this experience: e.g. label, advertising What grocer must do to help communicate this resulting experience: C: Accept P. label D: Premium price
Price to primary entity		
Revenues to Perdue (through grocer)	Costs to Perdue of making above happen, including costs of supporting VDS to grocer	

Supporting VDS to one other entity in the chain, e.g. grocer		
Value proposition	How resulting experiences will be provided by Perdue to grocer	How resulting experiences will be communicated by Perdue to grocer
Timeframe: Immediate Supporting entity: grocer What we want grocer to do (A, B' and (C, D')(from primary VDS) Grocer's alternative: no change		
Resulting experience: Attract more consumers by doing what Perdue asks (A, B, C and D)	What Perdue must do to help bring about this experience to grocer (products, services, assets, processes that must be deployed)	What Perdue must do (message; vehicles) to communicate experience to grocer
Price to grocer		
Revenues to Perdue (part of primary VDS)	Costs of making above happen (part of costs in primary VDS above)	

Supporting VDSs are not *businesses*. Only the primary VDS, which includes the supporting VDSs, is a business. Supporting VDSs therefore should not be considered at all independent from the primary VDS, but rather as integral parts of it. Organizations rarely have this perspective. Rather, they frequently treat each customer relationship in the chain as if that relationship were a separate business. Thus, often a Sales Force can be found delivering some value proposition to an immediate customer entity which is quite independent of the proposition that marketing or R&D may be trying to deliver to a customer entity further out on the chain.

These two *de facto* value propositions may be in conflict. That is, the value proposition that sales tries to deliver to the immediate customer may undermine the one marketing tries to deliver, which in turn undermines sales' *de facto* proposition. Only one level in the chain is primary: the level where the primary entity is found. Once this level is determined, the conflicting functions must be managed to deliver jointly the appropriate primary VDS and corresponding supporting VDS. There must not be ambiguity as to which of these VDSs is primary. Typically, though, no such discussion occurs and both functions continue to undermine one another. When things go sour in the market place, guess who each function blames?

Recognizing the importance and appropriate roles of off-line entities and suppliers

Off-line entities may also require a supporting VDS. For example, Glaxo (see Chapter 9) successfully delivered a supporting value proposition to several influential gastroenterologists (GEs). Glaxo wanted these opinion leaders to study Zantac carefully and justifiably conclude that Zantac was more effective than Tagamet in long-term maintenance therapy. The opinion of the GEs was an important vehicle in communicating Zantac's primary value proposition to the GP physician. The GEs got the resulting experience of being able to conduct important, well designed clinical studies of importance to their specialty while enhancing their reputations. All of this came with no ethical compromise (i.e. they weren't paid to draw or support any conclusion and were free to conclude that Zantac was inferior). To provide this proposition to the GEs, Glaxo made available funding and other support with no strings attached. To communicate it to the GEs, Glaxo proposed the studies and convinced the GEs that the studies would be important, adequately funded and supported, yet independent.

Off-line entities are easy to miss when thinking about a value delivery chain, because their role can be indirect and subtle. This is especially true when the off-line entities are only *potentially* important. For example, Australian steel maker BHP might like the construction industry to use more steel, replacing in part forest products. Currently, local governments usually play little role in BHP's businesses. However, modifications in local building codes could facilitate builders' greater use of steel materials. Navigating the Byzantine rituals of local government decision making well enough to influence local codes systematically requires significant resources. But it might facilitate a much more attractive value proposition from BHP to the builder.

Off-line entities don't naturally fit into the buy/sell, product-supply framework, since they usually don't buy anything sold in the main portion of the value delivery chain. However, their potential importance is easier to recognize as part of the value delivery framework, for they often so pivotally affect the delivery of value in the chain.

Recognizing discontinuities caused by off-line entities

In the late 1970s, Mr Clean, the household cleaner made by Procter & Gamble, was in a slow, apparently irreversible, long-term decline in the US and in most other countries where it was sold. Other liquid cleaners' success had diminished Mr Clean's reputation for cleaning efficacy; various spray and aerosol products had surpassed it for convenience.

Meanwhile, a seemingly small new cloud appeared. Consumers were writing letters to P&G complaining that P&G cleaners had damaged their new floors. The R&D community looked into the situation and found that installers of a new kind of polyurethane flooring, called no-wax floors, were getting complaints from consumers that their new floors had become dulled. Some installers were telling these consumers that conventional household cleaners, including P&G's, could be doing the damage.

Mr Clean's volume was concentrated in kitchen floor cleaning. For over 30 years, most kitchen floor surfaces had been made of linoleum, a plastic sheet attached to a wood or concrete floor. Consumers had traditionally waxed these floors. Maintaining a waxed linoleum floor required stripping the wax periodically (about every two weeks), which required a floor cleaner. Between waxings, the floor was lightly cleaned, again with floor cleaner. The wax surface trapped dirt easily, so a reasonably strong cleaner was required. So household cleaners were all formulated with phosphates. These chemicals comprised a vitally important, highly developed technology across many P&G products. For floor cleaners, phosphates allowed the cleaner to penetrate the wax and either strip it or free the embedded dirt particles to be removed.

No-wax floors were different. Their polyurethane surface meant no need to wax ever again. Also, these floors could be cleaned more easily. Phosphates, however, left a creamy film on the surface of polyurethane, unless the consumer rinsed the floor thoroughly. This same film was deposited on wax but would sink into the surface of the wax unnoticed. On top of a polyurethane surface, phosphates made a freshly cleaned floor look like its shine had been dulled. The culprit was the phosphates in household cleaners!

There is an old *New Yorker* cartoon from the 1930s showing, supposedly, the 'Natatorium at Procter & Gamble' with worried young executives peering into the swimming pool, with the caption 'The Day a Bar of Ivory Sank.' Thus did some in the household cleaner division feel that dark day in 1976 when this disturbing news emerged. To appreciate this scene fully, the reader needs to understand the emotions surrounding phosphates. In the 1970s, they were a cause celebre in Procter & Gamble. Blamed by environmentalists for degeneration of streams, legislation in about 10 percent of the US banned their use. P&G used phosphates in most of its cleaning products and top management believed that phosphates from these products were not a significant source of the environmental phosphate problem. The company was engaged in major public relations battles to dissuade governments zero-phosphate (zero-P) legislation.

The Mr Clean brand group conducted research on no-wax floor consumer ownership and buying intentions. As of 1976, only about 12 percent of US kitchens had a no-wax floor, but over 90 percent of consumers claimed that their next kitchen floor surface would be a no-wax floor. Given the life span of linoleum, this suggested that by the early 1980s, over 85 percent of kitchen floors might be no-wax. A *discontinuity* had emerged in the environment of the business, changing the usage environment of the primary entity and probably the appropriate primary VDS. In this case, it came from an off-line entity in Mr Clean's relevant value delivery chain.

The brand group wondered, 'Rather than *sue* the no-wax floor makers, perhaps it would be wise to determine if a winning value proposition for consumers with these floors could be delivered by Mr Clean?' After all, Mr Clean was dying slowly but surely, despite the fine new perfume. A strat-

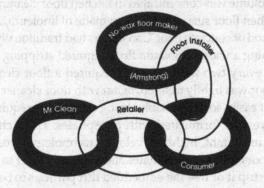

egy tying Mr Clean to a soon-to-be ubiquitous floor surface might have more long-term promise than fragrance or fighting a losing battle over cleaning power on obsolete, waxed surfaces.

But it would be important to understand why consumers were so enthusiastic about this new surface. Additional research revealed an insight largely missed. While consumers didn't like waxing, they *did* like floors to have a bright shiny look. That's why they tolerated the drudgery of waxing all those years. Yet household cleaner brands at the time did not view a shiny floor as a desirable result of the floor-cleaning process. In retrospect this oversight is understandable. Household cleaners did not shine floors; wax did. Wax was seen as a different product category, a different market. When consumers were asked to name the resulting experiences they wanted from a floor cleaner, they never mentioned shine. By exploring the interest in no-wax floors, however, it became clear how important the resulting experience of shine had been all along. When consumers cleaned their floor, they wanted it clean, of course. But they also wanted the floor to be shiny.

The floor installers knew that household cleaners seemed to dull no-wax floors. Therefore, they told consumers to add a few drops of Ivory dishwashing liquid to a bucket of water and use that to clean the floor. This left no apparent dulling. However, the R&D engineers working with the brand group pointed out that this method (essentially cleaning with plain water) did *not* adequately clean the floors. It left particulate matter that could be ground into the surface, eventually *permanently* dulling it.

It became clear that the right answer was this: a household cleaner that was strong enough to remove the surface dirt without leaving a phosphate film and that required no rinsing. R&D studied and experimented, and then concluded that the easiest way to provide this cleaner was to use a formula with no phosphates. Because of the Zero-P legislation, a no-phosphates Mr Clean formula already existed for sale in banned areas. It cleaned traditional floors much less well than phosphate based cleaners, but cleaned polyurethane very well. Why not use this Zero-P formula to re-launch 'New Mr Clean, formulated to keep no-wax floors shining?' Sounded reasonable, but this new strategy was almost killed by the perceived affront to phosphates.

The remaining problem with the strategy was credibility. How could the team convince the consumer that new Mr Clean was appropriate for these floors, especially while the installers continued to discourage use of so-called harsh cleaners? The brand decided to try to win the cooperation of the manufacturers P&G so recently meant to attack.

Armstrong had the largest share of the no-wax floor market and by coincidence used Sun imagery in the names of their floors: Armstrong Solarian no-wax floors. This went well with Sunshine Fresh Mr Clean. The brand group and its immediate management approached Armstrong and offered, in effect, a supporting value proposition. The team argued that Armstrong had a problem: if consumers used conventional cleaners, which left a film and apparently dulled their floors, they would be unhappy with Solarian. If consumers were urged to rinse two or three times after each cleaning, the whole labor-saving purpose of Solarian would be defeated. Yet, if Armstrong allowed installers to continue recommending a drop of Ivory Liquid in a bucket of water, the Solarian floor would be *permanently* damaged over time, also a disaster for Armstrong.

The team presented evidence indicating that New Mr Clean was ideally suited for cleaning no-wax floors and asked Armstrong to *endorse* it. In return, Mr Clean would run advertising featuring Solarian floors. The ads would tell the New Mr Clean story and would feature a no-wax floor installer - with Armstrong's name on his uniform - recommending Solarian and the use of New Mr Clean for No-Wax Floors.

But the strategy met an unexpected complication. Armstrong had been worrying for some time about this cleaning problem. Knowing that conventional cleaners left a film and that inadequate cleaning would eventually lead to damage, Armstrong had created its own floor cleaner, intended to clean adequately without leaving a dull appearance. Unfortunately, a whole team of Armstrong R&D people had become attached to this project. Those team members fought to save their own project. Once again, a customer entity of importance in an organization's chain may have individuals and groups within it who have different agendas from the whole customer entity.

The Mr Clean team argued that household cleaning was a difficult and not so profitable market in which a large sales and distribution network like P&G's was very helpful. Armstrong would do better to focus on the flooring business. Plus, if Mr Clean were to solve their cleaning problem, Armstrong had no strategic reason to enter such a market. Moreover, by cooperating with P&G's strategy, Armstrong would get the second superior experience of new, effective communication of their own primary value proposition. Armstrong was still fairly small and inexperienced in television advertising, whereas P&G, obviously very experienced in this area, was offering free advertising developed with P&G's skills. After some internal struggle, Armstrong decided to accept the Mr Clean value proposition. As for the installers, they only wanted to avoid the cleaning problem; if Armstrong backed up the Mr Clean solution, the installers were generally happy to go along.

In a successful test market and later nationally, Mr Clean was re-launched as 'the best cleaner for no-wax floors, because it was specially formulated to safely help keep no-wax floors shining.' The product now universally used the '0-P' formula and R&D developed a different appearance: a clearer, more golden color. The brand group rewrote the label to focus on the no-wax floor shine and safety story. The advertising developed by Mr Clean's agency featured Solarian floors installed by a professional, who told the consumer that Armstrong specifically recommends 'New Sunshine Fresh Mr Clean for No-Wax Floors.' Armstrong sent installers back-up literature and letters urging them to recommend Mr Clean specifically to consumers.

This new strategy successfully turned Mr Clean around; market share grew significantly for the first time in some 15 years. The brand remained focused on the resulting experience of shiny looking surfaces and within a few years returned to a leadership position in the household cleaner category. A discontinuity had occurred. Off-line entities, the floor manufacturer and installer, suddenly became crucial players in Mr Clean's primary VDS, and inspired its successful redesign, which included the redesign of the appropriate supporting VDSs to these off-line entities.

Multiple interrelationships – like an ecosystem

In his 1996 book, *The Death of Competition*, James F. Moore applies some of the concepts of biological ecosystems to an understanding of how business organizations interact with the environment. This analogy to an ecosystem complements the value delivery chain perspective. Moore argues that simple head-to-head competition between players in the same industry is 'dead.' That is, he believes that business organizations survive and thrive or perish as a function of the co-evolution of all of the relevant competitors, customers, suppliers, and other interested parties, including players in other industries. Thus Microsoft is part of an ecosystem that includes makers of chips and hardware systems, not just other software companies. More recently, a prominent participant in Microsoft's ecosystem is the US Justice Department. Moore argues that an organism, a business organization, must be aware of the whole ecosystem and try to influence or even lead its co-evolution.

Moreover, he points out the need to understand and anticipate dynamics within the ecosystem; this is equivalent to the need for considering dynamics across the whole value delivery chain. An organization may correctly analyze customers at an important level in a chain and focus the right value proposition at them. However, if another level is currently changing or about to undergo transformation, that other value proposition may not stay viable for long. In this way, Moore's rich analogy to an ecosystem is helpful for understanding the interconnected nature of long, complex value delivery chains.

***

The value delivery chain is a two-way street. Supplier-entities should, under many circumstances, understand and be part of the VDS the organization is trying to implement. Compaq and Conner peripherals worked together as if part of the same large VDS, which they were. However, conventional strategy doctrine articulates competitive advantage in terms of a zero sum battle between suppliers and customers; one must pick the other's pocket or become the pocket picked. Many in the buying function have been taught to follow strictly this supposed path to competitive advantage. They therefore are loath to give anything useful to suppliers, including information the supplier could use to make the buyer's organization more successful.

Of course, organizations must be careful about confidentiality in explaining their strategies to suppliers, but this concern is generally exaggerated. As a result, the buying function keeps suppliers, who could make a bigger, more creative contribution to the organization's success, in the dark. Understanding that suppliers are part of an organization's primary value delivery system, rather than the enemy, helps an organization more effectively navigate the complexities of the chain.

John Prescott, then-CEO of the giant Australian corporation BHP, once commented on the supplier-customer relationship, saying that typically the two most inappropriate people from the two organizations dominate the dialogue - the sales rep and the buyer. These two, he observed, tend to focus far too narrowly on the specific product and delivery demands of the buyer, the product features the rep wants to extol, and, of course, price. Prescott argued that the two organizations should comprehend each other on a deeper level, share an understanding of their strategies, and have plenty of dialogue involving functions other than sales and buying. This mentality sees the business-customer less as the buyer of a product and more as a whole enterprise. This requires approaching any business-customer not as if the buying department were the whole enterprise. Rather, an organization must have the larger and more profitable purpose of improving the customer's entire VDS.

Chapter Twelve

Don't *Sell* to Business-Customers: Improve Their VDSs Instead

When approaching a business-customer, whether a primary or some other entity, organizations frequently misunderstand the real identity of the customer. They make the implicit assumption that the customer is the *buyer*, including the buying function and other decision-makers and influencers of the buying process. This mistake leads organizations to deliver value propositions primarily aimed at satisfying the customer's buying criteria. While this approach is not automatically inappropriate, it usually foregoes taking advantage of much better opportunities to improve the way in which the customer's whole enterprise delivers value.

Focusing on the buying process or on any other function that is only a *part* of the customer's relevant VDSs clearly misses the big picture. Such misplaced emphasis is typical of the internally-driven, customer-compelled philosophies and the product-supply framework. Organizations should stop asking the traditional questions, 'How does the customer buy? On what key factors does the customer base its decision? How can we influence the buying process?' Instead, they should ask, 'What would make the customer's whole VDS more successful? What is the value proposition we should deliver so that they will more profitably deliver value to their customers?'

Because conventional perspectives implicitly equate a business with making and selling a product, they also imply that what is important in the customer organization is how and why they *buy* that product. *DPV*, however, equates a business with delivering the resulting experiences the entire customer *entity* would value. So what's most important from the *DPV* perspective is how that entity might obtain those resulting experiences. A winning value proposition may be, and often is, experienced by parts of the customer's organization involved neither in making nor in influencing buying decisions. Therefore, constructing a winning proposition often requires a focus on these non-buying functions, processes, and individuals. Unfortunately, organizations rarely realize this, and thus misunderstand the customer's identity within the entity.

In the beginning, Compaq Computer wanted to make a computer compatible with IBM's PC but so compact that a user could actually carry it from place to place. Achieving this portability meant making everything smaller, including the hard disk and disk drive. The company put out feelers, but major disk drive makers were not interested - they didn't see a market for such a thing. Phineas Conner, however, a small start-up himself, liked the Compaq value proposition and expressed interest in making the smaller disk drive. However, Conner made a further proposal to Compaq. It seemed probable that customers would see a portable computer as convenient but likely of poorer performance than a regular desktop PC. What if Compaq were not only smaller but also *faster*?

Conner reasoned that, with a smaller disk drive, it might be possible to design both the drive and the computer itself in such a way as to allow faster data transfer. But to take advantage of this opportunity, Compaq would have to change its design and focus. Conner Peripherals would likewise have to design the smaller drive in tandem with the Compaq changes. Together this would improve Compaq's VDS and value proposition. Both prospered handsomely from this redesign of the VDS of Conner's customer.

Buyers and actual users in a business-customer

A primary or supporting VDS should deliver a winning value proposition to the customer's organization. This is quite different from trying to please or satisfy *all* of the interested parties within that customer's organization or even those closest to the buying decision. It may even mean significantly displeasing this piece of the customer entity.

The department responsible for buying and sometimes managing the relevant product in a large customer organization may sometimes be best understood as an intermediary in the chain. A different group within the customer entity may be the *actual user* of the product. Actual users are groups or individuals within a customer entity that most directly use and are most impacted by the resulting experiences that are or could be delivered by an organization's VDS. Actual users can and often do have internal customers within the organization. For example, if a large law firm is a primary entity for Xerox in the copier market, the law firm's IT department may be considered the buyer, while secretaries may be the actual users. The lawyers may be the secretaries' internal customers. For a railroad, a customer's transportation department may be the buyer of shipping service, while that customer's sales force is the actual user. In these cases, it may be very possible to deliver a value proposition to the customer's business that advances the agendas of both buyers and actual users. In some situations, however, the buyer's agenda conflicts with a proposition that would help the actual users make a bigger contribution to the customer's whole business.

For example, after Fidelity's great success in taking mutual funds direct to individual investors (see Chapter 11), they were quick to recognize an additional opportunity in the pension fund market. Until the mid-1980s, firms offered employees Defined Benefit (DB) plans only. Employees were essentially guaranteed some financial benefit as their pension. The firm's board of directors determined how much the firm would contribute to the pension fund, a sum usually in proportion to an employee's salary. A pension fund manager, usually an investment bank or insurance company, invested the fund's assets.

A firm usually employed a pension and employee benefits administrator, playing the roles of both buyer and actual user. This benefits administrator might have been an HR manager or a finance officer, such as the corporate treasurer. Often a Pension Committee of some sort, including HR, treasury, and sometimes employee representatives, evaluated and selected the fund managers and oversaw the administration of pension-benefits. Achieving reasonably good returns without much risk was the typical objective of the firm's pension-and-benefits administrator.

Then the US Defined Contribution (DC) plans emerged, along with what are called 401-K plans. These committed a defined amount of contribution, which the employee could supplement, and the opportunity for the employee to self-direct the investment of this contribution. The firm gave no guarantee of performance and thus of financial benefit. This allowed the employees the opportunity to invest more aggressively at their own risk. It also shifted a significant portion of pension cost directly onto the employee's shoulders.

Fidelity realized that, in effect, this shift allowed them to treat employees, rather than the pension administrator, as actual users. Many pension fund managers, however, were not prepared to interact with a large number of individual employees, having traditionally cultivated relationships with the administrators, committees, and perhaps the board. Insurance companies, also active in pension fund management, did have the ability to handle interaction with large numbers of employees but were not known for stellar investment performance.

Fidelity already had an expert infrastructure in place for exactly this kind of interaction. The company's well-educated representatives could handle complex inquiries via toll free telephone at all hours. And Fidelity's performance reputation, earned through its well managed mutual fund business, was far stronger than that of the insurance companies. Fidelity also offered a large number of mutual funds and other investment vehicles, so employees would have numerous investment choices with Fidelity as fund manager. Senior management in primary entity firms had become an especially important group of actual users, for they now had a considerable personal stake in the pension fund's performance. Fidelity recognized the opportunity this situation presented and aggressively courted senior managers, essentially circumnavigating the buyers — the pension administrator and pension committees. Senior managers could easily see the case for using Fidelity, and many therefore successfully endorsed Fidelity's appointment as manager of their firm's DC plan.

Delivering the winning value proposition to the employee did *not* deliver the value proposition desired by quite a few benefits administrators. Some administrators were no doubt interested in giving employees this value proposition but were hesitant to accept the less significant role it carried for them. However, Fidelity allowed the customer-organization better to accomplish its objectives of motivating employees while off-loading pension costs and risk to the employees. From the perspective of the firm, the primary entity, Fidelity's value proposition was superior. By recognizing that the primary entity was the entire customer entity, not the buying function, Fidelity delivered a very profitable value proposition.

***

This discussion of the value delivery chain allows a more complete understanding of the idea that a business is a value delivery system. A business is a primary value delivery system, often including one or more supporting VDSs. This leads to a yet broader question - what is a firm? How should a firm be understood, and what therefore should the guiding framework be for corporate strategy? The answer, from the *DPV* perspective, is that a firm is its businesses, its primary VDSs, and that corporate strategy consists of deciding what those businesses should be.

Chapter Thirteen

Define the Firm's VDSs: Key Task of Corporate Strategy

Since a firm's businesses generate its wealth, the firm's most fundamental strategic decision is to define clearly what its primary VDSs, its businesses, will be. When a firm operates only a single VDS, a single business, the firm's strategy *is* that one primary VDS. The strategy of a firm operating numerous businesses should consist of the disciplined choice and design of those numerous primary VDSs it will implement. These choices must take into account the interrelationships, both complementary and conflicting, among the businesses. This includes ensuring that the sum of the company's businesses does indeed create wealth.[1] It also includes ensuring that capabilities needed across various businesses are identified and supported appropriately at the corporate level. These choices must be continuously reconsidered and refined. This definition of the firm's VDS should be understood as the substance of corporate strategy.

Yet, in many major corporations, senior managers do not and *could* not articulate their corporate strategy in these terms. They could discuss the firm's products, technologies, customers, competitors, competencies, and broad goals, but could not describe the primary VDSs the firm intends to execute. As a result, single-business firms often poorly deliver their one value proposition. For multi-business firms, this lack of awareness of the value delivery framework also leads them to misunderstand the interrelationships among businesses. They put priority on building and leveraging resources or on achieving economies across the firm, inadvertently hurting the businesses to which these objectives should be subsidiary.

Thus traditional corporate strategy is formulated backwards, in ignorance of the real heart of business. Encouraged by the internally-driven and customer-compelled philosophies, many managers define their businesses by what they see in the looking glass. They confuse their own organizational entities, functions, products, assets, and capabilities with businesses. Instead, a firm must define its businesses as the winning combination of primary VDSs, which *include* the resources to implement them.

Losing the businesses

In the 1920s, Alfred P. Sloan led the young GM out of chaos and imminent disaster. To do so, Sloan brilliantly defined a set of distinct though related businesses, thus formulating GM's corporate strategy. To guide long term management of the businesses, he introduced principles of balancing centralized and decentralized decision-making. These principles served GM well in some ways for over 40 years, but they also allowed the firm gradually to lose the clarity by which the businesses were defined and, to some extent, the businesses themselves.

In 1921, Sloan described Ford's strategy, manifested in the Model T, as 'a static model at the lowest price in the car market.'[2] Ford's philosophy was to maximize the economies of mass production by producing totally uniform products. At the time, Ford had 60 percent (in units) of the total car and truck market. Chevrolet had 4 percent, the other GM cars even less. GM, Sloan concluded, could not compete on Ford's terms.

As Sloan saw it, GM's lines randomly overlapped one another in price and characteristics, except for the high-end Buick and Cadillac. His strategy called for a varied line of cars, each delivering a different value proposition, coordinated as one coherent overall strategy. This coordination among the different propositions and their delivery was meant to achieve economies of mass production previously thought possible only with a single uniform product. The product policy, as Sloan called it, was the 'concept of mass-producing a full line of cars graded upward in quality and price.'[3]

> 'First ... produce a line of cars in each price area, from the lowest price up to one for a strictly high-grade quantity-production car, but ... not ... fancy-price ... with small production; second ... price steps should not ... leave wide gaps in the line, and yet ... keep their number within reason, so that the greatest advantage of quantity production could be secured; and third, there should be no duplication by the corporation in the price fields or steps.'[4]

Sloan made Chevrolet, Pontiac, Oldsmobile, Buick, and Cadillac fairly independent profit centers, while establishing a centralized policy-setting power, including a strong, centralized finance function. The subsidiary car companies were allowed to operate as divisions with control over engineering, manufacturing, and selling. Fisher Body, also an independent subsidiary, was a leader in the important innovation of *closed body* designs. It kept its independence as the car divisions did. The General Motors Acceptance Corporation (GMAC) was also formed as a separate company, which provided innovative dealer and motorist financing.

The old car companies became known as the 'selling divisions.' Each was given responsibility to deliver a different value proposition. Each proposition was clearly bounded by price and quality, and together the propositions ranged from lowest to highest in the market. 'The new set of price classes meant that the car line should be integral, that each car in the line should properly be conceived in its relationship to the line as a whole.'[5]

The strategy combined product line variety with mass production and called for coordinating aspects of design and production across divisions. This was first demonstrated in the Pontiac, developed in the early 1920s to fill the gap between the low-end Chevrolet and the Oldsmobile. GM conceived of combining a six-cylinder engine, unlike Chevrolet's four, with 'such Chevrolet body and chassis parts as would fit the new design.'[6] The Chevrolet division developed and tested the prototype, then assigned it to the division that became Pontiac. Sloan saw great importance in this success.

> 'Physical co-ordination ... is, of course, the first principle of mass production, but at that time it was widely supposed from the example of the Model T, that mass production on a grand scale required a uniform product. The Pontiac, coordinated in part with a car in another price class, was to demonstrate that mass production of automobiles could be reconciled with variety in product. ... If the cars in the higher-price classes could benefit from the volume economies of the lower-price classes, the advantages of mass production could be extended to the whole car line.'[7]

The strategy worked exceptionally well, albeit with some help from Henry Ford. First created by his genius, Ford Motor was nearly destroyed by his implacable refusal to change anything in response to GM's challenge. When urged to match GM's cars in various colors, Ford's founder chuckled, saying that motorists 'can have any color of car they want, as long as it's black.' Meanwhile GM delivered a wide range of value propositions much better than the one offered by the basic Ford. As used Model Ts became ubiquitous, GM helped consumers use those cars as their entry-level, bare-minimum-transportation purchase. For those ready for something a bit more comfortable or faster or more stylish, there was no point in buying a new Model T; they could trade up for one of GM's lines instead. Rather than compete directly against Ford on Ford's terms, GM had offered a car

> '... much better than the Ford, with a view to selling it at or near the top price in the first grade ... The strategy we devised was to take a bite from the top of his position, conceived as a price class, and in this way build up Chevrolet volume on a profitable basis. In later years, as the consumer upgraded his preference, the new General Motors policy was to become critically attuned to the course of American history.'[8]

For years, this proved a winning strategy for GM. But because GM never adopted the discipline of defining exactly what its businesses were, the company risked losing sight of the first principle behind its success: offering consumers a distinctive variety of motoring experiences while searching for opportunities to share resources that did not undermine that variety.

As Maryann Keller recounts in her book *Rude Awakening*, the distinctive character of the GM divisions lasted well into the 1960s, but by that time signs of decay had begun to emerge. In 1964, General Motors Assembly Division (GMAD) was created, some say, to dodge government anti-trust action. This meant that manufacturing, a vital element in all of the businesses, was now an independent entity with its own agenda. Meanwhile, corporate finance increasingly dominated decision-making for GM. Keller quotes another writer on the same phenomenon in Ford Motor:

> 'The competing culture is one of statistical technicians, the number crunchers left over from the days of [Ford's] whiz kids, who believed that anything could be quantified. These people swarm over the company trying to knock off 50 cents from the manufacturing cost of a bumper and another 75 cents off a fender – cost savings that can mean millions of dollars to the company. But this process collides with the bettors who are trying to get out the best car with the newest features. Unless the company has ... very strong ... values that encourage everyone to work for the same identifiable goals, these competing tendencies can easily turn into internecine wars. Where key people focus more on internal wars and less on keeping their organization in tune with the business environment, then it is possible for the market-place to pass them by.'[9]

Similarly, in the memoirs of his GM career, *On a Clear Day You Can See General Motors*, John De Lorean complained that corporate staff interfered with and slowed many decisions in the car businesses. He claimed that 'capricious, almost mindless marketing decisions' were routinely imposed by what he called 'upstairs.' Despite De Lorean's later questionable escapades, he had been a fast rising star at GM, and his testimony seems plausible.

By the 1970s, the differences among the de facto value propositions delivered by GM's car businesses were increasingly blurred. The car divisions ostensibly controlled engineering, other than body design and except when corporate finance intervened. They controlled marketing, except when the dealers were able to dictate their preferences or when finance intervened. GMAD, which became more than ever a world of its own, controlled assembly (except when you-know-who intervened). And the divisions competed, looking to grow by expanding into each other's businesses. They all began making increasingly similar small, medium, and large sized cars in more and more models. Corporate finance pushed them to achieve higher efficiency by using the same parts and components, with little concern for the impact on the motorist's experiences. Neither the car divisions nor anyone else was designing or articulating the firm's primary VDSs, and decisions were no longer made in context of any coherently defined businesses.

Then came the oil shocks and Japanese small cars with small prices but big-car acceleration, tight, sporty handling, excellent gas mileage, buttons that didn't break, doors that usually closed, less cheap looking plastic interiors, and numerous big car features. Meanwhile, the Germans enthralled high-end consumers with more sophisticated, less bulky, more efficient, posh, reliable, high-performance sports-touring and luxury cars. What was GM's response? Make its cars less distinctive, of course. It downsized the entire fleet, cutting length and the weight of parts. Two new small-car designs were quickly developed: the X-car and the J-car. The X-car became a quality disaster. The J-car was supposed to be an import fighter, but the joke was on GM. To save cost, J-car models were quite similar to the X-car and to each other. For the US market, the J-car was grossly under-powered by an obsolete engine design that allowed use of parts from the X-car. CEO Roger Smith defended J-cars' inadequate engine as follows: 'I always live in deadly fear of the day the light turns green and you don't get across. This one, before that light gets warmed up, it will be across.'[10]

GM cars had achieved a remarkable state of sameness, what Keller called a *look-alike* and *feel-alike* problem. Product design had been reduced to 'badge-engineering,' which differentiates a car by changing a nameplate and a few chrome curlicues (at least until they peel off). A retired Oldsmobile chief engineer explained the *feel-alike* problem:

> *'The use of common parts across the car lines impairs the ability of GM to make products that are truly distinctive in terms of drivability and character - the things under the skin that make the personality of the car so important. Developing uniqueness in the feel of a car was much more straightforward when all the components were different.'*

When 1977 Oldsmobile owners discovered they had Chevrolet engines, they were, well, disappointed. The media dubbed it Chevymobile, and GM blamed the media for consumers' negative reactions. Yet, the J-car was used to make a Cadillac, the ridiculous Cimarron. According to Keller, *nothing* distinguished the Cadillac Cimarron from a Chevrolet Cavalier except for leather seats and a luggage rack. The *Wall Street Journal* greeted Cimarron: 'Cadillac is about to take the wraps off what it hopes will restore its injured pride … the Cimarron, a front-drive, high-mileage little car that will bring gasps from the bluebloods who have driven big Caddies for years.'[11] Cadillac had historically delivered luxurious resulting experiences including a more spacious, roomy feeling in the plush interior, a slightly exotic opulence and feeling of power, and the comfort and handling that come from the most advanced technology and highest quality workmanship. No one could have articulated such a value proposition and then agreed to introduce a *compact* Cadillac – an automotive oxymoron – with a grossly under-powered engine, dull styling, and a cramped and cheap-looking interior.

In the first half of the 1980s, GM spent $45 billion on capital investments to achieve competitive advantage through technology. The firm broke up Fisher and GMAD and reorganized as two businesses, big cars and little cars, both of which proceeded to make big and little cars. They launched the dubious experiment called Saturn and talked of a bright future. Meanwhile US market share continued to decline steadily. In 1985, the Eldorado had been redesigned to be smaller and more sporty, thus targeting the BMW fans. *Motor Trend* magazine named the redesigned Cadillac Eldorado 'worst car of the year.' The magazine commented on GM's understanding of Cadillac's potential customer, 'The problem with the Eldorado stems from the basic GM credo to be everything to everybody … Longtime Cadillac owners won't like it. European sports-touring owners won't bother to look at it. Where's the market?'[12] The same year, CEO Roger Smith was named by *Chief Executive* magazine the Chief Executive of the Year. The magazine explained that he 'tore up a proud, if aging battleship and is rebuilding it into a squadron of guided missile cruisers and attack submarines.'[13] Too bad he didn't get the battleship to make better cars.

Badge engineering, the cosmetic attempt to fool customers into thinking two essentially identical cars were different, had made a mockery of Sloan's clear definition of the businesses. Sloan had a clear vision of a strategy, consisting of five distinct businesses. Unfortunately for GM, in the long run, the principles of balance between centralized and decentralized power survived but something far more important was lost. Even on a clear day, you could no longer see the businesses of General Motors.

It's after 10 pm – do you know where *your* businesses are?

Years ago a public service campaign asked parents this question about their children. Many firms have it worse. Often, a set of clearly defined VDSs that integrate the firm's resources is nowhere to be found.

This is because resources are mistakenly *equated* with businesses. Breaking the assumed equation between internal resources and a business is essential. To think forwards, primary VDSs are defined first, and they determine the resources needed.

Organizations are not the businesses they manage

From the *DPV* perspective, an organization is not a business. In some cases, there may exist a one-to-one correspondence between a single business and an organization. However, an organization may conduct multiple businesses; conversely, one business may require actions by several organizations. A primary VDS, a business, is the delivery of a value proposition, so it *includes* whatever organizations should manage and execute it.

A function is part of a business, not a sovereign state

One computer company creates divisions based on product lines. Each division includes R&D, marketing, manufacturing, finance, and HR functions. A separate sales division decides which products of which divisions merit attention. Because the divisions are encouraged to see Sales as their customer, they vie for meeting its needs. External customers are the property of Sales. Most marketing personnel spend little time with external customers - Sales' customers. Sales tells Marketing the product needs. Marketing dutifully passes these lists of features and performance attributes on to R&D. Yet each division has a P&L, as if it were managing a business.

Or consider a major oil company competing in the motor oil market, which treats its additives lab as a business and accords it profit and loss responsibility. The lab develops and sells additives to a marketing division that produces, names, and labels a finished motor oil, and also has a P&L. A marcomm department, with the help of an ad agency, develops advertising for which neither the motor-oil-marketing division nor the lab is responsible. A legal department determines what ad claims are acceptable to develop based on an assessment of competitors' likeliness to object. A few years ago, the lab developed a new additive formula and offered it to the marketing division, which asked Marcomm who, after consulting legal, ruled that the formula could not be used to make effective advertising. So the lab sold the formula to a much smaller competitor, which used it very effectively to build market share at the larger company's expense. The company's organizations are all busy making decisions, but no one manages a coherent business.

Functional entities that don't manage the whole firm should not formulate corporate strategy. All strategic decision-making tasks should belong to the organizations implementing the businesses, not to a free-floating strategic planning, corporate finance, or corporate marketing function. A business's management team should have the responsibility for selecting the markets in which to compete and for designing, implementing, and redesigning the primary VDSs in each market. Senior management must then play the role of resolving conflicts among the businesses. Of course, this is not to say that an organization operating a primary VDS has to *own* all the relevant resources. Important elements in a primary VDS are often owned by entities outside the firm.

In the mid-1980s GM undertook a much ballyhooed organization restructuring to correct its strategic malaise. The result was the formation of two new divisions – more or less Small Cars and Big Cars. This upheaval only underlined how badly GM had lost sight of its original vision of businesses as distinct, if complementary and synergistic, endeavors.

Chevrolet and Pontiac made up the small car division. But Chevrolet had already become a diffused attempt to be everything to everyone and therefore nothing to anyone. How would it help to add Pontiac and call it a Business? Meanwhile, Buick, Olds, and Cadillac made up the other group. But how could there be a Buick–Olds–Cadillac value proposition?

Years of continued floundering amid a relentless loss of market share were the upshot of GM's big rethink. What was still missing, lost in the decades of hubris since the days of Sloan, was a genuine corporate strategy that defined GM's businesses in terms of distinct value propositions to be delivered. Redrawing organization charts, creating and eliminating organizational entities, and shifting power do not, in a vacuum, address the real problem of poorly defined, disintegrated value delivery systems.

If it's a product or an asset it isn't necessarily a business

In consumer retail banking, typical products include checking accounts, credit cards, savings accounts, money market accounts, car loans, education loans, mortgages, and trust services. Each and any product *can* be managed as the sole product in a VDS that is quite separate from other VDSs in the bank. These products can even be used successfully as parts of independent businesses, without being operated by a bank at all, such as the Discovery credit card or numerous mortgage companies' products.

However, just because such bank products *can* be managed as the sole product in a separate business doesn't mean they necessarily should be. Many consumers are unhappy with the fragmented service they get from their bank and would appreciate having a single contact in the bank who could help manage their whole portfolio. Often a problem or question on one product involves another, and the poor, unaided customer is tossed from one phone extension to another, waiting in vain for a straight answer to stop the *hold* music. Also, many such consumers are not financially sophisticated and would appreciate more *proactive* assistance in choosing financial products. For this customer, defining several businesses, each based on a separate product, is altogether inappropriate. A single business should be defined around an integrated value proposition that ties together all the appropriate products and services into a profitable customer relationship.

Unfortunately, conventional management practice treats the products as businesses. This product/business equation interferes seriously with the ability to define and manage integrated VDSs.

Just as one VDS might entail several products, one product might be in several VDSs. In the bank, there may be more than one business using a combination of several products in its VDS. Some of those products are likely to be part of more than one VDS. And when the same product plays a role in more than one VDS, the products may have to be designed, operated, and priced to fit the priorities of several businesses.

A primary VDS *could* in some cases include just a single asset, but most VDSs include numerous assets. Equating an asset to a business in the name of Asset Management is a misguided venture. The managers in charge of each major asset are of course focused on maximizing the returns on their asset, not on maximizing the returns on each of several profitable value propositions that should be delivered *using* that asset. What generates a better return on *all* the relevant assets of an organization can be quite at odds with what will maximize the return for a single plant or other asset.

A forest products company acquired its own railroad to gain competitive advantage in transportation cost. The railroad business unit is empowered to ensure that this asset is utilized fully, so lumber mills must use the company railroad - often. This illusion of excellent asset utilization actually causes mills to distribute more slowly and unreliably and at a higher cost than if they chose their own transportation options. Utilization of the firm's total assets is damaged in the name of better asset utilization.

Defining businesses is not beneath strategy

When a firm's businesses are ill-defined, in any of the ways discussed above, managers frequently sense a basic disconnect between the organization and the actual resulting experiences customers have. Often, the marketing department is tasked to solve this problem by somehow satisfying customers more fully and communicating more persuasively. A less casual regard by a firm's leadership for defining its businesses effectively implies *redefining* the businesses and changing *all* functions and resources accordingly, not just delegating the problem to one of the functions.

Part of the reason for this relaxed attitude is that many managers have been educated to view corporate strategy as above the pedestrian concerns of defining and managing the firm's businesses. Corporate strategy supposedly should focus on more strategic issues, such as the firm's relative position against the competitive forces in its industry, its strategic intent, its corporate dream, and its need to nurture core competencies. In all of these, managers are taught that corporate strategy should not be distracted by the parochial issues of managing the lowly business units.

These approaches to corporate strategy appeal to many consultants and academics who promote them because they seem above the gritty work of understanding and building real businesses. Only by seeing corporate strategy, in its essence, as the clear definition of the firm's businesses can managers recognize the threats and realize the opportunities of true importance to the firm.

***

Using *DPV*, a firm's leadership must formulate strategy that can profitably deliver enough superior value to accelerate growth and generate wealth. The firm must design its VDSs and ensure their optimal support and coordination. Part Two of this book turns to *how* an organization should formulate and implement such strategy. However, it is important first to understand the *market-space*, the context within which VDSs must be identified, chosen, and managed.

Notes

1   This requires accurate measurement of each business' contribution to corporate wealth. It may also require financial engineering to achieve a low total cost of capital and to maximize free cash flow. This leads some to argue that a firm's businesses should each have a cost of capital. Since measuring this is an arcane time sink, senior management should adjust assumed cost of capital by business and then let managers focus on the value delivery that generates profits above that cost of capital.

2   Alfred P. Sloan, *My Years with General Motors*, Anchor, New York, 1972, p. 63.

3   *Ibid*, p. 76.

4   *Ibid*, p. 71.

5   *Ibid*, p. 74.

6   *Ibid*, p. 179.

7   *Ibid*, p. 181–2.

8   *Ibid*, p. 177.

9   M. Keller, *Rude Awakening*, Morrow, New York, 1989, p. 27.

10   *Ibid*, pp. 72–3.

11   *Ibid*, p. 74.

12   *Ibid*, p. 197.

13   *Ibid*, p. 197.

Chapter Fourteen

Define VDSs Within the Context of their *Market-Space*

In *DPV* terms, a group of related VDSs (current and potential) and the wealth that could be generated by them, comprise a market-space. A market-space is thus broader than the usual definition of a market – simply a group of customers. Rather, it is a set of possible VDSs. Each related potential VDS in a market-space is, in *DPV* terms, a value delivery *option*. Any market-space is thus a set of value delivery options. A firm must identify and understand its relevant market-spaces in this way, identifying and then choosing the VDSs it will implement from this group of options. And a firm must consider interactions among the potential VDSs when making this choice.

Related potential VDSs are a market-space

Delivering Profitable Value sees a group of related business opportunities – potential VDSs – as a market-space. A market-space thus includes customers but is not defined entirely by them. The opportunity to create successful, sustainable VDSs should be the focal point for a firm committed to profitable growth. Thus, such a firm should identify realms of opportunity, i.e. market-spaces, which consist of specific business opportunities, i.e. VDSs, that are related to each other in important ways for the firm.

Obviously, two VDSs are related if major elements in them are similar. The Compaq and IBM PC VDSs deliver similar propositions using similar delivery vehicles. Compaq cannot understand its strategy without considering the relevant market-space, which includes IBM's PC VDS.

However, two VDSs may use very different vehicles, yet still be related and thus part of the same market. For example, value propositions involving Paris-London travel can be delivered using trains or aircraft. The VDSs are different in major ways, but the value propositions are comparable. So British Airways and France's TGV train should take one another into account in formulating strategy. Competing value propositions can be delivered by quite different businesses. For example, a letter can be sent via overnight courier, facsimile, e-mail, or the post office. A strategy for one must take the others into account. Thus organizations must recognize the relevant market-space regardless of the boundaries of product and industry.

More specifically defined, a market-space is *the potential wealth that could be generated in some timeframe by some set of broadly related primary value delivery systems.* That potential wealth is a function of the potential demand among potential primary entities for some set of broadly related resulting experiences. It is also a function of the capabilities and costs of delivering those experiences.

This view of the context in which businesses – VDSs – may be developed, focuses on profit or wealth, not just revenue. Often harder to measure, a VDSs potential share of a market's total wealth is more important than its share of revenue. Also, this definition emphasizes *potential* wealth from *potential* demand among *potential* primary entities. Strategy is a decision: what to do now to shape the organization's *future*. Managers must define the relevant market-space by what could evolve and by what could be created, not solely by how things are today.

In some timeframe, how much money *could* this organization make *if* it implemented the most profitable primary value delivery systems possible for it to implement in this market-space? Managers answering this question based on what was sold last year or on what current customers say they want are placing harmful constraints on their business's strategy. It is also crucial to ask what experiences *would be* most valuable to some customers if delivered to them in some timeframe? These may only be *potential* primary entities, since they may not be aware of these experiences or may not appreciate or be able to derive value from them. Knowledge workers in 1975 were potential primary entities who could derive great resulting experiences from PCs, but they didn't know this and so weren't ready to use a PC.

Finally, a market-space is defined by *primary* VDSs, including their supporting VDSs. Gastroenterologists were part of the same ulcer therapy market-space as were GPs. The butchers and grocers who retailed Frank Perdue chickens and the consumers of those chickens were in the same market-space. Pension-benefits managers were in the same pension-fund management market-space as employees. Although intermediaries may be quite different from the primary entities and different from each other, they are part of one market-space, as defined by the similarity of the primary VDSs.

Potential businesses, *not* customer groups or products

The marketing literature usually defines a market as some group of customers. They may have some shared characteristics such as their supposed needs. This view is generally consistent with conventional management theory, which *separates* a business from its customers; in this usual perspective, it is to them that a business sells. *DPV*, however, treats customers as an integral part of a VDS – they are an integral part of a business.

In formulating strategy, an organization must ask the basic question, 'What are the most promising business opportunities, or potential primary VDSs?' This is different from asking, 'Which are the most promising customers to whom we might sell our product?' Sometimes markets are defined as the demand by some customers for some product or product-line. However, the underlying demand for a product is really the demand for the value propositions that can be delivered when a customer uses that product. It follows that the relevant market-space for an organization should be defined by those value propositions and how they might be delivered, rather than by a product.

For purposes of formulating strategy, market-spaces can be defined with narrow or broad boundaries. That is, almost any market-space can be seen as a part of a still larger market-space. At the lowest level within a market-space are strategic options, each a single potential VDS.

Thus, most market-spaces are really part of some larger one. An organization must decide the relevant boundaries for the market-space in which it will formulate strategy. An auto maker could formulate effective strategy for the next 50 years in a sub-market-space of transportation that excludes the VDSs using planes and boats. On the other hand, cars may be part of a sub-market-space that belongs to a larger market-space that includes light trucks. These two product classes can deliver such increasingly overlapping value propositions that the car maker needs to think about strategy beyond the sub-market-space where cars belong.

Formulate strategy by relevant market-space

An organization can be very successful competing in a VDS, a single option, in a market-space. However, the other current and possible VDSs in the same market-space can affect the success of that one business, so an organization should formulate its strategy in context of that whole market-space. Determining a firm's strategy includes designing the optimal set of VDSs for each market-space in which it competes or may compete. Based on the outcome, the firm must choose the optimal combination of these market-spaces to stay in or enter.

For some market-spaces, it is critical to compete in more than one value delivery option. Apple Computer appealed strongly in the 1980s to a small portion of customers in the market-space served by PC-class computers. By not delivering a superior value to the majority of the market-space, however, Apple paid a penalty in the part of the market-space in which it *was* successful. Since application developers, a crucial off-line entity, saw

Macintosh becoming a small niche operating system, it became less attractive to develop applications for it. Apple devotees are steadily giving up, unable to get as many applications as they want. Even schools in the education sub-market-space that Apple dominated for 15 years are now rapidly switching to PCs.

To choose which market-spaces to be in, a firm must first select market-spaces to *consider*. Market-spaces worth examining *require* resulting experiences an organization believes it may be able to profitably deliver or to build the ability to deliver. They must also offer a large enough profit potential to be worth the organization's time. For each market-space deemed worth considering, the firm should then determine the optimal set of primary VDSs it *would* implement in that market-space if the firm decided to enter or remain in it. Finally, it can decide if it will actually enter or remain in each market-space considered and analyzed. The organization must assess whether being in that market-space makes sense relative to its other options. In this way, a firm determines the market-spaces in which it will compete and what line-up of businesses it will use. It also understands why this is the optimal strategy and what capabilities the firm must therefore build and how.

Questions a corporate strategy should answer for the long- and short-term

1 What are the firm's one or more primary value delivery systems?
 • In what relevant market-spaces will the firm compete?
 • For each market-space, what primary VDSs will the firm implement?
2 To maximize the firm's success, why does this represent the optimal choice
 • of relevant market-spaces in which to compete?
 • of primary VDSs in each market-space?
3 What are the most important capabilities, of providing or communicating resulting experiences, that must be built, and how will they be built?

Of course, details will necessarily be less precise in a long-term version of these answers. Nonetheless, a broad outline of the salient features of the firm's major VDSs in such a timeframe is reasonable. For the short-term, especially within the coming year, firms should strive for a great deal of detail. Many firms do not articulate coherent, formally agreed-upon answers to these questions for either timeframe. Firms that do decide to tackle these questions, however, find that it is easier said than done. Part One of this book described where organizations ought to be. In Part Two, *Delivering Profitable Value* turns to the question of just how, exactly, to get there.

Part Two

How to Deliver Profitable Value

Part One of this book proposed that a firm's strategy should consist of its choice and design of the primary value delivery systems it will implement within each market-space. Part Two proposes a comprehensive methodology to formulate and execute such strategy. Part Two will detail and illustrate the methodology of *DPV* – how does an organization go about formulating and executing such strategy?

It starts with a radically different approach to identifying strategic options, an approach proposed as a wholesale replacement for the failed and confused traditional notions of market and industry segmentation. This more realistic approach to exploring market-space options and formulating profitable growth strategy is based on the *DPV* method of anthropologically *becoming the customer*. It is in lieu of conventional market research and also replaces traditionally internally-driven competitive analysis. The value delivery framework then calls for the articulation and analysis of the strategic options that emerge from this approach. The result: a disciplined choice of corporate strategy in each market-space worthy of consideration.

This *DPV* methodology helps an organization explore and act on its most fundamental long-term strategic options. It is thus appropriate to be used by a new firm, by a firm thinking of launching businesses in very different or new market-spaces, or by one thoroughly reexamining strategy in its current market-spaces. However, this same methodology, narrowed somewhat in scope, is also appropriate for continuously reviewing and improving one's current businesses. The methodology shows managers how to commit to and execute strategy by the use of real, value delivery business plans. Finally, managers are urged to take action.

Chapter Fifteen

Formulate Strategy by Identifying and Choosing Value Delivery Options

The *Delivering Profitable Value* methodology starts with a focus on current or potential market-spaces, to discover the groups of potential primary VDSs relevant to the firm. Conventional frameworks focus on the organization's position in an industry, concentrating on the organization's products and assumed competencies. They define businesses in these product suppy terms and then try to find targets for these (ill-defined) businesses.

Using *DPV*, an organization selects market-spaces worth considering, then explores for potential winning VDSs in them. The most promising combination of these potential businesses for the long-term comprises the organization's best strategy in that market-space.

This creative search, forward-thinking analysis, and disciplined strategic choice comprise 'value delivery option identification.' A value delivery option is a potential VDS. Identifying these options is quite different from conventional notions of segmentation. They define a segment more narrowly and for a less strategic purpose. Furthermore, they cluster customers in a logically backward, counterproductive fashion and produce unnecessarily complex, impractical segmentation schemes. *DPV* argues for dispensing with the terminology and counterproductive methods of segmentation

Value delivery options are primary VDSs

> A potential business = a potential primary VDS =
> a value delivery option within a market-space
> A market-space = a group of related value delivery options

In the early 1990s, the Natural Gas Business Unit (NGBU) of Chevron was responsible for natural gas in the US. The NGBU analyzed the US market-

There's segmentation and then there's ... value delivery option identification

	Conventional product supply segmentation	Value delivery option identification
Basic definition of a segment versus a value delivery option	A group of customers; or, a product type and a group of customers	A potential VDS *including* primary entitles and products
Purpose of segmentation versus option identification	Find possible sales targets for a product-defined business; or, a prelude to a business	Formulate strategy: identify and choose possible VDSs in a market space; create businesses
Basis for placing any customer in a particular segment; or, a value delivery option	They are part of a large identifiable group; any one or more demographic or product-usage variables can group them with other customers	The same resulting experiences, delivered in the same way, are appropriate to these customers
Where a value proposition fits	After defining a segment, figure out a value proposition to it	The right proposition, and how best to deliver it, define the option
What makes a segmentation or set of value delivery options actionable	Customers in each segment can be reached easily and efficiently	Each option is a distinct potential primary VDS that the organization can decide to pursue or not

space for industrial uses of energy, which was a sub-market-space of the total energy market-space. This sub-market-space included potential businesses focused on any industrial concern that did or could use natural gas or other energy sources in the production of some product. It excluded residential and commercial use (for space heating, for example). Potential users in this sub-market-space could include electric utilities and various kinds of product manufacturers who used energy as part of their processes. The organization posed this fundamental question, 'What potential businesses are there in this market-space that the NGBU should pursue?' Using the *DPV* methodology, Chevron analyzed 56 industrial companies, which were potential primary entities, to develop a preliminary option-identification in this sub-market-space (hereafter simply referred to as this market-space). Four options, understood as four distinct primary VDSs, were identified as likely worth pursuing and later thoroughly quantified. The organization subsequently restructured NGBU into businesses, according to these four possibilities.

The value delivery options ranged from the easiest to implement with the most limited long-term profitability potential to the most difficult to implement with the greatest long-term profit potential. The first of these possible businesses was informally called, in reference to the customers in it, *'Self-sufficient.'* This option was focused on delivering a value proposition to industrial entities that needed the least help from an energy supplier. The primary entities were typically large electric utilities that had many optional sources of energy and had invested hugely in developing great expertise in understanding energy and the use of various fuels. Selling them natural gas on the spot market (i.e. with no long-term contract) with no additional services of any kind and at the lowest possible price constituted the essence of the value proposition for this option.

The second value delivery option, called *'Help them Buy Smarter,'* was focused on primary entities who valued some assurance of an uninterrupted supply of gas over time and some help in managing price-risk. Some utilities and very large manufacturers belonged to this opportunity.

The third option, informally titled *'Help them Convert Gas Smarter,'* was focused on extensively helping potential users with two aspects of using energy: better managing the complex issues related to then fast-evolving environmental regulation and possible cogeneration projects.[1] Utilities, very large manufacturers, and some manufacturers with only modest-sized operations were in this option. The fourth option, called *'Help them Use the Smartest Energy,'* was focused on helping potential customers entirely reengineer the way they used energy in their manufacturing processes. The potential users were manufacturers with plants that usually were not extremely large. These firms were better off if they focused their attention on delivering their own value propositions with their products - paper or sugar or chemicals – and not on developing expertise in sourcing and using energy.

The *Convert Smarter* and *Use the Smartest Energy* options thus featured much more complex Chevron-customer relationships than did the first two. The most difficult primary VDS to implement, of course, was the fourth one, but it offered the biggest long-term opportunity to impact customers in ways other than price. The first value delivery option presented a relatively straightforward challenge. There were definitely opportunities to make value delivery in this possible business more efficient, and this opportunity was by no means trivial, but operating in this option was consistent with Chevron's traditional capabilities. To leverage its core competencies, NGBU should have remained riveted to the Self-sufficient option, but this was also the option most subject to increasingly intense price based competition. Thus this easiest value delivery option was also most likely to become unprofitable.

According to then General Manager of the NGBU, Steve Furbacher, successful implementation of this option identification and redefinition of the organization's businesses played a primary role in NGBU's substantial profit improvement during the early 1990s. By defining and pursuing four distinct VDSs, delivering different, appropriate value propositions, NGBU strengthened the profitability in the more basic businesses while developing the potential in the more difficult businesses. After further development, all four natural gas businesses and Chevron's liquid natural gas businesses were merged with another energy supplier, Natural Gas Clearinghouse (NGC), to form a major new force in the energy market-space.

Consider a quite different market-space, one focused on helping consumers keep their bodies clean with products such as bar soaps. In the US, Procter & Gamble implements several primary VDSs, each one a business, but also called a brand in this context. Each business is, in effect, a value delivery option P&G pursues. One is called Safeguard, focused on an experience of superior deodorizing. Zest is focused on leaving one's skin feeling cleaner by leaving no soap film behind; this result is provided by the fact that Zest is synthetic (a detergent). Zest also produces suds in hard water far better than other bar soaps. Coast is focused on a sort of exhilaration in one's morning shower provided by a high-impact perfume released in the shower and by distinctive, striated coloring. Camay is focused on enhancing the beauty of one's facial skin. Ivory offers a mild and natural cleaning, which is provided and communicated by the absence of any perfumes, dyes, or additive chemicals such as deodorants. Ivory is also less expensive than most other branded bar soaps. Lava gets the most grimy, toughest dirt, such as heavy grease. Lava provides and communicates this ability via its inclusion of volcanic pumice.

The purpose of identifying value delivery options is strategy formulation

Defining strategic options as potential VDSs actually *is* the creation, definition, and redefinition of an organization's businesses. In contrast, conventional market and industry segmentation merely *supports* some predetermined businesses or furnishes only a *prelude* to their creation.

Following conventional practice, organizations often start with what they call a business, defined by a product (or service or product/service line). Then they divide the potential customers for this product into conveniently

measurable groups, which they call segments. These groups are then analyzed to determine how the organization can best sell its product to them.
In another approach, customers are again divided into groups after which
their supposed product requirements or needs are determined, usually in a
customer-compelled fashion. Then the organization decides which groups'
requirements best match, or 'fit' the organization's strengths or which best
fit its core competencies or which it simply finds most comfortable.

However, it is fundamentally internally-driven behavior to segment a
market in order to reinforce and justify whatever the organization sees, and
likes most, in its looking glass. What made the organization decide that these
products, resources, processes, or competencies were part of a winning strategy? Likely they are what the organization finds comfortable. That comfort
will be cold, however, when they turn out to be inappropriate for too much
of the market.

The appropriate primary VDS: the *only* variable by which to group customers strategically

The customers in a value delivery option consist entirely and exclusively of
those for whom the same VDS would be right for the organization to implement. Conventional market segmentation assigns customers to segments
by many variables, but not by this one, the only one that really matters.

Discussions of conventional segmentation often insist that there is no
one right way to segment a market. As Kotler says, '... buyers ... may differ
in their wants, purchasing power, geographical locations, buying attitudes,
and buying practices. Any of these variables can be used to segment a market.'[2] The widely influential work of Bonoma and Shapiro, *Industrial Segmentation*, offered a 'nested approach.' 'One of the primary thrusts of this
approach is that there are many ways to segment a market and the best
way ... depends upon the specific situation.'[3] On the contrary, there really
is one most coherent, understandable, and useful method to analyze a market – identifying the potential winning primary VDSs in it. One can *then* see
what customer characteristics, if any, correlate with these options.

Market-spaces whose primary entities are businesses

The need to analyze market-spaces for strategic options seems to inspire segmentation analyses of great complexity, especially in industrial, business-to-
business markets. Often the resulting segmentation approach is impressively
intricate but counterproductive because backward and overcomplicated. For
example, Bonoma and Shapiro recommend five sets of industrial segmenta-

tion variables. These are nested, ranging from 'easily observable' to 'subtle, hard to assess': 'demographics (industry, company size, location), operating variables (technology, user-nonuser status, customer capabilities), purchasing approaches (organization of purchasing function, power structure, nature of organizational relationships, general purchasing policies, purchasing criteria), situational factors (urgency, application, size of order/part of an order), and personal characteristics (buyer-seller similarity, buyer motivation, individual perceptions, risk management strategies).'[4]

Contrast this complex web of nested variables with the more direct pursuit of options defined by VDS. When HP's CTD was first struggling to reverse its decline (see Introduction, pp. 4–7), the division launched an elaborate segmentation study. They followed the model then prescribed in the company's strategic planning process for segmenting a market. First, identify competitive strengths (or, core competencies) – what they felt they were relatively good at doing. Then divide customers by demographic and product usage variables into 'segments.' Then search for those segments that need the division's strengths.

CTD knew its strength was producing more network data. They divided protocol analyzer customers by: the buyer's network organization (Network Management or Network Development); the customer's industry (12 classifications); type of products used (distributed versus dispatched network management tools and stand-alone, specialized, or integrated development tools); and network technology used (10 classifications). This scheme literally produced hundreds of segments. They then planned to scan these segments for customers who wanted 'more data' and to ask buyers (network managers) in promising segments to indicate the features that would give them more data than CTD's competitors offered. This approach was a formula for expending many thousands of hours analyzing data but was not likely to discover any useful insights.

By systematically becoming the customer instead, CTD found a large portion of companies who would value the ability to isolate a problem quickly and then implement a fast, practical solution more than they would value another protocol analyzer with even more data. The division had discovered a potential VDS, a possible business, that the previous multivariate segmentation matrix and its hundreds of segments only obscured.

Thus, conventional segmentation of industrial markets is typically confused and wrongly focused on an array of partly irrelevant variables. It often obscures rather than reveals an insightful understanding of these often complex market-spaces' business possibilities. Identifying value delivery options does not ignore the industrial market's complexity, but it does focus on the few variables that matter - those that determine what value delivery systems the organization must implement to win in that market-space.

And now something different – consumer market-spaces

The approaches to consumer market-spaces suffer from the same failure to understand and focus on discovering real value delivery options. Traditionally, managers are urged to consider geographic variables, demographics (age, income, culture, family-structure), product usage behaviors, attribute ratings, psychographics (lifestyle, personality type, social class), and other variables in segmenting a consumer market.

This *may* produce customer groups that can each be described by a singular VDS appropriate for all customers within it. Instead, it may produce groups that are defined and distinguished primarily by attribute ratings, product usage patterns, or psychographics, for example. In effect, traditional segmentation methods *permit* but do not encourage, let alone demand, the identification of customer groups based on the distinct VDS appropriate to them. Not surprisingly, this approach produces lots of segments only loosely related, at best, to a value delivery strategy.

Even when conventional segmentation accidentally produces segments of customers for whom the same VDS would be appropriate, managers typically do not understand them in these terms. As a result, the organization probably won't discover what the right value proposition for those customers is. So it likely still delivers a wrong or suboptimal one.

Analyze, design, choose: practical methodology

The fashion pendulum in the business world seems to swing between two extremes regarding strategic analysis. On the one hand, many organizations conduct arduous analyses focused on such issues as industry structure, competitors' behavior, management's favored core competencies, customers' product requirements, or perhaps psychographic profiles. Often, managers find that while they have large files of crunched numbers, they have no clear business strategy. On the other hand, it is also in vogue to dispense with most analysis altogether, citing 'analysis-paralysis,' a state which is sometimes a source of genuine frustration for managers and sometimes merely a justification for not having to think too hard. A complete lack of analysis rarely produces coherent business strategy.

To formulate strategy by the principles of *DPV*, an organization must identify its value delivery options. This approach encourages a thorough, fact-based analysis of the organization's strategic alternatives with a long-term, imaginative perspective. However, it is also single-mindedly aimed at one practical objective – to make clear business decisions upon which the organization can act. Those decisions define the organization's businesses: what are the primary VDSs we will implement, and why is this the optimal choice for the organization? Within its constraints, an organization should base these decisions on the most profound and factual understanding of potential customers and of how the organization could profitably deliver superior value to them.

The methodology for identifying value delivery options consists of selecting market-spaces to explore, then designing winning businesses by deeply understanding potential customers, their alternatives, and the organization's limits, and finally selecting businesses and market-spaces.

Formulating strategy by identifying value delivery options

I   Select market-spaces to explore and define their boundaries
II   In each market-space, formulate optimal strategy
    A   For a sample, design preliminary primary VDSs
       1   Select a sample of potential primary entities
       2   For each entity in the sample, become the customer
          a   discover valuable potential experiences
          b   identify competing alternatives
       3   Assess costs and capability gaps
       4   Design preliminary winning primary VDS
    B   Complete description of value delivery options
       1   Verify preliminary VDSs among the sample
       2   Group results into VDSs and quantify
       3   Identify additional value delivery options
       4   Design supporting VDSs
    C   Determine optimal VDSs and market-space's attractiveness
III   Choose organization's optimal market-spaces, thus its VDSs.

The central analysis in this methodology is II.A.2 above, in which individual customers' current and potential experiences are systematically discovered and defined. This intuitive but unconventional search for business insight is generally the most crucial and difficult aspect of formulating strategy by identification of value delivery options. The specific methodology for conducting it, called *becoming the customer*, is detailed in the following three chapters. The entire process, of which *becoming the customer* is a part, is strategy formulation by the principles of *DPV*.

I   Select market-spaces to explore and define their boundaries

Any organization that already operates a business thereby competes in some market-space. In reviewing its strategy, an organization will want to analyze that market-space, assuming it plans to remain in it for the foreseeable future. However, many organizations seeking new growth need to explore market-spaces in which they do not compete as yet. In either case, an organization wishing to begin formulating strategy should first select the market-spaces it wishes to explore.

II   In each market-space, formulate the organization's optimal strategy

For each selected market-space, the organization determines its best strategy. The organization must answer this question: 'What lineup of businesses (none, one, or several) in this market-space would maximize the organization's success over the long-term?' To answer this, the organization must first identify options within the market-space by analyzing in depth a sample of potential primary entities.

II.A   For a sample of entities, design preliminary primary VDSs

Managers must study a sample of current or potential primary entities in adequate depth to determine what primary VDS would be most appropriate to them. This process begins with selecting the sample. Then managers apply the analysis of *becoming the customer*, the systematic attempt to identify the most important resulting experiences that should be delivered to the analyzed customer in order to win their preference. Then the organization analyzes each of these important resulting experiences and assesses the organization's costs and capability gaps to deliver them. Based on this analysis, managers then design a preliminary primary VDS to win the business of the analyzed customer.

II.A.1   Select a sample of potential primary entities

Managers should select a sample of current and/or potential primary entities from within the defined market-space. This sample should be statistically small; it is not intended to be representative of the whole market-space. Rather, it allows one to identify several options within the market-space.

These can be quantified and additional options identified later. The only criteria this initial sample need satisfy is that it contain potential primary entities of the subject market-space. *The appropriate size* of an initial sample varies with the diversity and complexity of the market-space. Typically, initial samples of 25–30 consumers or 10–15 business-customers are practical.

II.A.2 Become the customer

The first, major portion of this process, of designing a preliminary primary VDS for a sampled customer, is *becoming the customer*. One starts with discovery and analysis of the customer's current experiences and the creation of possible improved experiences (both discussed in Chapters 16 and 17). Then the analysis continues with the identification of the customer's likely best competing alternative experiences (Chapter 18). This analysis helps managers identify resulting experiences that would be part of a winning value proposition to the analyzed customer in one or more future timeframes.

II.A.3 Assess costs and capability gaps to deliver identified resulting experiences

After having *become the customer* for this primary entity and thus identified the most important potential resulting experiences, the organization must determine its potential to deliver the identified resulting experiences to this customer. One identifies how the organization would go about delivering these experiences and thus what the organization's costs *would* be and what capabilities it *would* need in delivering them. From this analysis the organization can define the gaps the organization may face in those capabilities and estimate its chances of closing those gaps. This analysis may also reveal conflicts and synergies in trying to deliver the various resulting experiences.

This approach to analyzing capabilities differs importantly from much of popular practice in which managers start with a definition of what the organization is good at doing or what the organization thinks it could do better than competition.

II.A.4 Design the winning primary VDS for this customer

Next, the organization preliminarily designs the winning primary VDS appropriate for the customer studied. This designed VDS is only tentative, but it should nonetheless be a completely designed primary VDS (see Chapter Nine, p. 136). Since it is a *primary* VDS, moreover, it must include the required actions and resources of other entities in the relevant value delivery chain and some idea of how this cooperation will be secured.

II.B Complete description of options

With a set of options identified, the organization should preliminarily verify these with the customers studied in the sample. Then the size and customer-composition of the most promising options should be analyzed quantitatively. In this process, additional options are often uncovered. From these remaining options, the organization must choose the most promising and design supporting VDSs for them. This completes the description of the options.

II.B.1 Verify the preliminary primary VDSs among the sample

Once an organization tentatively formulates value propositions that could be winners, it is often useful to go back to the analyzed primary entities to verify the hypothesis. Managers can describe in rich detail the scenario representing the preliminary value proposition and contrast it with competing value propositions. Thus one can verify that the value proposition is indeed superior.

II.B.2 Group the primary VDSs to define some options preliminarily, then quantify their size and composition

After this analysis of individual primary entities in the sample, managers must group the results by similar VDSs. This preliminarily identifies value delivery options. However, the analysis is not actionable until one learns the approximate size and customer-composition of each option. Who else, what other primary entities, belong to this option? What are their useful common characteristics, if any?

Potential primary entities in a market-space are part of the same option if two conditions hold: (1) the organization concludes that these entities would find the same value proposition superior if it were delivered to them; and (2) the organization would also provide and communicate it to them in essentially the same manner. So the whole primary VDS, not simply the value proposition, bounds a value delivery option. Three techniques are helpful to quantify the composition of an option.

1 *Quantitatively repeat the individual in-depth analysis.* Having analyzed a small sample of primary entities, it is possible to repeat this analysis on a much larger, quantitatively valid sample. This demands resources, but the required time can usually be reduced substantially after the initial sample, since teams become much more proficient and common customer-phenomena become increasingly apparent.

2   *Research a large sample of primary entities' reactions.* Often a much faster technique of quantification is possible. If the value propositions are well defined, rigorously articulated, and adequately detailed, a quantitative sample of primary entities can be researched, producing a quantitatively valid measure of each option.

A statistically representative sample, e.g. several hundred primary entities, can now be interviewed to get their reactions to the possible value propositions. To each, the researcher carefully describes in detail each of the value propositions, including the competing alternatives to them, identified in the initial sample analysis. In the quantitative sample, any primary entity who responds best to a particular primary VDS is *in* the option defined by it. So, if some portion of this quantitative sample responds best to one of the primary VDSs, so would roughly that portion of the marketspace.

The key to using these powerful research techniques effectively is to use well-defined resulting experiences. Far too often, managers conduct a few focus groups, which result in a perfunctory, often customer-compelled description of a set of so-called benefits. The statistical analysis of the data may be superb, but due to the weak definition of this crucial variable, the whole exercise is a waste. Garbage in, garbage out. Carefully applying the *DPV* methodology to a small sample of primary entities first, however, these quantitative techniques can yield successful results. Still, three more caveats should be noted: (1) potential customers may not easily appreciate new experiences, (2) in a business entity, one must get reaction beyond buyers, and (3) confidentiality concerns may inhibit sharing new concepts with customers.

3   *Surrogate variables.* It may be the case that the primary entities in a particular option share a particular set of characteristics, such as some demographic, product usage, or other behavioral trait. It may also be the case that all primary entities with those characteristics are in that same option. Once one becomes confident of this strong correlation, one can determine the size of the option simply by measuring how many customers with these characteristics exist. In this sense, these characteristics are surrogates for the truly important but more elusive variable – what VDS would most profitably win these customers' preference over the long-term? By discovering these surrogates, options can better be quantified, understood, and efficiently pursued.

Once managers have quantified the composition of each option, they can refine the estimated cost of pursuing it. If it turns out that a particular option is very small, the ratio of cost relative to potential revenue may be unfavorable. At minimum, one may have to increase the price and/or diminish the resulting experiences delivered. Shared economies or other synergies with other businesses could ultimately make the option attractive after all; otherwise, it may be unprofitable to pursue. Of course, the option may be more attractive if larger than initially assumed. Identifying surrogate variables may also affect cost estimates. For example, it may be less expensive to deliver the right value proposition to consumers with distinctive demographic or product usage characteristics.

II.B.3 Identify any significant additional options

The preliminary, non-quantitative analysis uses a small, non-representative sample. It is possible that significant options, not represented by any primary entity in that initial sample, do exist. The three quantification techniques discussed above will all identify at least some of any value delivery options not revealed in analyzing the initial small sample.

II.B.4 Design appropriate supporting VDSs

At this point, one must more fully consider the supporting entities in the value delivery chains of the primary entities analyzed. Quite often, in the analysis of the initial sample of primary entities, there are other important entities, such as intermediaries, off-line entities, and suppliers. These supporting entities must play various supporting roles in the implementation of the primary VDSs. Now that all or most options in the market-space have been roughly described, it should be clear what those supporting roles need to be. The organization now must study the supporting entities in greater depth and design the appropriate supporting VDSs to secure their coordinated cooperation.

II.C Based on the above analysis, determine the organization's optimal VDSs in this market-space and the market-space's attractiveness

The organization must finally assess the attractiveness of the identified options for the market-space being explored. Which, if any, should it actually pursue? How attractive would it be in net for the organization to pursue this optimal set of businesses for this market-space?

If a large number of options has been identified, it may be possible to eliminate some easily. Some may obviously represent little or no potential for the organization. Some may be too small to bother with. Or it may be highly unlikely that the organization could implement the required winning primary VDS.

For the remaining options, the manager must next roughly estimate the share of each that the organization could capture. This is necessarily a guess, but it is a guess one must make in order to estimate the wealth associated with pursuing an option. Obviously, estimating share becomes more difficult when dealing with a timeframe in the distant future, an unfamiliar option, or an undeveloped potential option, but it is imperative to make an estimate. This estimate involves two assessments: the organization's ability to stimulate growth of the option and the ability to win primary entities' preference. Before finally selecting the most attractive combination of value delivery options to pursue in a market-space, one must look at the possible interactions among them. Pursuing one option may impact, either negatively or positively, the success in another.

III   Choose organization's market-spaces and businesses

The organization must conduct the above analysis for each market-space to be explored. Just as potential businesses within a market-space may interact, positively or negatively, a similar analysis of interactions across market-spaces must also be made. The organization must then decide upon the market-spaces in which it will compete, taking into account these interactions. The net result is the entire organization's strategy, which includes all the businesses, or primary VDSs, that the organization will implement.

The need for thorough identification of strategic options, potential VDSs, is obvious when considering entry into a new market-space. However, an organization with well-established businesses still needs to review and update its strategy frequently. Identification of value delivery options does not require starting from scratch and ignoring existing businesses.

Consider HP's Vectra computer business. In the early 1990s, Vectra's small market share was diminishing, and the viability of the business was in doubt. Wondering whether the company should segment the entire PC market, the division's management were exposed to the value delivery framework. As a result, a route more appropriate to the situation's urgency emerged: try to discover an option that included some primary entities actually buying and using Vectras. After all, some machines were leaving Vectra plants and not returning. Assuming these weren't purchasing errors, someone was probably getting a good value proposition. Maybe there were other potential customers like them.

The Vectra team subsequently investigated a sale at Taco Bell, the Mexican fast food chain then pursuing a much lower cost structure. They operated each restaurant with a single PC, so it was essential that it did not malfunction. The HP team discovered that units using other PCs had experienced unacceptably high breakdown. Units using Vectra, however, were experiencing very few problems. Why? In an office, Vectras were no less likely to break down than other PCs. However, most PCs don't react well to something commonly found in the Taco Bell atmosphere but never found in an office: grease. HP is constitutionally incapable of designing and manufacturing equipment that does not have exceptional reliability, regardless of whether customers seem to want it. Without having thought about grease, the Vectra's design team had made it virtually impermeable to grease.

Thus, an option was discovered whose primary entities included fast food operators. But the fast food environment is not the only one in which keeping a computer up and running is at once vital and, due to some alien element, difficult. Many industrial or commercial environments include hostile elements such as heat, moisture, electro-magnetic noise, or vibration. Pursuing this connection, HP soon made another important sale of Vectras to an automobile assembly plant. This small option was large enough for Vectra to pursue, at least until the organization could get the business back on track. At the time, identifying other options would have been counterproductive.

***

A flow chart follows, depicting the DPV methodology for formulating strategy. It is shown below, with the first analytic step highlighted. It is then repeated on the following four pages, each page highlighting and detailing the next major step.

Formulating value delivery strategy

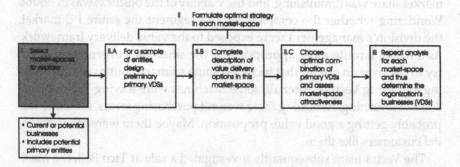

Formulating value-delivery strategy

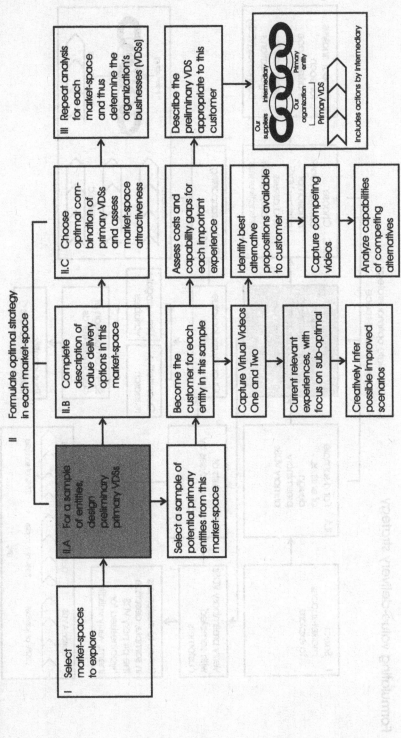

I Select market-spaces to explore

II Formulate optimal strategy in each market-space

II.A For a sample of entities, design preliminary primary VDSs

Select a sample of potential primary entities from this market-space

II.B Complete description of value delivery options in this market-space

Become the customer for each entity in this sample

Capture Virtual Videos One and Two

Current relevant experiences, with focus on sub-optimal

Creatively infer possible improved scenarios

II.C Choose optimal combination of primary VDSs and assess market-space attractiveness

Assess costs and capability gaps for each important experience

Identify best alternative propositions available to customer

Capture competing videos

Analyze capabilities of competing alternatives

III Repeat analysis for each market-space and thus determine the organization's businesses (VDSs)

Describe the preliminary VDS appropriate to this customer

Our suppliers Intermediary Our organization Primary entity

Primary VDS

Includes actions by intermediary

Formulating value-delivery strategy

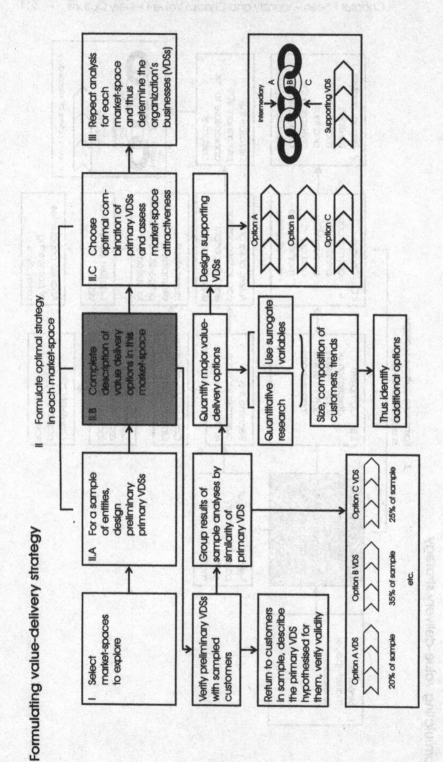

Formulating value-delivery strategy

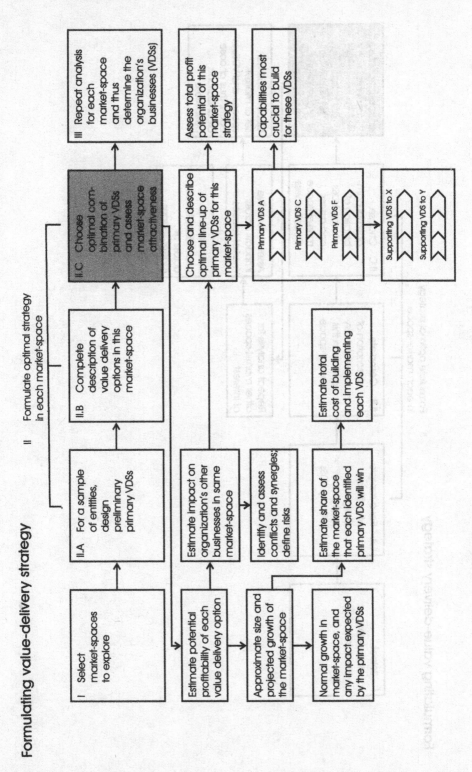

Formulating value-delivery strategy

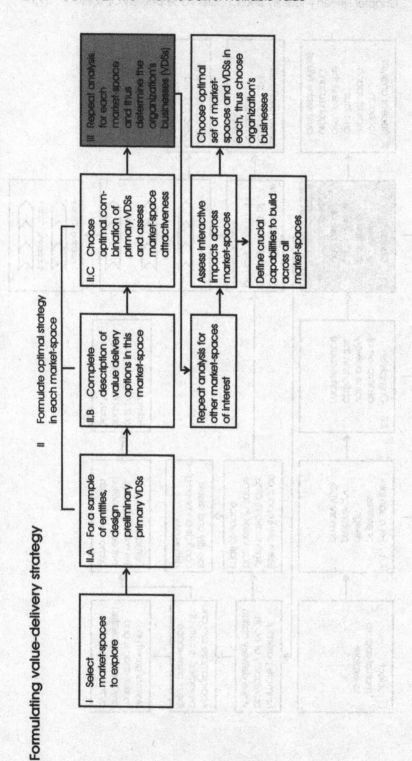

II   Formulate optimal strategy in each market-space

I Select market-spaces to explore

II.A For a sample of entities, design preliminary primary VDSs

II.B Complete description of value delivery options in this market-space

II.C Choose optimal combination of primary VDSs and assess market-space attractiveness

III Repeat analysis for each market-space and thus determine the organization's businesses (VDSs)

Repeat analysis for other market-spaces of interest

Assess interactive impacts across market-spaces

Define crucial capabilities to build across all market-spaces

Choose optimal set of market-spaces and VDSs in each, thus choose organization's businesses

***

Although it requires a serious commitment, analyzing market-spaces to identify value delivery options ultimately *saves* a great deal of an organization's precious time, since nothing wastes time more than a confused strategy. The ability to analyze individual customers insightfully – to become the customers – is essential to the exploration of market-spaces and is the subject of the next three chapters.

Notes

1   In a typical cogeneration project, an industrial plant produces enough energy for its own use and sells some excess back to a local utility.

3   Kotler, *op. cit.*, p. 265.

4   T.V. Bonoma and B.P. Shapiro, *Segmenting the Industrial Market*, D.C. Heath, 1983, p. 5.

5   *Ibid*, pp. 7–18.

Chapter Sixteen

Stop Listening: *Become* Customers to Discover What They *Really* Want

Despite the resources expended in the name of marketing, many organizations simply do not understand customers' experiences adequately. To see why this is so, it is important to appreciate the very real difficulty of the task. First, the study of customers is often focused on the wrong levels in the value delivery chain. Organizations may overly focus on intermediaries while giving inadequate attention to primary entities. Or, they may concentrate on the buying functions in the primary entity's organization, ignoring actual users and the customer's whole business.

But an even greater challenge than studying the right customers is unlearning the conventional modes of determining what they want. Conventional approaches gather customers' requests, which tell managers what customers think the organization should do. This sheds little light on the actual experiences that would be most valuable. Managers must learn to discover what customers *really* want, not obtainable by listening to them say what they want. Managers must learn instead to simulate living the current experiences of customers or *becoming the customer*.

In this chapter, the basic principles of becoming the customer are briefly illustrated and summarized. In the next two chapters, a discussion of the virtual video method and of this value-delivery-focused approach to competitive analysis is offered.

Hold the phone! Hunting for buffalo in the phone company

In the early 1990s, Kodak introduced its Photo CD system to consumers worldwide. Photo CD let a consumer capture images on a roll of film and then have those images transferred onto a CD. To accomplish this, photo finishers bought Photo CD laser writers that could scan the negatives into a computer and write the images by laser to a CD. This allowed consumers later to view the photos as still images on a TV or to incorporate them into a computer application. To view the images on a TV, the consumer bought a Photo CD player. The system was an impressive technological achievement. However, the substantial price of the player and of transferring images to a CD, plus the limited consumer appreciation for viewing photos on a TV, all added up to initial disappointment for Kodak.

At this same time, Kodak's Mass Memory Division (MMD) wanted to sell more of its large-scale data storage system, known as an optical disk library, in a non-consumer market. This system held a set of 14-inch laser disks that store data like a CD, but in larger quantity. The disks are stacked; robotic arms retrieve the disks in an arrangement reminiscent of a record jukebox. Using some of the Photo CD technology, this system allows a customer to record, store, and retrieve as needed large data quantities. An entire juke-box holds about a terabyte, or a thousand gigabytes of information. Users of the jukebox can retrieve data within 30 seconds, as compared to down-loading from a tape, which can take up to several minutes. While the juke-box is nearly as fast as on-line retrieval, where data resides on the computer's hard disk, it is less expensive. While MMD's main focus was the jukebox, it had prepared to explore possible industrial markets for Photo CD.

Also at this time, MMD's general manager, Don Strickland, wanted to apply the concepts and methodology of *DPV*. Strickland asked the MMD R&D manager, Dr Fred Geyer, to lead this exploratory effort. Geyer, a physicist, shared Strickland's desire to genuinely integrate R&D and other functions around a deep understanding of the customer. Whereas some felt that an R&D manager should stay in the lab, Geyer thought his real job should be tracking down business opportunities. Rejecting the usual functional pigeonholes, Geyer decided he wasn't really 'Director of R&D,' but rather, as his business card has subsequently stated, 'Buffalo Hunter.'

In this capacity, Geyer led one cross-functional team in a joint exploration with long-distance carrier MCI. Because such carriers must store huge quantities of billing data, MMD felt MCI might be a good user of the juke-box. The team explained to MCI's Information Technology (IT) department that MMD wanted to better understand the whole MCI value delivery system. MCI's value propositions had been centered on resulting experiences similar to AT&T's but at a lower price. AT&T's response to MCI's offering had been to make the journey with AT&T easier while keeping the difference in price small. AT&T typically delivered better information to the customer about their telecomm services. For the consumer market, this meant, for example, that AT&T had been ahead of the lower price carriers for some time in allowing immediate billing corrections. To better understand how MCI might improve its value proposition relative to AT&T's, the team therefore wanted to study the customer service function, in addition to IT.

IT agreed to work with the team to construct what the team called a 'video' of a 'Day in the Life' of the customer service department. Without literally making a tape, the team interviewed people in the department, documenting what actually happened during a billing inquiry. How often did customers make inquiries regarding bills that were no longer on-line? What happened next, with what consequences for the customer, department, and MCI? The team learned what actually happened, then analyzed what was missing, frustrating, or otherwise sub-optimal for MCI.

When a customer called MCI to make an inquiry about their bill, an MCI customer service rep would retrieve that bill. Current-month billing data was stored on-line, older ones on tape. If a customer inquired about a bill that was two months old, the service rep would not be able to answer the question during the initial phone call. The rep would have to call back, perhaps the next day, and would often fail to reach them easily and ultimately leave the customer frustrated. With Kodak's laser disk library, the customer service rep could possibly retrieve the two-month old data while the customer was still on the phone, arguably a better solution than on-line or tape storage. The jukebox clearly had a potential application in improving MCI's ability to respond to billing queries.

However, the customer service department did not only encounter this one situation, so the team asked them to describe others. This revealed other aspects of the billing process, including that for *corporate* customers. Here, customer service described a scene of great importance to them, the relevance of which to the jukebox was not immediately apparent. Corporate customers were sent their monthly MCI bills over telecomm lines directly into mainframe computers. From there, the customer could review the bill, in theory. However, a corporate customer typically includes scores of individual departmental entities, each of which accounted for part of the total phone bill. For a departmental entity to view the portion relevant to them on the mainframe was not easy, as is typical of data entombed in a mainframe system. Numerous customers had asked MCI to send the bill on floppy disks, so that departments could load these disks onto desktop computers and review their department's portion of the bill. This was no improvement, however, as a large corporate bill for a month required numerous floppies. Trying to distribute and manage these large sets created chaos.

The team did not ask, 'Could selling them a jukebox solve this problem?' Instead, they asked, 'What would an improved scenario be?' Only once that question was answered did they ask, 'And could we imagine helping them get to that better scenario? Maybe even profitably for us?'

Together, MMD and MCI's IT and customer service brainstormed a better scenario by imagining how it would look. A departmental manager would be seated at her PC. The bill for her department would somehow be easily, quickly, and accurately loaded onto her PC. The data would arrive at her desk, as easy to work with as if it were on only one disk. That was the better scenario they imagined.

Now they turned their minds to figuring out how this could happen and what it had to do with selling 14-inch laser disk jukebox libraries? It could happen if the manager had the bill written onto a CD and a CD ROM player attached to her PC. Maybe this didn't have anything to do with the jukebox, but it did have to do with a winning value proposition to MCI. If MCI were to have a CD writer with which they could efficiently write each customer's monthly bill, even large corporate customers' bills could be fitted onto one CD. At this time, CD ROM players were already nearly ubiquitous where PCs were found. Although MMD had not approached MCI with any intent of selling Photo CD, this same technology perfectly allowed MCI to realize a much-improved scenario for its corporate customer business.

MCI enthusiastically opted to buy the Photo CD product for use in its corporate customer billing process. Geyer's buffalo-hunting team had to improvise quite a bit to adapt the product to the MCI application, but managed to pull it off. As a result, MCI won an award from a telecomm industry trade group for the most innovative new product introduction in the industry for the year, and the Kodak product was featured on the cover of that year's MCI annual report.

The MCI case was a catalytic event for Kodak in developing the Photo CD technology for industrial markets. This success at MCI proved that some interesting and potentially profitable opportunities were out there waiting to be discovered, if only the enterprising hunting parties could be formed to find them. Kodak since uncovered a whole herd of buffalo, a wide range of industrial applications where frequently publishing customized data via CD delivers real value. Kodak subsequently created several related growing and profitable businesses based on such industrial applications.

Basic principles of becoming the customer

Managers should employ whatever works, within ethical and legal bounds, to enter customers' experiences imaginatively. *DPV* suggests a specific approach focused on seeing life as the customers do. This means learning to identify with the customers studied, seeing their goals, objectives, desires, and problems as if they were part of the manager's own life. The question is not what experiences you would want if *you* were in the customer's situation but rather if you *were* the customer.

Institutionalize the entrepreneurial perspective

Fairly often, successful entrepreneurs were literally in their customer's position prior to building their businesses. As a customer, they had a problem, created a solution to this problem, and translated the solution into a product. It is this aspect of entrepreneurial behavior and thinking that business organizations should strive to institutionalize.

Consider Steve Wozniak. He was working as an engineer for Hewlett-Packard in the mid-1970s. Computers were expensive machines that offered limited access for individual engineers. Steve wanted his own computer, one that he could program and control himself. So he proposed making a business out of personal computers, an idea HP rejected but one that he and Steve Jobs turned into Apple. Rollin King, prior to founding Southwest Airlines, was himself a frequent traveler on short business trips, frustrated by the current options available for this kind of travel. He couldn't help wondering, 'Why *couldn't* one make these trips in much less time, yet at no more than the cost of driving?' (See Chapter Eight.) Edwin Land was fascinated by photography. When taking a photograph of his young daughter, she demanded to know why *couldn't* she see the picture *now*? This question set Polaroid in motion.

Most organizations fail to emulate this behavior institutionally, even those led by successful entrepreneurs. Thus, organizations usually do not return to the market-space, genuinely to rethink the business from the perspective of customers. This rethinking has little to do with asking customers, 'What should we do next?' It is about behaving like a new firm with a nearly blank slate rather than an established firm trying to defend its competitive position. It is about institutionalizing the process of creatively observing customers to search for new business opportunities.

Act like an anthropologist

Becoming the customer is a mindset and process similar in some ways to that of an anthropologist or sociologist. Social scientists often gain their deepest insights by systematically exploring the actual behaviors, beliefs, and motivations of a population under study. An anthropologist may spend time actually living among the population, temporarily adopting their language, customs, and even their values in order to understand who they are and why. A sociologist must cumulatively spend years of a career observing and documenting behaviors and interactions of the social groups they study. Most social scientists would not even consider reporting conclusions about peoples or societies without this direct, in-depth, observational exploration. Managers must learn to conduct a similar kind of exploration if they want to get beyond a superficial and hazy comprehension of the most important population for their success – their customers.

In many businesses, managers cannot hope to do this well without being able to relate to and identify with people who are in fact quite different from themselves. At Procter & Gamble, most people in brand management, R&D, or the advertising agencies spent little time washing their sinks, floors, or clothes. But a brand manager, to be maximally effective, needed to spend time using the relevant products and closely studying consumers' experiences with those products. S/he also needed to convince managers in various other functions to do the same. For many, however, it was not natural to take the relevant life of the primary entity seriously, actually to *study* something as pedestrian as housecleaning. After all, they had opted for a career as sophisticated marketing or advertising professionals or chemical engineers. It seemed beneath them to listen to scores of consumers discuss floor cleaning in depth and even less so to pretend to be a typical homemaker who must frequently clean the kitchen floor. The most direct route to insights, however, is through these experiences.

In many industries, managers are less embarrassed by their product, but just as squeamish about entering the life of real users. For some managers in phone companies, business customers are important and exciting whereas most residential customers are the little old ladies in tennis shoes. Although managers in consumer imaging know they must understand consumers, many more naturally understand the male, advanced amateur photographer than the young mother of two who is not even a little intrigued by f-stops, chemicals, or emulsions. To become the customer, managers must get beyond their embarrassment and beyond their squeamishness.

The industrial lubricant oil company mentioned in Chapter Four is studying the use of lubricant oil from the perspective of an automobile assembly plant in England. What that plant would most value from a lubricant supplier may never surface in asking the plant to state their needs or desired lubricant oil benefits. The lubricant oil company must spend time living in that British assembly plant, understanding the context in which the plant performs lubrication tasks. That context is the broader issue of maintaining assembly machinery and maximizing the productivity of that plant. The key questions to ask do not focus on oil per se but on how well the machinery is maintained and how well it performs. How often does machinery go down or need repair, with what cost and other impacts on the assembly operation or on the quality of the vehicle? When and how are these results affected by lubrication procedures, including the amount and type of oil and how it is used? When lubrication procedures are sub-optimal, why? What would it take to change these sub-optimal procedures, and what ultimate potential value would this bring to the productivity of the plant?

The lubricant company has to imagine that it runs that auto plant and wants to improve machine maintenance and productivity. Like an anthropologist focused on machine maintenance, the lubricant company *becomes* the plant. In like fashion, the Kodak data-storage team learned to think like MCI customer service long and well enough to uncover opportunity.

Be in *the customer's business*

The lubricant company must learn to see itself as being in a different business than that defined by the product: the business of machine maintenance and efficient auto assembly. Sometimes managers become nervous at this idea because they are convinced they could never know the customer's business better than the customer does. But the lubricant company does not have to become a better auto manufacturer than the customer. It only has to shift its priorities from making and selling oil to better maintaining manufacturing equipment so that the plant more efficiently assembles vehicles.

Study relevant experiences, not primarily the buying process

Becoming the customer focuses on what the customer experiences in their world, rather than how they look at suppliers. In a business customer, buying entities specify products and features they want, need, or require from suppliers. As has been discussed, others in the customer's organization influence this buying process. Most traditional approaches assume that these entities, the influencers and the buyers, should be the principal subject of study. Becoming the customer eschews this all-absorbing interest in *buying* and instead focuses on the customer organization's potential for deriving resulting experiences of value.

For a maker of cardiac monitoring devices, an analysis of a hospital's buyers, influencers, and their key buying factors is not central to becoming the customer. The device maker must study, instead, what happens when a nurse monitors and a doctor diagnoses a patient's cardiac condition. How much time and money do these processes take? Are the data gathered sometimes inaccurate or difficult to interpret, leading to an incorrect or belated diagnosis? If so, what kind and frequency of false positive and false negative diagnoses occur, with what consequences? Studying the buying process may produce lists of desired features, such as disk capacity or printing speed, but little information and even less insight into these crucial experiences in the hospital.

This is not to say that the buying process is unimportant. It too may include resulting experiences that can be improved. For example, the organization could make it easier for the hospital's buyer to select, order, and pay for the monitoring devices, thus saving the hospital valuable time and hassle. Such experiences are usually less important in a winning value proposition than ones more essential to the customer's business, e.g. diagnostic accuracy for the hospital. Nonetheless, they should be part of becoming-the-customer. Moreover, once an organization has identified some potentially valuable experiences that could be delivered to a customer, it must consider how it would deliver those experiences. This includes how to *communicate* them, which requires understanding the buying process. However, the becoming the customer methodology pursues, most fundamentally, an understanding of what experiences would be most valuable to the customer organization, not the way in which buying decisions are made.

Accept no substitutes: become the primary entities

To understand primary entities, managers must directly *become* them. Unfortunately, some in an organization may wrongly assume that studying primary entities through intermediaries is adequate, or even preferable. After all, the specious reasoning goes, 'those are the *intermediaries'* customers, not ours; the intermediaries surely understand them better than we could; and we must satisfy our customers [the intermediaries] who did not ask us to talk to their customers.'

For example, consider a manufacturer producing a technologically complex product that is integrated into a larger system by intermediaries, such as resellers or other integrators. The manufacturer wants good relationships with integrators, sees a demographically bewildering array of users beyond these intermediaries, and so may declare, 'These are our partners – we must rely on their guidance.' But it is foolish to rely on intermediaries for insight into one's primary entities. If the primary entities are consumers, the reseller or manufacturer or retailer may have lists of consumers' supposed needs but only an incomplete, superficial understanding of the consumers' actual relevant experiences. Similarly, if the primary entities are businesses, the intermediary likely has at best a sketchy impression of the experiences of actual users, their internal customers, and others inside the primary entity. The intermediary may have a strong opinion as to what the *buyer* in the primary entity requests but a far weaker understanding of what actually happens in those entities beyond the buying function.

Even if it were true that intermediaries understand the organization's primary entities better than the organization can, this would miss the point. The organization that wants to manage based on facts must *itself* understand the primary entity as deeply as possible. This is hardly possible with second-hand accounts, even if they are from someone who understands these users. More frequently, the intermediary does *not* adequately understand the primary entity.

Therefore, asking an intermediary to describe video one is very often futile. Such a request often devolves into the intermediary's insistence that they know what their customers want and that the organization should be a good partner and simply meet the intermediary's requirements.

If the entity to be studied is a consumer, the organization may want to *become* the whole household, rather than only a single individual. One member of a household may buy a product, while a different member actually uses it and other members are ultimately affected by its use. Only interviewing and/or observing one member of a household may amount to relying on a substitute for some of the most important customers.

Other entities are also popular as surrogates in becoming the customer. For example, many high tech firms favor expert or supposedly leading-edge users. By asking this group of users to give direction, the organization hopes it is reading a prediction of how the rest of users will later think and react. The problem is that these users are wildly unrepresentative of the body of potential users. What this rarefied breed like, understand, can use, disdain, etc., may not be *ahead* of the rest of the market; it often has no resemblance to the rest of the market, present or future. Another popular but illusory short cut is to hire gurus and industry fortunetellers to predict future trends. Asking the so-called *experts* saves an organization the trouble of studying the real habits, objectives, and behaviors of potential customers. Unfortunately, too many experts rely on technology-driven projections, customer-compelled market research, or worse. Even if a professional prognosticator who reliably understands primary entities well enough to set the organization's strategy could be found, the organization desperately needs to understand those users itself.

Therefore, to manage a business based on a fact-based understanding of what customers really want, managers should study those customers directly and forsake the substitutes that promise an easier path.

Observe or virtually observe real behavior

Becoming the customer is a search for understanding of the customer's real behavior in their real life. That search is best conducted by getting as close as is practically possible to *direct observation* of that behavior. Since direct observation is often not practical, however, becoming the customer consists of collecting information that *would* be revealed if the manager literally observed the customer's life and real experiences.

Honda realized that it might be insightful to watch and record customers actually putting bags into their trunks (boots), rather than discussing their trunk needs or their projections of future trunk trends (see Chapter 2, p. 40). If Honda could not arrange to watch this scene directly, however, asking motorists to describe this same scene from memory, in as much detail as possible, would provide a reasonable simulation.

Consider a Caribbean-based systems integrator trying to understand the national power company for one of the Caribbean island-nations. The utility told the integrator that they wanted to revamp their information technology and spelled out what products and services they wanted to buy. But the integrator needed a factual understanding of the way information is actually used in the utility's operation. So the integrator asked managers at the utility to describe in detail the steps they had taken in trying to meet peak demand for electricity. The utility, because of its information systems, could not institute the pricing plans it knew would motivate electric customers to use less power in peak periods. The systems were incapable of precisely measuring peak usage by time or geography on the island and did not allow the company to monitor and accurately measure actual usage by customers. The integrator thus came to recognize the value of specifically redesigning the information systems to facilitate the needed measurements. This realization drastically changed the process of revamping the information technology that was initially requested by the utility.

Data from literally observing the customer's real experiences, especially when subjects are unaware of the observation, is usually richer and more reliable than an oral recounting. In the absence of this data, however, managers can and must get the most complete picture possible of what *would have* been seen by direct observation. Becoming the customer is therefore a methodology that constantly asks the customer to explain more about what happens in their business or life. Why did that happen, to what further events did it lead, with what results? This line of inquiry is meant to virtually record a video of real events and their significance in the customer's life, which provides the raw material for profitably creating improved scenarios.

By not listening, respect customers more profoundly

The idea that organizations should not listen to customers leaves some well-meaning managers aghast. Listening to customers is a big improvement over ignoring them or trying to force internally-driven solutions upon them. *DPV* is certainly not meant to encourage organizations to regress toward the primitive state of totally disregarding customers. However, simply listening to customers is altogether insufficient and frequently downright misleading. Listening conventionally pursues the wrong question – 'What do customers want us to do?' – and is based on a highly flawed two-part premise – 'customers know, and can tell us, what they really want.'

Often customers do not truly know what relevant experiences would be most valuable to them, despite any guesses they might venture when asked. So it is of doubtful utility to ask. Even more often, the customer does not know both the experiences they would most value *and* what products and services, with what attributes, would best provide those experiences. And still more often, customers are not likely also to understand how the organization could most effectively communicate these experiences to them, although again they may well guess. Yet, in the name of listening to customers or heeding their voice, managers are urged to ask customers what the organization should supply and how. Becoming the customer rejects such inquiries as facile but futile requests for instructions, an easy but counterproductive way to feel like the organization is tuned in to its customers.

Becoming the customer does not imply disregarding customers; on the contrary, it shows a more profound and genuine respect for them because managers practicing it must have a profound respect for the customer's beliefs, desires, and priorities. Managers often assume that the customer thinks and reacts in much the same way as they do. Or some may feel that the customer *should* behave in this way, and therefore the customer's concerns and aspirations may be trivialized, dismissed, or simply unnoticed. The concept here is *not* to imagine that the customer has become *you*, with all your perceptions and judgments, but rather the other way around. If the customer finds an experience difficult, irritating, and worrisome, it is – even if you don't.

Recently, for example, a team of engineers and marketers for a test and measurement business examined the trials and tribulations of some actual users, technicians, in several primary entity organizations. At first, the observing managers found it hard to imagine the users having difficulties with the test procedures in question, since the observing managers understood the procedures so well. They are, after all, so simple and obvious, they said. But they weren't so easy for the actual users, none of whom had spent years thinking about, let alone designing, this test equipment and its procedures. Only gradually did the observers realize the difficulty involved in learning these procedures, and they did so by assuming the perspective of the actual users.

Becoming the customer may lead to surprising results. To discover important but inconspicuous experiences, one must accept the likelihood of hitting a few dead ends. Not every imperfect customer experience will lead to an actionable insight. Moreover, sometimes those discoveries are unsettling and even frightening. If IBM had systematically become the customer in the late 1970s and early 1980s, it might have understood earlier that new and superior value propositions could be delivered outside the mainframe-centric model upon which the company was based. This insight would hardly have been easy to accept and use to guide action, however, since it meant rethinking and probably greatly changing the organization's entire strategy and culture. In addition, the insights discovered might produce scenarios that do not immediately please the customer who inspired the insights. Often, when customers are shown a new technology that would improve their lives, they respond at first with disdain, even though they later adopt it with enthusiasm.

Becoming the customer is about discovering and recognizing the experiences that would be most valuable to customers and that the organization may be able to deliver profitably. The methodology is designed to help managers achieve this understanding without being too distracted by their own or the customer's discomfort with unfamiliar results.

Don't ignore competitors – become customers, understand their alternatives

In formulating strategy by identifying value delivery options, managers will not ignore competitors. However, the focus of analysis and creative thinking must revolve around understanding what experiences customers may have available to them. It must not revolve around how to make the organization's operation different from or better than competitors' operations. Managers must determine the value propositions that the organization must beat. By becoming the customer, the organization can explore what alternative experiences the customer may be able to derive by selecting various competing alternatives.

***

These principles of becoming the customer are central to the overall approach of formulating value delivery strategy. But what is the specific method by which to put these principles into action in practical terms? The next chapter turns to the method of making virtual 'video tapes' of the personal and/or business life of the customer. Here is where managers truly stop listening to customers and delve more profoundly beyond the customer-surface, in the search for strategic insights.

Virtual Videos of the Customer's Life: Structured Method for *Becoming the Customer*

As part of the strategy formulation process discussed in Chapter Fifteen, an organization first defines the rough boundaries of the market-space it wishes to explore and then selects a sample of potential primary entities to study. Managers then become the customer for each primary entity in that sample. This begins with determining what individuals or groups within the primary entity to study. Then they construct a written description of scenarios from the customer's life that are relevant to the organization. This is much like capturing on videotape the customer's most relevant experiences. This virtual video arms the managers with the understanding they need.

Two versions of this virtual video are developed and written. The first, called Video One, explores what the customer's experiences currently are. The becoming the customer team asks, 'What happens today? Why? What were the customer entity's objectives and how well were they met? What aspects of Video One are imperfect or could conceivably be improved from the perspective of what the customer ultimately wants to accomplish?'

Video Two, in which the organization imagines and documents in writing a possible, improved scenario of experiences for the same customer entity, is then created. The analyzing team asks, 'What experiences *would be most valuable* for this customer and also possible for the organization to help bring about profitably? What scenario of experiences could optimally reduce or eliminate the imperfections, frustrations, and missed opportunities seen in Video One?' The output of this analysis is a clearly defined set of resulting experiences.

Deeply study the customer's current scenario: virtual Video One

Becoming the customer starts with Video One – understanding and critiquing what currently happens in the customer's life. The analysis is somewhat different when the customer is a consumer versus a business. If the entity in question is a consumer or household, then Video One is a description of a representative set of events, processes, or incidents from the life of that consumer or household. These descriptions are like scenes in the video. Each documented scene should be one where the consumer now or potentially could use or be affected by some products or services relevant to the market-space under study.

Thus, Kodak studying a household for the consumer imaging market-space selects some scenes in which some imaging events happen and photo products and services are used. Kodak might document a vacation in which one member of the subject household takes some photos. In a second scene, another household member picks up the photos from a retailer and orders some enlargements. In another scene, members of this household are at a party where no pictures are taken. In another, one of these consumers picks up some photos but does nothing with them beyond storing them in a shoebox. In yet another, we see Grandma, who lives in another state, moved to tears by a baby picture received in the mail. All of these scenes can be critiqued for frustrations, difficulties, disappointments, and opportunities lost that are potentially relevant to consumer photography.

If the entity is a business, then one captures scenes that allow analysis of that entity's businesses. The analyzing team critiques each such scene, looking for relevant imperfections in the customer's business. For example, Weyerhaeuser would gather scenes in which a furniture maker buys, stores, cuts, laminates, and otherwise uses particleboard. The team also studies the furniture maker's whole manufacturing process, its technical performance, quality standards, and its costs. Scenes that reveal how the customer sells to its customers and that shed light on the attitudes and priorities of those customers are studied as well. In all of these scenes, the team searches for sub-optimal, imperfect, or frustrating aspects of the customer's business.

One cannot study everything in the customer's life, but a starting point for selecting scenes to document is the usage of relevant products. The customer may already use a product much like that of the organization; if so, a few scenes of them using it should be captured. Glaxo can study doctors prescribing Tagamet and patients using it. Sun Microsystems can observe and analyze engineers using workstations. Fidelity can study young professionals using a broker or employees trying to understand their pension plans.

Sometimes, however, the customer may not now use the relevant type of product. Makers of an interactive television have little relevant experience to study. Many photographic consumers often do not use relevant photographic products in a situation where they *could*. Kodak must capture these scenes to understand what potential may exist for the consumer to start using the products in them. If they have no experience with the relevant product, one must learn what they do now that is relevant. What is their experience where such products could potentially be useful?

In addition to the potential use of some products or services, Video One scenes can often be productively focused on the primary entity's *journey*.[1] An organization, such as Novell or Microsoft, for example, that makes a network operating system (NOS) might study a set of corporations as primary entities. In each case, scenes of both the destination and the journey would be important. Video one scenes of the destination may include actual users in the information technology (IT) function making use of their current NOS to administer the network. The organization might also capture scenes of these actual users' internal customers, perhaps using their corporate Intranet. In addition, scenes of the journey would feature the events surrounding the selection and installation of a new NOS, its maintenance, its expansion, and its upgrading.

Making virtual Video One of a given customer starts with selecting some scenes such as these that may reveal issues, opportunities, and potential resulting experiences of value. In each scene, the analyzing team tries to determine the customer's objectives, what is imperfect in the pursuit of those objectives, and how important each such imperfection is.

Understand the customer's objectives

In gathering a set of these scenes, the analyzing team should strive to understand the root motivations underlying each scene. *What was the customer's objective in this scene? What did they hope or intend to accomplish? Why, for what further purpose?* The team must *accept* the customer's most important objectives and goals, even if the team does not *share* the customer's worldview or personal/corporate values. The team must examine customers' behavior and thought patterns to deduce their underlying objectives. This analysis identifies what the customer wanted or hoped to accomplish in this scene, regardless of their thoughts, if any, about this organization and its product.

It is important to distinguish between the objectives of an individual or group and those of the larger entity to which they belong. Often these are not entirely the same, and are sometimes quite opposed to one another. What an actual user or a buyer may want to achieve is sometimes inconsistent with the best answer for the whole customer-organization. Similarly, in a household, spouses may disagree or a child's wants may conflict with the parents' priorities. The analyzing team must understand these sometimes different objectives, searching ultimately to understand the whole entity.

Discover imperfections in the customer's pursuit of these objectives

Then the team must ask, 'What happened, in this scene, relative to the customer's objectives? What was successful and what was sub-optimal?' Some imperfect event or series of events may have happened. The scene may reveal various forms of compromise, waste, frustration, failure, or near-failures. And, some events may have occurred that achieve the customer's real objectives nicely. However, the team should *not* simply seek or accept the customer's assessment of the scene. Based on the customer's objectives and on what actually happens, the analyzing organization must infer in what ways the scene may be imperfect for the customer.

To understand better its opportunities to offer cellular phone service, one European phone company several years ago constructed multiple Video Ones for a series of sales reps who at that time did not have cell phones. The Video Ones showed that maximizing the productive use of their expensive time was the reps' objective. It also uncovered some imperfect events. For example, on occasion the rep would drive to the next appointment only to find that the customer had canceled. In some cases, the cancellation had been phoned into the rep's office over an hour earlier. A sub-optimal and possibly actionable event therefore was that the rep did not learn of the cancellation as early as she could have since she was incommunicado, in her car. The rep and her firm may not have complained about this situation, as they were not yet accustomed to using car phones. Nonetheless, the imperfect event was quite clear to the analyzing team.

One sub-optimal event may lead to another event or occurrence. In this fashion, we may need to peel the onion back, successively discovering subsequent layers of events. Consider a Video One in which doctors and nurses monitor a patient's cardiac condition and sometimes struggle to read the data accurately. This leads to difficulty in interpreting it. This in turn may eat up more time reaching a diagnosis for each patient. This time lost may impact the efficacy of the treatment ultimately selected and may increase total treatment costs. In a related but different final result, the same difficulty reading and interpreting the data could cause a misdiagnosis, leading in turn to adverse health effects and higher costs.

So what? Analyze the importance of these imperfect events

For this same imperfect event, one must then ask, 'So what? What end-result consequences result, of what importance to the customer? What is lost or not gained? Is some aspect of the customer's objectives thus frustrated or compromised?' The phone company rep did not learn of the cancellation for an hour; had she learned of it earlier, she might have gotten another appointment to fill the time or gone directly to her *next* appointment and finished some administrative tasks while waiting. Ultimately, the end-result consequence of the event is that the company lost money through the non-productive use of her time.

Then, to the extent possible, one must roughly quantify the importance of these end-result consequences. Sometimes one can quantify, even if only by estimating, the import of these consequences. If the sales rep loses an hour on average, one can fairly easily assign a cost. When the auto assembly plant experiences scheduled downtime, possibly affected by lubrication maintenance procedures, the cost of scheduled downtime is measurable, as is the more costly unscheduled downtime. However, when a hospital loses time providing a therapy, calculating the economic value of this result is more subjective.

It is nonetheless necessary to calculate this economic value, regardless of the difficulty involved. Frequently, for example, the hospital must incur additional costs due to a less desirable health outcome caused by the delay in therapy. Furthermore, the hospital and the various entities that pay for and authorize expenses must make numerous implicit judgments as to the value of improved health outcomes. These other judgments may allow the organization analyzing the hospital to estimate the value of this difference in health outcome caused by the delay.

To understand fully a sub-optimal event's importance, however, we must also learn the frequency with which it occurs. For the sales rep, how often does an appointment get canceled *and* the customer knows it an hour or so before the appointed time? Thus, how often does it happen that an appointment is canceled in time for reps to change their schedule productively, yet the reps are not informed until it is too late? How often does the auto plant suffer unscheduled downtime as a result of maintenance procedures? By modeling the rough frequency of these events, one can begin to see their real magnitude.

Below is an excerpt from a recent virtual video that was constructed by a British operator of petrol service stations. The primary entity interviewed was an English woman, Jane, who recounted her experience in using a station northwest of London.

Video One

Scene One: Driving in and filling the car with petrol

9 pm, November, in a middle class urban area. It's dark, raining lightly and rather chilly. Jane, a working woman, 35 years old, is on the way home in her company-owned car. She sees a Station X, near her home, the one she habitually uses. She has grown accustomed to this station and its familiarity makes it a bit easier to use, but she doesn't particularly like using it and has been considering trying a new Shell station nearby.

The layout is four pump stations. Jane pulls up to a pump slot with her preferred grade, Super Unleaded, with the pump on the side where her fill-cap is. She picks a slot nearest the shop, as is her habit, especially at night. Jane is not extremely frightened to use a filling station at night, but she knows they are not the safest place to be at night and is slightly uneasy, so parking nearest the shop makes her feel more secure. She gets out, locks it. The lighting under the canopy is, the team estimates, about 70 percent of the brightness under the canopies of Shell, the competitor with the brightest lighting. Jane can see but finds it a bit dim. There are shadows. This contributes to her finding the place a little depressing and slightly dirty and to her feeling faintly threatened and insecure. Making this a bit worse, as she glances around she can see that outside the canopy it is much darker still, as parts of the forecourt are not nearly as well lit as under the canopy.

Jane tries to look into the shop. She prefers to see who's in the shop - how they look - but various advertising signs and other obstructions block her view of large parts of the store. She remembers her friend Helen telling her at work the other day of pulling into her station late one evening and, unable to see well into the shop, deciding to pull out again and refuel in the morning. Both women have a low-level fear that either some drunken lout or worse could be inside and become a potential problem for them. Jane remembers one time when she did see a creepy looking creature about this time of night inside the shop, and she did drive off then. She shrugs and decides to take her chances as usual, as she hates refueling in the morning, she in a hurry and the tank low.

She has parked as close to the curb of the pump-island as she can, to minimize the struggle she foresees with the petrol pump and hose. By going to the same station most of the time, she's able to minimize the problem; by knowing the exact layout at this station (they're all a bit different), she knows just where to park and how to position her car. Fortunately the canopy is large and she will stay dry, she realizes, while refueling. Jane now proceeds to fill the car's tank. She doesn't find this very easy or comfortable. The hose is heavy, for her. She finds it awkward and a strain to get it to the fill-cap, though she certainly can do it. The pump handle and trigger are metal. It being a bit cold this night, she knows this will feel uncomfortably cold after holding it for a while as the tank fills. She remembers that one of the other two stations she sometimes uses, also a Station X, has a plastic handle and trigger; but not this one. The pump trigger is a big distance from the top of the handle, too big for the size of her hand to grip and pull the trigger easily. The trigger is also resistant, and after a while her hand gets fatigued.

She finds the smell from the fumes a bit obnoxious, as usual. Half-way through the refill, the pump shuts off. This has happened before; she pulls the trigger again, gripping it with her second hand to help now. A few seconds later, it cuts off again. She adjusts the position of the nozzle in the hole but it cuts off again. Now she tries reducing the flow of petrol, holding the trigger only three-quarters of the way pulled.

Jane does not understand *that 'blow-back' (of which she has not heard) has triggered the butterfly valve (which she doesn't know exists) to shut off the pump, nor that she is supposed to reduce the flow of petrol when this happens; nor that the pump is in fine working condition.*

When she puts back the nozzle, she has to try twice to get it to go into the holster properly. In the process, she catches the hose in a bit of her clothing and must untangle it, hoping it doesn't leave grease on her skirt, which happened once some months previous. Distracted, she slips slightly on the more slippery surface of the island, but doesn't fall. She glances at her hands, a bit darkened and ever so slightly glistening. Wrinkling her nose, she sniffs her hands to confirm that they now smell lightly of Super Unleaded.

(Video One) Scene Two: Paying

She unlocks her car, grabs her purse, closes and re-locks the car, and turns toward the shop, which she knows closes around now but she hopes it's still open. After a few paces she steps in a shallow puddle that has built up during the rain from cars dripping water. Men stepping into one of these puddles wouldn't notice, but Jane, like a lot of women, is wearing shoes with a low side edge, less than an inch above the ground. She gets water inside her shoe and it seeps through her tights, leaving her foot a bit wet. There are four or five of these small puddles on the forecourt, because small holes have been created when edges of the concrete blocks that make up the forecourt are damaged. This is largely caused by Heavy Goods Vehicles (HGVs), which are now more common on the forecourt than before Diesel sales began. This station apparently does not fix these holes immediately. Jane shakes her foot and moves on, but then catches the edge of her heel on the crack between two concrete slabs and almost trips. She remembers another Station X she used the previous summer had rubber joints sealing these cracks; since she was wearing higher heels that evening, one sank into the joint and stuck, causing her to step out of the shoe.

A few feet from the shop she sees a sign saying it's closed, so she goes to the payment window at the right end of the shop. As she stands at the window, a light spray of water drips on her, coming at a 45 degree angle; the canopy, though large, leaves a space between its edge and the shop building where rain can fall. She now stands at the window, purse in hand, unable to see behind her, feeling more vulnerable and insecure; she occasionally glances over her shoulder, wanting to know if someone is coming up behind her.

At the pay window, she occasionally gets some unwanted verbal attention from others in line or passersby. The glass screen has holes, a bit high for her five-foot-two height. The reinforced window is locked. Communication with the cashier is a little strained.

Invent an improved possible scenario: make virtual Video Two

By thinking forwards from the imperfections and frustrations of Video One to an improved scenario, a manager moves to the next step in becoming the customer: imaginatively construct a Video Two. It may be appropriate to construct two versions of Video Two that reflect different timeframes: a longer and shorter term. In each case, the team asks, 'Roughly how could the life of the customer look if improved to the maximum possible extent relative to their basic objectives, with our organization profitably helping?'

This question must be asked within the boundaries of the market-space under study and of what the organization judges possible in the timeframe selected. Video two is not science fiction in which the customer's problems or limitations magically disappear. The improvements conceived must be ones that the organization suspects could be delivered profitably – for a cost less than the potential value of the improvement. And finally, Video Two frequently includes *inferior* experiences as compared to Video One that the customer would need to accept to attain the improvements identified. For example, in SWA's Video Two for the Texas traveler, the frequent and punctual point-to-point flights also meant that connections would not be easy and that the passenger would not have the comforts of food or reserved seats.

This exercise is necessarily imprecise and iterative. Video two describes the maximum improvements in the customer's life that the organization might be able to cause. If the customer, this time, did not experience the frustrations or compromises of Video One, what would that look like? What events would unfold this time, with what consequences, compared to Video One? Thus Video Two is not the result of asking, 'How do we sell our product to this customer? Or, how can we use what we are good at doing to address this customer's needs?' Video two is not really about the organization conducting the analysis; it pertains only to the experiences the customer could possibly derive with the help of the organization.

Following are excerpts from a Video Two of the motorist Jane, in which the scenes from Video One are improved upon.

Video Two

Scene One: Driving in and filling the car with petrol

It is an evening similar to the one in scene one of Video One; Jane drives into the station. The layout is four-square. She pulls up next to a pump slot with her grade, Super Unleaded, with the pump on the side where her fill-cap is. She picks a slot nearest the road, because it was easier to stop there. She no longer makes a point of parking nearest the shop. At this station she feels very secure, as much as she does in the daytime. She gets out of the car but doesn't lock it. It seems to Jane as bright as daylight under the canopy. She can see clearly, and there are no shadows. This contributes to her finding the place clean-looking and apparently safe. She sees that outside the canopy it is also brightly lit; all of the station is fully lit.

Jane looks into the shop, feeling more secure by knowing she can see if anyone is inside. She sees no one but the cashier and a clear sign indicating the shop is closed. She is not worried about handling the hose and so didn't try to park as close as possible to the island. Moreover, she finds it helpful that this station has painted marks on the concrete to show the ideal location for most cars to reach the fill-cap easily with the hose. She has noticed that the parking routine is about the same at any Station X, which she finds helpful.

The canopy is large and she will stay dry, she realizes, while refueling. Filling the car's tank, she finds this quite easy, clean, and comfortable. Before starting, she grabs a pair of disposable gloves and puts on a disposable apron. A roll of paper towels is also available to her if the handle seems dirty. She sees pamphlets available on the island offering information on car care and simple advice and info on refueling. One concerns Station X's efforts to make stations secure; it discusses a video and audio security system. She looks up and sees a camera, speaker, and microphone that apparently allow two way communication with the cashier, if needed. She feels even more secure.

Although the hose is heavy for her, it is suspended by wire and arranged so that she needs only a finger's strength to guide the hose to her car's filler-cap. The handle and trigger are plastic, so they are warm in winter, cool in summer. The pump trigger is a short, comfortable distance from the top of the handle, easy for her hand to grip and pull the trigger. The trigger is very light to the touch with minimal resistance, although if she relaxes her slight pressure at all it instantly shuts off; so her hand does not fatigue during the refueling. A fan blows warm air from above and behind her towards the front of her car; this warm air is not unpleasant itself on this cold evening (and in summer this air is cool) but more importantly she realizes that this keeps the obnoxious fumes from being noticeable. Half way through the refill, the pump shuts off. She remembers that when she took the nozzle from the holster the instructions noted in bold red print that this happens by design as a safety measure and that she should reduce the flow rate of petrol when it happens. She had always thought that this just happened because of poorly maintained pumps.

When she puts back the nozzle, it again moves easily, and the nozzle slides into the holster without a glitch. As she replaces the nozzle, the wire seems to guide the hose and keep it well clear of her and her clothes. She notices that the hose and handle are remarkably clean. After this, she takes off and discards the gloves and apron and sees that her hands are as clean as when she drove in. She smells no petrol either.

(Video Two) Scene Two: paying

Jane takes her purse from the car, locks it and heads for the pay window. Despite rain outside the canopy, she notes that the concrete slab of the forecourt, though damp, has no puddles. As she walks toward the window, she steps on a crack between slabs, without incident, as the joint is sealed with a smooth plastic (that doesn't become soft in summer).

At the window, she stays dry. A special small canopy has been extended over the window ensuring that even in a steady downpour she will stay dry. A mirror slightly above her lets her see behind her. The window is wide open and she can see the cashier smiling at her. The cashier can close and lock this window if he sees fit. He is clean cut. At the pay window, she may get a little unwanted verbal attention from others in line or passersby. The cashier might ask someone else in line to tone it down; if need be the cashier is prepared to call police for help, as the pamphlet mentioned. The conversation is simple and professional, the cashier reassuring and pleasant. She pays.

In contrast, consider a different group of motorists also revealed in this same market-space analysis. A typical motorist in this different group was Roger, a sales rep who recounted some of his common experiences using petrol stations. In Roger's case, Video One was about being in a hurry. On his way to his first sales call in the morning, Roger may need to fill up. He pulls into a station, sits behind another car while it is filled, then pulls up and proceeds to start pumping petrol. This takes a couple of minutes, including some minor delays. Then he goes inside the shop to pay and waits in a line while the register clerk sells crisps (potato chips) and dispenses trading stamps to the others in front of him. After turning down the crisps and stamps he gets to pay and leave, but only after spending a total of 8–12 minutes to get petrol.

Video Two for Roger is quite different than for Jane. The whole issue is time spent. Roger would go out of his way (hint: he would pay more in this supposed commodity business) to save as much of that 12 minutes as possible. The logical conclusion: Roger shouldn't spend *any* time in the petrol station. The extreme version of Video Two would see the organization regularly deliver petrol to Roger's car by special van, during the night. His car would be filled and his account charged while he slept and in the morning he would spend zero minutes in the petrol station on the way to his first sales call. In a less radical Video Two, Roger would pull into a station with at least part of its facilities devoted to one issue – speed. He would pull into an express lane, an electronic sensor would read a smart card on his car and automatically authorize use of the pump, which would be designed for much more rapid fuel pumping, after which he would leave, having only spent perhaps two minutes at the station. And in the least radical but still improved Video Two, Roger would still have to pay inside, but in an express line with no purchases of junk food or negotiations over trading stamps.

Part of what was interesting in these different results of becoming these motorists is how clearly they belong to different value delivery options. Yet, conventionally designed market research had categorized both of these motorists in the same 'benefits-based market segment.' Why? Because they were given a survey that asked them to rank their desires for several petrol station 'benefits,' including: 'brands,' 'friendly service,' 'car wash,' 'reduced time in-and-out of the station,' 'best petrol' and 'wider selection of convenience foods.' Of course, both Jane and Roger voted for reduced time, but this does not mean that they should have been classified in the same market segment. Once their real Video One experiences were properly understood, the entirely different VDSs appropriate to each of them were clear.

Techniques for becoming the customer

When this methodology is used to support strategy formulation, an organization's leaders and a rich cross-functional mix of managers must actively participate. Which managers? The managers who directly participate in choosing, providing, and communicating the organization's value propositions should be directly involved in becoming the customer. Managers at all hierarchical levels in an organization should be involved in gathering Video One data, and managers across all important functions should then debate and interpret Video One to convert it into Video Two. To get the best information, an organization must make becoming the customer the job of all strategically significant functions.

In most organizations, the bulk of creative intellectual activity is directed at the central production and selling tasks, the development of products, packaging, manufacturing processes, the redesign of logistics, and the creation of advertising. But this same reservoir of talent can create an exciting and important Video Two. Too many organizations prefer to conduct market research without involving this creative talent and intellectual capability. In an example of parochial turf protectionism, market research is often made the possession of one function, marketing. The other functions are then given 'the answer.' Thus they accept a prescription rather than participate in finding or even deeply understanding the best answers. Similarly, it is folly to farm out this extremely important task to outsiders. Yet consultants and outside market research firms are regularly paid to 'find out what customers want and come back and tell us.' Use a research firm to help, but an outside service firm is not better positioned to understand what you should do to win customers' preference profitably. This is your business. Get up and go find out yourself.

How? What follows are several techniques for both gathering Video One data and constructing Video Two.

How Video One data should be gathered

In most cases, Video One should initially be developed by interviewing individuals. The length of Video One interviews must vary by the marketspace being explored and the complexity of the customer's relevant experience. However, in general the interviews are much longer than conventional market research interviews, typical sales calls, or customer visits.

Interviews are usually best conducted by two-or-three person teams. During interviews, it can be helpful to diagram what the customer describes. Make notes on flip charts to which all can later refer. Draw a flow chart linking events and their end-result consequences. If the entity is a business, sketch one or more of its *de facto* VDSs. Numerous analytical, factual questions will arise in an interview that the interviewee may not be able to answer, at least on the spot. Keep track of the hypotheses and issues for further analysis as they arise, while keeping the interview on track in order to complete the narrative description of each series of events in each scene.

Although these techniques apply to interviews used to analyze both consumers and businesses, there are significant differences between consumer and business-customer interviews.

Analyzing consumers

A typical consumer interview will run one to two hours per individual. Often one may want to interview several members of the same household. There can be advantages to interviewing these several members simultaneously, if the events to be described happen to a group. Often, however, it is necessary to interview separately. The interviews must usually be conducted in person, given their length and the need to make the subject comfortable discussing numerous events in great detail. Moreover, it may be useful to conduct the interview in its relevant physical context, such as the consumer's home or the place where they experience some relevant service, so that the consumer can more easily remember and refer to details of the relevant events.

Few interview questions should be closed-ended, e.g. asking the consumer to select from a menu of responses or to give ratings. It should primarily consist of the consumer telling a set of stories - what happened, what they did, why they did it, how they felt about it, and what the consequential results were. The interviewers must react to the open-ended responses, so writing a script of questions to ask is impractical. These interviews ordinarily cannot be conducted as a focus group, where a collection of unrelated consumers is interviewed together. It is impossible in a focus group to have each individual recount detailed scenes, especially with the requisite candor.

In some cases, it is important to go beyond consumers' descriptions to validate and sometimes quantify the experiences they report. A manager can accomplish this by observing them. The British operator of petrol service stations, for example, found it helpful literally to videotape numerous aspects of motorists' experiences in using these stations. Other, somewhat indirect means can be used to gather additional factual information. For example, analyzing well-used products or the nature of services performed on products may reveal much about how customers actually used them. The soft-goods retailer who reengineered its shirts asked consumers to show interviewers their closets. The consumer would then help the interviewer analyze the frequency and type of occasions on which garments were actually worn. This helped discover by inference, for that consumer, the characteristics of clothes that were worn a lot versus those left hanging in the closet.

Analyzing business entities

For business customers, the initial stages of constructing Video One may entail anywhere from one-half to two days. Getting in-depth interviews with individuals beyond the buying function requires hard work and commitment. In some customer entities, the right interview simply cannot be obtained; often, primitive attitudes still common among some individuals in the buying role are the root cause. Encouraged by the supposedly sophisticated, *real politik* concepts in traditional industrial-organization oriented strategy theory, the buying function has often learned to view suppliers as a competitive force that must be kept in the dark at all costs. However, the right interviews usually *can* be achieved in enough customer entities to understand a market-space. If approached in a thoroughly professional manner, more customers will cooperate than many managers at first assume.

Often the resistance from buyers or other gatekeepers is due in part to concerns and misconceptions that can be dispelled. It is crucial to convince the buying function that becoming the customer does not include any *selling* and that the purpose is not to survey them – again – about their opinions and needs. Most buyers can be convinced that becoming the customer is a serious effort to understand their businesses far more deeply than ever before. They can and must be convinced that only through such an investment of time can the organization gain the fresh insights that can benefit both parties.

However, the customer's buying function usually interacts with the organization's sales force. This everyday relationship should usually *not* be the focal point for the process of becoming the customer. A sales rep knows only too well that calling the buyer and saying, 'Hello there! I hope you won't mind if I bring a team by your place to spend a day or two interviewing people throughout your organization?' will be met with a poor reaction. It is quite common for buyers to use their strong relationship with reps to decline easily. The rep must worry about next week's order and can hardly be expected to risk this relationship just to get an interview. It is far easier to come back empty handed. Similarly, asking non-buying functions to commit time to a supplier puts the buyer in a difficult position. The buyer is under pressure to protect manufacturing, R&D, marketing, and other people from calls by vendors and market researchers conducting yet another survey.

Therefore, to establish the contacts needed for this exploration, it is often most effective for neither the organization's sales force nor the customer's buying function to play a central role, although they must be informed and involved. It is often much more appropriate for managers in other functions, who are at a suitably high level in both organizations, to conduct the negotiations. Professional firms specializing in recruitment can sometimes obtain interviews more efficiently than the organization itself, if those firms are trained properly in the relevant aspects of the becoming the customer method.

Once the analysis is agreed upon in principle by the appropriate parties, it frequently makes sense to start interviewing the people who would ordinarily execute a relevant purchase. Usually, it helps to see the big picture of the entity's businesses as the buyer understands it. How does the buyer describe the entity's VDSs? Where does the buyer see the role in these VDSs of the processes, products, or services most relevant to the organization? Ask the buyer to help draw the value delivery chain, including the buying structure within the customer entity. This may only confirm assumptions or open a new understanding of what entities and individuals must be studied. Then it is often useful to document one or two scenes in which the buyer is directly involved. After this, however, it is essential to proceed with a series of interviews of people in other functions and entities within the customer organization without a buyer present.

A classic formula for a wasted customer visit starts with the buyer orchestrating the day. Usually, the interviewing team is ushered into a room where the buyer plays master of ceremonies. A series of representatives from various functions comes in and gives a slide presentation on various topics – trends in our industry today, new technologies, problems we have with you, etc.. The interviewing team (now reduced to listening, not becoming) may be asked to give a boring presentation of their own, which is usually about how great their company is. The buyer directs traffic, making sure that purchasing-correct messages are conveyed.

Excluding the buyer from a large portion of the interviews does not constitute going over the head of the buyer. The organization is not trying to sell the product or get a higher price. The actual users, their internal customers, and others inside the entity are what the analyzing organization must observe or virtually observe. These characters must describe the scenes; someone whose job it is to control suppliers must not. The sooner that the analytic team conveys that it is trying to understand the customer's business more thoroughly, the better. Also, interviews often lead one to interview other people not initially on the interview list. If an interviewee comments on tasks that affect someone else, it is often useful to talk to that someone else about it.

As with consumer interviews, supplementing interviews with actual observation can be helpful in some cases. Where possible, walk through the plant, ride with the customer's sales reps, and sit in the lab with their engineers. Construct experiments to quantify critical issues. Help and if necessary pay the customer to gather more facts. For example, a maker of computerized manufacturing controls needed to know precisely how often quality control inspectors make a visual error on a high-speed line. The customer agreed to rig a high-speed camera, at the computer maker's expense, capable of making the measurement.

Additional techniques can supplement interviews and observation. For example, managers can use the relevant products as real customers would. This often requires adopting a different mindset. If the manager is an expert and the customer is not, the manager must simulate the customer's state of inexperience. Consider General Motors. At least until the late 1980s, GM executives always drove new GM cars in pristine condition. They never even came close to a dealer floor or a service department. Ross Perot, during his unwelcome stay on GM's Board, articulated this evidence of the internally-driven nature of General Motors' culture:

> 'We ought to cut out this business that if you're an executive your car comes into the garage every morning and the mechanics take it, and if there's anything wrong with it they fix it. You don't know what reality is. Your car is perfect. Buy a car. Negotiate for it. Have the engine fail. Have the transmission fall out. Have the tailpipe fall off.'[2]

To address this and related problems, GM threw Perot off the Board.

Finally, using competing products can be helpful. Many industries are populated by managers with little or no experience in using competing products. It is rare that one will find an executive in a high tech company using a competing computer or peripheral product. IBM or Compaq executives, for example, who order a Dell computer and go through its very different purchasing and support experiences, are in a better position to study and understand real users and the alternative Dell represents. Well into the 1980s one hardly ever even *saw* a foreign car in Detroit, even though one out of five cars in the US was un-American. Looking out the window of one's perfectly tuned Detroit-mobile, many Detroit auto execs could easily avoid pondering most of reality.

Video Two: learning to think like a 12 year old – forwards

The more deeply managers understand Video One, the better chance they have of creating a Video Two full of greatly improved resulting experiences upon which the organization can build its strategy. Video two is the solving of a problem posed by Video One. Somewhat like detectives solving a mystery, managers must gather evidence about the customer's current problems and opportunities through Video One and then simply construct the scenario in which those problems are solved and opportunities realized. The question in Video Two is not, 'How can we most easily sell them our stuff?' but rather, 'What *would* we make happen, perhaps with help of others in the relevant chain, if our sole objective were to solve problems posed by Video One?'

By imagining an improvement for the customer, an organization is not obliged to deliver it. Video two is not an exercise in committing but rather an exercise in imagining valuable possibilities. Deciding what to do comes later with more evidence. However, managers accustomed to the norms of internally-driven thinking can easily lose their way the first time they try to move from Video One to Video Two. The great temptation is to return to the organization's comfort zone. 'Now that we understand customers, let's talk about our products and how we can sell them.' To think forwards is to start with Video One, then invent a scenario in which its problems and frustrations are reduced or eliminated, and then to imagine what capabilities, including features and characteristics of products and services, would be needed to cause that scenario. Only then should a manager ask, 'Do we have such capabilities? If not, could we build them?'

Managers would do well to think more like a twelve-year-old, unfettered by formulae that supposedly should guide strategy. Think unconstrained by the noise that clutters the adult, educated, modern manager's head. Temporarily forget the supposed Corporate Strategy; forget the supposedly enormous difficulties the organization would have in selling the customer a new solution; forget what the latest voice of the customer research said are the six top requirements of customers; forget the new eight corporate initiatives; and forget the organization's supposed core competencies. Just reverse what happens in Video One, so that its major imperfections are suppressed, contained, or obliterated. Ask what would it look like if some entity deliberately focused all of its attention on making these improvements happen. How much improvement is realistically imaginable?

In the Emperor's New Clothes, it is a young boy who points out, to everyone's horror at first, that despite all the fine description of the Emperor's new robe, he is in simple fact riding through the city stark naked. Sometimes, like Alice in looking glass land, the child's perspective may be more sane than that of the adults. Therefore, it is helpful in Video Two to suspend preconceptions and restrain one's impatience to get back to one's *real* job.

Once a potentially promising Video Two is constructed, it is usually very important to test it. Customers can react fairly reliably to Video Two if it is brought to life well enough that they can really imagine the improved experiences. It may help to use physical prototypes, drawings, photos, or an actual video. In some cases, however, until customers undergo the experience, perhaps several times, they cannot appreciate it. Sometimes, moreover, the customer needs various kinds of reassurance, such as the approval of peers that this new behavior is OK.

Ultimately, an organization must design and test one or more whole VDSs. However, often only elements of Video Two are possible to research or market test. This grossly underused tool can validate and refine the most important conclusions of Video Two at greatly reduced cost and risk.

Reinvent the business-customer's value delivery system

When the entity studied is a business, whether a primary entity or another entity in the chain, it helps to start Video One by constructing a rough sketch of that entity's current VDS. This can be done without explaining the whole value delivery framework in any depth to the customer. Simply ask the customer, in some detail, 'Who are your customers? What do they experience as a result of doing business with you rather than with your competitors? How does your organization actually cause them to have those experiences? How do you tell them, if you tell them, what results they get by doing business with you?'

This initial sketch of the customer's VDS can help identify the most important, potentially insightful scenes to explore. In addition, after exploring those scenes in depth, it is often very helpful to come back and document the customer's VDS more fully. In this case, Video One consists both of the scenes described and the customer's VDS.

When a business-customer is the subject and Video One includes description of its VDS, it is the *de facto* VDS that should be studied and documented. It is also important to understand how the customer would like to improve its business, but such desired outcomes are most relevant to constructing Video Two. Video one should not primarily describe a theoretical business that the customer *wishes* executed (or perhaps even imagines executed). It must capture what actually happens, which means that this *de facto* VDS may be highly imperfect in various respects. By realistically describing the current business of the customer, the analyzing team structures its study of the business-customer's real objectives and the imperfections, frustrations, or opportunities missed, thus drawing a picture from which to select interesting scenes to study in depth. As Video One is documented, one can continuously refer back to the customer's VDS. Anything sub-optimal about Video One experiences should be understandable in terms of the VDS: some cost in delivering the value proposition is incurred or some opportunity is missed in order to deliver more valuable experiences and thus to generate more revenue.

Then the team can construct Video Two, an improved version of Video One scenes and of the *de facto* VDS. Video two thus conceives of improvements in the customer's business, such as ways for the customer to reduce the cost or increase the effectiveness of the delivery of the value proposition.

The business-customer may implement numerous VDSs, in which case studying a representative sampling of these businesses may be appropriate. It is often possible to describe a *generic* VDS that adequately captures

Video One: scenes studied from typical Australian camera store serving snapshooters

1 Owner reviews past year's declining business results; increased price pressure from other retailers; traditional customer base declining; expert staff expensive and hard to hold.

2 A snapshooter (woman, 34 years old, mother of two - 7 and 5 years) comes into store on a Saturday morning with the kids in tow, shopping for film for a weekend outing; tries to sort out what film to select; tries to get help.

3 Another snapshooter (male tourist from Melbourne) comes in on a Friday with a damaged camera (lens filter bent and jammed, obscuring lens); needs camera repaired quickly for weekend visit in Sydney; asks staff for help; directed to nearby repair shop.

4 Another snapshooter (woman, 55, grandmother) comes into store on a Tuesday, picking up a developed roll; wants to open envelope; goes out and comes back; waits in line again, then expresses some disappointment with prints; clerk explains her faults as a photographer.

5 Snapshooter from scene 2 comes in next Saturday morning; drops off a roll; comes back in afternoon with a friend; pays for finishing; wants to open envelope, but staff is focused on next transaction and won't let consumers mill about; they leave.

6 Staff (two men, mid-20s) on break, discuss irritation of ignorant people with no intention of buying a decent camera, who wander into store and ask silly questions.

7 Owner and two staff discuss current window displays, debating if worthwhile to clean accumulated mess and dirt from under cameras; discuss where to put new promotional posters, since all window space currently occupied.

the crucial elements of several or all of the customer's businesses the organization needs to understand. Frequently, after understanding primary entities' VDSs, one must analyze intermediaries in like fashion. Kodak in Australia analyzed the Camera-Specialty retailer in the early 1990s in this way. First Kodak thought through the primary value propositions it wanted to deliver, to the snapshooter and the enthusiast, its two main groups of primary entities. Then the organization designed the corresponding primary VDSs to deliver these propositions to these users. These primary VDSs included required actions by retail channel entities, including camera-specialty stores. Now, how to motivate and help these retailers perform the required actions? Kodak needed to deliver a supporting value proposition to these retailers. To determine what that supporting proposition ought to be, the organization then became the retailer, studying the *de facto* value propositions these retailers delivered to the snapshooter and enthusiast consumers. Below are listed some of the typical scenes that revealed these stores' *de facto* VDS to snapshooters. These scenes were captured and analyzed based on interviews of owners, staff, and snapshooters and were supplemented with the use of some in-store observation.

As an example, an analysis of Scene Two follows.

Video One, Scene Two:
Snapshooter with kids, looking for the right film

What happened?

A woman comes into the store with two kids. It's crowded, as it's Saturday morning; about 10-12 customers and 3 staff members are present. She and her family plan to go to a park, camp out for the night, do some boating, and return home on Sunday. She wants to get a roll or two of film to capture some of these adventures, but is unsure of what kind or film speed or whatever she really needs. Behind the counter she sees what seems to be a lot of different types of film. There is no information that explains these different types of film. She spends about two–three minutes trying to read the boxes and study the options, but is still unsure.

After about a five minute wait for her turn, she tells the clerk behind the counter that she needs some film, but she's not sure what's best. He rolls his head to the side, rolls his eyes slightly and asks her: 'Color or black and white? Slide, 35, or 110? 24 or 36? You want Fuji?' 'Well, that's just it,' she explains; she's not sure. She tries to explain about her weekend outing, and he asks some more questions about her camera and the shooting conditions, but she doesn't know all the answers. The kids are tugging at her; one gets loose and she gives chase. When she returns he somewhat impatiently gives her two rolls of 35 mm Fuji 24, assuring her that this should do the trick, charges her for the purchase, and turns to the next customer.

A little unsure about loading the film, the consumer also had questions about using her camera, since the last roll she took resulted in some disappointments. But she realizes the clerk isn't too impressed with her photo knowledge and decides she better just leave and hope for the best.

What apparently were the primary objectives of this camera-specialty retailer in this scene? What was the retailer trying to accomplish? What were the apparent goals of the retailer in this scene?

Overall, the store wanted to sell the consumer whatever film she needed efficiently. The store wanted her to appreciate the good selection of products and good service of the store and therefore return often in the future. The staff thinks primarily in terms of serving enthusiasts and selling/talking cameras and photo-technology; they feel they can't waste too much time on small-purchase novices, so the clerk wanted the consumer to specify quickly what she needed, rather than chat about her weekend.

What events, incidents, or processes that occurred are imperfect or sub-optimal, from this retailer's perspective? What was the consequence for the retailer of these sub-optimal events?

This snapshooter couldn't tell, from the shelf display and point-of-sale, what kinds of film she was looking at, so she got no help in deciding which kind to buy. The variety of film types made this confusion worse. The lack of help discourages her from shopping there in the future and will sometimes result in her using the wrong film for the occasion, thus producing overall disappointment with imaging and possibly further discouraging her from returning to this store.

The clerk compounded her frustration, didn't help her solve her problem, intimidated her, and drove her away without answering her questions. This discourages her from engaging in photography or from using this store in future. In consequence, the store loses revenue opportunity; her total consumption is inhibited and she may take her photo business elsewhere. The store's whole VDS ignores her and delivers mostly inferior experiences to her.

How frequently does it happen?

Perhaps 50 snapshooters per week experience such a scene.

Based on the analysis of such scenes, the Kodak team came to understand the typical camera-specialty retailer's *de facto* VDS to the snapshooter quite well (see exhibit on p. 249).

The Kodak team then went on to design, with the participation of many of these retailers, a Video Two – an improved VDS from these stores to the snapshooter. This is the VDS that Kodak wanted the camera-stores to implement for the snapshooter and which represented a major improvement for these stores over the Video One version (see exhibit on p. 250).

Video One: typical Australian camera-specialty store *de facto* VDS to snapshooter consumers – circa 1992

(De facto) value pro-position, camera-store to snapshooter	How camera-store pro-vided each resulting experience to snapshooter	How camera-store com-municated each resulting experience to snapshooter
Intended customer: store focused on enthusiast; did not deliberately pursue snapshooter Resulting experiences: by using camera-store, versus Kodak Express (KEX), Fuji Plaza, Pharmacy, K-Mart) snapshooters got following:		
Resulting experience #1: Good 1-hour processing, other processing, in many of these shops; *equal*	Resulting experience #1: Most offered 1-hour on-site and other processing, did not belong to of Quality Monitoring Service (QMS)	Resulting experiences #1 & 2: Occasionally advertised developing & processing (D&P) service and range of cameras, usually emphasizing price andnew technologies
Resulting experience #2: Could find everyday film and cameras, but lost some time due to confusing array of specialized products; *modestly inferior*	Resulting experience #2: Carried wide range of film, cameras, related products; snapshooter had to understand products (but did not) or ask staff, who explained using techno-jargon, which snapshooter did not understand	
Resulting experience #3: Made to feel somewhat intimidated and/or insulted by interaction with staff; *inferior*	Resulting experience #3: Staff held snapshooters in some contempt; focus was selling cameras, not trivial needs; paid scant attention to snapshooter; to questions, responded impatiently, using jargon	Resulting experiences #3 & 4: • One or two visits is enough, especially if Snapshooter ask for advice, info, or other help beyond a purchase • Appearance, layout of shop • Staff appearance, body-language • Word-of-mouth
Resulting experience #4: Put-off by clutter, semi-dirty, male-nerd ambi-ance; *Inferior*	Resulting experience #4: Keep shop floor overstocked, disorganized, slightly dirty	
Price: Somewhat higher		
Revenue: Value inferior; minor part of store's total revenues	Cost: minor part of store's total costs	

Video Two: improved Australian camera-specialty store VDS to snapshooter consumers (possible by 1994)

Improved value pro-position, camera-store to snapshooter	How camera-store would provide each resulting experience to snapshooter	How camera-store would communicate each resulting experience to snapshooter
Snapshooter now would be an intended customer; and by often using Wizard-member camera-store rather than other retail options, would get following:		
Resulting experience #1: End-result look of prints is as hoped, significantly more often than when obtained from outlets not Kodak-quality-controlled; *Superior to many, equal to KEX/other Kodak*	*Resulting experience #1:* Store joins Wizard program including KEX, thus controlling D&P process, and using equipment selected and serviced by Kodak; both process and equipment superior to non-Kodak processing	*Resulting experience #1:* Staff communications directed to snapshooter, with help of KEX advertising, quality guarantee, in-store QMS signage; word of mouth
Resulting experience #2: Feels more successful, proud of photos taken, confident to do more with picture-taking in future; *Superior versus all other*	*Resulting experience #2:* a. Prints are somewhat better (#1 above) b. Staff actively appreciate, reinforce success of consumer c. Store layout encourages immediate, leisurely enjoyment of prints on spot (e.g. chairs, tables, space to examine prints)	*Resulting experience #2:* Look of store, actual experi-ence with staff; word of mouth
Resulting experience #3: Can easily, quickly find everyday film and cameras, while much better understanding appropriate products by situation; *Superior*	*Resulting experience #3:* 'Open' merchandising,[3] self-service, point-of-sale info, proactive informative service of trained staff	*Resulting experience #3:* Actual experience; staff; store advertising and point-of-sale; word-of-mouth
Resulting experience #4: Feels comfortable, respected, and welcome in clean store; *Superior*	*Resulting experience #4:* • Staff interaction, attitude • Organized, inviting, clean layout	*Resulting experience #4:* Look of store; Actual experi-ence; staff, store advertising; word-of-mouth
Resulting experience #5: More prints can be improved, shared, displayed, in new, safe, easy ways; *Superior*	*Resulting experience #5:* • Image Magic, proactively promotes, demonstrated by trained staff • Proactive frames, gifting emphasis	*Resulting experience #5:* Image Magic and store advertising; merchandising of Image Magic and frames; staff; word-of-mouth
Price: Significant premium		
Revenue: Superior value, produces major new revenues	*Cost:* substantial new investment, but well below new revenues	

Why steady ain't spikey and TAT's not the key

In the mid-1990s, Hewlett-Packard's North American Distribution Organization (NADO) performed the order fulfillment function for HP's very fast-growing PC, small printers, and toner/ink supplies businesses. The primary entities were individuals and organizations using these products while the intermediary supporting entities were the distribution channels, what HP terms *resellers*. HP's older, traditional products, such as instruments, components, and larger computer systems, were distributed either directly to the using customer entities or through specialized value-added-resellers. These newer, mass market products, however, went through a variety of resellers with which HP was less experienced. These included computer- and office-product-superstores, and increasingly the consumer mass merchant outlets, such as Wal-Mart. Supplies were also distributed through contract stationers, resellers that contracted with corporate customers to meet their office supply needs.

The supplies product-divisions and the HP sales force wanted to encourage more reseller sales-promotion. However, HP's rapid growth and relative lack of experience with mass market retailing had led to numerous instances where orders were not filled on time to support a retail promotion, leaving the resellers unhappy and shy about aggressively promoting HP products. Moreover, if a reseller was too low on stock, the product divisions thought it important to be able to fill that order very quickly. And when surveyed as to their needs and satisfaction, the number one issue the resellers raised was the speed of order fulfillment. Therefore, there was pressure on NADO to increase its ability to fill orders quickly.

Not surprisingly, upper management of this products group set NADO the clear task of improving 'TAT' – turn around time for an order. This measured how long it took from the receipt of an order in NADO until it was shipped – the moment it left HP's dock. A series of initiatives was launched to change NADO's operations across the board and achieve shorter average TAT. NADO was tasked with reducing TAT for each class of reseller: computer, office-supplies, stationer, etc.

At this time, NADO decided to apply the *DPV* approach to formulating its strategy. The organization conducted a series of value delivery analyses using the *becoming the customer* methodology. NADO tried to understand the resellers' different VDSs. What were the implicit strategies of these channels? What value proposition did they implicitly try to deliver to their customers and how do PCs, printers, and ink/toner supplies fit into this picture? How do HP's products in particular and order fulfillment especially, fit this picture? What is wrong with this picture? What would it look like if HP's businesses grew more rapidly and profitably while the resellers' businesses were better supported by HP's order fulfillment practices? Improving TAT was neither assumed to be right or wrong.

For each of some 20 major resellers, NADO analyzed the virtual videos and thus thought through the value proposition that should be delivered to each studied channel-entity and how. The team found that the answers fell into two broad categories. Some resellers promote heavily and frequently, to generate business either in existing stores or in conjunction with a new store opening. To support this promotional behavior, this first category of channel entities experienced a pattern of volume characterized by periodic spikes. The second category promoted much less, if at all, and their volumes moved much more steadily.

However, the actual HP order patterns of these two categories differed less than one might expect. The 'Spikey' reseller was cautious about aggressively promoting HP, for fear that the product would not show up in time for the promotion. On the other hand, the 'Steady' reseller, finding HP's delivery performance erratic, ordered more than they needed, thus creating excess inventories. Then they would reorder and if that order was late they would run out-of-stock and put in another large order. Thus, the Spikey reseller's orders were steadier than they should have been, while the Steady reseller's orders were more spikey than they should have been. These mismatches, moreover, were not entirely caused by HP. Resellers would try to outguess the system by ordering more than they needed. Sometimes they were not ready to accept a delivery on the day the HP shipment arrived, thus putting it back another day or more and adding further chaos to the system. The costs to HP's logistics continued to climb while the promotional effectiveness of Spikey resellers lagged far behind its potential.

The needs of the two reseller categories were clear. Spikey resellers needed to periodically order very large quantities and know with absolute certainty that the product would arrive on time. The Steady resellers needed to be kept in stock without carrying excess inventory, so they needed to get a totally reliable, steady supply of product. In neither case, however, was faster order turnaround time particularly relevant. Faster TAT is always useful, but it does not come without cost nor without conflict with other more important objectives. It would address the symptoms of the problems rather than the problems of the resellers. Two entirely different patterns, two different value propositions delivered differently, were needed. One so that Spikey resellers could be spikey, and one so that Steady ones could be steady. Both propositions would build HP's businesses and reduce distribution inefficiencies.

NADO's focus shifted to ensuring that the two kinds of reseller actually received the right quantities at the right time. NADO had great success with this strategy, with the earliest progress among Steady resellers in the highly profitable and rapidly growing supplies businesses. NADO communicated and provided a proposition to these resellers that meant orders would henceforth arrive consistently in five days, with every order complete. As a result the Steady resellers derived three superior resulting experiences. They were able to cut inventory levels substantially while reducing out-of-stocks, thus increasing total sales (i.e. reducing *lost* sales) significantly. Third, at the same time the Steady reseller was able to cut costs because complete orders meant fewer receipts against an order, fewer invoices to match, etc. To get these clearly superior experiences, Steady resellers had to accept the tradeoff with the inferior experience of changing their ordering processes. They had to switch ordering systems (adopting SAP), order supplies independently from the hardware (printers and PCs), order in bulk, with some restrictions (rather than being able to place very small orders for some items) and consistently accept orders on the scheduled date and time.

As a result of all this, HP's out of stocks and thus sales improved with these resellers, while its distribution costs declined. The product lines now manage distribution logistics separately, rather than through a single NADO organization. The supplies business is therefore a more fully integrated VDS and is continuing to build on the earlier value delivery insights into distribution and broader strategy.

***

Having constructed Video Two, an organization has identified some of the most valuable experiences that could potentially be delivered to the customer analyzed. Then the organization must become the customer again, with a focus on competing alternatives. Competitors may offer some version of the experiences identified in Video Two. Moreover, the customer may see alternatives beyond both the organization and its competitors. The next chapter discusses becoming-the-customer in order to understand these competing alternatives.

Notes

1 See Chapter Two, p. 52.
2 *Fortune*, February 15, 1988, p. 49.
3 Many stores previously kept film and other products behind the counter to reduce shrinkage (theft) and to maintain more control over consumer choices (which were sometimes influenced by manufacturers' incentives). Kodak recommended *open* merchandising to let the consumer see and examine products.

Chapter Eighteen

What's Competition Got to Do with It? Understanding Customers' Alternatives

The only good value proposition is a superior value proposition. In *DPV* therefore competition plays a very important role, but not the role it often plays in management practice. Formulating strategy by identifying value delivery options does not *start* with competition. Traditional approaches may analyze competition intently, well before (if ever) defining the experiences customers would most value. Conventional approaches ask, 'What will our competition do?' The *imitation-inspired* organization reflexively strives to match costs, abilities, and characteristics of leading competitors, hoping not to be left in their dust. The product-supply approaches advocate knowing what the competition will do so that the organization can achieve lower cost, differentiate its product, or invest in competencies difficult for competitors to equal. Looking glass firmly in hand, traditional competitive analysis compares 'us' to competitors.

In *DPV*, a different question is posed, 'How well will competing alternatives deliver the most valuable experiences? What alternative value propositions will customers have, which we therefore must beat with a *superior* proposition?' Thus organizations should not be concerned with *competitors* but rather with the *customer's competing alternatives*.

Make competing videos of the customer's life

In any timeframe customers usually have several scenarios, including Video One, from which they can select. The *becoming the customer* team must construct the best competing videos of that customer's life. In the chosen timeframe, if customers *didn't* select the value proposition offered by our organization, what would they most likely select? For the intended Southwest customers, if they reject SWA's value proposition for a short-trip, they would drive, fly some other airline, or possibly not even take the trip.

So, alternative scenarios may come from a competitor similar to the organization or from subtler origins. Makers of entirely different technologies might deliver an attractive alternative value proposition. The best alternative sometimes is for the customer to do or make something themselves; systems integrators frequently compete with an intended customer's own information technology department, for example. Sometimes, the best alternative is Video One – changing nothing. A winning proposition must be superior to all of these alternatives, as they are understood by that customer.

A team becoming a potential primary entity or a supporting entity constructs a competing video for each possibly viable alternative scenario the team can identify. To construct such a competing video, a team must identify some competing alternative. The alternative may be that represented by another firm or organization, in which case that entity must of course be identified. In some cases, however, the alternative is controlled by the customer entity itself. In either case, the team asks, for the relevant timeframe, 'How well would this competing alternative *be able to* deliver this experience?' After answering this question for all the experiences of Video Two, the team must assess the inclinations of the entity offering the alternative and the likelihood that this competing entity will pursue the delivery of such experiences. Out of this analysis, the team must estimate the value proposition that this alternative will represent for the customer under study.

These are of course speculative questions that force one to make an informed guess. Obviously, the further in the future the timeframe of Video Two, the more difficult and subject to error these guesses will be. Moreover, to make these guesses, one must also predict trends in the environment, such as technology, geopolitics, regulation, and broad customer tastes, that may affect competing entities. Nonetheless, it is not possible to formulate a *superior* value proposition rationally in a vacuum. An organization must make the best estimate it can of the alternative value propositions it must beat. Moreover, one should not assume omnipotent competitors, unconstrained in their options. Constructing competing videos is an important tool in realistically anticipating competitive response.

In hi-tech markets, managers sometimes despair of assessing competitors' likely future value propositions because rapid changes in technology make prediction too hard. In fast changing markets the more distant future videos are difficult to construct accurately, but managers despair too easily. Resulting experiences of value don't change nearly as much or as quickly as the technology by which those experiences can be delivered. Organizations that invest heavily in understanding the experiences customers would most value can better interpret and react to technological change.

Whatever one's uncertainty about competitors, strategy must focus on delivering a value proposition *superior to* some assumed alternative customers will have. Consider Federal Express's failure to use this logic in their ill-conceived response to fax – Zap Mail. With the advent of fax, FedEx, in a panic-induced paroxysm of internally-driven thinking, asked the wrong questions. What capabilities do we have by which we could defeat fax? Can we use FedEx's resources to provide improved fax services? With our communication lines built for the tracking system, why not pick up a document and fax it digitally to a FedEx office in the destination city? This would produce a letter-quality copy at the other end, which would be *better* than a regular fax. Voila: 'Zap Mail!' For $28, FedEx offered the excitement of a *letter* quality document in under four hours.

But customers could send a fax, with more than adequate image quality for the vast majority of documents, in two minutes for about $2. Or, they could send the original, overnight, for $10. Thus, Zap Mail could never deliver a superior value proposition for most of the documents threatened by fax. It lost the company several hundred million dollars. FedEx could have avoided this failure if they had analyzed the threat by *becoming the customer* again, analyzing customers wanting to send a document. This would have revealed some customers who would: greatly value sending an original-quality document; not mind if it's not the *actual* original; and greatly value getting it there immediately or at least on the same day. Zap Mail seems to deliver a superior value proposition to them. The problem is that the number of documents sent by customers in this situation is only a tiny percentage of the total. The vast bulk of documents were under conditions where either fax quality – readable – was quite adequate or where only the actual original would do or where delivery had to occur within minutes. The organization, understanding the value propositions they had to beat, could have recognized that Zap Mail could only deliver superior value in a small portion of cases.

A different approach to competitor analysis

The *DPV* approach focuses on the competition's ability to deliver superior value to the customer. This question is much more focused and useful than a wide ranging analysis of every fact one can dig up about competitors. Yet some strategy consultants love such customer-blind competitor analysis, as it allows them to churn through huge quantities of data and impress clients with the sheer magnitude of numbers they found. One of the classic such analyses is called SWOTs: Strengths, Weaknesses, Opportunities, and Threats. The current convention is to determine core competencies and use these as the Strengths. Identifying SWOTs sounds good, but this analysis is almost invariably conducted as a basis for formulating strategy, *before* the question of what customers would really value is posed (if it ever is). SWOTs should be understood in the context of a customer and the option they represent, once these are fully identified. Then a strength or weakness can be expressed in terms of the organization's ability and cost to deliver the most important resulting experiences. An opportunity can then be understood in terms of delivering a winning value proposition; a threat as the potential that a competing option will deliver one instead.

The imitation-inspired mentality is fueled very effectively by the way competitive *benchmarking* is often practiced. Benchmarking commonly compares an organization's products and features, manufacturing or operating costs, and various production and selling processes to those of its competitors. Often these comparisons are made without reference to any specific resulting experiences for any particular customer. Thus most benchmarking is performed in a resulting-experience vacuum. Without first defining carefully some specific resulting experiences and measuring how well the competitor can deliver these, benchmarking will naturally and often counterproductively stimulate imitation. If a competitor performs a process faster or cheaper, this might be bad news, since it *may* mean that the competitor can deliver some value proposition more fully or at lower cost. On the other hand, it may just mean that it can perform the process better, and this may have little relevance to the delivery of any important value proposition. Rarely does an organization begin benchmarking with a consideration of the importance of a product feature, cost, or process to delivering some value proposition that would win the preference of customers.

This perspective applies as well to the practice of benchmarking companies in non-competing industries. In this case, it is popular to determine 'world class' performance for some vague process. Thus, other companies are studied for their quality or cost reduction or customer service processes. Again, it is more pertinent to start with a broadly defined notion of the resulting experiences of most importance in a market, and only then to find other companies or whole industries that deliver those experiences well.

Consider a US regional bank that benchmarked its mortgage approvals against car dealers. Not a vague comparison of customer service, this analysis benchmarks the speed with which customers can get approved for credit in the range of $100,000. For a Mercedes dealer, the collateral on an $80,000 asset drives off the lot, is difficult and costly to repossess, and depreciates instantly in resale value. With a $120,000 mortgage, the house can't leave town and usually appreciates in value. Yet the bank takes two weeks to approve the mortgage, while the car dealer approves a loan in two hours. There are technical differences, but two weeks versus two hours? The regional bank stands to learn something valuable about how to provide a better experience (faster mortgage approval) from such benchmarking, because it is focused on a particular resulting experience.

Identifying customers' best alternative propositions

- Considering the most important resulting experiences that emerged from Video Two, determine the competing alternatives which could potentially deliver such experiences to this customer in the Video Two timeframe.
- For possible alternatives, estimate the potential ability, cost, and inclination of the relevant entities to deliver these resulting experiences.
- Determine how fast competing alternatives could match or surpass delivery of these resulting experiences by imitating the organization.
- Describe the best value proposition the customer will have available in this timeframe; Video One could be that best alternative; several different value propositions may be about equally valuable and thus best.

Relevance of becoming the customer

Identifying the customer's best alternatives completes the process of becoming the customer. That process and method has proven powerful in at least four important application contexts, all of which support designing explicit winning value delivery systems. First, even if an organization does not revise its VDS for a customer it studies, becoming the customer, executed and documented properly, can be a powerful way for improving an organization's implementation of a VDS. The virtual videos of the customer's life can help people throughout an organization see the direct link between actions and the customer's actual resulting experiences.

Second, R&D scientists and engineers who learn to use this technique usually find it both exhilarating and liberating. Most of these people want to create not just cool technology but cool technology that is actually useful to someone. Becoming the customer lets them discover for themselves what would be useful, which is a vast improvement over depending on other functions for technology requirements that are developed in a vacuum, usually wrong, usually lacking in imagination, and usually meaningless to the engineer or scientist.

Third, when customers are themselves businesses, becoming the customer can be a powerful means of strengthening the direct relationship with them. The technique is highly effective in better understanding the business of the customer and in demonstrating the organization's willingness to invest in that understanding. Many customer entities are enthusiastic to find a supplier who genuinely wants to know how they operate and what their opportunities are. The approach can transform a typical sell-buy relationship that is overly focused on price haggling, hard selling, and relationship-building between the sales rep and a buyer, to a more integrated, organization-to-organization partnership aimed at profitably making the customer more successful. In fact, business-customers often find the exercise of thinking about what value proposition it delivers, and how, to be very useful in its own right. Helping a customer perform this exercise is sometimes the basis for the most productive of supplier/customer relationships.

This technique is also highly applicable to a sales force's approach to customers. Sales can and in many cases should learn to use the becoming the customer method to drive their ongoing relationship-building efforts with business-customers. This allows a sales force to tailor the implementation of a disciplined VDS to the varied situations of specific customers without wandering away from the chosen strategy for the business. It also allows Sales to play a more proactive, creative role in shaping the VDS.

Fourth and most fundamentally important, becoming the customer is the central information-gathering mechanism in the value delivery methodology for strategy formulation. To analyze a market-space strategically, the hypotheses produced by becoming a small number of customers must of course be validated and refined quantitatively, as was discussed in Chapter Fifteen. Becoming the customer, however, is a realistic means to identify and develop these strategic hypotheses based upon a creative and thorough analysis of customers' actual lives and businesses. This approach is considerably more trouble than proceeding with strategic hypotheses that are based upon a woefully inadequate and superficial understanding of customers' experiences. It is also much more likely to produce winning strategies.

**

The last four chapters have outlined how an organization should formulate a genuine value delivery strategy. Having conducted this analysis and made the disciplined choice of what market-spaces to enter or stay in, what options in each market-space to pursue, and thus what businesses to operate, the organization must now make the formal commitment actually to implement the chosen primary VDSs. It must now articulate and execute a real business plan.

Chapter Nineteen

Make Disciplined Choices: Implement VDS-Structured Business Plans

Having formulated a strategy in value delivery terms and identified the capabilities necessary for each value delivery system, the organization can proceed to actually building those VDSs and delivering the chosen value proposition in each business. Though often poorly written and widely reviled for the wrong reasons, business plans are an essential instrument of implementation of a genuine value delivery strategy. These plans must articulate the designed primary VDSs in detail and must incorporate plans to build the necessary capabilities. Those plans must then actually be executed with line management authority and discipline. Their execution should be monitored closely and their real impact in the marketplace measured. As a result, managers learn how to improve the business plans continuously and support the never-ending cycle of freshly reexamining strategy. Thus, implementing value delivery strategy entails four interrelated acts.

Implementing a value delivery strategy

1   Commit in real business plans to execute the chosen primary VDSs.
2   Don't just write it – *execute* the business plan.
3   Monitor and measure – what actually happened and why?
4   And finally – start *DPV* all over again: continuously improve, test, and recreate value delivery strategy.

---

1   Formally commit in real business plans to execute the chosen primary VDSs

Once a strategy is formulated, it must be translated directly into a formal, detailed commitment by the organization to implement the specific primary VDSs chosen in that strategy. Otherwise, formulating strategy is likely to be no more than an abstract exercise. A common reason why so many business plans are useless is that no real strategy has been formulated. If an organization has not chosen a value proposition for each business, writing a meaningful business plan is indeed problematic. For the organization at least roughly following the principles and methodology of *DPV*, however, a real business plan follows easily from strategy formulation. The business plan need simply document the decision of which VDSs to implement, expressed as the organization's clear commitment to action.

Build the capability bridges needed by the strategy

A real business plan, based on the principles of *Delivering Profitable Value*, must be a direct manifestation of corporate strategy. It must consist of a decision and commitment to implement one or more businesses, where each business is rigorously defined as a primary VDS. However, a winning VDS for some future period will often be one that the organization is not yet fully capable of implementing. It usually lacks capabilities that it must have in order to implement its strategy successfully.

The design of VDSs as documented in real business plans therefore must include identification of the most important of these capability gaps and how the organization will close them. This may include building altogether new capabilities and/or significantly strengthening existing ones. To implement such a strategy includes closing these capability gaps.

Once an organization understands and chooses real VDSs, it can identify its capability gaps in implementing them. Then, four powerful aspects of the organization must be managed to bridge these gaps and thus enable the organization to implement profitable VDSs.

Four bridges to value delivery capabilities

1 Align the organization's *criteria for success* with the long-term delivery of profitable value – unambiguously reward implementation of chosen VDSs.
2 *Structure* the organization explicitly by its chosen VDSs – make the organization structure directly reflect the businesses defined in the strategy.
3 Develop *value delivery resources* – create, modify, or obtain the providing- and communicating-vehicles needed in the chosen VDSs.
4 Design and develop *value delivery processes* – use the VDSs to determine key processes and change the job roles that perform these.

A business plan for each primary VDS

For each primary VDS to be implemented, an organization needs a well-written business plan for the relevant timeframes. Two are usually appropriate: one for the medium-to-longer-term, such as three years, and one for an more distant future. For any business that is already operational, a plan for the immediate year is also needed. Obviously, a longer-term plan will be less specific, but it will still cover the same basic issues. When an organization operates several businesses in the same market-space, the several individual business plans need to be consolidated into a larger plan that can address the issues cutting across those businesses.

Clarify criteria for success and organization structure

A business plan for a primary VDS should indicate that the organization's criteria for success align with implementing that VDS. It thus should express the general objective of the plan in terms of its intended financial impact on the firm and then should make clear that its more specific objective is to execute the VDS as designed and described within the plan.

The organizational structure corresponding to this VDS should also be described within the plan. The organizational entities involved in the implementation of the primary VDS should thus be identified, including those that may be exclusively allocated to the business as well as those that the business will share with others. The organizational entity with direct managerial responsibility for this business must also be identified. This is the team or individual dedicated to play the role of the business management function for this business. If the primary VDS includes supporting VDSs, the entities within the organization that have managerial responsibility for each of these supporting VDSs should also be identified.

State the primary value proposition

The plan should then proceed to articulate the primary VDS for the timeframe of this plan. This begins, of course, with stating the chosen primary value proposition in such a way that it specifically answers the questions of the *Complete Value Proposition* (Chapter Four). In answering the first of these questions, the timeframe indicated will be that for the whole business plan. The second question asks for the intended customer, which in this case is the primary entity. Thus the plan should describe the group of primary entities who are part of the market-space option that is this primary VDS. These are all the current and potential primary entities for whom the VDS described in this plan is most appropriate. It is also helpful to clarify the structure of the whole relevant value delivery chain into which this primary entity fits.

Of course, in describing each of the resulting experiences in this proposition, in answer to the fifth question, it is essential to adhere to the principles that define this fundamental concept, as expressed in the *Criteria for a Resulting Experience* (Chapter Two).

Describe how each experience will be provided and communicated

Following the complete statement of the primary value proposition, the plan must specify how it will be delivered. Broadly speaking this means satisfying the three characteristics of *The Completely Designed VDS* (Chapter Nine). More specifically, it means that each resulting experience in the value proposition should be discussed in detail, including a description of how it will be provided and how it will be communicated. Inferior and equal experiences must be described as fully as superior ones. This description should indicate what must actually happen such that the experience will be provided and communicated. Thus, the providing- and communicating-vehicles must be described, including the relevant resources and processes that must be produced and performed. Here, the implications for the one or more relevant products and services must also be detailed.

This description must also clarify who is responsible for these elements of the required delivery vehicles. That is, what organizational entities must take action, devote resources, or otherwise cooperate such that each delivery vehicle is created and used as required? Of course, the entity responsible for this primary VDS usually must play some role. In some cases, the primary entity must also allocate resources or perform certain actions and processes in order for a resulting experience to be provided. In addition, some supporting entities in the relevant value delivery chain may need to play a role. And some other entities in the chain, within the business unit or firm owning this business, may need to play a role.

The description of the primary VDS, in the business plan, thus includes the actions required of other entities in the chain. For some of these entities, securing their cooperation is usually non-trivial. They may need to be convinced and perhaps helped to develop and devote the needed resources and processes that would support this primary VDS. Therefore, supporting VDSs must also be articulated in the business plan. In this section of the plan, only the *actions* needed from each supporting entity should be described. A description of the actual supporting VDSs follows in a separate section.

For each resulting experience, the plan should indicate the most important capability gaps that must be closed, at least in part, by the time the VDS is to be implemented. This portion of the plan should highlight required resources and processes that are not yet fully in place. The plan should indicate how the organization intends to close the capability gap. The organization may describe a specific program to close this gap or may refer to a supporting VDS or capability-building effort detailed separately.

Include estimated costs to deliver the resulting experience

In the statement of the value proposition, the plan has provided a rough estimate of the value of each experience. The plan should in this section compare this estimate to an estimate of the cost of delivering these experiences, which should be made up of the costs of the various actions necessary to deliver each experience. In some cases, of course, it is difficult to determine accurately the costs of delivering a particular resulting experience. Several experiences may be simultaneously provided and/or communicated by the same vehicle. Allocating these costs to individual experiences is necessarily inexact. But managers can and should make a rough approximation of the total costs, because the organization must have some sense of the relationship between the cost of delivering a particular resulting experience and its contribution to the value of the total proposition.

It is useful to distinguish between two elements of cost in delivering an experience. One is the ongoing operational cost, after any capability gaps in delivering it have been closed. The second is that of any effort to close capability gaps. If a major capital investment is involved, this cost may even dwarf the operational costs. Therefore, it is important to estimate these separately to understand the economics of the VDS. Estimating costs is an iterative aspect of writing a real, value delivery business plan. At this point in the plan, supporting VDSs and capability-building efforts have not yet been described fully. These must be designed and their costs estimated before an allocation of their costs can be made to each separate resulting experience.

Describe supporting VDSs

Any supporting VDSs required for the primary VDS should be described by this plan, whether they are exclusive to this primary VDS or shared by other businesses in the same firm. Each supporting VDS should be described in the same way as the primary VDS. Thus the criteria for success and the organizational structure for managing the supporting VDS should be articulated. Then the supporting value proposition focused on the supporting entities, followed by a description of how each resulting experience will be provided and communicated to the supporting entity, should be stated. Included in this description, key capability gaps and plans to close them must be identified. Finally, an estimate of the organization's costs to deliver each experience must be made.

How primary-VDS capability gaps will be closed

Earlier in the plan, the discussion of how each resulting experience in the primary value proposition will be delivered identified the gaps and the plans to close them. So did the descriptions of the supporting VDSs. Here it is useful to aggregate these required capability-building efforts, since some may apply to more than one element of the primary VDS. Thus, the key resources, including products and other assets, and the key processes that must be created, changed, or otherwise obtained in support of this primary VDS should be summarized along with the principal plans to do so.

Summarize requirements by resource: products, functions, other entities

The plan should extract from the earlier sections and aggregate in this one all the requirements for each product, asset, and functional entity involved in the primary VDS. Providing one resulting experience may make one requirement on the main product; delivering another experience may make a different requirement on the same product. Likewise for the impact on the sales force, R&D, or Human Resources. Here, the plan summarizes the implications of the primary VDS for each of these concerns in the aggregate. It also shows the required actions of other entities in the value delivery chain (e.g. intermediaries or off-line entities or the organization's suppliers). These are the actions that the supporting VDSs must make happen. Without this aggregation, it is difficult to understand the whole set of requirements for each product and functional entity within the organization and for each relationship with other entities in the value delivery chain. This aggregation of product, functional and other-entity requirements is generically depicted in the exhibit on the following page.

One of the advantages of aggregating these requirements of the primary VDS by resource is that this can illuminate conflicts and opportunities not immediately visible within the framework of a VDS. This may lead not only to executing the designed VDS better but also to improving its design as well.

Throughout this iterative process, it is the VDS framework that drives and expresses strategy. The by-resource view of the same requirements facilitates execution and refinement of that strategy. In contrast, in the conventional approaches that dominate much of management practice, the by-resource view is the *only* perspective used. It is the automatic result of using the product-supply, rather than value delivery, focus.

Assess the impact of this primary VDS and define metrics

Based on this entire discussion, the plan must indicate the intended impact on the organization, including the risks, of implementing it. This last section of the plan should therefore answer the questions of the *Checklist for a Winning Business* (Chapter Nine). In addition, the plan should outline the metrics by which the plan will be measured against the criteria for success. This includes a description of how information will be gathered and analyzed to determine what value proposition is actually delivered, how it actually compares to competing alternatives, the resulting revenues and costs for the organization, and other key results of executing the plan.

A combined business plan for multiple businesses

When one BU manages a group of businesses in broadly related market-spaces, a combined business plan should be written to address the issues

Requirements from primary VDS, aggregated by resource

Resource	Requirements	Reason for requirement	Cost	Issues
Products				
Product A	A1P	Provide experience #1	—	Problem with A2
	A2	Provide experience #2	—	
	A1C	Communicate exp. #1	—	Can do more than B1
Product B	B1	Provide #1	—	
	B2P	Provide #2	—	
	B2C	Communicate #2	—	
Functions				
Manufacturing	Man1	Provide #1	—	Man1 can be improved
	Man2	Provide #2	—	
Distribution	Dist1	Provide #1	—	
	Dist2	Provide #2	—	
Supporting entities	**Requirements**	**Reason for requirement**	**Supporting VDSs**	
Retailer X	X1P	Provide #1	VDS to X	
	X2P	Provide #2		
	X1C	Communicate #1		
Retailer Y	Y1P	Provide #1	VDS to Y	
	Y2P	Provide #2		
	Y1C	Communicate #1		Cannot achieve Y2C
	Y2C	Communicate #2		
etc.				

Primary VDS – first iteration

Primary value proposition	How to provide	How to communicate
Resulting experience #1	Product A — A1P Product B — B1 Manufacturing — Man1 Distribution — Dist1 Retailer X — X1P Retailer Y — Y1P etc.	Sales force — Sales1 Product A & package — A1C PR — PR1 Advertising — Adv1 Retailer X — X1C Retailer Y — Y1C etc.
Resulting experience #2	Product A — A2 Product B — B2P Manufacturing — Man2 Distribution — Dist2 Retailer X — X2P Retailer Y — Y2P etc.	Sales force — Sales2 Product A — B2C PR — PR2 Advertising — Adv2 Retailer X — X2C Retailer Y — Y2C etc.
Resulting experience #3	etc.	

Primary VDS – second iteration

Primary value proposition	How to provide	How to communicate
Resulting experience #1 (now better than the first iteration)	Same, but features of product B enhanced by new B1 and better Man1	Same
Resulting experience #2 (may be weaker)	Reduced performance due to A2 problem	Will not communicate effectively in Retailer Y (Y2C problem)

cutting across these businesses. At a minimum, this combined plan should consist of the individual business plans for each of the primary VDSs. However, several aspects of these plans are likely to overlap or interact in ways that should be described by the combined plan. It may be at least an option to share various resources, such as supporting VDSs, products, manufacturing assets, R&D or sales force, among businesses. To the extent possible, such resources of value delivery should be *dedicated* to each business separately, so the business unit avoids the compromises and challenges inherent in sharing resources. Managers reading this may fear offending the gods of efficiency, but dedicated resources can facilitate a much more focused and coherent delivery of a well-chosen value proposition. However, the scarcity and cost of resources often make such a separation impractical (though probably less often than the internally-driven mind perceives). BU management should describe a proposed allocation of resources in its combined multi-business plan. The allocation should reflect the optimal balance between the cost and the effectiveness of value delivery. The resolution of any conflicts among VDSs should be articulated in the combined plan as the best way to maximize the organization's long-term success in the relevant market-space.

The combined business plan should also delineate the shared tasks of capability-building. Often the development of a needed resource or process, which is vital to the success of several primary VDSs, must be led by BU or firm management. Here, Prahalad and Hamel's original insight about the importance of capabilities above and beyond individual businesses is so important. Often a single business may not be able to generate enough wealth to cover the cost of developing some expensive capability, while several businesses that share the capability may easily justify it.

Finally, a combined business plan should explain why the combination of businesses represents the best strategy for the firm in the relevant market-spaces. As noted in the discussion of corporate strategy earlier, most firms do not but should explicitly articulate why their choice of market-spaces in which to compete and their choice of businesses in each market-space represent the optimal pursuit of long-term profitable growth. The combined business plan is the appropriate context for such articulation.

2 Don't just write it – *execute* the business plan

Each function and entity that will help execute a designed VDS should actively participate in the formulation of strategy and its manifestation as a real business plan. Often, not all parties will agree with the final business plan. But once adopted, the business management function for each primary VDS must work with all other parties to ensure that the VDS adopted is actually executed as designed, unless and until that design is formally changed. Enforcement of the agreed business plan is made possible not so much by the authority of the business management team as by the authority of the business plan itself. Focusing on implementing a well-designed primary VDS reduces the arbitrary political power of both opposing functions and senior management.

Empower but also enforce: a VDS must be Implemented

Following the Kobe earthquake of 1995, many Japanese citizens complained bitterly that hundreds of police and military troops stood around for days instead of proactively distributing water and other desperately needed supplies. Officers explained that they could not act because they had no clear orders. Lack of empowerment in an organization has a similar detrimental effect: employees await the command structure to specify each move. A primary VDS in a business plan does not regiment each employee's day, but it does allow them to understand what the business team, to which they belong, is trying to accomplish and how. It is thus a means of empowering people to help develop and execute strategy. However, this is quite different than empowering people to do whatever occurs to them.

The business management function must take responsibility for how well all other entities actually perform the actions indicated by the business plan's articulation of the primary VDS. This does not mean that the business management function should give orders to R&D or the sales force. It does mean, however, that the function should inquire into the other entities' activities and should understand how well these activities support the primary VDS. Are the appropriate R&D resources actively developing the specific features and attributes most crucial to improving the providing-vehicle for one of the highest priority resulting experiences in the chosen value proposition?

Is the sales force actually telling the immediate customers the agreed-upon story about why they should cooperate with the organization's new product offering to the primary entity?

If the lab manager's answer is, 'No, the lab is working on another priority,' the business manager for that VDS should demand that R&D do one of two things. Either the lab must change priorities or R&D must make the case why the business plan and thus the design of the primary VDS should be changed. If the sales force answers, 'No, but we're handling the customers just right; we don't know what each rep tells customers, but we sell effectively,' the business management team should invoke the corporation's decision to implement the business plan. The team must insist on knowing what the sales force is communicating to customers. If the messages they convey do not correspond to the designed VDS, once again, one of two things must change: the sales force's actions or the business plan.

This mentality is not about one function's dictating behavior to others. It is about taking a business plan seriously. Empowering people in an organization is vitally important. But they must be empowered to contribute to strategy formulation and then to its implementation, not to act randomly. To make this approach possible, business plans must be seen as the incontrovertible decision of the firm to implement a specific primary VDS, until the firm changes the plan. Few business plans are so empowered.

Give real power to the business plan itself

A real business plan has power. One of the reasons typical plans have little affect beyond numbing the minds of managers in a pointless number-crunching ritual, is that no one takes them seriously after they are finally approved. There must be a stupider way to waste managerial time, but the theoretical rationalization for it hasn't been published yet. Many business/marketing/strategic/operating plans don't state a clear intent to do anything in particular; they usually stop after paying homage to some platitudes and promising faintly unrealistic financial results. However, when plans do describe a coherent scheme to take some particular course of action, many organizations casually disregard such plans. Senior management may whimsically kill various initiatives and launch new ones halfway through a planning period, laying waste to what few clear intentions had been articulated. Middle managers may likewise arbitrarily ignore supposed plans in cultures where senior management does not hold them to any real adherence.

If a business plan is to be taken seriously, it must be specific about the value propositions to be delivered and exactly how they will be delivered. Beyond the numbers, most business plans are intellectual exercises and do not reflect serious decisions as to which actions to take. By describing the primary VDS in detail, a business plan can be a real tool of strategy implementation; but it must be given adequate and genuine line management authority. A business plan must be given the power of a firm commitment that flows down from the corporate level.

3 Now monitor and measure - what actually happened and why?

Most organizations do not learn what de facto value proposition each of their businesses delivered, how they delivered them, and sometimes what it cost to deliver them. They likewise do not know what the competition delivered. This partly stems from the fact that most organizations do not develop, debate, and then adopt a real business plan in the first place. For an organization serious about profitably delivering superior value, however, implementation of strategy demands not only developing and committing seriously to a completely designed primary VDS for each business but also continuously and carefully studying what actually happened.

Managing includes analyzing what happened

Monitoring a VDSs implementation, which must be done by the business management function, requires asking whether the value proposition was actually delivered. Did the intended primary entity do what the organization wanted and did they actually get the resulting experiences chosen in the proposition? To the extent that this did not happen, why not? Was the chosen value proposition not a superior one after all? What did competing alternatives offer, and was this different than the plan assumed? Did the organization fail in some respects to deliver the resulting experiences? Which experiences, and why? For each experience not fully delivered, was this a failure of providing it, communicating it, or both? If a failure to provide it, did the organization in fact deploy the planned providing-vehicles? If so, how were these wrongly designed? If not, where was the breakdown – in a key resource or a key process?

Armed with an understanding of what actually happened in the customer's world, the organization can analyze what happened internally. Was the cost of delivering the proposition in line with the plan? Where did actual delivery depart from the plan, in terms of the delivery vehicles for each resulting experience? Why did these occur? Was an identified capability gap not closed? If so, was that because the organization did not implement the planned gap-closing effort or because the effort was insufficient or ill conceived? Did the organization have an unrecognized important capability gap in some aspect of profitably delivering the resulting experiences? In either case, how fast, at what cost and risk, could the remaining crucial gaps be closed? Is this fast enough to repair the VDS?

Note how this perspective differs from the traditional. Managing the delivery of the Frank Perdue primary value proposition, for example, one should monitor, among other issues, whether Perdue chickens *actually* tasted more tender to the intended consumers, consistently over time. If not, why not? Did the organization breed, hatch, feed, process, package and distribute the chickens as planned to bring about this experience? Did it incur the planned costs of providing this experience? These are altogether different questions than focusing on shipping cost per kilo or the portion of consumers who count themselves 'totally satisfied' with Perdue chickens.

Elude the bugaboo of precise financial measurement

The difficulty of measurement is a major perceived stumbling block to the implementation of many value delivery systems. Often, a VDS cuts across resources in such a way as to complicate measurement seriously. Accounting methods, of course, have evolved to measure the resources and processes of the product-supply process. Costs and revenues associated with products, assets, and functions are inherently easier to measure precisely than those associated with the delivery of value propositions. The most appropriate value proposition for an organization to deliver, the one that would profitably deliver the most value over time, may be one that makes use of parts of several products, assets, and functions. Accurately allocating these parts is of course more difficult than dealing with them in isolation. This helps managers rationalize the definition of their businesses in terms of these neatly measurable entities. As a result, managers inadvertently elect to more accurately measure the wrong strategies rather than suffer imprecise measurement of the right strategies.

If accounting is to meet the needs of an organization practicing *DPV*, it needs to do a little work. Radically new methods that overhaul the field's approach to measuring costs, revenues, and profit must be developed. Managers need better, more consistent techniques for linking the performance of processes and the use of resources with the actual resulting experiences derived by customers. Until the accounting profession moves aggressively in this direction, however, organizations can and must improvise.

Common sense modeling of the relationship between actions taken and value propositions delivered can provide a rough basis for a logical allocation of costs and revenues. Current accounting methods allocate costs for various applications. Methods such as Activity Based Costing can aggregate a set of related resources and processes. Allocating the cost of a product, asset, resource, or function among several primary VDSs is not wildly different than many such allocation exercises. The proportion of revenue associated with a given VDS can also help allocate costs. Although resisted in many organizations partly on the grounds that it is too expensive, market research can measure revenues by VDS. Market research is not perceived as a way to measure the revenues of a business, but only because businesses are usually defined in easily measurable product and asset terms.

Of course, the harder the shared resources are to disaggregate, the less accurate these allocations will be. However, the revenues and costs associated with the VDSs using these resources must add up to the total revenues and costs associated with these resources. If the organization has made a good choice of value propositions to deliver, then the grand total of financial results for all businesses will be better than it would have been otherwise.

4   And finally – start *DPV* all over again: continuously improve, test, and recreate strategy

The fourth key act in implementing a value delivery strategy is using the learning that emerges from monitoring and measuring its execution. As execution of a business plan unfolds, an organization may need to refine the design of the VDS, and thus continuously improve it. Simultaneously, organizations must also revisit the fundamental strategic questions that led them to design the VDS, such as 'In what market-spaces should we compete, and with what businesses?'

Redesign plans to accommodate reality

As an organization monitors the implementation of a business plan, it will often conclude that the primary VDS needs work. The value proposition may prove less well chosen than the organization had hoped, in which case one must consider changing it. Or, the means of providing or communicating the proposition may prove inadequate; although it may remain viable if its delivery can be improved. Or the basic VDS may be well designed, but the capability-building efforts may need revamping.

The concept of continuous improvement, created by Demming as part of total quality management, is quite useful in the context of implementing a value delivery system. Organizations should continuously improve their understanding and definition of each value proposition they intend to deliver. They should continuously improve the design and deployment of the required vehicles for providing and communicating that proposition. And they should continuously improve their efforts to close the most crucial value delivery capability gaps.

Don't improve by just guessing and hoping for the best - test the elements of a VDS when possible (which is often)

A primary VDS should be managed with discipline, yet with great flexibility as well. To succeed in the unpredictable environment of competitive markets, an organization must continuously search for new insight into how it can improve its one or more primary VDSs. A key tool in developing such improvement rapidly yet with limited risk is also a woefully underused tool by many organizations: the seemingly simple notion of *testing* the elements of a VDS among potential customers.

Few delivery vehicles are more important to test than the product or service and its most salient features. In many cases, organizations can preliminarily test products in isolation, without using an actual test market, by putting the product or a prototype into the hands of potential users. The scientific market research methods, including blind product testing and other techniques, are well suited for gauging customer experiences with and reactions to new or changed products and services. As compared to a test market, this approach reduces time, money, and the risk of tipping one's hand to competitors, but it is obviously less representative of reality. In addition to and often following such product-usage testing, the new or improved product can be fully tested in a test market.

Since products must be understood, in the logic of *Delivering Profitable Value*, as providing- and sometimes communicating-vehicles for resulting experiences, they must be tested in this context. Rather than simply asking, 'Do customers like or prefer this product?' one must also more pointedly explore, 'How well does this product actually provide the one or more experiences in the proposition that it is supposed to help provide? How well does it play the role it is meant to play in the VDS?'

Carefully testing products with potential customers seems to come naturally to organizations in some industries. These industries include pharmaceuticals and some other technology-intensive businesses with long product life cycles and some consumer-oriented businesses such as packaged goods. However, a great many firms that should extensively test products among customers fail to do so.

The high-tech world, for example, frequently launches new products or product improvements with only limited testing in the form of beta testing. Beta testing consists of putting well-developed prototypes into the hands of some potential users and gathering their input. However, this testing is often conducted among an unrepresentative sample of leading edge customers or especially heavy users, in the poorly founded belief that winning preference among these users indicates likely acceptance among less sophisticated or lighter users. In some cases, beta testing is used largely to identify some of the innumerable bugs in new versions of products, especially software. However, it is more rare to place a product into a test market, a limited geography, or other portion of a market in order to learn about customers' experiences and reactions.

More extensive product research and test marketing is usually dismissed by high-tech strategists because, supposedly, things are moving too fast. The logic goes something like this: if we did a test market, the product life cycle would be over before we rolled out the product. This is correct if one conducts test markets for a year or two at a time. Even in very fast changing markets, however, test markets lasting two–three months would generate important insights that could lead to improvements.

Another popular argument for not testing high-technology products is that doing so won't save much cost. Before a product is available for testing, a huge investment is required; by then, most of the money has been spent. Therefore, so the logic goes, test marketing won't save much anyway. However, following this faulty logic is hardly brilliant. Why blow another $250 million distributing and advertising a losing product just because $2 billion has already been lost developing it? Moreover, it may be embarrassing to develop a product at great cost, test it, and quietly withdraw it, but insisting on rolling out a bad idea for everyone to see hurts the firm's reputation and credibility far more.

In the past 15 years, Kodak has three times introduced new photographic technology with disappointing results – the Disc Camera, Photo CD, and the Advanced Photo System (APS). Each time, the company has taken the big-bang approach, introducing worldwide on virtually the same day with a public relations and media blitz. In each case, things went awry soon thereafter despite, in the latter two cases, impressive technology. For each project, one or two test markets, each conducted in a single city, would have revealed the imminent problems. While many focus groups and various kinds of product testing had been conducted, a full-scale launch in an actual test market was not. While testing could not have eliminated all of Kodak's problems with these projects, it would have allowed the company to reduce and manage them better.

Such mistakes are not exclusive to high-tech products, however. With all the consumer-marketing literature on test marketing and various forms of product testing, one might assume that the best consumer marketers use these techniques with skill and aplomb. Yet even some companies renowned for marketing competence often fail to perform competent product testing. Coca-Cola has become one of the few truly global US companies. Its impressive performance of the past fifteen years under the guidance of the late Roberto Goizueta reflected brilliant, performance-focused management of operations and bottler/distributor relationships worldwide. The formula for Coke is one of the most popular products in history. The company's accompanying reputation for marketing genius, however, was blemished by the mid-1980s New Coke fiasco.

This blunder, replacing the traditional Coke with New Coke, was maximally magnified by the company's insistence on simultaneous national expansion of an untested plan. Faced with a consumer revolt, replete with actual demonstrations of people demanding the return of old Coke, the company was eventually forced to reinstate the original formula. All the while, the firm constantly cited hundreds of thousands of taste tastes as proof that New Coke's taste was really preferred by consumers. The company explained that consumers were so nostalgically attached to old Coke that they could not tolerate any changes to it. Thus, it was claimed, consumers rejected a taste they actually preferred. Most marketing pundits accepted this assertion that consumers really preferred New Coke's taste but just wouldn't admit it. These commentators argued that consumers were outraged at having their 'brand' taken from them, that Coke has underestimated consumers' brand loyalty. It appeared to many casual observers, on the other hand, that most consumers at the time actually *thought* New Coke didn't taste so good. Those who were around during that time will remember that consumers did not complain about losing something called a brand; they complained that New Coke tasted flat. It is not impossible that they were right. Regardless, those taste tastes were no substitute for thorough product testing or for a test market of the new product.

New Coke had a sweeter formula than old Coke, a change aimed at regaining some market share lost to Pepsi. Pepsi is a little sweeter than Coke, and in thousands of taste tests had trumpeted its (slight) win over Coke. Teenagers in particular, the heaviest users, seemed to prefer sweeter Pepsi. The company had gained some market share among these young swillers in those markets where it bragged of its win. So, New Coke was formulated to beat Pepsi in such taste tests and recover ground among teens. Thirty-second taste tests of food and beverage products, however, are well proven to produce sometimes unreliable results. In particular, in the US marketplace and even more so among US teenagers, any product in a taste test is likely to win if it is sweeter than an otherwise similar product. Consumers in a taste test are looking for a clue – which one is the one that's supposed to win? Sweetness is a discernible clue, but it does not automatically produce actual preference in real usage over time, when consumers are drinking much more than two sips and are no longer trying to guess the right answer.

In addition, a win in a taste test or any other product test can conceal subtler problems. For example, imagine the testing of two products A and B among 100 consumers. Imagine that about 65 consumers actually find the two nearly equal. Of these 65, also imagine that most, say 55, slightly prefer product B, while the other 10 slightly prefer A. But imagine also that, of the 100 consumers, 35 absolutely hate product B and strongly prefer A. If this were the case, the test results would show a 55–45 percent win for product B. Fifty-five slightly prefer B; ten slightly prefer A; thirty-five strongly prefer A. But these results, which may encourage the manufacturer to rush product B into the market, are potentially misleading. Changing to such a formula, about which two-thirds of consumers are nearly indifferent but one third are strongly negative, is dangerous at best. In addition, Coke's tests were aimed at the target audience with which it was then most obsessed – teens. Protests upon introduction of New Coke seemed to come primarily from adults. Therefore, it is also possible that the taste tests largely reflected indifference among teens and that many adults hated New Coke's taste.

After the taste tests, New Coke should have been tested in-home in extended use testing. Over several weeks, a sample of consumers would have consumed several cases of New Coke, old Coke, and Pepsi. In some research the products could have been unidentified – e.g. cola A, B, and C – and in other research, identified. It is possible that this more realistic use testing would have revealed many consumers' dislike of New Coke. If this testing had instead shown no strong negative reaction by even a loud minority of drinkers, the product could then have been tested in an unannounced ship test. Using this technique, the company would have shipped the New Coke formula in old Coke bottles into one or two test cities. By design in such a test, no one, beyond a few bottling plant employees, would know that the formula had been changed. Then properly conducted pre- and post-ship-test research would have picked up any negative reaction among consumers. Had New Coke passed this last hurdle, then the company could have conducted a full-fledged test market, introducing the product into a single city, accompanied by all of its marketing hoopla. If Coke drinkers in Seattle and Richmond, for example, had happily embraced New Coke, with no signs of a vocal and intensely negative minority, the company would have been very sensible to proceed with a rollout. Had the Coke-consuming citizenry of those two towns loudly rejected New Coke, however, then the company would have been wise to hesitate before rollout.

Even then, an additional product analysis would have been in order. It is conceivable that Coke, perhaps inadvertently, changed the New Coke formula after the taste tests. The formula in all those taste tests may have been a prototype. Often a formula must be changed somewhat in going from prototype to large-scale production. Upon facing rejection in a test market, the company would have been smart to check that the large-scale production formula was still a blind-test/in-use-test/ship-test winner.

If the conventional wisdom is right about New Coke, however, then all the product testing described above, conducted prior to and after full test markets, would have confirmed that consumers actually preferred the taste of New Coke, as long as they didn't know it was called New Coke. Consumer rejection in Seattle and Richmond would then indeed support the popular explanation of New Coke's failure, that it was unrelated to actual taste. Nonetheless, finding this out first in a test market, rather than after rollout, would have still saved most of the cost, embarrassment, and risk of New Coke.

If the company and most marketing experts who have discussed this case are right, all of those irrational consumers really prefer the taste of New Coke but are emotionally incapable of accepting such a change. There must be other examples of consumers going insane en masse because a product was improved, but none come to mind. When old Coke, re-christened Classic Coke, was returned to the market, New Coke volume quickly dwindled to less than one or two percent of Classic. Some people want to believe the usual spin on this tale, which is that even though everyone secretly preferred New Coke *no one* would forego old Coke to drink it. More skeptical managers may want to consider rigorous and thoughtful product testing in their organizations, instead.

In many industries, other VDS elements, such as distribution approaches, after-sale-service offerings, sales force initiatives, and advertising, are tested even less often than the product. Chapter Seven discussed the aversion to measuring the effectiveness of advertising and developing it through testing. Similar rationalization discourages a testing-oriented approach to the development of other functions and resources. Just as managers have their own rationales for not testing products or advertising, many sales force managers, for example, will protest the supposed impracticality of test markets that might measure and help develop sales programs. Their argument often is that each sales district is quite unique. These managers can go on at length about all the variables among districts – customers, competitors, local regulations, the weather; *everything* is so different, one just can't test anything. It is true that test markets and their controls must be carefully chosen, and it does takes a bit of work to minimize the interference of extraneous variables. However, the notion of a controlled experiment via the scientific method is robust and fully capable of accounting for a multivariate problem. Sometimes test markets will indeed produce misleading results or prove unreadable, but far more often they can, with hard work, discipline, and logic, be controlled properly and provide extremely useful learning.

Organizations with no clearly designed VDS often read test results based on inappropriate criteria for success. Without a clear understanding of the impact on value delivered to customers, a manager may declare the test successful if costs are reduced. Such a cost victory can be Pyrrhic. Similarly, a manager may read test results based entirely upon customer satisfaction ratings, awareness of brand name, or advancement of a core competency, all without evaluating the value proposition consequently delivered.

Testing in the marketplace among potential customers goes hand-in-hand with designing specific VDSs. Once a VDS is designed, it is vitally important and a powerful tool for creative improvement to test its elements rigorously. Conversely, without using the value delivery framework, testing is more problematical. With a designed VDS, an organization can make the maximum use of the techniques for testing which have been so well developed but inadequately used by many businesses.

Recreate strategy: again answer the questions of Delivering Profitable Value

At the end of the long journey to formulate and implement value delivery strategy, an organization will find itself in a place that looks like the beginning. The questions of *Delivering Profitable Value* must be asked all over again. This time, they must be answered with at least the same courage and, one hopes, increased wisdom and skill. There is no rigid timetable by which strategy should be rethought and recreated, but it must happen often; it is essentially a continuous process, a way of business life.

The organization must revisit its definition and understanding of the markets in which it competes. Within those markets, the organization must continuously update and deepen its understanding of customers. For current and potential customers at various levels in the value delivery chains, the organization must continue becoming customers, steadily expanding its knowledge of customers' real life experiences, the most valuable potential experiences that could be delivered to them, and the best competing alternatives they will have. In this way, the organization must reexamine its value delivery analysis. What are the businesses that it could implement?

In this effort to recreate strategy, organizations must fight the natural tendency to justify everything they currently do. They must search for and be open to the completely new perspective of an outsider considering the business for the first time. This open perspective must lead to identifying and developing new value propositions. And these propositions and the means to deliver them must be tested.

Then the organization must make the disciplined choice: which businesses in which markets should the organization actually pursue? For each such business, what is the primary VDS which must be implemented and the needed supporting VDSs? Across all the businesses, what are the most crucial capability gaps that must be closed? What capability bridges must be built to close these gaps? As the result of engaging in this most fundamental analysis, a business organization answers the basic questions of *DPV*. It may not answer them all correctly, but by answering them as well as it can, an organization has the best chance it can to succeed in generating sustained long-term growth. And thus, it takes responsibility for its own fate.

The questions *of Delivering Profitable Value*

I   What are the one or more market-spaces in which the organization will compete over the next five years? Describe for each the current and potential primary entities and the relevant kind of resulting experiences they would value.

II For each market-space, what are the important value delivery options? For each, briefly and broadly describe the primary entities, the value proposition appropriate to deliver to them, and the most salient elements in the primary VDS.

III Which options will the organization pursue as businesses in this market-space in the long-term (i.e. next three–five years) and short-term (i.e. the upcoming year)?

IV For each of these businesses, for the long-term and for the short-term, what is the primary VDS the organization intends to implement? For each VDS for each of these timeframes, this means answering the following:

   A   Clarify the criteria for success for this business

      1   How will the organization measure the contribution of this business to wealth generation for the firm over its intended timeframe?

      2   Beyond this first criteria of wealth generation, will success be judged entirely by the extent to which the organization delivers the chosen value proposition at the cost and as designed in the business plan for this primary VDS?

   B   Describe the organization structure relative to this primary VDS?

      1   What organizational entity will have the line business management responsibility for this primary VDS?

      2   What other entities within the business unit and/or firm must play a role in this VDS and are exclusively part of this VDS?

      3   Which entities must support this VDS but also other businesses? What other entities or managers must agree to the needed specific actions of support by these shared entities?

   C   What value proposition will this business deliver?

      1   What is the specific *timeframe* for delivering this proposition?

      2   Who is the *intended primary entity*?

      3   What does the organization want them to do for the experiences they will obtain?

      4   What is the best competing *alternative*(s) they will have?]

      5   What specific, measurable resulting experiences, whether superior, equal or inferior, including price, *will* they derive? That is, describe each experience as follows:

         a   What event or events will happen in the user's life?

         b   What will be the user's end-result consequence from this event or events, compared to their alternative experience, with what value to them?

   D   If the organization can deliver it to intended primary entities, would they perceive this proposition to be superior to their alternatives?

/Continued

E What is the estimated total revenue the organization would thus gain?

F For each chosen experience, how will the organization deliver it?

    1 How will the organization *provide* it to the primary entity?

        a What providing vehicles must interact with the primary entity so that they actually have the experience? For each:

           i What resources, such as products, does the organization need?

           ii What processes does the organization need?

           iii For each product and process, what attributes, features and characteristics must it have?

        b Who must use and help develop the vehicle: primary entity, supporting entities in the chain, and/or the organization?

        c What is the best estimate of the cost of providing this experience?

        d What capability gaps must be closed to provide it?

    2 How will the organization *communicate* it to the primary entity?

        a By what communicating vehicles will the organization convey to them:

           i What the resulting experience is?

           ii The reasons they should believe it will be provided?

        b For each vehicle, what resources and processes does the organization need?

        c Who must use and help develop this vehicle?

        d What is the estimated cost of communicating this experience?

        e What capability gaps must be closed to communicate it?

G For this whole primary VDS, what are the requirements in total for:

    1 Each significant product or service involved

    2 Each major asset and process involved

    3 Each function that is part of the VDS

    4 Each other entity involved within the firm

    5 Each significant set of supporting entities in the chain.

H For each important set of supporting entities that must be influenced, what is the supporting VDS to them (questions in F and G above must all be answered)?

I How will the organization measure progress versus success criteria?

    1 What techniques and devices will the organization use to measure this progress?

    2 What entity, with what resources and cost, will do this measuring?

J Across this primary VDS what are the most crucial capability gaps, the programs to close those gaps, and the estimated cost of those programs?

K Is this primary VDS a winning business for the firm?

    1 What is the estimated total revenue the organization would thus gain?

    2 Can the organization close the crucial capability gaps at roughly the estimated cost, quickly enough for the selected timeframe?

/Continued

3   What is the total estimated cost of delivering the proposition as designed above, including all resources and capability bridges?

4   What is the estimated profit contribution of this business as designed, in the selected timeframe?

5   What impact will this primary VDS have on the organization's other businesses?

6   What impact will it have on this option in different timeframes?

7   What discontinuities may impact its success and sustainability?

8   Should the firm implement this primary VDS?

L   What new elements or improvements in the VDS are being developed for future timeframes, and how are they being tested during this timeframe? What are the cost and profit implications of this testing in this timeframe?

V. For organizations implementing multiple businesses, a combined business plan should aggregate the individual primary VDSs and also address:

A   What are the requirements in aggregate across all the businesses for each common element listed in G above?

B   For each supporting entity that must be influenced across businesses, what is the appropriate supporting VDS?

C   What crucial capability gaps cut across the businesses?

D   What key capability bridges must be built to close these gaps:

1   Changes in criteria for success?

2   Implications for organization structure?

3   Key resources that must be developed or obtained?

4   Key processes to create or build, including any appropriate pivotal job change programs?

E   What is the total revenue, cost, and profit impact on all the businesses?

VI Finally, what is the organization's plan to reexamine its strategy in each market-space?

***

All management activities should reflect either the organization's answers to these questions of *Delivering Profitable Value* or an on-going effort to find the answers. Yet managers should ask whether in their organization, despite talent, intelligence, and energy, this is really the case. If not, where should leadership start, to realize the potential of this philosophy, framework, and methodology? What should a leader ask the organization to do first, in practical terms, to start *Delivering Profitable Value*?

Chapter Twenty

What to Do Monday Morning?

If *DPV* is broadly and pervasively applicable, how can an organization assess its own starting point – where is a manager to start, come Monday morning? Is it more realistic for organizations only slowly and partially to adopt *DPV* in a carefully limited context, or should organizations wholeheartedly embrace its full implications?

The last framework this book offers is the first framework managers will use in leading their organizations toward *Delivering Profitable Value*. This philosophy implies that no formulaic, one-size-fits-all answer can be useful. To determine the right first steps toward *DPV*, an organization should first assess its current situation. Real change is difficult to achieve unless managers share a consensus that the organization should, but does not currently, apply the principles of *DPV*. Then, leadership must commit the organization to applying the mindset and methodology of *DPV* wholeheartedly.

Assess the organization's current situation

Once leadership has internalized the principles of *DPV*, it should assess the extent to which the organization currently understands and uses them. Then it must determine the extent to which, in contrast, the organization operates under internally-driven and customer-compelled principles.

To what extent is this organization value delivery focused?

A few simple questions can assess the extent to which managers understand the most fundamental concepts of *DPV*. This assessment can be made for an entire corporation as well for individual organizations within a firm. Leaders making this assessment can answer each question below. On the scale of one to five, one means 'managers in this organization are not at all familiar with this concept as defined in *DPV*.' Five means 'managers have a thorough understanding of this concept as defined in *DPV*.'

Understanding Value Delivery

How well do managers understand the following DPV concepts?

1 A resulting experience   1 2 3 4 5

2 A real value proposition   1 2 3 4 5

3 Providing and communicating resulting experiences   1 2 3 4 5

4 A value delivery system   1 2 3 4 5

5 That the chain of suppliers and customers is best seen as a
   value delivery chain, with primary and supporting entities 1 2 3 4 5

6 That a business is best understood, defined, and managed
   as a primary VDS, including its supporting VDSs   1 2 3 4 5

7 That a market-space is a set of related potential businesses
   and that a strategic option is a potential primary VDS   1 2 3 4 5

8 Formulating strategy by identifying value delivery options –
   analyzing markets to discover their potential businesses   1 2 3 4 5

9 *Becoming the customer* for samples of primary entities
   and supporting entities, and then quantifying results   1 2 3 4 5

10 That criteria for success, organization structure, and
   development of resources and processes must entirely
   reflect chosen VDSs   1 2 3 4 5

After thus assessing managers' understanding, one can then determine how well these concepts are actually applied. Leaders can assess the extent to which the *Questions of DPV* (Chapter 19, pp. 279–81) are answered. Determining whether the organization has answered these questions should not be confused with ascertaining whether people simply use some of the language of *DPV*, such as 'value proposition' and 'value delivery system.' If an organization answers these questions, it is useful to ask the more subjective question of how well. Are these questions analyzed as factually and as deeply as they need to be? Do all elements in the organization understand and accept the answers as the basis for all operations?

Most organizations, of course, will find that they are not thoroughly value-delivery focused. It is useful then to characterize how the organization *is* managed. Even organizations that have absorbed some of these concepts and do answer many of the *Questions* well will benefit from knowing whether decisions are made in an internally-driven or customer-compelled fashion.

To what extent is this organization internally-driven?

This assessment is about the extent to which the organization makes decisions based upon what it likes to do or what it thinks it could do better than competition. Customers are rarely ignored altogether in the internally-driven organization. However, they are understood as a marketing or sales issue, one that should be addressed after strategy has already been determined. The organization and how it compares to competition provide the main focus in such a culture. It is implicitly assumed that understanding what customers want and what will be valuable to them is trivially obvious – the clever stuff is in figuring out a position in the industry that is superior to competitors. If the organization is lucky, the de facto value proposition delivered can be superior, even though it is the result of internally-driven agendas. Few organizations are so lucky. The internally-driven organization does not understand that a business must be created and managed as a relationship with the customer and their experience. Rather, bolstered by most of modern management theory, this perspective starts and ends in the looking glass and is focused on the organization's own resources, characteristics, and outputs, as they compare to those of competitors.

Internally-driven thinking can be manifested in many behaviors In some cases, the focus is on cost-control, to the exclusion of the outside world. Many organizations in high-tech find it difficult to be driven by anything other than technology, such as any real consideration for the value delivered to users. The finance function and the constraints of the annual budget can also be the subject of the internally-driven mentality. Even a strong marketing department can behave in a highly internally-driven manner by directing great energy and money toward marketing activities without a clear value delivery strategy. It is useful to evaluate the degree to which the organization exhibits this internally-driven behavior by rating the organization on a scale of one to five. A score of one would indicate that the organization does not exhibit the behavior, while a five would indicate that the organization very much behaves in this manner.

To what extent is this organization customer-compelled?

This third assessment helps determine the extent to which an organization tries to correct internally-driven behavior by trusting the customer to show the way. Customer-compelled philosophies follow an enduring tradition of trying to save organizations from dissatisfying their customers. Like internally-driven philosophies, this thinking manifests itself in several behaviors.

The suggestion-boxed organization asks customers for input on how to manage a business. It is important to learn from customers, but the suggestion-boxed organization is trapped in pursuit of the wrong essential questions: 'What do you suggest, or desire or demand, that we should make and sell to you? How do you suggest we better supply it to you?' Another customer-compelled philosophy is the assumption that the organization should never deny customers anything good. Delivering a tradeoff is viewed as a failure rather than a potentially creative strategy. Such organizations find it difficult to say no to virtually anything. Promising customers total satisfaction is another customer-compelled facade. The organization guarantees or emphatically assures the customer that they will be satisfied without limits. Promising everything, the organization has not committed itself to much of anything. Behind this facade is usually a beehive of unadulterated internally-driven behavior. In the misguided effort to make an organization customer-driven without constraints, employees are empowered to react to customers. All functions, not just marketing, are encouraged to reach out rather randomly to customers and to ask them what they want from that function. What is not decided is what value proposition will be delivered or how.

Again, managers would do well to use a 1–5 rating scale when evaluating their organizations for evidence of customer-compelled behavior.

To what extent is this organization both?

Most organizations are neither entirely internally-driven nor entirely customer-compelled. Many find that, over time, they have swung back and forth between these two approaches. Often, organizations find a midpoint that mixes internally-driven behavior with a strong dose of customer-compelled behavior. This only creates more confusion.

A method for resolving this contradiction has become widely popular. The organization determines its internally-driven preferences, its core competencies and competitive advantages in supplying products. It also gathers a customer-compelled list of what customers supposedly want. Then the organization meets whichever of these customer demands happen to coincide with the organization's preferences. This approach only ensures that the organization will retain the worst of both approaches.

A framework for all businesses and functions

Some managers, uncomfortable with the magnitude of change required by *DPV*, will wonder if perhaps their firm or their particular function is outside the bounds of realistic application. Every firm, every business, every market, is indeed *different* from every other in significant ways, but the fundamental principles of business success are no different from industry to industry. The concepts of *DPV* apply to any enterprise that must succeed in part by influencing the behavior of some customers. Some examples of organizations where *DPV* applies, despite a common perception to the contrary, are high tech, commodities, health care, those selling to the government, financial services, regulated or quasi-governmental organizations, government, and other non-profit organizations.

There are no universal, all-purpose value propositions that cut across any market. Nor is it likely that a meaningful classification of types of value propositions could be devised. Of course, an abundance of platitudes and vague generalities, which offer strategy-without-thought for today's executive in a hurry, are regularly churned out. But these attempts at pre-cooked, all-purpose answers are nonsense. The *DPV* perspective assumes that the winning VDS in every business is necessarily unique. However, although diversity in the *answers* to the questions of *Delivering Profitable Value* is critical, the questions and methodology for answering them should not much vary.

Managers may also wonder at *DPV*'s application to some functions within a firm. Among the numerous such entities are the following: manufacturing and logistics, finance, information technology (IT), human resources, market research, and last but not least, purchasing. *DPV* is indeed relevant for all these functions. *DPV*, which is focused on generating wealth through improving customers' experiences, aims to accomplish this in part by the integrated involvement of all resources. The VDS gives every function a voice in the disciplined choice of a value proposition and empowers them and every employee to help profitably deliver that chosen proposition.

For each primary VDS, a business management function should play the leading role in the formulation and coordinated execution of strategy. None of the other functions exclusively owns the value proposition or its delivery. All must share responsibility for and contribute to value delivery. Because *DPV* is highly focused on customers, managers in functions other than sales and marketing may wonder if *DPV* is less applicable to them. Not so. Every function can and must help profitably deliver value.

Learn to run before walking

In most countries of the Soviet Union at the time of its disintegration, a majority of people believed that their society needed to adopt the principles of free market economics. The debate in large part has been whether to move slowly and cautiously or rapidly in allowing private property, establishing financial markets, privatizing state-owned enterprises, and otherwise reforming the economy. Poland and the Czech Republic moved more quickly while others, such as Russia, were swayed by the argument that they should learn to walk before trying to run. While countries that liberalized rapidly have hit bumps in the road, they have made great progress and seem unlikely now to reverse course. Those that played it safe have not yet learned to walk and now risk losing momentum as reactionary forces regroup and try to sabotage reform.

Similarly, managers who are serious about putting the principles of *Delivering Profitable Value* into action must reject the temptations of timidity in leadership. Once understood, the scope of the change required by *DPV* might seem daunting, but half-hearted, overly cautious attempts to implement it are more likely to produce failure than to reduce risk. As a former student of *DPV* once pointed out, a thirty-foot gorge is not often crossed by three well timed ten-foot leaps. The timid instincts of many in a leadership position can easily produce such counterproductive compromises that undermine rather than advance the chances of implementing *DPV*.

One such instinct is to co-opt rather than adopt *DPV*. To do this, one drafts some statement misnamed a value proposition and adds it to an internally-driven and customer-compelled strategy or plan. The organization does not design a VDS nor does it understand the chain of customer entities as a value delivery chain. In some cases, the organization may conduct a traditional market segmentation study, identifying groups of customers by demographic or product usage or lifestyle variables, and then assign teams to write 'value propositions' for each so-called segment based on superficial and customer-compelled research. Or an organization may develop its list of core competencies and then assign teams to write 'value propositions' that will best rationalize these competencies to customers. In some cases, an organization's leadership goes so far as to conduct a handful of 'a day-in-the-life of the customer' studies, but stops there. This taste of becoming the customer may result in self-congratulation among managers who order the study, but rarely threatens business as usual.

***

This chapter gives leaders a starting point, a way to put their organizations on the path to *Delivering Profitable Value*. But managers wishing to generate wealth over the long-term must go further - toward institutionalization of this framework, methodology, and philosophy. This is no easy task but with the long-term commitment and managerial will to make it happen, it is possible, as discussed in the Conclusion.

Lead Beyond a Few Improvements, Build a Great Company: Institutionalize *DPV*

A prime intent of this book has been to kindle in its readers a deep natural instinct that is often repressed and underdeveloped. This instinct is that of understanding a business as a competitive, sometimes complex and sometimes baffling relationship between an organization and the real experiences of potential customers. I have tried to convince readers to move once and for all beyond the business paradigms that either ignore or trivialize this all-important relationship, paradigms that recognize only deterministic processes of supplying a product. However, this book is also meant to inspire managers to take action, to not only think in a fundamentally different way but to use this value delivery framework to build their organization's ability to succeed consistently.

DPV may be intuitively obvious, but some will wonder if it is really practical for many organizations to be managed in such a different way. Are firms only able to deliver profitable value sporadically, or can this mentality, framework, and set of business-management capabilities be institutionalized, thoroughly inculcated into a culture over time? This Conclusion suggests answers to these questions, answers meant to embolden managers to make *DPV* their organization's way of business life, to focus their organization single-mindedly on dramatically accelerating growth and generating wealth by improving customers' experience, and thus to lead their organizations beyond the looking glass and into the real heart of business.

While managers can decide to apply *DPV* only to one business within an organization or only temporarily for short-term improvement, business leaders should be far more ambitious. They should aim to internalize the *DPV* principles, frameworks, and methodology throughout the corporate culture with the intention to build a company of lasting greatness. To reach this goal, the organization's leadership should learn to *institutionalize* the mindset, framework, and collection of tools that make up *DPV*.

This book contains numerous examples of organizations that success-fully used some of the principles of *DPV* to improve parts of their busi-nesses. Among them were Kodak Consumer Imaging in Australia, numer-ous divisions of HP, Chevron's US natural gas business, some of Weyerhaeuser's composite product businesses, Glaxo's Zantac, and some of Kodak's industrial imaging businesses. Some of those firms are moving steadily down the road to deeper and broader application, while others have moved more slowly. The road to thoroughly institutionalizing such a fundamentally different approach is long. Moreover, *DPV* has only been completed as a comprehensive framework and methodology within the past few years. Thus, most innovative business leaders and thinkers have not even been exposed to it yet.

So the jury is still out on whether large complex organizations can thor-oughly institutionalize the perspective and capabilities of value delivery as put forth here. However, there exist firms that have adopted, in effect, many of the *DPV* principles. Southwest Airlines, FedEx, Perdue, Glaxo Wellcome, Procter & Gamble, Fidelity, British Airways, Honda, Microsoft, Sony and others have been cited here for demonstrating some of the fundamental principles underlying *DPV.* Others, who are among some of the most ad-mired companies and also demonstrate the ability to institutionalize some of these principles include General Electric, ABB, Disney, Coca-Cola, and Toyota. Though all these achieved success without being aware of or delib-erately using the specific *DPV* methodology presented in this book, some of *DPV's* underlying principles seem to have been ingrained in the culture of these firms over time.

Perhaps one of the greatest, most historically important firms to illus-trate the power of many of the fundamental principles articulated by *DPV* is Microsoft. Randall Stross's brilliant history of Microsoft in the 1990s, *The Microsoft Way*, debunks much of the mythology surrounding the company. That mythology spins a fantasy tale of how Gates imposes his evil will on the helpless victims. Microsoft may have had some negative impact on so-ciety. Its power and at least the potential for its abuse are cause for legiti-mate concern. But the mythology of Microsoft forcing itself on millions of customers, usually by some vague form of cheating, obscures how well Microsoft has deliberately sought, with spectacular success, to profitably deliver superior value propositions to its potential primary entities.

Microsoft is at the center of one of the more interesting phenomena of the computer/digital revolution over the past 30 years. For, it turns out that software, not hardware, is probably the richest source of profit from digital technology, an insight always understood by Microsoft but persistently missed by most major players for many years. In the mid–late 1980s when

Microsoft was first trying to get beyond its initial operating-system success, as Stross points out, few people thought the company able to dominate the industry or even dictate the next generation of operating system for PCs. Most others assumed that hardware, where the big capital investments and the big prices were, held the key to power and wealth. Software ultimately proved so important, not because of magic or foul play but because of what Gates and Microsoft always understood so clearly: software dramatically affects the most important resulting experiences for the primary entities, the users of PCs.

The company has single-mindedly focused on delivering user experiences of the maximum value that can be delivered and still generates wealth for the firm. Microsoft, far better than Apple and the long-clueless IBM, understood and aggressively pursued the far better experiences made possible by the Macintosh/Xerox-invented approach to operating systems – the graphical user interface with its mouse, windows and other features. It is Microsoft who has insisted on much lower prices than conventional wisdom dictated, while investing in R&D at higher relative levels than almost any other player.[1] A crucial manifestation of this attitude is the company's brilliant invention of a suite of software applications, which simplified the purchase and interactive use of the basic desktop applications priced much lower than the market would bear for each one separately.

Microsoft has, especially since the late 1980s, institutionalized some forms of *becoming the customer* in order to guide product development. In 1988, a key executive, Nathan Myhrvold, argued that Microsoft should develop what he called 'User Modeling,' an approach that does not rely on asking users what to make. User modelling would

> '... collect data on how computer users actually went about ... whatever they had set out to do. The research would note not only keystrokes and menu choices but also more subtle measures such as disc utilization, network traffic and recourse to on-line help. Microsoft should no less intensively study the real-world use of competitors' products, Myhrvold suggested, to give developers another source of empirical data [to improve] Microsoft's products.'[2]

The firm's Usability Lab, first created in the early 1980s, allowed developers to observe and analyze users attempting to use various products. The Lab grew steadily in importance until by 1992 it was 'so well established and highly regarded that its anteroom was jammed with product managers waiting' to test their programs.[3]

The company has also been very successful in exploring and pursuing the value delivery options in new and unfamiliar market-spaces, including business application software, publishing via CD ROM, consumer software for education and entertainment in the home, Internet applications and others. Rather than gazing at its own navel to discover the core competencies it could leverage, Microsoft has identified potential to deliver valuable experiences to users and invested in understanding that potential and developing the capabilities.

> 'Gates also proved to be shrewd in recognizing at the time of the CD-ROM's appearance what he and the others at Microsoft did not know. He intuitively understood that to fully exploit the medium would require entirely new skill sets that had yet to be devised. Moreover ... he was not certain [that CD-ROMs could be profitable] but he was willing to spend ... to find out ... [He] confided ... that he was willing to lose $200 million to find out whether a market existed.'[4]

In addition, the company has masterfully understood the value delivery chains in which it must operate. In CD-ROM development, publishing and other areas, the company worked brilliantly with competitors, suppliers, related industry players and others to create consensus, momentum and cooperation with Microsoft's own strategic agenda. One amusing exception has been the company's insistence on maximally alienating the anti-trust lawyers of the US Justice Department. By and large, however, the firm has understood and proactively managed its value delivery chains, staying focused all the while on delivering superior value to users, the primary entities.

As a quite different and somewhat more detailed example, another great firm that has indeed institutionalized many of these *DPV* principles over the long term is Procter & Gamble. P&G has always conducted its core businesses in market-spaces not known for dynamic growth or dramatic product changes. Yet, the company has a very long track record (well over 100 years) of profitably differentiating and branding its businesses in such mundane categories as soap. Given its size, age and rather slow-changing market-spaces, P&G has generally ranked highly over time among US industrials for financial performance. For example, it ranked number 20 for the greatest growth in earnings per share over the past 10 years; only one of the 19 companies ranked above it were as large in revenues. It ranks ninth in total market value. Its stock rose nearly nine fold over the past decade, about double the rest of the stock market.

Some firms have outperformed P&G in recent years, of course, but not many have its long-term record. In the early 1970s in the US, there was a famous set of blue chip stocks known as the 'nifty fifty' among investment managers who believed in pouring funds into these 50 companies. One was P&G, but very few of the others (which included Polaroid, IBM, Xerox, Kodak, Avon, and McDonalds) would be considered nifty today, while P&G still would. Similarly, P&G is one of the few companies named 'excellent' by *In Search of Excellence* (1982) which would still be considered so.

In addition, P&G has achieved its performance over a long period of time marked by the leadership of numerous CEOs. It is interesting to note that the highly admired companies of Microsoft, Intel, and Berkshire Hathaway have all had essentially only one CEO. And GE, Coke, Disney and ABB have excelled only since the helm was taken by the current or most recent CEO; while these companies' performance over the past 15 years has certainly been outstanding, they have not yet demonstrated the ability to sustain great performance under more than a single leader. P&G is interesting partly because it has managed to institutionalize a winning approach in a difficult set of market-spaces, across the past 50 years under six different CEOs.

At P&G, a brand is understood and managed as a business and very much like a primary VDS. Although managers in P&G do not articulate the idea in quite these terms, the company places a central strategic importance on the primary entity (the consumer in this case) and on making a disciplined choice of how to deliver a superior set of experiences. The concept of the brand also treats a business as the resources and processes, including in P&G's case the product and package, advertising and distribution, that are needed to deliver those experiences profitably to the primary entity.

Thus, P&G exemplifies some of the most important concepts of *DPV*. The company's success in institutionalizing important aspects of this approach provides encouragement to business leaders seeking to institutionalize *DPV*. With competent, focused leadership, the systematic approach of *DPV* can be inculcated thoroughly into an organization.

This isn't like soap, you know

Many strategy consultants and similarly educated executives seem to think that packaged goods companies are on an entirely separate planet of their own. Principles followed by P&G have no application to companies outside packaged goods, these thinkers would say. However, while the planets in our solar system are indeed different from each other, they do revolve around the same star and obey the same laws of physics. Yet, some managers strongly resist analogies between the general framework for a business and a brand, especially a brand that may involve soap. Many managers, in fact, are so convinced that their industry operates under unique economic laws that they deride any sort of analogy from outside their industry. But managers would do well to relax and learn more easily from other industries.

Of course, P&G is only an example of the value delivery framework in a particular context – consumer packaged goods, or fast moving consumer goods. Applying the consumer brand management version of the *DPV* framework in a high-tech, heavy industry, or financial services business would work about as well as trying to get a nice tan on the moon. Instead, managers are urged to apply *DPV,* a generalized framework and method, to their own type of business.

So packaged goods are different. However, the principles of operation that any organization wanting to adopt *DPV* fully must strive to institutionalize over time are the same. P&G's success in firmly entrenching some of these principles in its culture indicates that the same success institutionalizing *DPV* is possible for any organization.

Following are some basic principles that characterize P&G's culture. These principles were established firmly within the culture as a result of consistent reinforcement over many years. They are described in somewhat generic terms in order to relate them specifically to the equivalent concept of most general relevance to *DPV.*

Everyone knows: consumers are the real priority

The general lesson to learn from this shared mindset is not that the first priority in any company should necessarily be consumers but rather that it should be the primary entities, whoever they are. In the case of almost all of P&G's businesses, of course, the consumer is that primary entity.

The important decisions in this company are made with the highest priority placed on the consumer. This means that the impact of any decision or action on consumers must always be considered thoroughly and seriously. And if a proposed action may adversely impact consumers and their attitudes toward the company's businesses, that proposal is exceedingly difficult to sell. Throughout the organization, individuals have no doubt about the source of its wealth: P&G's relationships with consumers.

P&G managers are taught and continuously reminded that understanding, developing, and protecting those relationships and giving the consumer a clear reason to prefer and trust the company's brands is the wellspring of the corporation's success. They are also convinced that this is not a commitment at some vague corporate, public relations level. Rather, a manager's personal success is directly related to nurturing that consumer relationship, even if his efforts affect that relationship only indirectly. This mindset pervades more than just brand management, the business management function for each P&G business. Sales managers focus on retailers but understand that underlying the retail relationship are the goals of winning and holding consumer preference. R&D focuses on products but does so entirely within context of their impact on consumers. Manufacturing managers are trained to understand their role within the context of the strategies for building consumer preference for each brand.

The philosophy of the consumer as first priority is reinforced in many ways. For example, the company, like may others, aggressively pursues cost savings. Managers are well rewarded for identifying cost savings opportunities. However, to avoid subtly reducing the value delivered to consumers, a proposed change cannot qualify as a cost savings opportunity unless it can be demonstrated to have no adverse impact on the experiences the consumer will derive.

P&G often makes decisions that clearly forego short-term opportunity in order to deliver long-term improvements to consumers. In some cases, these decisions even risk profit. In the early 1990s, P&G radically changed its approach to sales promotion. At that time, retailers were purchasing increasing portions of all products as part of a promotion. One day a brand would sell for $4.50, and a week later it would be on sale for $2.99. The whole distribution system was wasting huge costs by buying large quantities of goods for promotions, thus increasing inventory, handling, shipping, and other costs. The more packaged goods manufacturers engaged in this process, the more promotionally priced volume most retailers demanded. The player really paying for this game was the consumer. So P&G simply ended most promotional pricing and lowered everyday prices on all of its brands. This risked losing favor with some retailers and some short-term market share to competitors willing to continue aggressive price promotion. But eventually, retailers became convinced that P&G did this for the good of retailer. Of course, consumers paid less on average for all P&G brands.

Similarly, in recent years the company developed concentrated versions for many of its products. A concentrated box of detergent or bottle of fabric softener is now less than half of its conventional size. This amounted to giving away shelf space, an asset that packaged goods manufacturers traditionally fight to protect, but it also reduced cost and pantry space for the consumer. So it was an easy decision for P&G.

At P&G, primacy of the consumer isn't a customer-compelled commitment to satisfy every consumer desire or to seek instructions from them on how to manage the businesses. Rather it is a belief in placing great importance on understanding the consumer and making every decision with an eye to the sometimes complex and subtle impact it may have on them.

Strategic obsession with the user's experiences and the choice of a superior value proposition

Managers, especially those in the brand management function, R&D, and the company's advertising agencies, are continuously reminded to think about business *strategy* for the one or more brands on which they work. They are taught that strategy is centrally focused on the question of what consumer benefits and price to give target consumers. In effect, while the language and to some degree the concepts are different, P&G's managers are taught that understanding the user's experiences and choosing a superior value proposition are at the heart of business.

This lesson is not taught, however, by issuing an occasional statement of corporate philosophy or by sending managers to a training course to learn some buzzwords. It is taught by constantly asking the management of each brand – each business – to clarify and defend its strategy in these terms. Senior managers continuously ask middle managers to describe the evidence they are gathering and how they are analyzing it to understand better the current and potentially valuable experiences of consumers. Managers are bombarded with questions about their brand – how is the intended consumer defined, how are they changing, what are their behaviors and attitudes, how do they use relevant products and services, where are they frustrated or disappointed or missing opportunity. Likewise, they are challenged to articulate the brand's strategy in response to this background. They are asked to explain in depth what benefits the brand intends to deliver to these consumers currently and in the future, at what price, and how this all compares to the consumer's competing options. Managers in brand management, R&D, and the agencies cannot operate (for long) without thinking about these questions. If they don't think about them often, they risk being unable to answer them convincingly.

People learn a new language most quickly and easily if they have to learn it to get by. Similarly, P&G institutionalized the capability to understand customer experience by making it a necessary requirement for managers to survive. It is simply not possible for these managers to get anywhere at P&G without being able to discuss coherently and justify factually their understanding of strategy for the brands they affect. P&G's supporting VDSs, which are focused on the retailer, are equally demanding. Managers in the Sales Department[5] must understand, articulate, and explain what the company wants retailers to do, what their alternatives are, and what resulting experiences P&G will deliver to them.

But the company not only demands that its managers think in these terms. It also continuously invests in the research and market testing that can further managers' knowledge and understanding of customer experiences.

Compared to many markets, consumers in most of P&G's markets change relatively little. Yet, the company spends far more resources than almost any other corporation studying the experiences, including the behavior, habits, and attitudes, of its primary entities and other customers.

Integration of all resources and activity around delivery of each brand's value proposition

In effect, each P&G brand is managed as a value delivery system - the choice and integrated delivery of the brand's value proposition. The resources and processes needed to deliver a brand's value proposition are designed and articulated clearly as that brand's business plan. In many cases, important elements in the brand's VDS, such as manufacturing and sales, must be shared with other brands. In all functions to the extent possible, however, resources are dedicated to specific brands. The sales function manages its relationships with retailers as supporting VDSs. The company institution-alizes this understanding of businesses by making it the only framework within which managers can function.

Each brand group – brand manager and team of assistants – works with all other functions to develop a proposed business plan. That plan is recom-mended to senior management. Occasionally a functional group will not agree with the plan a brand group and its immediate management recom-mend. In these cases, senior management will ultimately resolve the issue, but all concerned are strongly motivated to arrive at consensus before that point. Once the plan is approved, however, it takes on the authority of a real business plan. The brand group has the leading responsibility to en-sure that it is implemented as designed, to monitor and measure its success, and to recommend on-going improvement. It is not so much the brand manager/group or even the upper middle managers heading the brand management department that have actual power. The business plan, ap-proved by top management of the company, has power.

Of course, battles among functions do occur. R&D, manufacturing, sales, or an agency may question the wisdom of a particular action specified by an already approved business plan. The ensuing debate may result in the consensus that the action in question conforms to the intent of that plan. Other times, a plan is changed. Often, the function challenging the plan will win the debate because the struggle is not about the political clout of one department versus another. It is about the merits of one approach to designing or implementing the brand's VDS versus another.

Upper management asks managers many questions about how each brand's value proposition is delivered. Managers are unable to gain agree-ment to any initiative in the marketplace, to any expenditure, to any change in product, distribution, manufacturing, advertising, or pricing without relating the proposal to the VDSs of the one or more brands affected.

Clear success criteria

P&G's criteria for success are not at all ambiguous. Managers know that ethical behavior generally, and honesty and a respect for the truth most specifically, are inviolable company principles. There may be some unspoken cynicism about this principle, but even cynics know that managers found violating it usually don't last long. Beyond this requirement, managers are judged on two criteria: their contribution to building the one or more businesses, i.e. brands, that they impact and their success in developing the potential of people reporting to or influenced by them.

The people-development criterion is not at odds with the business-building criterion. That is, proper people development is not seen as a compromise that will reduce business performance but rather as a way in which to enhance it. So managers are expected to meet both criteria. Therefore, the only real constraint on the criterion that defines success as building the business is that one cannot pursue it dishonestly.

The clarity of the business-building criterion plays a major role in creating a high performance environment at P&G. Generally speaking, senior management establishes a simple to understand financial requirement for each brand, which usually varies somewhat according to the capital structure of the category. The requirement might be a return on sales ratio. Managers are expected to maximize the growth, in market share and volume, of the brand while maintaining that financial ratio. They will not gain agreement to business plans which produce a return below that target, nor are they rewarded for exceeding that return. The objective is to maximize the growth of the business at a return that generates wealth – the more volume and market share, the more cash flow and long term strength.

Managers who are in a position to significantly affect the business results of one or more brands are partly evaluated based on those results. P&G has a weakness in that the rigor of the relationship between real career reward or punishment and business results is not as great as it should be. Still, this principle is upheld for the most part. In addition, all employees, whether or not they strongly impact measurable business results, are evaluated based on the nature of their contribution to the business. Once business plans are agreed upon, every employee can be measured against reasonably clear objectives for execution.

In effect, the primary VDSs of the brands establish a set of actions that, if executed as planned, are assumed to make a positive contribution to the business. Thus each department, team, and individual can be evaluated for how well they execute as planned. In this way, the company makes it clear that objectives that do not support building the business, long and short term, are not acceptable. The one exception, of course, is those objectives that develop people, which is still not an acceptable excuse for failing to contribute to building the business.

With such an unambiguous focus on building the business, it is not easy for objectives that interfere with building the business to take hold. Such counterproductive objectives that are internally-driven include: achieving technology leadership, leveraging core competencies, winning total quality awards, winning advertising creative awards, differentiating products and other resources, or achieving industry cost leadership. Some similarly counterproductive, customer-compelled objectives are: winning advertising popularity contests, pursuing customer satisfaction ratings, adding product or packaging features or sales promotions based primarily on consumer requests for them, or even winning popularity contests with retailers.

Of course, P&G does not scorn superior technology, low costs, customer input, or close working partnerships with their retail customers. However, the company understands – and ensures that every manager understands – that these things are not goals in their own right. They are only justifiable if they directly help increase the brand's market share and volume at a rate of return that generates wealth. If a P&G manager has to use an inferior technology, fail to utilize an officially designated core competence, ignore a clearly stated consumer request, increase costs, come in dead last at this year's Cannes Faux Art Ad Awards, or even irritate a grocery buyer in order to build the market share and long-term strength of a P&G brand, s/he will only be rewarded. At least, in principle. The place isn't perfect, after all.

Focus on building capability in key delivery vehicles

Of course, like any great company, P&G prides itself on its efforts to be world class in virtually all significant aspects of its operation. Obviously, as indicated above, the company invests heavily in building its ability to analyze and insightfully understand its primary entities and supporting customers. Its abilities as a global manufacturer are indeed world class. In recent years, its whole distribution, sales, and logistics operations have been dramatically changed to align better with the evolving worldwide retail environments. However, two delivery vehicles are especially important in most P&G businesses and historically have been the focus of some of the most intense ongoing capability building. These are the product and advertising.

A few years ago, HP had an informal alliance with P&G. Both companies had committed to working closely together and to learning from each other, a commitment which was an excellent choice for both to make. This alliance generated a story, perhaps apocryphal but representative of the truth, of a discussion between the two CEOs, HP's John Young and P&G's John Smale. At dinner one evening, Young explained that, while HP was a *product company*, he wanted to make HP more like P&G, a *marketing company*. Smale replied that P&G is *not* a marketing company – it's a *product* company.

If John Smale said this, he was right. Young may have found it hard to believe that this reply came from the CEO of the soap opera company, but he apparently understood it and made a point of relating the story inside HP. The simple truth in Smale's comment is that P&G focuses on the relationship between a brand's consumers and its product, not on the processes of marketing. Managing that relationship includes creating and developing the product to deliver the right experiences and reinforcing that delivery through packaging, advertising, and other vehicles. But the focus is on that relationship and the experiences that result for the consumer, as the consumer understands them, due to using the product.

In this context, the company devotes huge resources to product research and development. Only a handful of companies in the world hire as many hard-science PhDs, and few of these scientists end up in the sales force or designing promotional coupon mailings. P&G's extensive R&D effort aims specifically to develop products that are superior in their actual delivery of the experiences most valued by consumers.

However, managers, especially those in other industries, commonly assume that all packaged goods products, especially soap products, are *really* exactly the same, that marketing companies – like P&G – just use advertising to fool the gullible consumer. Each executive expressing this attitude usually has washed about five loads of clothes and cleaned about three kitchen floors over the last decade. These people are not the intended primary entity for P&G's businesses. The target consumer, who might wash 12 loads of clothes per week, is far more discerning than popular mythology would suppose. In fact, P&G assumes that without products that deliver noticeably superior end-results to these users, the company would eventually go out of business.

Generally speaking, the company principles prohibit introduction of new brands into a test market without a product blind test win against leading competition. Similarly, product changes aren't allowed without at least a blind test win against the current version of that product. In other words, 'New and improved' means new and improved. In a blind test, a win means that the sample population preferred one product to the other by a statistically significant margin. It means that more target consumers prefer the experiences, in net, that the tested product delivers, than prefer the other.

But winning a blind test is not enough justification for P&G to introduce a new or improved product. It must also be proven a winner in a test market. These standards create a fairly unambiguous and demanding criterion for the product development function. A product may be declared superior by some internally-driven engineering criteria, perhaps inspired by the latest benchmarking, or declared superior by some customer-compelled criteria from consumer requests. But that product will get nowhere if it cannot win in a blind test and in a test market. This constraint works well to concentrate the minds of R&D, the brand group, manufacturing, and others on developing products and product changes that will actually improve delivery of the experiences chosen as important for that brand to deliver.

Of course Procter sometimes imperfectly executes its own principles and develops a bad product. But a deep respect for the integrity of products in their role of helping to deliver a winning value proposition has been well institutionalized. This principle and the energy it takes to institutionalize it have little to do with soap. It is a natural implication of the company's broader philosophy of delivering real superior value to its primary entities.

Many deride P&G's approach to the second crucial delivery vehicle, advertising, even more so than its approach to product. Even analysts who generally admire the company are likely to note that, 'Despite all it does well, P&G's advertising is atrocious and totally lacking in creativity.' P&G is actually happy with this state of affairs, since the less the outside world understands what it does, the more difficult it is for competitors. The reasons for this condemnation of its body of advertising, despite its incontestable track record of generating wealth, are somewhat complex. However, it provides another good illustration of how dimly the communication functions are comprehended by conventional management thought.

Some pundits of the mystified advertising arts profess to be stumped by the supposedly big question, 'Does advertising really work? Can it increase market share or can it only increase awareness of name and image?' P&G, more than a century ago, proved to itself beyond any doubt that advertising certainly can work, at least in its businesses. But good advertising works and bad doesn't. What P&G has institutionalized is, in part, a systematic, rational approach that, as with product development, demands development of advertising that is proven to work.

The company extensively analyzes its enormous worldwide experience with advertising to explore the key question, 'What works?' The P&G staff function called Copy Services, which has been traditionally managed by two or three of the smartest managers senior leadership could find, has built and analyzed a large data base involving thousands of advertising campaigns in the whole range of the company's product categories and geographies. These campaigns are analyzed against two basic results: business building in the market and communication to consumers. In other words, ads and campaigns are classified as to whether or not they were associated with reasonably sustained periods, such as 12 months, of growth in market share. They are further classified for how well they scored on standardized research measures of communication. This includes how well the advertising was recalled by the target audience and also, more specifically, what portion of consumers recalled the most important benefits in that brand's advertising strategy. Thus, how well the resulting experiences in the value proposition were communicated is thoroughly analyzed.

Copy Services then characterizes each advertising execution or campaign by as many variables as seem relevant to understand. For example, they compare the business building and communication results of advertising that includes a competitive product demonstration to advertising which does not, and find that this factor correlates well with advertising that works. Or, they compare ads with singing jingles to those without and find an inverse correlation. Though P&G's specific findings may not translate to non-packaged-goods industries, its philosophy does. P&G has institutionalized the following rational principle. The company studies and tries to understand what works in advertising. Brands and the agencies are strongly encouraged to use these findings to develop more effective advertising. Any advertising campaign or execution must be proven to perform in the market place, both in its measurable ability to communicate the brand's value proposition and in its impact on market share, before it is used broadly.

Make decisions based on principles, facts and logic, in clear written form

The final principle inculcated in P&G managers is perhaps best described as the principle of using principles. Every human organization is inescapably political in nature, in the sense that at least some decisions will be made based upon power relationships. However, P&G's culture represents a serious effort to minimize the political factor in decision-making in favor of the objective application of carefully articulated principles.

When employees want to propose some course of action, their success will in large part depend upon how well they relate their proposal to company principles. They must clearly articulate, usually in writing, a logical argument for their proposal that is backed by factual evidence and proves the proposal to be more consistent with the company's relevant accepted principles than any alternative. The proposal might be unconventional in some respects or might suggest some course of action that goes against the instincts of many of the managers who must judge it. The manager proposing it may even be unpopular. However, if the proposal demonstrates a logical and factual connection to the accepted principle, it has an excellent chance of flying.

This style of decision-making also reflects the hierarchy of principles established within the company. Suppose an R&D manager working with a brand group wants to pursue a particular new formulation of a product. Perhaps this product direction is inherently controversial, which makes the proposal a tough sale. The engineer cannot simply argue that the new formula would build the business, but must demonstrate the evidence for why this is so. If no alternative use of the resources needed for this proposal is shown to be likely to improve delivery of the value proposition, this proposal should win approval through a stage of development and technical testing. If that testing shows the new formula able technically to out-perform the current product, this will justify blind testing which, if won by the new formula, will in turn justify a test market. If the new formula convincingly builds the business in that test market, the case can be made for its broader expansion into the market.

At the end of this process, the senior vice president or even the president of the company may hate something about the new formula. But if the case that it's a winner has been well articulated and documented, that senior manager is more often than not likely to approve it anyway. This de-politicized, largely meritocratic style of decision-making sometimes falls prey to political forces, of course. However, this principle is well upheld, partly because of several supporting elements.

First, the culture insists on constant analysis of results and frequent experimentation in pursuit of knowledge of what works. The ever-present questions are, 'What approaches to product development, packaging, sales and distribution to retailers, pricing, advertising, promotion, etc.., actually work to build the business? What works to provide the experiences in this brand's value proposition better? What works to communicate these experiences better?'

Second, the organization insists that answers to these questions be based on factual evidence that is carefully gathered, measured, and analyzed. The company puts an extraordinarily high priority on protecting the integrity of facts relevant to the businesses. Sloppy or analytically incompetent handling of facts has sidetracked many careers; evidence of disregard for the truth ends them instantly. Most companies would say they have the same high regard for factual analysis and accuracy, but few really do. Still fewer institutionalize it by documenting so much factual analysis in writing.

The third characteristic of the P&G culture that supports principle-based decision making is the insistence on writing concise, cogent, prose documents. Most business correspondence has gone the route of consultants' presentations – sentence fragments, sound bites, topics, and partial phrases. Coherent, logically structured, unambiguous ideas are rare. Moreover, managers in most firms spend unbelievable hours *talking* in meetings, often focusing on largely incoherent overheads. Whatever factual, logical discourse does occur is lost into thin air. Small wonder that so many decisions are made arbitrarily, with few managers in the organization understanding their rationale. P&G managers spend much more time than most companies writing and reading carefully argued proposals and analyses. This lets them much more easily clarify and contemplate the business principles, facts, and logical argument upon which a proposal or analysis is based.

Finally, institutionalizing these principles requires leaders to take responsibility for teaching them to the organization. Leaders do this partly by questioning. When a proposal goes to senior management in P&G, a set of questions usually comes back. The questions may ask for more clarification as to the basic principles on which the proposal is based, or they may ask for more facts or additional analysis or clarification of the logic. This teaches managers how to think and articulate their arguments as well as how to anticipate the questions. When middle managers recount their meetings with a P&G President, CEO, or other senior type, they rarely dwell on pearls of wisdom they received. Instead they recall vividly the questions they were asked. These questions subtly teach a way of thinking about business.

***

P&G is certainly far from ideal. It is not always able to adjust its own culture successfully to suit some markets it enters. The company has a history of creating some dubious products in its relentless effort to succeed in processed food, for example. Only with great pain was it able to salvage something from its elaborate effort to make a synthetic simulation of a potato chip, Pringles. The company lost a moderate fortune on cookies that were chemically altered to have the softness of a fresh-baked cookie, a disturbingly unnatural feature, given the weeks they spent on a grocery shelf. No takers could be found for paper cups with embedded cola, to be released by pouring water into the cup. The company makes plenty of other errors as well, and growth has not been spectacular in recent decades.

Still, Procter is a great company worth study and appreciation, despite the business world's snobbish dismissal of it as just a company selling soap to idiots. Its particular markets and delivery vehicles are obviously different from many other companies. However, P&G shows that the kind of managerial behaviors and attitudes fundamental to DPV can indeed be made an integral part of business life throughout a large global corporation. This successful institutionalization consists of inculcating principles that are independent of the nature of markets, their primary entities, or their delivery vehicles – it's not a question of packaged goods, soap, or television. It is a matter of committing an organization to the profound study of primary entities and their experiences, to formulating strategy as the disciplined choice of value propositions and the design of their delivery, to unambiguous success criteria that demand and reward building the businesses, to focusing on the capabilities most needed by the appropriate delivery vehicles, and to making decisions through a clearly articulated, factually and logically rigorous argument.

DPV and leadership: the hedgehog or the fox?

Institutionalizing *DPV* is clearly a function of real and sustained commitment to major *change* by an organization's leadership. Yet *DPV* is inherently a fundamental and discomfiting challenge to business-as-usual in most organizations. Cultures typically react to such a serious challenge by first ignoring it, then denying its validity, then marginalizing its relevance, and finally trying to co-opt it. Managers who want to succeed in institutionalizing *DPV* must have the focus and persistence to overcome all of these powerful forms of cultural resistance.

In an essay on the subtle but great leadership of Abraham Lincoln, historian James McPherson argues that Lincoln was one of history's foremost hedgehogs, in contrast to the numerous foxes among his contemporaries. The hedgehog, an animal similar to the American porcupine, is noted for its distinctive defense, its sharp spines. As the Greek poet Archilochus wrote, 'The fox knows many things, but the hedgehog knows one big thing.' McPherson points out that this can simply mean that the fox's cleverness and varied tactics are insufficient to overcome the single but decisive defense of the hedgehog. However, British philosopher Isaiah Berlin perceived a deeper meaning. McPherson recounts that Berlin saw the hedgehog as a thinker or leader who 'relates everything to a single central vision...a single, universal, organizing principle' whereas the fox 'pursues many ends, often unrelated and even contradictory.' According to McPherson,

> 'More than any of his Civil War contemporaries, [Lincoln] pursued policies that were governed by a central vision, expressed in the Gettysburg Address, that this "nation, conceived in Liberty, and dedicated to the proposition that all men are created equal...shall not perish from the earth.' Lincoln was surrounded by foxes who considered themselves smarter than he but who lacked his depth of vision and therefore sometimes pursued unrelated and contradictory ends. Two of the most prominent foxes were William H. Seward and Horace Greeley. Both were more clever than Lincoln, more nimble-witted and brilliant in conversation. They shared Lincoln's nationalism and his abhorrence of slavery. But while Lincoln navigated by the lodestar that never moved, Seward and

> *Greeley steered by stars that constantly changed position. If they had been at the helm instead of Lincoln, it is quite likely that the United States would have foundered on the rocks of disunion.*[6]

Lincoln believed deeply in the supreme importance of liberty and consistently pursued this single, universal, organizing principle. After the South rebelled, however, Lincoln focused on saving the Union. The 'central idea pervading this struggle...[was the necessity]...of proving that popular government is not an absurdity.' Allowing the South to secede would 'go far to prove the incapability of the people to govern themselves.' He was acutely aware that 'our popular government has often been called an experiment' which would fail if the Confederacy succeeded, ending that 'last best hope...[for] maintaining in the world...government of the people, by the people, for the people.'[7] Despite suggestion from some of the foxes to let the slave states 'go in peace' rather than risk war or more pro-slavery compromises, Lincoln steadfastly insisted upon ending the insurrection.

On the other hand, emancipation of the slaves would only be a lever to be used as appropriate to support the central strategic vision of holding the Union together. When the war broke out, he made it clear that he was *not* trying to free the slaves. He wrote Greeley, 'If I could save the Union without freeing any slave, I would do it.'[8] In the early months of the war he revoked orders by Union generals emancipating slaves in some areas. Numerous foxes castigated him for not moving immediately to end slavery, but Lincoln realized that emancipation at that early stage in the war would simply drive the border slave states into the Confederacy and probably lose the war. In 1864, the right moment, the moment when Lincoln had more to gain by striking at the South's labor supply than by continuing to appease the border states, arrived. He proclaimed emancipation *because* it furthered the central aim – winning the war and restoring the Union, and *thereby* furthering the cause of liberty.

In like fashion, those leaders of enterprises who have thought deeply about the principles of value delivery and who have the ambition and courage to attempt to institutionalize *DPV* should strive to be hedgehogs rather than foxes. At its essence, *DPV* is the notion that an organization generates wealth and sustained growth as a function of the value propositions that it delivers. The fox may use many clever, supposedly sophisticated questions, techniques, and stratagems, but the hedgehog concentrates on the single central issue that matters – formulating and executing the organization's winning primary VDSs. Single-minded focus and persistence is required to lead an organization that is deeply entrenched in the traditional product-supply paradigm to the *DPV* way of business life. Some foxes will want to make *DPV* another element in their panoply of clever theorems and techniques, which in the aggregate prove that the leader has a sophisticated grasp of all the latest management fads and buzzwords. The hedgehog will recognize that this cleverness only dilutes the energy and unwavering focus needed for real change, for genuinely institutionalizing *DPV*.

This clarity of strategic vision and strength of direction as a leader should not be confused with simple-mindedness. As McPherson noted:

> *'[His partner] conceded that while Lincoln "thought slowly and acted slowly," he "not only went to the root of the question, but dug up the root, and separated and analyzed every fibre of it." In a legal case or ... political debate, recalled [an observer], Lincoln would concede non-essential points to his opponent, lulling him into a false sense of complacency. "But giving away six points and carrying the seventh he carried his case ... the whole case hanging on the seventh ... Any man who took Lincoln for a simple-minded man would wind up with his back in a ditch."'[9]*

The one big thing hedgehogs know: their value proposition

McPherson writes that 'Lincoln expressed this hedgehog philosophy of concentrating on the one big thing, to the exclusion of non-essentials, in a speech to an Ohio regiment. 'No small matter should divert us from our great purpose ... [Do not] let your minds be carried off from the great work we have before us.'[10] Managers must learn that choosing and delivering the value proposition is that great purpose.

Institutionalizing *DPV* means, in part, teaching the organization to focus not on the means but rather the end. The fox assumes that the end – the value proposition that must be delivered – is obvious. The fox concentrates on the means – the resources and processes that will provide and communicate the value proposition – without having adequately considered and articulated the end. Consider two companies, one managed in the spirit of the fox, the other more like the hedgehog – Apple and Microsoft.

It is now common to speak of poor management and strategic errors at Apple, but during the 1980s most spoke glowingly of Apple's brilliant strategy and marketing. With the Macintosh operating system and hardware architecture introduced in 1984, Apple had a chance to deliver a spectacularly winning value proposition. However, it was Bill Gates who clearly understood the power of this proposition and, hedgehog-like, pursued its delivery until the clever foxes of Apple were completely vanquished.

To millions of knowledge workers, Macintosh could have delivered a much easier and faster learning experience on a PC, versus the DOS/Intel environment. As an end result, users could in fact do more with their computers, thus obtaining far more utility from them. If these experiences were delivered at a price no higher than that of the DOS-based alternatives, the world's businesses would have had a strong reason to prefer the Mac system. If it had started capturing a large share of personal computing, software developers would likely have continued writing software for it. Primary entities would have had little basis for preferring the DOS standard.

Apple, however, repeatedly outfoxed itself; it consistently failed to understand and commit clearly to this value proposition. When Mac was introduced, it was presented as a historic opportunity for business people to escape the oppressive domination of IBM. The introductory ad '1984' showed the target business person as mindless slave to Big Brother (hint: this is IBM); Macintosh was shown as the revolutionary destroyer of Big Brother. This ad was hailed at the time as one of the creative pinnacles of all time and recently was named the single greatest in television advertising history by Ad Age and CBS. A similar ad ran a year later depicting the target customer as lemmings mindlessly following IBM over a cliff. Unfortunately, there were two problems with this brilliant marketing: (1) the vast majority of business people did not realize they were mindless slaves desperate to escape the IBM-compatible-world's vise and (2) this story failed to give people so much as a hint about the above-described value proposition.

After wasting about two years in this manner, Apple turned to a niche market – desktop publishing. Apple reveled in its brilliant niche marketing strategy, but this only reinforced the impression that Mac was not for mainstream computing. This brilliance was followed in the late 1980s by advertising that explained that Mac was for people who are afraid of technology. By then, most corporate buyers had categorized Mac as a computer for non-serious work – good for children, hippies, maybe graphic artists, but not for mainstream knowledge workers doing word-processing and crunching numbers.

During this period, Apple considered licensing the Mac operating system (OS) to other manufacturers who could make Mac clones and lowering system prices, but decided against both. To deliver the winning value proposition described above, Apple would have had to lower the price to one comparable with the DOS/Intel world. But Apple thought doing so would be like IBM's mistake in losing control of the PC. But IBM's mistake had been in letting Microsoft and Intel own the OS and chip. Apple owned the OS and the patents on the hardware architecture and could have sold these truly proprietary delivery vehicles. Then other manufacturers could have made the hardware at a low enough cost for a winning value proposition. Letting other manufacturers make the Mac system also would have meant sacrificing a little of the tight integration between OS and hardware, but this tradeoff would have been a winner. The Apple foxes, however, cleverly kept the hardware exclusive and prices and margins sky high.

Poor hedgehog Bill Gates, on the other hand, was laughed at by the chic foxes of Apple. Apple was confident that Microsoft could *never* get close enough to Mac to matter. Gates understood, however, that it takes an entire value proposition, not just a delivery vehicle, to win. He priced DOS, and later the Windows imitation of Mac, at a low price aimed at maximizing market share, so more applications were written for it and more support provided by PC hardware vendors. Primary entities had increasingly greater options with DOS/Windows than with Mac. Corporate environments became heavily committed to Windows/Intel, making it increasingly painful to shift to Mac. As successive versions of Windows better emulated the Mac OS, the entire value proposition was increasingly superior to that of the Mac.

The organization led by the instincts of the fox is prone to the backward logic that justifies internally-driven and customer-compelled practices. Such an organization may develop technologies that accomplish little in the marketplace but nonetheless make the fox proud of its triumphs of strategic-partnering or competence-leveraging. The fox deploys advertising that fails to build the business but brags about its creativity and even succeeds in winning praise and admiration for its brilliance. Alice would recognize this internally-driven, backward logic from her adventures, such as at the royal court.

There, the Knave of Hearts is accused of stealing tarts made by the Queen of Hearts. The King calls for a verdict, but is persuaded to allow the evidence first, a letter of pure nonsense verse that proves nothing. When the Knave protests that he didn't write it and that it can't be proved he wrote it, since it is unsigned, the King concludes 'that only makes the matter worse. You *must* have meant some mischief, or else you'd have signed your name like an honest man.' Finally it seems time for the jury to consider their verdict. 'No, no!' said the Queen. 'Sentence first – verdict afterwards.'[11]

Sentence first, then verdict, then evidence (for which nonsense will do nicely, thank you). Surely sophisticated management theory at the turn of the twenty-first century is not backward? Still, Alice might recognize the logic of that theory as often taught and practised: decide on one's core competencies, then create a product which the competencies allow, then segment customers by many variables, and ask each segment for their needs (for which customer-compelled research will do nicely, thank you).

The fox pursues customer satisfaction ratings, quality awards, or perhaps ISO9000 quality process certification. Each function is urged to find customers, to ask their requirements, and to meet them diligently. Elaborate techniques gather detailed input from customers on every feature of every product. Focus groups and highly advanced quantitative marketing research is conducted. A frenzy of customer-driven, customer-defined, customer-specified activity provides the fox-manager a sacred blessing: no one can say this organization is not customer driven. The only things missing are any clues as to the nature of the actual experiences customers have now, their alternatives, the value proposition the organization should deliver, and how exactly this should be done.

In the world of the Looking Glass, many characters are chess pieces. The Red and White pieces play in opposition to each other but without understanding the purpose of the game, thus approximating the noisy debate between the internally-driven and customer-compelled philosophies of business. Make this product with this feature – our customers request it! No, make this product; it better leverages our competencies! Let's improve the quality of our process-improvement process; that should improve our quality! Cut off everyone's head, as the Red Queen likes to order – our strategy is cost leadership! No, let's do something different from competitors; then our strategy can be differentiation!

When frustrated that things are not going well, the fox likes to increase the pressure on the rest of the organization. When the Mad Hatter cannot remember the testimony he is supposed to give, the King helpfully clarifies the reward system, 'Don't be nervous, or I'll have you executed on the spot.'[12] Top management promises growth or a return to profit, with no clear idea of the strategy needed to make it happen. When it does not materialize, managers are given impossible targets, which distract them and drive them to take desperate short-term actions. Results soon collapse, at which point all their heads are cut off. Bottom line leadership.

DPV is a path away from self-absorbed, backward logic. It consists of putting down the looking glass altogether, deeply analyzing the real lives of customers, and then making a disciplined choice of a single value proposition for each business. The hedgehog manager must have the fortitude to reject the temptation to pursue many unrelated and contradictory ends. McPherson recounted the description of Lincoln's mind by a contemporary:

> 'Herndon visited Niagara Falls some time after Lincoln had ... Telling Lincoln his impressions ... Herndon waxed eloquent in typical nineteenth-century romantic fashion, declaiming of rush and roar and brilliant rainbows. Exhausting his adjectives, he asked Lincoln [his impression]. "The thing that struck me most forcibly ... was where in the world did all that water come from?" Herndon recalled this remark after nearly forty years as an example of how Lincoln "looked at everything ... His mind, heedless of beauty or awe, followed irresistibly back to the first cause ... If there was any secret in his power this surely was it."'[13]

It is this searching for first causes that characterizes the spirit of *Delivering Profitable Value*. And it is an essential element in the character of a leader who would guide an organization through a metamorphosis that takes it out of the looking glass and into an institutionalized mastery of the principles, frameworks, and methodology of *DPV*. Such leaders must be focused and able to inspire others to focus likewise on the first causes that explain the behavior and attitudes of potential customers. They must focus on finding the first cause, the essential aspects of a resulting experience that would be of superior value to a customer. Such leaders must teach their organizations to understand that a value proposition must be chosen for each business and that the proposition must be based on those first causes of customers' motivation. And then such leaders must show their organizations how to use that chosen value proposition, not the distracting agendas of internally-driven and customer-compelled thinking, as the first cause of every resource, process, and action taken in that business.

To become the customer, to analyze objectively the experiences and alternatives of the customer, to think forward from those experiences to superior ones and, without undue bias, to a business design that could profit by delivering them, is to think much like a twelve-year-old. Unencumbered by the sophisticated elaboration of the grown-up fox, the child's mind is open to seeing many things as they really are. Managers are hectored to tow the line of current conventions; sweeping away the confusing and misleading doctrines that beckon organizations into the looking glass goes against that grain. But managers who want to be leaders and to build great organizations should take heart from young Alice, who is astounded by the backward logic of the trial at the end of her *Adventures*.

> '"Stuff and nonsense!" said Alice loudly. "The idea of having the sentence first!" "Hold your tongue!" said the Queen, turning purple. "I won't" said Alice. "Off with her head!" the Queen shouted at the top of her voice. Nobody moved. "Who cares for you?" said Alice ... "You're nothing but a pack of cards!" At this the whole pack rose up into the air, and came flying down...[whereupon she finds herself back in reality].*[14]*

Deep in the heart and mind of the manager who loves being in a business is the clearest, most fundamentally intelligent instinct of humankind: to engage in a mutually beneficial cooperation with other people. Stand up and act with courage on that instinct, like the hedgehog, and many of the obstacles in the way may turn out to be little more than a pack of cards.

Notes

1 Microsoft spent $1.17 billion, 31st in the world in absolute R&D spending, in 1997; this was a higher portion of sales (16.9 percent) than any

of the 30 firms that spent more (British Department of Trade and Industry, cited by *International Herald Tribune,* July 4, 1998, p. 15).

2 Randall E. Stross, *The Microsoft Way,* Addison-Wesley, Reading, MA, 1996, p. 59.

3 *Ibid,* p. 95.

4 *Ibid,* p. 65.

5 Now Customer Business Development, where customer means retailer.

6 McPherson, J.M. *Abraham Lincoln and the Second American Revolution,* Oxford University Press, 1991, p. 114; I. Berlin quote from *The Hedgehog and the Fox: An Essay on Tolstoy's View of History,* New York, 1966.

7 Quoted by McPherson, *op. cit.,* p.116.

8 *Ibid,* p. 127.

9 *Ibid,* pp. 114–15.

10 *Ibid,* p. 115.

11 Carroll, *Alice's Adventures in Wonderland,* Macmillan, pp. 94, 96.

12 *Ibid,* p. 88.

13 McPherson, *op. cit.*

14 Carroll, *op. cit.,* p. 98.

Glossary of *DPV* Terms

Becoming the customer   *DPV* method of studying customers' relevant real current experiences, to discover valuable potential ones and competing alternative ones; learning to think like the customer.

Building Market-Focused Organizations/BMFO   Course on DPV concepts, taught by Lanning, Phillips & Associates since 1987.

Being in the customer's business   Learning to improve their business rather than sell them goods.

Business plans   Organization's commitment to implement one or more primary VDSs.

Business   A primary VDS.

Buying process   What marketeers often study instead of understanding the customer's whole business; the mechanisms by which a customer's buying function decides on suppliers.

Capability   An organization's potential to choose, provide and/or communicate some resulting experience.

Capability bridges   Key aspects of an organization that must be managed/redesigned to close *capability gaps*.

Capability gaps   Shortfalls in the organization's ability to implement an element of a VDS.

Choosing a value proposition   First function in a VDS (business); requires senior management to answer the questions of a *complete* value proposition and make formal commitment to actually deliver it.

Communicating   Third function in a VDS; ensuring that customers actually understand *what* each resulting experience is and *why* they should believe it will be provided; requires *communicating vehicles* – the means (e.g. sales force) by which a resulting experience is communicated.

Competing alternative   An experience or whole value proposition a customer may be able to select; an alternative to which an organization's value proposition must be superior.

Complete value proposition   The answer to the questions of: timeframe, intended customer, what we want them to do, their alternatives, and the experiences they will derive as a result.

Corporate strategy   Choice and design of a firm's primary VDSs and the capabilities needed for them.

Cost controlled Form of internally-driven behavior that equates strategy and business with cost reduction.

Customer An organization's customer is an entity that does/could derive resulting experiences from the organization; can be a primary entity, intermediary, primary entity's customer, or off-line entity.

Customer-compelled behavior Making decisions based on what products/services customers say the organization should supply, and how; and, believing that customers must be given everything they want; in contrast to discovering and choosing a winning value proposition.

Customer's resulting experience Some actual event or series of events that a customer has, with some end-result consequence for them, as a result of doing business in some way with the organization; the consequence has some value in comparison to the customer's competing alternatives.

Delivering profitable value Delivering one or more superior value propositions at a total cost (including that of capital) below the total revenues thus generated; making money in business.

Designed value delivery system A VDS reflecting a disciplined choice of a complete value proposition and of how each resulting experience in it will be provided and communicated.

DPV Abbreviation for *Delivering Profitable Value*.

Entity or customer entity An organization (firm or division) or individual in a value delivery chain.

Experience(s) see **customer's resulting experience**.

Internally-driven behavior Making decisions based primarily on what seems to leverage resources, be more convenient, or be superior to competitors, without adequate consideration of value delivered to customers.

Intermediary entity Entity in a value delivery chain between the organization and primary entities.

Level Position in a value delivery chain where a set of entities are at the same distance from the organization; e.g. all grocers are at intermediary level, consumers at primary-entity level.

Listening to customers The conventional methods by which customers are solicited for their opinions; asking customers what the organization should do, as opposed to *becoming the customer*.

Looking-glass A mirror; Lewis Carroll's Alice went through one into a backwards world.

Market-space A set of related potential businesses (VDSs) including the customers in those VDSs.

Off-line entities An entity in a value delivery chain that affects the organization's success but does not buy or use the products or services in which the organization is involved; e.g. a regulator.

Organization   A firm or division or other entity conducting or considering a business.

Primary entities   Strategically, the most crucial entities in a value delivery chain; those entities that must be delivered the right value proposition for the organization to win.

Primary value delivery system   A business; the VDS which delivers a winning value proposition to the primary entities; often *includes* supporting VDSs.

Primary value proposition   The proposition to the primary entities.

Product-supply focus/system   The conventional management paradigm, versus that of *DPV.* Expressed variously as the value chain, marketing mix or business system, it sees a business as developing, producing and selling/marketing products/services, versus choosing, providing and communicating a value proposition. Focused on *supplying products/services,* not *delivering resulting experiences.*

Providing   Second function in a VDS; ensuring that intended customers actually get the resulting experiences; requires providing vehicles (e.g. products and services) to make the experience happen.

Resulting experience(s)   see **customer's resulting experience**.

Strategy   Decision as to what primary VDS or VDSs to implement.

Strategy formulation   Identification of value delivery options in each market-space worth exploring; assessment and disciplined choice among these options, thus commitment to primary VDSs.

Strategy implementation   Writing, execution, monitoring, and measuring of real business plans that specify the one or more primary VDSs, including supporting VDSs.

Success criteria   How an organization and its people are measured for reward purposes.

Supplier   Any entity that may deliver some value proposition to the organization.

Supporting entities   Entities other than primary entities in a value delivery chain, including intermediaries, suppliers, off-line entities, sometimes primary entities' customers.

Supporting value delivery system   The VDS by which the organization will secure the coordinated cooperation of some set of supporting entities, in delivering the appropriate primary value proposition.

Supporting value proposition   The proposition appropriate to deliver to some supporting entities.

Thinking like a 12-year old   Seeing the reality of customers' experience and simply imagining a better scenario, rather than rationalizing why the customer should support the organization's agenda.

Tradeoff A combination of resulting experiences in a value proposition, some of which are superior and some inferior compared to competing alternatives; characterizes many winning value propositions.

Value The net desirability customers perceive in some resulting experience(s), in comparison to some alternative; what those customers should be willing to pay accordingly.

Value delivery Choosing, providing, and communicating some resulting experience(s), including price.

Value delivery chain The entities of relevance to a business, including suppliers, intermediaries, primary entities, their customers, and off-line entities; understood as delivering value to each other and as one interconnected set of relationships.

Value delivery focus Understanding business in terms of choosing, providing and communicating some set of resulting experiences to potential customers rather than in terms of supplying products/services.

Value delivery framework The whole set of questions and corresponding actions of the primary and supporting VDSs, understood in context of the value delivery chain.

Value delivery option identification Exploration of a market-space to discover what primary VDSs would be viable in it; in contrast to conventional market segmentation.

Value delivery system (VDS) Understanding of a business as the choosing, providing and communicating of a real (complete) value proposition; see **primary** and **supporting**.

Value proposition The combination of resulting experiences, including price, which an organization delivers to a group of intended customers in some time frame, in return for those customers buying/using and otherwise doing what the organization wants rather than taking some competing alternative; the essence of a business, properly understood, in contrast to the conventional implicit assumption that products and services (or, vaguely, customers) are that essence; *not* the trivialized and garbled notions that have been wrongly ascribed to this term.

VDS Value delivery system; a business, in *DPV* terms.

Virtual videos Part of the methodology of *becoming the customer*.

Video One The discovery, description, documentation and critical analysis of the current or base-case relevant experiences of a customer

Video Two The inferred, creative invention of a maximally-realistic improved scenario of experiences for the same customer.

Competing videos Capture what scenarios the same customer may have available from competing sources.

Index